EURIPIDES

HERACLES AND OTHER PLAYS

Translated by JOHN DAVIE,
with an introduction and notes by
RICHARD RUTHERFORD

T0204487

PENGUIN BOOKS

PENGUIN BOOKS

Published by the Penguin Group
Penguin Books Ltd, 80 Strand, London WC2R ORL, England
Penguin Putnam Inc., 375 Hudson Street, New York, New York 10014, USA
Penguin Books Australia Ltd, 250 Camberwell Road, Camberwell, Victoria 3124, Australia
Penguin Books Canada Ltd, 10 Alcorn Avenue, Toronto, Ontario, Canada M4V 3B2
Penguin Books India (P) Ltd, 11 Community Centre, Panchsheel Park, New Delhi – 110 017, India
Penguin Books (NZ) Ltd, Private Bag 102902, NSMC, Auckland, New Zealand
Penguin Books (South Africa) (Pty) Ltd, 24 Sturdee Avenue, Rosebank 2196, South Africa

Penguin Books Ltd, Registered Offices: 80 Strand, London WC2R ORL, England

www.penguin.com

This translation first published 2002

2

Translation copyright © John Davie, 2002
Introduction and notes copyright © Richard Rutherford, 2002
All rights reserved

Set in 10/12.5 pt PostScript Monotype Bembo
Typeset by Rowland Phototypesetting Ltd, Bury St Edmunds, Suffolk
Printed in Great Britain by Antony Rowe Ltd, Chippenham, Wiltshire

PENGUIN  CLASSICS

HERACLES AND OTHER PLAYS

EURIPIDES, the youngest of the three great Athenian playwrights, was born around 485 BC of a family of good standing. He first competed in the dramatic festivals in 455 BC, coming only third; his record of successes in the tragic competitions is lower than that of either Aeschylus or Sophocles. There is a tradition that he was unpopular, even a recluse; we are told that he composed poetry in a cave by the sea, near Salamis. What is clear from contemporary evidence, however, is that audiences were fascinated by his innovative and often disturbing dramas. His work was controversial already in his lifetime, and he himself was regarded as a 'clever' poet, associated with philosophers and other intellectuals. Towards the end of his life he went to live at the court of Archelaus, king of Macedon. It was during his time there that he wrote what many consider his greatest work, the *Bacchae*. When news of his death reached Athens in early 406 BC, Sophocles appeared publicly in mourning for him. Euripides is thought to have written about ninety-two plays, of which seventeen tragedies and one satyr-play known to be his survive; the other play which is attributed to him, the *Rhesus*, may in fact be by a later hand.

JOHN N. DAVIE was born in Glasgow in 1950, and was educated at the High School of Glasgow, Glasgow University and Balliol College, Oxford, where he wrote a thesis on Greek tragedy. From 1975 to 1984 he taught Classics at Harrow, before moving to St Paul's School to become Head of Classics, where he still teaches. He is the author of two articles on the problems of writing favourably about monarchy in a democratic society such as fifth-century BC Athens. He is a member of the Hellenic Society's visiting Panel of Lecturers.

RICHARD RUTHERFORD was born in Edinburgh in 1956, and was educated at Robert Gordon's College, Aberdeen, and at Worcester College, Oxford. Since 1982 he has been Tutor in Greek and Latin Literature at Christ Church, Oxford. He is the author of a number of books and articles on classical authors, including a commentary on books 19 and 20 of Homer's *Odyssey* (1992), and *The Art of Plato: Ten Essays in Platonic Interpretation* (1995).

CONTENTS

GENERAL INTRODUCTION

'I portray men as they should be, but Euripides portrays them as they are.'

(Sophocles, quoted by Aristotle, *Poetics*, ch. 25, 1460b33–4)

'Whatever other defects of organization he may have, Euripides is the most intensely tragic of all the poets.'   (Aristotle, *Poetics*, ch. 14, 1453a28–30)

'I am really amazed that the scholarly nobility does not comprehend his virtues, that they rank him below his predecessors, in line with that high-toned tradition which the clown Aristophanes brought into currency . . . Has any nation ever produced a dramatist who would deserve to hand him his slippers?'

(Goethe, *Diaries*, 22 November 1831)

'What were you thinking of, overweening Euripides, when you hoped to press myth, then in its last agony, into your service? It died under your violent hands . . . Though you hunted all the passions up from their couch and conjured them into your circle, though you pointed and burnished a sophistic dialectic for the speeches of your heroes, they have only counterfeit passions and speak counterfeit speeches.'   (Nietzsche, *The Birth of Tragedy*, ch. 10)

I

Already in his own lifetime Euripides was a controversial figure. Daring in his theatrical innovations, superbly eloquent and articulate in the rhetoric which he gave to his characters, closely in touch with the intellectual life of his time, he has stimulated and shocked audiences and readers not only through the unexpected twists and turns of his plots, but also by the alarming immorality of many of his characters. But before exploring these and other aspects of his work in more detail, we must briefly put him in context, by giving an outline of the earlier history of the Athenian genre of tragedy, and the work of Aeschylus, his great predecessor, and of Sophocles, his older contemporary.

Unlike epic poetry, which was a traditional form familiar throughout the Greek world, tragedy was a relatively new invention in the fifth century BC, and one which was particularly Athenian. Its origins and early development are obscure: if, as Aristotle believed, it originated in a form of choral song, the 'dithyramb', a song in honour of the god Dionysus, then it had already been transformed before the time of Aeschylus. Ancient tradition held that contests between tragic playwrights had become an established part of the festival known as the City Dionysia (held in March) some time in the 530s, and that the key figure of these early days was a dramatist called Thespis. Our earliest surviving tragedy is Aeschylus' *Persians*, performed in 472, a full sixty years later. The dramas which have survived span the rest of the fifth century, a period of intense political activity and social and intellectual change. Hence generalizations even about the extant dramas will be dangerous, and we must always bear in mind that we have only the tip of the iceberg.

The Athenian tragedies were performed in the open air, in a theatre enormous by modern standards: some experts believe that it could have contained more than 14,000 people, as it certainly could after reconstruction in the fourth century.[1] This large audience was probably composed mainly of men (it is likely that women could attend, but probable that not many did so). Those attending paid for admission, but the price was low, probably less than half a labourer's daily wage; in the fourth century even this charge was paid for out of public subsidies. The stage-arrangements were sparse: a building set behind the main area where the actors moved would represent a palace or other such building according to the needs of the play. Perhaps on a lower level (though the layout is much disputed) was the open area called the *orchestra* ('dancing-space'), in which the chorus stood or danced. The events were presented as happening out of doors, theatrically necessary but also more natural in Mediterranean life. Entrances along passages on either side of the theatre were loosely conceived as leading to different destinations – country or city, army camp or seashore, depending on the plot. Actors were all male (even for female parts), normally Athenian citizens; all wore masks and dignified formal dress; speaking actors were almost invariably limited to three in number, but could take on different roles during the play by changing costume and mask offstage. Stage equipment and props were few; the action was largely stylized, even static, with the more violent action conceived as taking place offstage, then being reported to the actors, often in a long narrative speech. All plays were in verse, partly spoken and partly sung; although Euripides made several strides towards more 'realistic' drama, the effect of a Greek tragedy in his time would still have been to move the audience to a distant world, where great figures of the mythical past fought and disputed over momentous issues.

Every Greek tragedy had a chorus, a team of twelve or fifteen singers representing the community or some other body concerned with the events of the drama. It may be that originally tragedy consisted wholly of choral songs; if so, the key innovation, whether Thespis or another was responsible, must have been the introduction of an actor who engaged in dialogue with the chorus, who could withdraw and take part in events offstage, then return to inform them of developments. Aeschylus is said to have introduced a second actor, Sophocles a third. There the tragedians stopped, though as the century passed the three actors were often expected to play more roles, and 'mute' actors (domestic slaves, attendants or soldiers) were permitted. In general, the importance of the actors and the size of their role in the play increased, while that of the chorus declined; but in the work of the three great tragedians the chorus was never unimportant, and their songs or 'choral odes' do far more than fill in time or allow an interval: these odes comment on the action, react to it and ponder its significance, placing it in a larger perspective, chronological and religious. Some of the finest poetry in Greek tragedy comes in the choral odes.

We tend to think of the theatre as a recreation, and one which is available more or less any night of the year. The position in ancient Athens was quite different. Drama was part of a civic occasion, the festival of Dionysus. Although the city held many religious festivals, tragedies were performed only at a few, and at fixed points in the year. It was not possible for a dramatist to stage anything he liked at any time; he had to apply to the proper authorities and be 'granted a chorus', given permission to compete and financial support. (It is true, however, that we also have evidence for theatrical activities in rural Attica, where procedure was perhaps less formal than at the great civic festivals.) In the earliest times the dramatist would also play a part in his plays, though Sophocles is said to have given this up because his voice was weak. Still more important, the author was also the producer, working together with his actors and choruses and training them. At the City Dionysia three tragedians would compete for the prize every year; each of them would present three tragedies – sometimes but not necessarily a connected 'trilogy'. Aeschylus favoured these trilogies (as his master-piece, the *Oresteia*, illustrates), but they seem to have gone out of fashion after his death, and the overwhelming majority of surviving tragedies are self-contained dramas. After that each competing dramatist would also put on a 'satyr-play'. This last was a wild and fantastic tailpiece, usually shorter than a tragedy: it always had a chorus of satyrs, the bestial entourage of Dionysus, and usually treated mythological themes in a burlesque and bawdy way. The only complete example to survive is Euripides' *Cyclops*, an amusing parody of the story told in Homer's *Odyssey* about the hero's encounter with the one-eyed monster.

What of the content of the tragedies? Perhaps the most significant fact is that the subjects are almost always mythological.[2] The only surviving exception is Aeschylus' *Persians*, though we know of a few others in the early period. The *Persians* commemorates the victory of the Greeks in the recent war against Xerxes, king of Persia, and in particular the battle of Salamis, which had taken place only eight years earlier. But this exception in a way proves the rule, for the play is not set in Greece, but at the Persian court, presenting the subject from the Persian viewpoint. Nor is it mere jingoism: the theme is almost mythologized, raised to a grander and more heroic plane. No individual Greek is named or singled out for praise: the emphasis falls rather on the arrogant folly of a deluded king, who has led his people to defeat. There is, as always in tragedy, a supernatural element: the ghost of Xerxes' father, summoned back to earth, pronounces stern judgement on his son's rash ambition. In the rest of the tragic corpus, the dramatists use myth to distance their stories in time, and so give them universality. Instead of setting their actors the task of impersonating living generals or politicians confronting contemporary crises, the tragedians, like Homer, show us men and women who are remote from us in their circumstances, yet vividly like us and real in their hopes, fears and desires.

Secondly, Greek tragedy is civic in emphasis: its plots, that is, deal with kings and rulers, disputes and dilemmas which have vital implications for the state as a whole. If Oedipus cannot find the murderer of Laius, the plague which is already devastating Thebes will destroy it. If Odysseus and Neoptolemus cannot recover Philoctetes and his bow, Troy will not fall. Consequently tragedy normally deals with men and women of high status – monarchs and royal families, tyrants and mighty heroes. Characters of lower rank generally have smaller parts. As we shall see, however, this is one area in which Euripides showed himself an innovator: 'I made tragedy more democratic', he is made to say in the satirical treatment of tragedy in Aristophanes' *Frogs*, produced after his death.

Thirdly, complementing and often conflicting with the political dimension, the family is regularly the focus for tragic action. Part of the lasting power of Greek drama lies in the vividness with which it presents extreme love and (still more) intense hatred within the family: matricide, parricide, fratricide, adultery and jealousy, even incest and other forbidden passions. Duty to family and duty to the state may come into conflict: can Agamemnon bring himself to abandon the expedition against Troy, or must he take the terrible decision to sacrifice his daughter for a fair wind? Loyalty to kin is central to *Antigone*; conflicting obligations to different members of the family create many of the dilemmas in the *Oresteia*. The list could easily be extended.

Fourthly, there is the religious aspect. We know too little of early tragedy to confirm or deny the theory that it concentrated mainly on the myths of Dionysus, in whose honour the plays were performed; but by Aeschylus' time the scope has obviously broadened. But no Greek tragedy is secular. Although the dramatists normally focus on the actions and sufferings of human beings, the gods are always present in the background. In early tragedy they figure quite frequently on stage as characters (as in Aeschylus' *Eumenides*). Sophocles seems to have been much more restrained in this, while Euripides normally confines them to the prologue (where they do not usually meet any mortal characters), or to the conclusion of a play, where a god may appear on a higher level, above the stage-building. Sometimes this seems to be a matter of the god standing on the roof of the building, but more spectacular still was the use of a crane-like device to allow the divinity the power of flight. From this remote position of authority the god would declare his will, *ex machina* as the phrase has it, intervening to resolve or at least impose a conclusion upon the events on earth.

Even when gods do not appear, they are frequently invoked, addressed in prayer, called to witness an oath, sometimes questioned or challenged. With the awesome powers of Olympus watching and influencing events, human affairs gain a larger significance: these are not trivial wars or petty crimes if they attract divine attention and even retribution. Yet because the humans often seem helpless pawns or puppets in the divine game, the greatness of the heroes can seem sadly insignificant, and their proud boasts or ambitions may often be ironically overturned or frustrated. The wiser players on the tragic stage sometimes draw this pessimistic conclusion. 'I see we are but phantoms, all we who live, or fleeting shadows,' says Odysseus in Sophocles' *Ajax* (125–6); or as the chorus sing in *Oedipus the King*, after the horrible truth is out:

Alas ye generations of men, how close to nothingness do I count your life. Where in the world is the mortal who wins more of happiness than just the illusion, and after the semblance, the falling away? With your example, your fate before my eyes, yours, unhappy Oedipus, I count no man happy. (1186–96)

One last general point should be made. Greek tragedy was intended for performance: although texts undoubtedly circulated, the primary concern was production in the theatre.[3] It is important to try to reconstruct the stage movements, the points at which characters enter and exit, observe one another, come into physical contact, pass objects to another person, and so forth. Major questions of interpretation may hinge on these seemingly small-scale puzzles: to take an example from the plays in the first volume of this series, does Hippolytus ever address Phaedra or not? It all depends on how we envisage the staging, and relate it to the words, of a particular scene (*Hippolytus* 601–68, esp. 651ff.). The case of *Andromache* is particularly striking: in the original performance, the character Andromache either appeared in the final scene or she did not. Since she speaks no words in that scene, the text gives us no guidance; but her mute appearance, recalling to the audience her previous suffering and the miseries of Troy, would modify the effect of the end of the play, in which so much is made of the death of Neoptolemus, one of the sackers of Troy.

Moreover, the tragic performance involved music and dancing by the chorus, of which we can recover next to nothing – a few descriptions in ancient prose authors, a handful of papyri with musical annotation, and pictures of dramatic productions on vases do not get us very far. To compare our situation with that of an opera-lover confined to studying a libretto would be unfair to the tragedians, for the spoken dialogue of tragedy is far richer and more significant, demands far more attention from the audience, than the interludes between songs in opera. But we should not forget that, particularly in the choruses and the other lyrics, we have lost what the original cast and audience would have regarded as a vital part of the production.[4]

II

To try to sum up the work of Aeschylus and Sophocles in a few paragraphs is to risk pure banality.[5] The attempt must be made, however, if we are to see Euripides in relation to his great predecessors. Seven complete tragedies attributed to Aeschylus survive, including his monumental trilogy, the *Oresteia* (*Agamemnon, Libation-Bearers, Eumenides*). One of the others, *Prometheus Bound*, has recently been subject to close critical scrutiny, and on the basis of this analysis many authoritative judges think it spurious; but if so, its author shares something of Aeschylus' grandeur of conception and magnificence of language. As already explained, Aeschylus tended to use the trilogy form, which permitted him, as in the *Oresteia* and in the series of which the *Seven against Thebes* is the third, to trace the history of a family through several generations, showing how the sins of the elders are re-enacted or paid for by their descendants. Inherited guilt, ancestral curses, persecuting Furies, vendetta and religious pollution – concepts such as these permeate the world of Aeschylean tragedy, a world of dark powers and evil crimes, in which humans must pray and hope for justice and retribution from the gods, but may pray in vain, or find that the gods are slow to respond. Austere in its characterization, eloquent yet exotic in its polysyllabic style, dominated by long and complex choral songs, his drama often seems to belong to a much older world. Yet this is only one side of a complex artist; Aeschylus, born in the sixth century BC, is also the poet of democratic Athens, deeply concerned with its ideals of reasoned discussion and decision-making. By the end of the fifth century he was established as a classic (his plays were re-performed in recognition of this), though he could also be regarded as remote and difficult. Aristophanes' *Frogs*, which dramatizes Dionysus' quest in the underworld for a great poet to bring back to life, presents Aeschylus as a symbol of the good old days, but also as a composer of grandiose and incomprehensible lyrics. In the next century, Aristotle in the *Poetics* uses examples from Sophocles and Euripides far more than from Aeschylus.

To sum up Aeschylus as a poet of archaic grandeur would, however, be quite misleading. He is capable of much lighter and even humorous passages: particularly memorable are the sentimental reminiscences of Orestes' nurse in the *Libation-Bearers*, or the complaints of the herald in *Agamemnon* about the awful time the common soldiers had at Troy (it is significant that both of these are lower-class types; the great tragic figures are not allowed these more chatty interludes). More important, in his presentation of the doom-laden world of the heroic age he not only shows us horrific events and catastrophe, but also allows his characters to work towards a difficult resolution. In Aeschylean tragedy there is a strong emphasis on the power of the gods, particularly the will of Zeus, who oversees human lives and may bring blessings as well as destruction. Not all the dilemmas faced by Aeschylus' characters are insoluble, although the final outcome may be preceded by further hard choices or disasters. The city of Thebes is saved from invasion, but only through the death of Eteocles, its king. Above all, in the *Oresteia*, the one trilogy which we can study as a magnificently unified whole, Aeschylus dramatizes the contrast between a darker world of vendetta and savage intrafamilial conflict and a society in which the rule of law has an important place, where argument and persuasion may prove superior to hatred and violence. It is a society which mirrors or idealizes his own: the refugee Argive Orestes, pursued by the monstrous Furies, finds sanctuary in a mythical Athens where Athena presides over an archetypal lawcourt. In this trilogy, although the suffering and crimes of the past are not forgotten, the final emphasis is on the enlightened justice of the present, and the reconciliation of opposed factions among the gods promises prosperity in the future. Aeschylus as a boy had seen the overthrow of the Athenian tyrants; he had fought at Marathon, and in his later years saw the transformation of his city into a democracy and the centre of an empire. It is no surprise that ideals of political debate and civic harmony are prominent in his work; but in view of the darker side discussed above, it would be facile to label him an optimist, either about human nature or about human society. The tragic power of his dramas is not diminished by his central recognition that something positive may, in the end, emerge after or out of suffering.

Whereas Aeschylus' characters (*Prometheus* apart) are above all members of a family or of a larger community, Sophocles tends to focus on individuals set apart from their society or at odds with those who care for them: Ajax, Antigone, Electra, Philoctetes, the aged Oedipus. With him, more than with the other two tragedians, it makes sense to speak of tragic heroes and heroines. Again we have only seven plays, selected in late antiquity for school study, and we know that this represents less than a tenth of his output; moreover, those we have are mostly impossible to date. Obviously generalizations must be surrounded with cautious qualifications, but we can recognize a number of other differences from Aeschylus (to whom he nevertheless owed much). The abandonment of trilogy-form has already been mentioned. The role of the chorus is somewhat reduced, though some of the odes which reflect on human achievement and its smallness in relation to the timeless power of the gods have a poetic splendour to match almost anything in Aeschylus. The characters have more depth and subtlety: as an anonymous ancient biographer said of Sophocles, 'He knows how to arrange the action with such a sense of timing that he creates an entire character out of a mere half-line or a single expression.' Partly because he makes more varied use of the third actor, Sophocles constructs scenes which involve more shifts of attention, more realistic and sophisticated interplay between characters, than we can easily find in Aeschylus. Another difference is in the religious atmosphere. Aeschylus regularly brought the gods on stage and allowed them to converse with humans (the Furies, Athena and Apollo in *Eumenides*, Aphrodite in the lost third play of the *Supplant Women* trilogy); Sophocles does so only rarely, and even then the gap between man and god is emphasized: Athena is remote and haughty with Odysseus in *Ajax*, Heracles commanding and superhuman in *Philoctetes*; both are probably out of reach, above the human level. In general, the gods do not communicate plainly or unambiguously with mortals: oracles and prophecies offer mysterious and misleading insights, and even Oedipus, the most intelligent of men, can find that his whole life has been lived on completely false assumptions. The limitations of human knowledge allow ample scope for dramatic irony, where the audience understands the double meanings or the deeper truths behind the superficial sense of the words. Central to Sophoclean tragedy is the gap between reality and appearance, understanding and illusion; his characters often discern the truth about their circumstances, or themselves, only when it is too late to avert disaster.

Sophocles has sometimes been seen as a particularly 'pious' writer or thinker. In part this results from a very partial reading of certain selected passages which have been taken to express the poet's own opinions (always a dangerous method); in part it derives from information about his involvement in Athenian religious life, for instance the cult of Asclepius. But within his plays, although the power of the gods is beyond question, and those who doubt that power or reject their oracles are swiftly refuted, it is hard to see any straightforward scheme of divine *justice* at work. Divine action is characterized as enigmatic and obscure. There is an order in the world, as is shown by the fulfilment of oracles; but the pattern is often too elusive for men to grasp. The gods are not indifferent to humanity: they punish Creon in *Antigone*, they grant a home and honour to Oedipus at the end of his life (*Oedipus at Colonus*).

But there are also mysteries which remain unanswered: why does Antigone have to die? Why did Philoctetes suffer agonies in isolation on Lemnos for nine years? Any open-minded reader of these plays will acknowledge that Sophocles does not give us a simple or uniform account of human life or of mankind's relation to the gods and fate. Had he done so, the plays would probably not have remained so hauntingly powerful over two and a half millennia.

Sophocles is justly regarded as the greatest master of formal structure – no mere mechanical technique, but a vital aspect of his art. The development of each scene, in each play, is beautifully paced; the contrasts of style and mood between successive scenes, or between one scene and the choral song which follows, are achieved with seemingly effortless brilliance. These skills are combined with deep understanding of character in the scenes between Neoptolemus and Philoctetes, with mastery of tension and irony in the advancing quest which will lead Oedipus to self-discovery. On a more minute level of style, *Oedipus the King* also shows his subtlety of technique in the exchange which culminates in the revelation of the hero's identity (1173–6): here each line is divided between Oedipus and the herdsman whom he is questioning, and as the truth becomes plainer, Oedipus' questions become shorter and more faltering, the servant's responses fuller and more desperate. This flexible handling of dialogue form is only one small example of the complete command Sophocles has over his medium. Appalling hatred and unbearable loss are expressed in formal verse of wonderful lucidity and sharpness; only rarely do the eloquent lines dissolve into incoherent cries of pain, as they do when Philoctetes is overcome by his repulsive wound.

III

We turn now to our main subject, the third of the great tragedians. It is far too commonly supposed that Euripides comes 'after' Sophocles, and this can easily lead to a simplifying formula which sees Aeschylus as primitive, Euripides as decadent, and Sophocles as the apex of perfection in between. In fact, although Euripides was clearly younger, he and Sophocles were competing together, often against one another, for most of their lives, and Sophocles died within a year of his rival. Both were very much younger than Aeschylus, though they will certainly have seen some of his later productions. Sophocles in fact competed against Aeschylus with his first production, in 468 BC, and won; Euripides first put on a tetralogy in 455 with a less satisfactory result, coming third. We do not know his competitors on that occasion. From that point on Euripides was constantly in the public eye, putting on a total of around ninety plays up to his death in 406 (his last plays, including the *Bacchae*, were produced posthumously).

We know very little about his life, and what comes down from antiquity is often unreliable (a great deal seems to be derived from the comic treatment of the dramatist by Aristophanes). There is a long-standing tradition that he was unpopular and unsuccessful in his career. We are told that he was melancholy, thoughtful and severe, that he hated laughter and women, that he lived in a cave looking out to the sea from Salamis, that he had a substantial library. None of this amounts to much more than doubtful anecdote. A more concrete statement, which probably rests on inscriptional evidence, is that he won the first prize four times (once posthumously) in his whole career. This sounds more dramatic than it is, since prizes would be awarded to the tetralogy of plays as a whole: in other words, sixteen out of about ninety plays were winners. Even with this reservation, however, there remains a contrast with the other two tragedians: Aeschylus and Sophocles were each victorious with over half their plays. In the end Euripides is said to have emigrated to Macedonia, where King Archelaus was gathering a circle of poets and intellectuals to give tone to his court. It may be doubted whether he left Athens purely because he felt unappreciated; the hardships of life in a city engaged in a long war which she now looked likely to lose might be a more pragmatic explanation. He died in Macedonia, an event again elaborated in wild anecdotes (he was allegedly torn to pieces, like Actaeon in myth, by a pack of hunting-dogs). We should not attach too much importance to the figure about his victories, for it is clear that he was repeatedly granted a chorus, and that the Athenians enjoyed and were fascinated by his work. The constant parodies and references to his plays in

Aristophanes' comedies are not only satirical criticism but a kind of tribute to a playwright whose work he obviously knew intimately and whose significance was beyond question.

We happen to have more plays by Euripides than by the other two tragedians put together: the complete total is nineteen, but that includes the satyr-play *Cyclops* and also *Rhesus*, a play widely thought to be a fourth-century imitation. This larger figure is partly accidental, the results of the hazards of transmission through the ages, but partly reflects the popularity of Euripides in the educational tradition – his language is easier, his speeches were more suitable for aspiring orators to study, and his plays, with their heady mixture of intellectual and emotional appeal, might be found more immediately accessible.[6] We can also put fairly firm dates to a good many of the plays, because of information which survives in copies of the original inscriptions recording victories in the contests and citing the names of annual magistrates of Athens. Where external evidence for dating is lacking, the date of a play can be determined within limits by stylometry, that is, the statistical analysis of the poet's changing linguistic and metrical habits, using the firmly dated plays as a framework.[7] This means not only that we can say something about Euripides' development as a poet, but also that it is possible to identify, or at least speculate about, passages which touch on or allude to Athenian politics and other contemporary events. This is naturally most tempting with plays such as the *Children of Heracles* and the *Suppliant Women*, which are set in Athens and present a mythological image of the Athenians as benefactors of others. But there are many other passages which, without naming Athens, use the language of contemporary politics or ideology. A good example comes in *Orestes*, in which a detailed account of a meeting of the assembly of Argive citizens includes lines which remind the reader of historical and rhetorical texts of the period – of the historian Thucydides' portrayal of Athenian demagogues, for example (*Orestes* 866–952, esp. 902–16). Although the importance of this approach has sometimes been exaggerated, and the tragedies are not allegories of history, it is a mistake to rule out such allusions on principle.[8]

None of the plays we possess in entirety is from the earliest stage of Euripides' career; the first, *Alcestis*, was produced in 438 BC, when he was already in his forties. The great majority of surviving plays come from the last three decades of the fifth century, the period of the great war between Athens and Sparta, a time in which the cultural and political prominence of Athens was still conspicuous but no longer unchallenged, and by the end of the period increasingly under threat. Euripides did not live to see the defeat of Athens, but several of his later plays suggest growing pessimism about political and military leadership, about civic deliberation, and about the conduct of the victors in wartime. These are not novel themes, in poetry or in life, but they have an added resonance in the light of fifth-century history.

The sheer range and variety of Euripides' plays is extraordinary. Perhaps if we had as many of Aeschylus' or Sophocles' plays they would seem equally difficult to categorize; but it is tempting to see Euripides as particularly innovative and trend-setting. Like Sophocles, he seems to have worked mainly on sequences of self-contained plays, though it looks as if the *Trojan Women* was the third of a trilogy concerning the Trojan war from its origins to its conclusion. Unlike Sophocles, he does not generally take a single heroic figure to form the focus of a play – only *Medea* easily fits this pattern. There is a strong tendency to divide the play between major characters: thus in *Alcestis* the heroine gives way to Heracles, the sufferer to the doer; in *Hippolytus* Phaedra dominates the first half of the play, Hippolytus the second; in the *Bacchae* the action is polarized, with the mortal Pentheus and the disguised god Dionysus in conflict throughout. Other plays extend this experimentation to the overall structure. Thus in *Andromache* we begin, as we might expect, with the widow of Hector in difficulties, but as the action advances Andromache is forgotten and other events follow, with different characters taking the limelight. In the *Trojan Women* the continuous presence of Hecabe, the grieving queen of Troy, seems to mark her out as the 'heroine', or at least the principal sufferer, but she is a figure who can achieve nothing. As the play unfolds we are shown a series of scenes which embody the suffering and ruin accompanying the fall of Troy, a sequence which adds up only to further misery. Other plays multiply characters and divide our attention still more: *Helen* has eight human characters with full speaking parts, *Orestes* nine, the *Phoenician Women* eleven.

The plays of Euripides, although they still work within the traditional range of myths, do not generally dramatize heroic initiatives and triumphant achievements. His are tragedies of suffering rather than of action (*Medea* again is a special case, a partial exception). Phaedra, Andromache, Hecabe, the Trojan women, the chorus of mothers in the *Suppliant Women*, the guilt-ravaged Orestes, are all presented as victims, whether of war or other persecution, human folly or divine antagonism. Even when they do attempt to take the initiative, to assert themselves through action, the consequences are rarely presented positively. Phaedra's efforts to preserve her good name bring about Hippolytus' death without achieving her objective; Electra and Orestes in *Electra* destroy their mother, but with psychologically devastating results for themselves; in *Orestes*, the young man's matricide makes him an outcast, and his efforts to take revenge on his mother's sister Helen are first frustrated, then turned to near-farce. Even when Euripides is reworking material which had been treated grimly enough by Aeschylus, he regularly gives his own version a new twist. The brutal sacrifice of Iphigenia at Aulis, so that the Greek fleet may sail for Troy, was presented by Aeschylus in an unforgettable choral song as a terrible necessity, an agonizing decision reluctantly taken by Agamemnon, and one which will have momentous consequences. In Euripides' version, *Iphigenia at Aulis*, Agamemnon and Menelaus chop and change, other members of the expedition seem to have more authority than the leaders have, Iphigenia herself changes her mind, and, most disturbing of all, there is the off-stage presence of the army, an uncontrollable mob of soldiers panting for blood. *Iphigenia at Aulis* is a fast-moving and constantly attention-grabbing play, but one in which the high seriousness of the Aeschylean ode is dissipated, and the tragic sacrifice becomes wasteful self-deception. As A. P. Burnett put it: 'In these plays the poet shows men scaled for comedy trying to live in a world still ruled by the gods of tragedy.'[9]

Some of the ways in which Euripides made old subjects new have already been mentioned. This practice was not simply a perverse desire on his part to alter tradition. Between 480 and 430 BC some five hundred tragedies would have been staged; a middle-aged man in his audience might have seen over two hundred.[10] The Athenians, like any audience, enjoyed innovation: indeed, originality and novelty were at a premium in the second half of the fifth century, as new ideas and new literary styles made their appearance in Athens. Euripides was in part responding to audience demand (though it is only fair to add that a sizeable portion of his audience would be more conservative, and that Sophocles clearly did not feel the need to innovate so ostentatiously). By the middle stage of Euripides' career Aeschylus looked archaic: in his *Electra*, the younger tragedian unmistakably parodies a recognition-scene from Aeschylus' *Libation-Bearers*, in which the discovery of a lock of hair at Agamemnon's tomb was taken as evidence of Orestes' return (513ff.). It is interesting to note that the grounds for criticism are improbability, lack of realism, violation of common sense. Aeschylus and his audience had been above such concerns; by Euripides' time it was more natural to apply to tragedy at least some of the standards of everyday life.[11] Nevertheless, the parody is two-edged: it turns out that the Euripidean Electra's scepticism is misguided, and the deduction from the Aeschylean token remains valid. The allusion to Aeschylus need not be merely dismissive.

Innovation can also be observed in the composition of Euripides' plots. It is natural for us to think of the myths as fixed and organized, as they are in the modern summaries which we find in handbooks; but in fact the fluidity of the legends is surprising, and the tragedians already found variations in the epic and lyric accounts which they inherited. Euripides often uses less familiar versions of myths, or combines stories normally kept apart. Although the loss of so much earlier literature makes firm assertions dangerous, it seems likely that he is modifying the legend in making Medea kill her own children deliberately (in an earlier version it was the Corinthians who took their revenge upon her offspring). In the legends of Heracles it was normally held that the hero's labours were a kind of penance for killing his children in a fit of insanity. Euripides reverses the sequence, making Heracles return home to his family triumphant after his labours are ended – then, the crowning horror, madness and slaughter follow. In his *Helen* he adopts the bizarre version of the lyric poet Stesichorus, which made Helen a prisoner in Egypt throughout the Trojan war, while Greek and Trojan armies fought for ten years over a phantom. The unexpected becomes the rule, in both plot and characterization: women behave manfully, slaves show nobility and virtue, barbarians express civilized sentiments.

Even when he is closer to the traditional versions, he often introduces new characters or explores the implications of legends with a fresh eye: thus in *Orestes*, Menelaus, Tyndareus, Hermione and Orestes' friend Pylades all have prominent roles, and the effect is quite different from earlier versions of this myth. Characterization can also be modified: in Aeschylus' *Seven against Thebes*, Eteocles, king of Thebes, is a noble figure, though labouring under a curse; in Euripides' *Phoenician Women*, he becomes a power-crazed tyrant. In the *Electra* of Euripides it is even possible to sympathize with Clytemnestra and Aegisthus, the murderers of Agamemnon. Sharp changes of direction and unexpected shifts of personality are also common: in *Andromache*, Hermione at first seems a cruel and malicious princess, but later becomes a sympathetic victim. In *Medea*, the heroine vacillates throughout much of the play: loving mother or merciless avenger, which side of her character is to prevail? Aristotle in his *Poetics* (ch. 15) found fault with these startling reversals of character, singling out *Iphigenia at Aulis* for criticism: 'the girl who pleads for her life is quite different from the later one', he complains, referring to the scene where Iphigenia, after earlier begging for mercy, resolves to sacrifice herself in the name of Greece. Euripides also plays variations on his own earlier work: our extant *Hippolytus* is a second version, in which the portrayal of Phaedra is made more sympathetic and her character more complex.

In some ways Euripides can be seen as more self-consciously literary dramatist than his fellow-tragedians. It is not accidental that it was he who was said to have a large library. He seems regularly to modify the conventions of his genre and adapt the work of his predecessors, sometimes even drawing attention to the changes he has made. The parody of the Aeschylean recognition-scene has already been cited; similarly, later in *Electra*, the trapping and killing of Clytemnestra within the hovel in which Electra and her husband have their home is a re-enactment of the killing-scenes within the palace of Agamemnon in Aeschylus' trilogy: humbler setting, unheroic characters, dubious morality all work together. In *Helen*, the heroine proposes that they contrive an escape by pretending Menelaus is dead and mourning him. Is that the best you can do?, asks Menelaus; 'Your plan is hardly very original' (1056). The point is that the trick has been tried often before in tragedy: the character is given the critic's fastidiousness. Aeschylus and Sophocles are also experienced in reshaping and adapting traditional motifs, but Euripides goes far beyond them in playing with conventions and exploiting the spectator's awareness of the dramatic situation. While shocked and moved by the events on stage, we are nevertheless frequently reminded that this is 'only' a play.[12]

As the example from *Helen* just quoted suggests, Euripides' plays are not devoid of lighter, humorous touches. Indeed, his wide repertoire includes not only starkly 'tragic' plays in the stricter sense, such as *Medea*, but also dramas which are harder to categorize. *Alcestis*, with its fairy-tale plot and happy resolution, seems to belong to a kinder and less threatening world than most tragedies. Later plays, notably *Iphigenia among the Taurians* and especially *Helen*, have often been classed as tragi-comedies. In both plays, after many misfortunes, the principal characters are reunited in a far-off setting (Helen is held captive in Egypt, Iphigenia in the Crimea), recognize one another after many false steps, and plan a successful escape back to Greece, outwitting their barbarian opponents. Hair-breadth escapes and cliff-hanging moments are common, as when Iphigenia is about to sacrifice her unrecognized brother to the goddess Artemis. We know that similar scenes occurred in lost plays by Euripides: in *Cresphontes*, a mother is on the point of killing her son with an axe, but the danger is averted, the potential tragedy dissipated.

There is much here which looks back to the *Odyssey*, with its complex plot full of deceptions and recognitions. Moreover, plays of this kind also look forward to later comedy, the types of plot favoured by Menander, Terence and eventually Shakespeare (not to mention Oscar Wilde).[13] These plays are sometimes called escapist, misguidedly; there remains a strong sense of suffering and waste in the past, and they undoubtedly still qualify as tragedies. But they do show the versatile Euripides experimenting with new types of play, and these experiments are accompanied by a lighter and more ironic tone, providing a very different kind of pleasure from the cathartic experience provided by the *Oresteia* or *Oedipus*. Euripides is plainly interested in variations of tone, juxtaposing scenes of very different emotional intensity. A 'comic' element may be found even in much grimmer plays, but there it is often used to reinforce the seriousness of the rest of the action. The self-pity and bad temper of the downtrodden Electra, for example, provide some humour as we sympathize with her husband, the long-suffering farmer; but their conversation also contributes to our understanding of Electra's tortured psyche. Far more macabre is the delusion of Heracles, who believes he is journeying to Mycenae, arriving there, punishing Eurystheus – when all the time he is in his own home, slaughtering his sons. The effect is intensely powerful: this madness would be funny if it were not so horrible.

In reading a plain text, and still more a translation, of Euripides it is easy to overlook the formal and musical aspects of the dramas. Here too we can see that he went beyond the earlier conventions of the genre, in ways which were exciting to the audiences, but also often controversial. Greek tragedy is broadly divisible into spoken verse and sung verse: the former is the medium in which the actors converse with one another or with the chorus-leader, the latter is most commonly found in the songs of the chorus. Already in Aeschylus there are plenty of exceptions: actors can sing solo parts or participate in lyric dialogue. In *Agamemnon*, the prophetess Cassandra voices her god-given insight in emotional song, to the bewilderment of the chorus; still more wild and agitated are the lyric utterances of Io, tormented by pain, in *Prometheus*. But Euripides seems to go further in giving his actors lyric passages, often highly emotional and linguistically rich (no doubt these were also striking in their musical accompaniment). The solo passages, arias or 'monodies', are often virtuoso pieces, and must have made huge demands on an actor: examples are rarer in the earlier plays, but there are several in *Hippolytus*. From the later plays the most memorable examples include Creusa's lament for the child she exposed years ago and now believes dead, the ecstatic suicide-song of Evadne, and (as in Aeschylus) the prophetic raving of Cassandra (*Ion* 859–922, *Suppliant Women* 990ff. and *Trojan Women* 308ff.). In *Orestes* of 408 BC we find the prize example, a *tour-de-force* narrative of the attempt on Helen's life, sung by a Phrygian eunuch in a state of extreme panic, exotically foreign in its linguistic and rhythmical looseness, and no doubt accompanied by violent gestures and mime. The brilliant lyric parody in

Aristophanes' *Frogs* (1309–63), which lifts lines from *Orestes* and elsewhere, shows how extraordinary audiences found his style in these arias. Other formal features of the drama would take too long to illustrate, but the general impression is of sharper and more prosaic or argumentative dialogue style combined with a more self-consciously 'poetic', decorative, image-laden, almost romantic style in lyrics.[14]

Several other aspects of Euripides' work can be illuminated by Aristophanes' *Frogs*, in which Aeschylus and Euripides compete against one another in the underworld. Although it is unsafe to use this play to establish Aristophanes' own aesthetic position, it is first-rate evidence for at least some of the things in Euripidean drama which made most impression on contemporary audiences. In the *Frogs*, Euripides is made to boast that

as soon as the play began I had everyone hard at work: no one standing idle. Women and slaves, master, young woman, aged crone – they all talked . . . It was Democracy in action . . . I taught them subtle rules they could apply; how to turn a phrase neatly. I taught them to see, to observe, to interpret; to twist, to contrive; to suspect the worst, take nothing at its face value . . . I wrote about familiar things, things the audience knew about . . . The public have learnt from me how to think, how to run their own households, to ask 'Why is this so? What do we mean by that?' (948–79, tr. D. Barrett)

In Euripidean drama others besides kings and heroes play major roles; a large number of plays are named after, and focused on, female characters. Indeed, it has been pointed out that most of Euripides' *thinkers* are women: certainly Creon, Jason and Aegeus are easily out-classed by Medea, and in both the *Trojan Women* and *Helen* Menelaus is inferior to his quick-witted wife.[15] Lower-class characters are more prominent and more influential: the Nurse in *Hippolytus* is a perfect example. In *Electra*, the downtrodden princess is married to a mere farmer, who respects her in her adversity, and has not slept with her. The farmer comes from a noble family now impoverished; his low status is contrasted with his honourable behaviour, but the latter still has to be explained by his noble birth. In both *Hecabe* and the *Trojan Women*, the decent herald Talthybius is sympathetic to the captive women, and shocked at the misdeeds of his social superiors. Mention should also be made of the many messengers in Euripides, several of whom are vividly and sympathetically characterized.

The other point which the passage in the *Frogs* emphasizes is the way these characters talk. Here we come close to one of the central aspects of Euripides' work, his fascination with argument, ideas and rhetoric. In the later fifth century BC professional teachers were instructing young men, in Athens and elsewhere, in the art of rhetoric, which in a small-scale democratic society could justly be seen as the key to political success. Types of argument were collected, methods of refutation categorized. It was possible, one of these experts claimed, 'to make the worse case defeat the better'. Euripides gives his characters the inventiveness and articulacy which these teachers sought to impart. This is particularly clear in the so-called *agon* ('contest' or 'debate'), at least one example of which can be found in most of his plays. The *agon* is a scene in which two (occasionally more) characters express their antagonism in long, highly argumentative and sometimes ingenious speeches: rhetorical skill is combined with energetic emotion. Examples are Jason versus Medea, Theseus versus Hippolytus, Helen versus Hecabe (in *Medea*, *Hippolytus*, *Trojan Women* respectively). These scenes sharpen our understanding of the issues, and often challenge us to adjudicate between the parties involved. There is rarely a clear winner, either on the arguments or under the prevailing circumstances in the play: often considerations of power and self-interest matter more than who is in the right. As a result, tragic conflict-scenes seldom lead to a resolution, but tend rather to heighten the antagonism of those involved.[16]

Perhaps all drama suggests larger issues beyond the particular experiences enacted on stage, but Euripides' plays articulate these more abstract and universal concerns to an unusual degree. Although the characters on stage are not mere types – what could be called typical about Medea or Heracles? – their situations and dilemmas often suggest larger questions, more general themes and problems inherent in human life and society. When does justice become revenge, even savagery? Can human reason overcome passion? Should right and wrong be invoked in interstate politics, or is expediency the only realistic criterion? These questions are not left implicit: the characters themselves raise them, in generalizing comments which are often given special prominence at the opening of a speech. The audience, like the characters, must often have been uncertain which side was in the right, and their attitude would naturally change as the drama unfolded. Many, perhaps most, Athenian theatre-goers would also have served as jurors in the law-courts (Athenian juries were often very large, five hundred or more); many would also have voted on proposals in the democratic assembly. They were used to moral and verbal contests, real and fictional, public and private, forensic and literary. Indeed, Athenians were notorious for their addiction to debate: the contemporary historian Thucydides makes a politician call them 'spectators at speeches', a telling paradox.[17] It is no coincidence that this agonistic aspect of Athenian society is so vividly reflected in the dramas. Euripides may have taught the audience to be glib and clever, but he was responding to a development already well advanced.

Perhaps no question has been as prominent in criticism as the nature of Euripides' beliefs, his philosophy. This may seem strange: why should we expect a dramatist to adopt a philosophic position, still less to maintain it from play to play? The reason that this issue seems to many people particularly important is that Euripides frequently introduces abstract ideas or theoretical arguments, sometimes drawing attention to the oddity of his character's language or thought. In the *Suppliant Women*, the Athenian Theseus and the Theban herald argue at length about the relative merits of democratic and monarchic government (399–456). Even if we allow that Theseus, the favourite hero of Athens, is no ordinary monarch, the anachronism involved in placing such a debate in the heroic age is obvious. In *Hippolytus*, Phaedra discourses on the power of passion and how it can overwhelm the mind's good resolutions: her calmness and the abstract tone of her words seem strange after her earlier frenzy. More striking still are the many passages in which characters question the nature, or the very existence, of the Olympian gods. In the *Trojan Women*, Hecabe, in need of inspiration in the *agon*, prays as follows:

O you who give the earth support and are by it supported, whoever you are, power beyond our knowledge, Zeus, be you stern law of nature or intelligence in man, to you I make my prayers; for you direct in the way of justice all mortal affairs, moving with noiseless tread. (884–8)

These lines echo both traditional prayer-formulae and contemporary science; they involve contradictory conceptions of the supreme deity; they even hint at the theory that gods are merely externalizations of human impulses. Little wonder that Menelaus remarks in response, 'What's this? You have a novel way of praying to the gods!'

In passages of this kind Euripides plainly shows his familiarity with the philosophic or metaphysical teachings of a number of thinkers: Anaxagoras, Protagoras, Gorgias and other figures known to us particularly through the writings of Plato and Aristotle. Influence from philosophy or abstract prose has occasionally been detected in Aeschylus and Sophocles, but any such cases in their work are rare and unobtrusive; with Euripides we are dealing with something new. This introduction of modern ideas coheres with his general tendency to make the characters of myth less remote and majestic, more like ordinary mortals with human weaknesses. Unsettling and bizarre these passages may seem, but they are clearly meant (as in the plays of Ibsen and Shaw) to surprise and stimulate: it would be absurd to suppose that Euripides did not realize what he was doing, or that he was incapable of keeping his intellectual interests out of his tragedies.[18]

Ancient anecdote claimed that Protagoras, an agnostic thinker, gave readings from his work in Euripides' house, and that Socrates helped him write his plays. Although these stories are rightly now recognized as fictions, the frequency with which Euripides introduces philosophic or religious reflections still needs explanation. An influential tradition of criticism has maintained that Euripides was a disciple of one or other of these thinkers, and that his dramas represent a concerted endeavour to open his countrymen's eyes to the moral defects of men and gods as represented in the traditional myths. In the earlier part of the fifth century BC, the lyric poet Pindar had questioned a myth which told of divine cannibalism, and in the fourth century Plato was to censor epic and tragedy in the name of morality. The myths were also criticized by

Euripides' contemporaries on grounds of rationality and probability: how could sensible people take seriously stories of three-headed hounds of Hades, or other monstrous creatures? There is, then, no reason to doubt that Euripides could have seen reasons to be sceptical about some of the myths: he makes Helen doubt whether she was really born from a swan's egg, and Iphigenia question whether any deity could conceivably demand human sacrifice (*Helen* 18, 259, *Iphigenia among the Taurians* 380–91).

It is much less plausible to suppose that he was urging total scepticism about the gods or the supernatural, and proposing some alternative philosophical or humanist view in their place. It is difficult for the modern student to appreciate how different Greek religious thought and practice were from the Judaeo-Christian tradition.[19] There was no creed, no sacred books, no central priestly establishment. The city performed its sacrifices and paid honour to the gods, as had always been done; sometimes new gods were admitted to the pantheon; but cult was not the same as myth, and it was well known that myths contradicted one another and that poets made up many stories – many lies, as the Athenian Solon once said. To express doubts about one particular myth did not shake the foundations of religion. Outright atheism was rare and freakish. The more open-minded attitude of the great traveller Herodotus may have been commoner: he declared that all men were equally knowledgeable about the divine.[20]

Certainly there are serious difficulties in treating Euripides as an unbeliever on the evidence of his plays. This is not simply because, alongside the more questioning attitudes in the passages quoted, we find many speakers expressing profound faith and devotion, and choral odes which invoke the Olympians in magnificent poetry: one could always argue (though with some circularity) that these characters possessed only partial or erroneous insights into religion. More important is the fact that without the existence of the gods the plays simply do not work. How is Medea to escape if the sun-god, her grandfather, does not send his chariot to rescue her? How will Theseus' curse destroy his son if Poseidon is a mere fiction? How will the plot of *Alcestis* even begin to work unless death is something more than natural, unless there is a personified being against whom Heracles can do battle? A full discussion would also have to consider the numerous scenes in which gods appear at the end of plays to bring events under control: here, rationalizing interpretations truncate the dramas.

But if Euripides the anti-clerical atheist cannot stand, neither can he simply be forced into the straitjacket of traditional piety, even if that piety is defined in terms flexible and sophisticated enough to include Aeschylus and Sophocles. There remains overwhelming evidence that Euripides, in this as in other respects, was an innovator: just as he introduces new and often unfamiliar characters into traditional myths, or views familiar tragic situations from unexpected angles, so he combines traditional mythical and theatrical conventions about the gods with disturbing new conceptions and challenging ideas. Sometimes the contradictions become acute and paradoxical, as in a notoriously baffling passage of *Heracles*. In this play Heracles, son of Zeus by the mortal woman Alcmena, has been brought to his knees by the goddess Hera, who persecutes him because she resents Zeus' adulteries. Theseus, befriending Heracles and seeking to comfort him, refers at one point to the immorality of the gods, whereupon Heracles bursts into a passionate rejection of this concept:

I do not believe that the gods indulge themselves in illicit love or bind each other with chains. I have never thought such things worthy of belief and I never will; nor that one god treats another as his slave. A god, if he is truly a god, has no need of anything; these are the wicked tales of poets. (*Heracles* 1340–46)

This outburst comes near to rejecting the very premises that underlie the play and Heracles' own experiences within it. Is Euripides showing us something about Heracles' psychology? Insisting, in Plato's manner, on the moral inadequacy of the myths? Alluding to the poetic and fictional quality of his own play? Or all of these at once, and more? The passage, and the issues it raises, is likely to remain controversial.[21]

Although all such labels are bound to oversimplify a many-sided artist like Euripides, we may find more valuable than 'atheist' the term proposed by E. R. Dodds, one of the most gifted interpreters of Greek literature in the twentieth century, who dubbed Euripides 'the irrationalist'.[22] By this Dodds meant that Euripides was interested and impressed by the achievements of human reason, not least in the fields of rhetorical argument and philosophic theory, but in the end felt that they were inadequate both as explanatory tools and as instruments to enable mankind to deal with the world. Reason versus passion, order versus chaos, persuasion versus violence – these antitheses are present in all Greek tragedy, but Euripides seems more pessimistic about the limits of man's capacity to control either himself or society.[23] The demoralizing and brutalizing effects of a prolonged war surely play a part in the development of his outlook: the *Suppliant Women*, *Hecabe* and the *Trojan Women*, or a decade later the *Phoenician Women* and *Iphigenia at Aulis*, all dramatize the suffering and callousness which war makes possible or inevitable. Even *Helen*, for all its playful irony and lightness of touch, implies a bleak and pessimistic view of human action: the Trojan war, far from being a glorious achievement, was fought for a phantom; and although Menelaus and Helen are finally reunited, that partial success cannot compensate for the countless lives thrown away on the plains of Troy.

On this reading, Euripides does not assert the independence of man from divine authority; he is neither an agnostic nor a humanist. Rather, he acknowledges that there are forces in the world which mankind cannot understand or control. They may sometimes be described in the language of traditional religion, or referred to by the names and titles of the Olympians, though even then he often suggests some new dimension: 'she's no goddess, then, the Cyprian, but something greater', cries the nurse when she learns of Phaedra's desire (*Hippolytus* 310). At other times he will make his characters speak of nature, or necessity, or chance: as Talthybius asks in *Hecabe*, 'O Zeus, what am I to say? Do you watch over men or are we fools, blind fools to believe this, and is it chance that oversees all man's endeavours?' (489–91). Or again, a speaker may throw out the suggestion that 'it is all in the mind': 'when you saw him your mind *became* the goddess. All the indiscretions of mortals pass for Aphrodite . . .' (*Trojan Women* 988–9). The supernatural, however it is defined, embraces those things which are beyond human grasp. The author of the following speech, again from

Hippolytus, may not have been a conventional Greek thinker, but he understood how to communicate religious longing.

It's nothing but pain, this life of ours; we're born to suffer and there's no end to it. If anything more precious than life does exist, it's wrapped in darkness, hidden behind clouds. We're fools in love – it's plain enough – clinging to this glitter here on earth because we don't know any other life and haven't seen what lies below. (*Hippolytus* 189–96)

No play of Euripides raises these questions more acutely than the *Bacchae*, surely his greatest tragedy. It is also his most controversial work: it has been read as evidence of a change of heart, a conversion of the ageing playwright to the truths of religion, while others have preferred to see it as a denunciation of ecstatic cult, expressing the tragedian's deep distrust of irrational action.[24] It would be quite impossible to do justice to the play here; what can be done is to sketch a few of the ways in which, for all its special qualities, it is quintessentially Euripidean.

The *Bacchae* describes the coming of Dionysus, still a new god in the mythical world of the play, to his native city of Thebes, accompanied by a chorus of loyal bacchantes. The god seeks recognition in his own land, but comes in disguise, as gods often do, to test the citizens; even the chorus suppose him to be a human priest. The youthful king Pentheus, ignoring good advice from older heads, proceeds to defy the god, little knowing the power he is confronting. At first Dionysus plays the part of an innocent captive in Pentheus' power, answering his questions and leading him on; but he soon escapes from captivity and in a series of scenes gradually gains ascendancy over the king. In the end Pentheus is completely in his power (magic? hypnosis? or something in Pentheus' own heart that answers the Dionysiac summons?). The god, still not revealing his identity, leads him to the mountains where the Theban women are running wild in bacchic frenzy. A messenger reports the horrifying outcome: Pentheus is dead, literally torn to pieces by the women, with his own mother Agave in the lead; in her madness she believes she has slain a wild beast. The bacchic chorus rejoice that their divine master has been vindicated; but even they feel some pity and distress when Pentheus' mother brings on the head of her son and is slowly coaxed back to sanity and misery by her father Cadmus. The whole royal house is to be punished for their unbelief; Dionysus, appearing finally without disguise, *ex machina*, drives Cadmus and Agave into exile, and his pitiless speech contrasts with the tender parting of father and daughter. The cult of Dionysus will now be celebrated in Thebes, but its inauguration has been achieved through the slaughter of the opposing king.

The theme is traditional. Tragedy may have originally focused on Dionysiac subjects; in any case, we know that Aeschylus wrote a trilogy on how the god overcame his early opponents, which Euripides seems to have imitated. In this play Euripides to some extent abandons many of the stylistic and rhetorical features which made his late work so striking: there is no *agon*, for example, and the choral odes are more directly relevant to the play as a whole. Other aspects discussed above are well represented, however: the touches of sophistic argumentation (especially in the pompous lecture by the prophet Tiresias, who claims to know the 'true' nature of Dionysus); the brilliantly vivid and often gruesome narrative of the messenger; the macabre black humour of the scene in which Dionysus clothes Pentheus in female bacchic dress, and in which the king preens himself in his new outfit, unaware that he is being attired as a ritual victim.

Furthermore, the overall treatment of the theme is very different from anything we can imagine from Aeschylus' hand. The play could have been a straightforward tale of *hubris* punished, an evil man struck down by a proud but just god. What is different in the *Bacchae* is the presentation of Pentheus as a weak and unstable young man, psychologically more interesting than the standard tyrant-figure. As already mentioned, the scenes between him and Dionysus are hard to interpret: on the one hand the god is playing with the foolish king like a cat with a mouse, but on the other Pentheus seems eager to fall in with Dionysus' suggestions, pruriently keen to visit the maenads, perhaps even sexually attracted by the almost feminine beauty of the stranger. Euripides, as we have seen, is interested not only in the decisions and actions of his characters, but also in their inner psychology.

As for the god himself, unusually present on stage throughout, he too is hard to evaluate. The chorus sing beautifully of the delights of Dionysiac worship: 'O blessed he who in happiness knowing the rituals of the gods makes holy his way of life and mingles his spirit with the sacred band, in the mountains serving Bacchus with reverent purifications' (73–7). We recognize here the playwright's understanding of religious devotion, just as we do in the lines in which Hippolytus prays to his beloved Artemis (73–87), or in the fragments of choral ecstasy from the lost *Cretans* (fragment 472). But the joy of union with nature is the inverse side of the madness that leads a mother to slay her own son – this, too, at Dionysus' bidding. Dionysus values honour from mankind, and relishes his revenge: is this what a god is truly like? The broken Cadmus entreats the god for mercy at the end of the play, in terms which echo the words of earlier plays.[25]

CADMUS: Dionysus, we beseech you. We have done wrong!

DIONYSUS: You were late to understand us. When you should have, you did not know us.

CADMUS: This we have come to recognize; but your reprisals are too severe!

DIONYSUS: Yes, because I am a god, and you insulted me.

CADMUS: Gods should not resemble men in their anger!

DIONYSUS: Long ago Zeus my father approved these things.

(1344–9, tr. G. S. Kirk)

It is not the business of a tragedian to solve the riddles of the universe, but to dramatize human experience in such a way as to arouse his audience's compassion and extend their imaginative understanding. This, and much else, is what Euripides offers to spectator and reader alike.

IV*

Of the plays in this volume only *Helen* is firmly dateable (to 412 BC); the others can be dated approximately, and probably range from about 415 to 409; *Heracles* is probably the earliest, but its chronological relation to the *Trojan Women*, firmly dated to 415, is unclear. Euripides in 410 would have been in his late fifties or older, and had been producing tragedies for over forty years. By the time of *Helen* he had only a few years to live, and would spend most of them at the court of Macedon, far from his native Athens. Yet his final decade was a period of extraordinary creativity and innovation in his tragic technique.

This was a bleak period for Athens. After the disintegration of the Peace of Nicias, war had been renewed with Sparta and her allies; in 413 the disastrous expedition to Sicily had failed, with immense loss of life and waste of resources. In 411 the democracy had been overthrown from within by a revolution which attempted to set up a more narrowly based government. Although the coup was shortlived, and the democratic constitution was swiftly restored, the episode left Athens full of distrust and divided as to the future of the war. There were setbacks overseas, with subject cities in revolt; there were repeated invasions of Athens' territory from the north; there were problems in leadership, with Athens' most charismatic general, the gifted Alcibiades, in exile and unscrupulously currying favour at Sparta and in Persia: even when he rejoined the Athenian side he was distrusted. The growing involvement of the Persian king and his subordinates in the war which Athens and Sparta were pursuing in Ionia would eventually lead to decisive intervention on the side of Sparta. By this stage no Athenian could have been cheerfully confident of victory; many may have doubted the wisdom of continuing the conflict while being reluctant to accept any diminution of Athens' remaining naval and imperial power.

This grim background is not clearly reflected in any of the plays in

*Sections I–III of this introduction are reproduced, with minor modifications, from the corresponding General Introduction in earlier volumes of this series. Section IV adds a few more specific comments on the plays which figure in this volume, to be supplemented by the prefaces to each play.

this volume except *Helen*, and even there the connections are indirect: the play undoubtedly alludes to the wastefulness of war in general and the futility of the Trojan war in particular, but no passage necessitates an application of these judgements to the Athens–Sparta conflict. Athens is however a recurring presence in the plays, though without occupying centre stage. In *Heracles*, Theseus, Athens' favourite hero, offers consolation and refuge to the broken Heracles. In *Ion* and *Iphigenia*, Athenian rituals and traditions are prominently mentioned; in both, the principal characters are setting out to Athens at the end of the play, and in both, Athena appears as *deus ex machina*, but in none of these plays is Athens actually the scene of the drama. This group of plays includes no case like *The Children of Heracles* and *Suppliant Women*, in which we saw Athens engaged in heroic warfare in defence of the innocent. There is a sense in which the characters are disengaged from politics: Theseus in *Heracles* is more important as friend than as king; the emotional and moral focus of *Ion* is on the relationship of parent and child, although the need of Athens for a legitimate heir is also genuine; in *Helen*, with the realization that the Trojan war was fought in vain, the reunion of husband and wife becomes all the more precious. When characters in these plays do talk politics, the note is one of disillusionment; even in Ion's inexperienced view there is much to criticize in the Athenian way of life (*Ion* 585–647). In the later plays, especially the *Phoenician Women* and the *Orestes*, the bitter scepticism about political debate and the motives of politicians goes further.

Three of the plays grouped in this volume clearly have much in common: *Ion*, *Iphigenia* and *Helen* (*Helen* may indeed be composed as a piece of self-imitation, on the model of *Iphigenia among the Taurians*). The accident of survival may lead us to exaggerate the importance of this grouping: recognition and happy endings are not new in Euripides, or in tragedy as a genre. Nevertheless, it seems reasonable to accept that these plays show a new, or a renewed, preoccupation with a particular type of ironic and complex plot, in which the emphasis is on deception and illusion, leading finally by devious means to recognition between those close to one another: in *Ion*, mother and son; in *Iphigenia*, brother and sister; in *Helen*, husband and wife. Euripides' exploration of these relationships in *Electra* was darker and bleaker; in these plays more is made of the positive aspect. Misapprehension or failed recognition is combined with deliberate or malicious deception, in a variety of ways. In *Ion*, because Creusa is unaware of Ion's real identity, she conspires to murder him. By contrast in the other two plays, the conspiracy is positive, involving deception as a means of escape: once accidental misunderstanding is over, trickery of one's captor can lead to a happy homecoming. The escape-plot is shared also with the satyric *Cyclops*, in which the giant is deceived by comic means (Odysseus gets him drunk), and the subsequent violence is also treated as comic. In all of these respects *Heracles* stands apart: in its unrelieved presentation of undeserved suffering, in its horrific presentation of divine malignity, it belongs to a different tragic sphere. The other plays of this volume flirt with comedy and comic themes: Euripides' tirelessly inventive mind seems in his later period to be ever more restless within the generic boundaries of Athenian drama.

The same innovative tendency can be seen in the formal and stylistic aspects of the plays. The intervention of the gods half-way through *Heracles*, though it seems to have a precedent in Sophocles' *Niobe*, is almost certainly more abrupt and unexpected than in that lost play, and breaks with all Euripides' own conventions. There is a general tendency to bold experiment and to extremes of style. The standard verse used by the characters, the iambic trimeter, is more freely handled, with a larger number of syllables being freely introduced; messenger speeches and sung lyrics by actors are multiplied; the choral odes become more purely lyrical, less easy to connect with the play's main themes and plot. The style of the playwright's lyrics becomes more exotic and extravagant, with long and loosely structured sentences, invocations, repetitions, novel words and rhythms. Some have attributed these changes to the influence of the little-known lyric genre of dithyramb, and especially to a contemporary poet called Timotheus; but where so much of fifth-century poetry is lost, little can be said with certainty. What is clear is that Euripides' dramas in this period have a new quality: stylistically innovative, adventurous and even outrageous in plot, full of unexpected twists and changes of fortune. The mood of these dramas is impossible to characterize: they swing from lamentation to celebration, from tragic intensity through ironic misapprehension to

tongue-in-cheek witticism. If we are to seek a concluding generaliz-
ation, it can only be imperfect and in need of further qualification.
Euripides portrays a world of inherent instability, which he invites us
to view with scepticism that does not exclude compassion.

NOTES

1. On the festivals and theatrical conditions, see above all Sir Arthur Pickard-
Cambridge, *Dramatic Festivals of Athens* (2nd edn, Oxford 1968); E. Csapo and
W. J. Slater, *The Context of Ancient Drama* (Michigan 1995); more briefly
E. Simon, *The Ancient Theatre* (Eng. tr., London and New York 1982), pp. 1–
33; O. Taplin, *Greek Tragedy in Action* (London 1978), ch. 2. A readable account
of the theatrical context is provided by R. Rehm, *Greek Tragic Theatre* (London
1992). See also J. R. Green, *Theatre in Ancient Greek Society* (London 1994).

2. For an excellent discussion of the types of myths favoured, see B. M. W.
Knox, *Word and Action: Essays on the Ancient Theater* (Baltimore and London
1979), ch. 1.

3. O. Taplin, *The Stagecraft of Aeschylus* (Oxford 1977); D. Bain, *Actors and
Audience* (Oxford 1977); D. Mastronarde, *Contact and Discontinuity* (London
1979); M. Halleran, *Stagecraft in Euripides* (London and Sydney 1985); Rehm,
Greek Tragic Theatre.

4. See M. L. West, *Ancient Greek Music* (Oxford 1992). On dance, see Pickard-
Cambridge, *Dramatic Festivals of Athens*, ch. 5.

5. For fuller essays, see R. P. Winnington-Ingram and P. E. Easterling in *The
Cambridge History of Classical Literature*, vol. 1, ed. P. E. Easterling and B. M. W.
Knox (Cambridge 1985; paperback 1989); also the pamphlets by S. Ireland and
R. Buxton in the *Greece & Rome New Surveys* series (Oxford).

6. Revivals of older tragedies became a regular feature at the festivals from
386 BC onwards: see Pickard-Cambridge, *Dramatic Festivals of Athens*, pp. 99–
100. Euripides' plays were frequently chosen. For the possibility of performances
outside Athens already in the fifth century BC, see P. E. Easterling, *Illinois
Classical Studies* 19 (1994), pp. 1–8.

7. This work is highly technical, but the essentials can be gleaned from A. M.
Dale's introduction to her commentary on *Helen* (Oxford 1967), pp. xxiv–
xxviii.

8. See further G. Zuntz, *The Political Plays of Euripides* (Manchester 1955), chs.
1–3, esp. pp. 78–81. Some more recent approaches, which all seek in different
ways to put tragedy in an Athenian context, can be found in the collection

Nothing to do with Dionysus?, ed. J. Winkler and F. Zeitlin (Princeton 1990), and *Greek Tragedy and the Historian*, ed. C. B. R. Pelling (Oxford 1997).

9. From the jacket blurb of Anne P. Burnett, *Catastrophe Survived* (Oxford 1973).

10. I draw here on R. P. Winnington-Ingram, 'Euripides, *poietes sophos* [intellectual poet]', *Arethusa* 2 (1969), pp. 127–42. His points are further developed by W. G. Arnott, 'Euripides and the Unexpected', in I. McAuslan and P. Walcot (eds.), *Greek Tragedy* (*Greece & Rome Studies* 2, Oxford 1993), pp. 138–52.

11. In Aristophanes' *Clouds*, originally produced in 423 BC, the rebellious Pheidippides is asked by his father to sing a passage of Aeschylus, and scoffs at the idea, dismissing the older poet as a bombastic and incoherent ranter. When asked to produce a modern alternative, he shocks his father by reciting a passage from Euripides' *Aeolus* defending the merits of incest!

12. This aspect of Euripides has been emphasized, sometimes to excess: see e.g. S. Goldhill, *Reading Greek Tragedy* (Cambridge 1986), esp. ch. 10.

13. Knox, *Word and Action*, pp. 250–74 ('Euripidean comedy').

14. Good summary, with further references, in C. Collard, *Euripides* (*Greece & Rome New Surveys* 14, Oxford 1981), pp. 20–29.

15. The reference to Euripides' thinkers comes from E. R. Dodds' essay 'Euripides the Irrationalist', *Classical Review* 43 (1929), pp. 87–104, reprinted in his collection *The Ancient Concept of Progress and Other Essays* (Oxford 1973), pp. 78–91. On women in Athenian literature and society, see further J. Gould, 'Law, custom and myth: aspects of the social position of women in classical Athens', *Journal of Hellenic Studies* 100 (1980), pp. 38–59; Goldhill, *Reading Greek Tragedy*, ch. 5; and the essays in A. Powell (ed.), *Euripides, Women and Sexuality* (London 1990).

16. For a very helpful essay on this side of Euripides, see C. Collard, 'Formal Debates in Euripidean Drama', in McAuslan and Walcot, *Greek Tragedy*, pp. 153–66; also M. Lloyd, *The Agon in Euripides* (Oxford 1992).

17. Thucydides iii.38, 4. It is particularly striking that the word translated as 'spectator' is the regular term for a member of the theatrical audience.

18. A. N. Michelini, *Euripides and the Tragic Tradition* (Madison, Wis. and London 1987), part 1, gives a well-documented history of the debate over Euripides' views. A seminal work, still enjoyable and stimulating, is G. Murray's short book *Euripides and his Age* (London 1913).

19. See the useful collection of essays edited by P. E. Easterling and J. V. Muir, *Greek Religion and Society* (Cambridge 1985), esp. J. Gould's contribution, 'On making sense of Greek religion'.

20. Herodotus 2.3, 2. On this subject in general, J. Mikalson, *Athenian Popular Religion* (Chapel Hill 1983) and *Honor thy Gods* (Chapel Hill and London 1991) are valuable collections of material, but tend to draw too firm a line between what happens in life and what appears in literature.

21. T. C. W. Stinton, *Proceedings of the Cambridge Philological Society*, NS 22 (1976), pp. 60–89; reprinted in Stinton, *Collected Papers on Greek Tragedy* (Oxford 1990), pp. 236–64; H. Yunis, *A New Creed: Fundamental Religious Beliefs in the Athenian Polis and Euripidean Drama* (Göttingen 1988), esp. pp. 155–71.

22. Dodds, 'Euripides the Irrationalist'.

23. Classic (over-) statement in K. Reinhardt, 'Die Sinneskreise bei Euripides', in *Tradition und Geist* (Göttingen 1960); also available in a French translation (K. Reinhardt, *Éschyle; Euripide*, Paris 1972).

24. E. R. Dodds' commentary on the Greek text of this play, *Euripides. Bacchae* (2nd edn, Oxford 1960) remains essential for serious study; see also R. P. Winnington-Ingram, *Euripides and Dionysus* (Cambridge 1948).

25. See esp. *Hippolytus* 114–20.

CHRONOLOGICAL TABLE

As explained in the Introduction, not all of the plays of Euripides (and fewer still of Sophocles) can be firmly dated. This table shows all of the extant Greek tragedies for which we have fairly certain dates, and also lists most of Aristophanes' surviving comedies and some major historical events to put them in context. Conjectural dates are given with question-marks, and are usually fixed by analysis of metrical technique: they may well be three or four years out either way.

Year BC

c. 535–2	Thespis competes in first tragic competition		
		490	Darius' invasion of Greece
		480–79	Xerxes' invasion
472	Aeschylus' *Persians*		
468	Sophocles' first victory, on his first attempt		
467	Aesch. *Laius*, *Oedipus*, *Seven against Thebes*, *Sphinx*		
463?	Aesch. *Suppliant Women*, *Aigyptioi*, *Danaids*, *Amymone*	c. 462	Radical democracy established at Athens

458	Aesch. *Agamemnon*, *Libation-Bearers*, *Eumenides*, *Proteus*		
456	Death of Aeschylus		
455	Euripides' first competition: third prize		
438	Eur. *Alcestis*		
431	Eur. *Medea*	431	War begins between Athens and Sparta
c. 430?	Eur. *The Children of Heracles*	430	Great Plague of Athens
		429	Death of Pericles
428	Eur. *Hippolytus* (surviving version)		
		427	Aristophanes' first play (now lost)
425?	Eur. *Andromache*	425	Arist. *Acharnians*
		424	Arist. *Knights*
pre-423?	Eur. *Hecabe*		
423?	Eur. *Suppliant Women*	423	Arist. *Clouds* (original version)
		422	Arist. *Wasps*
		421	Arist. *Peace*; death of Cleon; peace of Nicias
c. 417–415	Eur. *Heracles*, *Electra*		
		416	Athenian massacre at Melos

415	Eur. *Trojan Women*	
		414 Arist. *Birds*
		413 Athenian expedition to Sicily ends in disaster
pre-412?	Eur. *Ion, Iphigenia among the Taurians*	
412	Eur. *Helen*	
412 or later?	Eur. *Cyclops* (satyr-play)	
		411 Arist. *Lysistrata, Women at the Thesmophoria* Oligarchic revolution at Athens
c. 409?	Eur. *Phoenician Women*	
409	Soph. *Philoctetes*	
408	Eur. *Orestes*	
406–405	Death of Euripides in Macedonia; death of Sophocles	
after 406	Eur. *Iphigenia at Aulis, Bacchae* (posthumously produced)	
		405 Arist. *Frogs*
		404 End of war, with Athens defeated
401	Soph. *Oedipus at Colonus* (posthumously produced)	
		399 Execution of Socrates

NOTE ON THE TEXT

We have no manuscripts in Euripides' hand, or going back anywhere near his own time. If we had, they would be difficult to decipher, and would lack many aids which the modern reader takes for granted: stage directions, punctuation, clear indications of change of speaker, regular divisions between lines and even between words. In fact, although some parts of his plays, mostly short extracts, survive in papyri from the earliest centuries AD, no complete play is preserved in any manuscript earlier than the tenth century. Moreover, the textual evidence for the various plays differs greatly in quantity. Three plays were especially popular in later antiquity, namely *Hecabe*, the *Phoenician Women* and *Orestes* (the so-called 'Byzantine triad'). These survive in more than 200 manuscripts. The plays in the present volume, however, all fall into a group which derives from a single fourteenth-century manuscript known as L, unaccompanied by ancient commentary. In a different category come the many quotations from Euripides in other classical authors, which sometimes preserve different readings from those in the direct tradition of Euripidean manuscripts.

This situation is not unusual in the history of classical authors. No ancient dramatist's work survives in his own hand: in all cases we are dealing with a text transmitted by one route or several, and copied many times over. In an age which knew nothing of the printing-press, far less the Xerox machine, all copying had to be done by hand, every copy in a sense a new version. The opportunities for corruption of the text – that is, the introduction of error – were numerous. The reasons for such corruption include simple miscopying or misunderstanding by the scribe, omission or addition of passages by actors in later productions, efforts to improve the text by readers who felt, rightly or wrongly, that it must be corrupt, accidental inclusion of marginal notes or quotations from other plays, and very occasionally bowdlerization of 'unsuitable' passages. Problems of this kind were already recognized in antiquity: efforts were made to stabilize the texts of the tragedians in fourth-century BC Athens, and the ancient commentaries or 'scholia' to some of Euripides' plays make frequent comments on textual matters, for instance remarking that a line is 'not to be found' in some of their early manuscripts, now lost to us. In the same way, when a modern scholar produces an edition of a Euripidean play, there are many places where he or she must decide between different versions given in different manuscripts. Sometimes the choice will be easy: one version may be unmetrical, ungrammatical or meaningless. But often the decision may be more difficult, and in many cases it is clear that no manuscript preserves the lines in question in the correct form. Hence the editor must either reconstruct Euripides' authentic text by 'conjecture', or indicate that the passage is insolubly corrupt.

A translator is in a slightly more fortunate position than an editor. The editor must make a decision what to print at every point, and uncertainty may prevail as to the exact wording even when the overall sense is fairly clear. In this translation James Diggle's excellent Oxford Classical Text has normally been followed: when he has marked a word or phrase as probably or certainly corrupt, we have usually adopted a conjectural reading, whether made by him or a previous editor, even though we often agree that there can be no certainty that this is what Euripides actually wrote. In cases where the corruption is more extensive, we have tried to give a probable idea of the train of thought. These problems arise particularly in choral and other lyric passages, where the language is less close to everyday speech, and where unusual metre and dialect often misled copyists.

Many of the smaller problems involving variations of words or uncertainty over phrasing will be unlikely to cause difficulties to readers of this translation. More noticeable are the occasional places where it seems that something has dropped out of the text; usually this can be explained by the accidents of miscopying or by damage to some of the manuscripts from which our texts descend. The problem is not acute in the plays in this volume, but occasional gaps, mostly of no more than a line or two, are indicated in the text by daggers, and glossed in the notes. Where words are supplied to fill an apparent gap in the text, the additional matter is indicated by curly brackets thus: { }. Similarly, copyists sometimes misplaced and transposed passsages: an example of this is to be found at lines 860–70 of *Heracles*, where the text has been adjusted accordingly; hence the disruption of the marginal line-numbers (p. 29).

A much more serious problem which affects criticism of Euripides is that of interpolation. This is the term used to describe the inclusion of alien material in the original text, expanding and elaborating on the author's words. Sometimes the new material betrays itself by its very unsuitability to the context, and we may suppose that it has been included by accident (for instance, parallels from other plays were sometimes copied out in the margin, then found their way into the text in subsequent copies). Sometimes lines may be present in one manuscript but omitted in others: if they seem superfluous in themselves, they may well be a later addition. Sometimes a speech may seem unnecessarily wordy, and we may suspect without feeling certain that it has been expanded; here textual criticism merges with literary judgement. It has often been suggested that some passages in the plays have been 'padded out' by actors seeking to improve their parts: although this phenomenon has probably been exaggerated, it would be a mistake to rule it out altogether. One speech which has fallen under suspicion on these grounds is Medea's famous soliloquy as she wavers over the killing of her children (*Medea* 1019–80: the boldest critics would excise all of 1056–80). In the present volume there is no case of such central importance for the interpretation of a play, but interpolation has certainly been diagnosed in many places. In the translation our normal policy is to follow Diggle's text, and consequently we omit passages which he brands as interpolated, but we have not accepted all of his judgements, and in particular we retain, though with cautionary comments in the notes, certain parts of *Helen* where his determination to excise the irrelevant may be thought to have gone too far. We also print the choral tail-piece which ends that play in the manuscripts, even though it also appears at the conclusion of several other Euripidean plays. It is customary for the chorus to have the final word, and to omit this moralizing conclusion brings the action to a rather abrupt halt. We are not convinced that it is impossible that Euripides should have ended several plays with the same choral tag. As with many such questions, there remains much room for argument; but Diggle's intimate familiarity with the author and clear-headed judgement demand respect, and despite a few disagreements of this kind, our high opinion of his text has only been enhanced by closer study.

FURTHER READING

W. S. Barrett, *Euripides: Hippolytus* (Oxford 1964), pp. 45–84: a detailed account, requiring some knowledge of Greek and technical terms.

C. Collard, *Euripides* (*Greece & Rome New Surveys* 14, 1981), p. 3: a good one-page summary with bibliography.

L. D. Reynolds and N. G. Wilson, *Scribes and Scholars: A Guide to the Transmission of Greek and Latin Literature* (3rd edn, Oxford 1991).

D. Roberts, 'Parting words: final lines in Sophocles and Euripides', *Classical Quarterly* 37 (1987), pp. 51–64.

M. L. West, *Textual Criticism and Editorial Technique* (Stuttgart 1973), part 1.

TRANSLATOR'S NOTE

A new translation of an author as great as Euripides needs little justification, perhaps, but it may be useful to point out certain respects in which this translation differs from those of the late Philip Vellacott which Penguin published in four volumes between 1953 and 1972. In these, for the most part, the translation was deliberately broken up into verse-like lines, creating a certain stateliness that reflected the dignity of the original but often resulted in the kind of English which could only exist on the printed page. My aim has been to produce a version that conforms far more to how people speak, and for this the medium of continuous prose was essential.

A further consequence of the earlier approach is that all the characters speak the same form of stylized English, whether they are princes or slaves. By adopting continuous prose I have tried to achieve a tone that is more relaxed, less stylized and less close to the Greek word-order, while remaining true to the original. There is a wider range of tones and moods in recognition of the fact that, for all the uniformity of the Greek, not every character maintains a wholly dignified register of speech. Some employ a more colloquial and fast-moving style, even verging on the humorous (for example the Old Woman in *Helen*), others require a more dignified style because they are arrogant or demented or divine.

In the lyric passages, especially the choral odes, I have aimed at a certain archaic formality of language in recognition of their emotional or religious content, but the overriding concern has been to let the freshness and beauty of the poetry come through to the reader as directly as possible. These elements of song in Euripides' work were much admired by his contemporaries and by later generations, and here, if anywhere, the translator's responsibility weighs particularly heavily.

There is a change of presentation from the first and second volumes. In order to mark more clearly the distinction between spoken and sung parts in the plays, all lyric sections have been put in italics and where appropriate separated more distinctly from what was spoken. The areas chiefly affected are the choral odes.

Euripides is intensely interested in human nature in all its different forms and a modern translation must therefore try to take some account of the richness of his character portrayal and psychological insight. It is this belief that underpins my attempt throughout these plays to find and express variety of tone; I have tried to think of the words as being spoken by real persons rather than literary creations, remembering the remark attributed to Sophocles that, whereas in his plays he showed men 'as they should be', Euripides showed them 'as they are'.

This said, it remains true that the language of Attic tragedy, even in the case of the modernizing Euripides, was never that spoken in the streets of Athens in the poet's day. As with Homeric epic, it is essentially a literary creation that aims predominantly at a certain grandeur in keeping with the dignity of its subject-matter. This inevitability imposes limits on how natural a style should be attempted by a translator. However modern Euripidean tragedy may seem compared with that of Aeschylus and Sophocles, its language was still sufficiently grand for Aristophanes to parody it relentlessly in his comedies as high flown and pompous.

As with the first and second volumes, I have not attempted to produce an entirely modern idiom in these translations (except in the special case of the satyr-play *Cyclops*, which contains considerably more colloquialisms per spoken line than any Euripidean tragedy); the overall tone remains, I hope, essentially dignified, as Greek tragedy demands, and I have tried hard to be faithful to the original both in letter and in spirit, taking heart from the excellent prose translation of Virgil's *Aeneid* for Penguin Classics by Professor David West, and the sensible remarks he makes on translating poetry into prose in his own introduction to that book.

No dramatist of any age can be content to live solely within the confines of the printed page, and it is gratifying that my translation of *Trojan Women* has been used for a performance on the London stage. I hope that other plays in these versions may catch the eye of modern producers and that the reader who comes fresh to Euripides in this volume may feel that his voice deserves to be heard more in the modern theatre.

My warmest thanks go, once again, to my collaborator Dr Richard Rutherford of Christ Church, Oxford, not only for his introductory essay, prefaces and notes, but also for his generosity in casting a scholarly eye over my manuscripts and rescuing me several times from 'translationese'. Any remaining infelicities are to be laid firmly at my door. I am also grateful to Professor David Kovacs, translator of Euripides for the Loeb Classical Library, for sharing his thoughts with me on the problems and pleasures of translating this elusive author; to Professor Robert Fagles of Princeton, translator of Aeschylus and Sophocles for Penguin Classics, whose generous remarks on the first volume were much appreciated by a comparative novice in the art of translation; and to Pat Easterling, Regius Professor Emeritus of Greek at Cambridge, for her encouragement and advice in the early stages. I must not forget my students at St Paul's School, who have played their part in sharpening my focus on the plays and several times made me think again. Five plays remain to be translated out of a total of nineteen, in a project that began in 1994 – *kamatos eukamatos*.

Finally, I would like to dedicate this book, as ever, to my children, Lorna and Andrew, and to Gill.

J.N.D.

HERACLES

PREFACE TO *HERACLES*

Heracles is one of Euripides' darkest plays. We are introduced to the mortal father of Heracles, Amphitryon, to his wife Megara, and to her children by the hero, all of whom are imperilled and have been abandoned by fair-weather friends. In their wretched state they have taken refuge at an altar: we recognize the recurring pattern of a suppliant drama (as in *The Children of Heracles* or *Andromache*; Helen's situation at the opening of *Helen* is similar, though less fraught with danger). Where there is a suppliant, there is normally a rescuer; but the family of Heracles have virtually lost hope that their preserver will ever return from the land of the dead, where he has gone in order to fulfil one of his terrible labours for King Eurystheus. After several scenes of despondency advancing to despair, the play presents the return of Heracles, triumphant at the end of his labours, rescuing his family in the nick of time from the cruelty of the tyrant Lycus, whose very name means 'wolf'. It seems that the family are reunited and that Heracles has proved the saviour of his father, wife and children. But at the peak of his good fortune, when all his cares seem to be at an end and the tyrant is slain, horror and madness ensue. This madness has been sent by the goddess Hera, through her agents Iris and Madness; under its influence Heracles kills his wife and children, destroying the palace in the process, and collapses into unconsciousness. The remainder of the play shows him regaining both consciousness and sanity, and confronting the full horror of what he has done. Can he even bear to go on living after this?

Before considering the closing scenes, we should consider how unusual this handling of the story is. There is good reason to think that Euripides has made considerable innovations in the mythological plot of *Heracles*, firstly in inventing the character of Lycus and the dilemma of the hero's family, but more significantly in the overall chronology of his career. In most sources the killing of his children in a fit of madness comes earlier in his life: indeed, the labours are represented as a form of punishment or expiation for this atrocity. Here the sequence is reversed, so that the fortunes of Heracles and his household, having been at a low point when the play begins, rise to an apparently positive peak, and then are cast down once more to still greater disaster. The destruction which Lycus would have inflicted on Heracles' kin is brought about by the hero himself.

No less startling is the structural technique of the drama. The play seems to have reached a satisfactory resolution, and the concern of the gods both for Heracles and for justice in the human world seems to have been vindicated. 'Hail Justice!' cry the chorus; 'Hail the tide of fate that flows from heaven! . . . Tears of grief have turned to joy, this happy change has given birth to new songs' (739, 765–7). Less than a hundred lines later they are singing a very different song. The turning-point of the play is reached when at line 815 the chorus cry aloud in fear and distress at the sudden appearance of the menacing figures of Iris and Madness. There have been no ominous forebodings, no doubts about Heracles' future, since he returned as the saviour-figure of the play. Few other Greek tragedies involve such a markedly unexpected change in the course of events. It is also unusual in Euripides, though not unparalleled in earlier tragedy, for an epiphany to take place in mid-play: in most other cases the divine intervention is confined to the opening or, more relevantly, the close of the play. Here the structural anomaly emphasizes the disruption of Heracles' mind and life; it also brings home to the audience with drastic force how little the expectation of divine justice is justified in the sombre world of this play.

The most impressive part of the play for many modern readers is the last four hundred lines, in which first Amphitryon helps Heracles to recognize what he has done (a scene of considerable psychological insight), and then the Athenian hero Theseus, a late arrival on the stage, proves himself a true friend by urging Heracles to live rather than freeing himself from humiliation and grief through suicide. This part of the play shows us human suffering rather than heroic prowess; the

Heracles whom the chorus described with lyric enthusiasm earlier in the play, the hero who overcame the hydra and the Nemean lion, is now a weeping, broken figure. His final 'labour' has been the execution of his children (1279). Outraged at the conduct of the gods, he repudiates his divine father, Zeus, and accepts Amphitryon, whom according to the familiar legend Zeus had cuckolded, as his real father (1264-5). Just as Amphitryon represents the love of a real human father, Theseus in this play represents true human friendship as opposed to divine malignity and eventual indifference. There is a pro-Athenian aspect to this (as in other dramas, Theseus shows civilized values and Athens proves to be a refuge for the unfortunate), but we recognize a respect for human compassion and fellow-feeling which goes beyond patriotic motives.

At the close of the play Heracles departs to Athens. Euripides leaves it unsettled what will become of him. In the tradition familiar to all Greek audiences, Heracles eventually became a god and was reconciled with Hera, his old enemy, marrying the goddess Hebe, whose name signifies youth and vitality. This tradition goes back at least as far as Hesiod. There is no hint of future deification in this play, though a few critics have struggled to find some compensatory note of this kind. It is true that Theseus declares that in days to come, when Heracles has gone down to Hades, the Athenians will commemorate him with stone monuments, a reference to the honours paid by the Athens of historical times to Heracles as a hero or a god. But the poet deliberately confines this to the human sphere, and no divine message at the end is permitted to soften the austerity of the conclusion.

Many readers have found *Heracles* a shocking play, and so it is; many critics have found it bizarre, because of its peculiar construction and its apparent neglect of Aristotelian principles of cause and effect. There is no clear reason for Heracles' suffering: occasional references suggest that we may supply Hera with her traditional motive of enmity to one of Zeus' bastard offspring, but the motif is hardly emphasized. No act or deficiency of Heracles himself seems to account for his downfall. The oddity of the *deus ex machina* in the middle of the play, and the new direction of the plot once Theseus appears, have already been mentioned. On the whole it is now admitted that the play does not fully abide by Aristotelian principles (which of course were not formulated until well after Euripides' death!), but that this does not mean the play is a failure. There are other forms of unity which can be traced in *Heracles*, including the recurring references to friendship, family ties and gratitude. There are also significant links between the imagery of the two halves of the play. A particularly powerful parallel is the comparison which is used in two places to describe one or more person's dependency on another: the metaphor of a small boat attached to a larger vessel and being towed after it. Heracles uses the image fondly and protectingly, to describe his own family as he guides them within the house – to their deaths, as it turns out. The image is reused at the close of the play, by Heracles again, this time describing his own relationship to his preserver Theseus (1424, echoing 631). Theseus provides the protection that Heracles tried but failed to give his family. Such verbal devices do not produce orthodox unity, but they do illuminate the powerful reversal involved in Heracles' catastrophic downfall.

Heracles is quite unlike the other tragedies contained in this volume: there is no room here for pleasant ironies and clever repartee. At the end of the play there is little sense of consolation: Theseus' friendship is important, but there is not much he can do to dispel the grimness of Heracles' experience. A comparison with the end of *Hippolytus* is apt: there too the cruelty of a god (Aphrodite) has brought grief and suffering, but there remains a small element of satisfaction for the audience, because Theseus and Hippolytus have spoken again and been reconciled before the latter's death. Human feeling balances divine neglect. Both scenes are indebted to the sublime episode in the last book of the *Iliad*, in which Achilles and Priam eat together and share their sorrow, recognizing that it is a bond between them, and part of the human lot. Both epic and tragedy dramatize man and woman facing adversity: both focus not just on the nature of the suffering but on how the victims come to terms with it.

CHARACTERS

AMPHITRYON, *supposed father of Heracles*
MEGARA, *wife of Heracles and daughter of Creon, the
former king of Thebes*
LYCUS, *the new ruler of Thebes*
HERACLES, *son of Alcmene and Zeus*
IRIS, *messenger of the goddess Hera*
MADNESS
MESSENGER
THESEUS, *king of Athens*
THREE YOUNG SONS *of Heracles*
CHORUS *of elders of Thebes*

[*The scene is one of suppliants at an altar.*[1] AMPHITRYON, MEGARA *and her* THREE YOUNG SONS, *shut out by Lycus from Amphitryon's house, sit in a group at the public altar of Zeus the Deliverer.*]

AMPHITRYON: Is there anyone on earth who does not know of Argive Amphitryon who shared his wife's bed with Zeus?[2] In bygone days Alcaeus, Perseus' son, fathered me, and I am the father of Heracles. This city of Thebes has been my home, where the earth-born crop of Sown Men[3] sprang to life and Ares allowed a small number of them to live and people Cadmus' town with their children's children. From this line came Creon, son of Menoeceus,[4] who was king of this land. Creon became the father of Megara here whose wedding all the Cadmeans celebrated in time past, singing in consort with the music of the pipe, that day when the renowned Heracles led her home to my house as his bride.

Later my son left Thebes, where I had settled, and the lady Megara here, together with all her family, and made it his aim to live in a fortified city of Argos,[5] the one the Cyclopes had built, from which I fled after killing Electryon.[6] Since he was eager to end my exile and to live in the land of his forefathers, he promised Eurystheus as the high price for his return that he would rid the earth of violent creatures. It may have been Hera's cruel jealousy or else the decrees of fate that forced these labours on him, no one knows.[7] All of them he has completed except for the last. He has now passed through Taenarus' jaws into Hades' realm to bring back the triple-bodied hound[8] to the upper world, but from there he has not yet returned.

There is an ancient tradition among Cadmus' folk that this city with its seven gates was ruled by Lycus, husband of Dirce, in the days before Zeus' offspring, Amphion and Zethus of the white horses, came to hold sway in Thebes.[9] This man's son, named after his father, was no Cadmean but hailed from Euboea. He attacked this town of ours when it was sick with party conflict,[10] killed Creon and became king of Thebes. As for us, our tie of kinship with Creon has proved, it seems, our greatest danger. As my son is in the depths of the earth, this Lycus, this parvenu ruler of Thebes, means to quench bloodshed with more bloodshed by murdering the sons of Heracles, after killing his wife and myself (if it is right to count a useless greybeard such as me as a man). His fear is that these children will one day reach manhood and seek revenge for the spilling of their family's blood.

My son left me here in the house to watch over his home and guard his children, when he began his journey into the earth's black gloom. I have tried to save the sons of Heracles from death by joining their mother in supplication at this altar of Zeus the Deliverer, which my noble son raised to commemorate his triumph in battle the day he overcame the Minyans. And here we keep our pious watch, denied the basic needs of life – food, drink, clothing – with only the hard ground for bedding. We are banned from the house and sit here with little hope of being saved. As for friends, some I see are not to be relied upon, while those deserving of the name are powerless to assist. So it is when men encounter misfortune. I pray that no friend of mine, even a mere acquaintance, may have this experience; there is no surer test of friends.

MEGARA: Old man, who once destroyed the city of the Taphians,[11] leading the army of Cadmus' people to glory, how veiled from our understanding are the gods' gifts to men! On my father's side I was no outcast from fortune; because of his wealth men hailed him once as great, and he had children too, and a throne, which rouses lust and makes long spears fly at the prosperous owner. He gave me to your son Heracles in a marriage that caught everyone's eye.

70   But now all this is no more, it has taken wing, and you and I are about to die, old man, as are these sons of Heracles I am keeping safe, like some mother-bird protecting her cowering young under her wings. And they question me, one on this side, one on that: 'Mother, tell me, where is father now? What part of the world is he in? What is he doing? When will he be here?' They are so young and miss their father; they do not understand his absence. I put them off by telling stories, but every time there is a noise at the gates, up they jump, each one of them, wondering if it is their father and they can run to clasp his knees.

80   So now, sir, what hope, what means of safety, can you provide? You are the one I look to. We would not get clear of this land's borders without being seen (there are frontier-guards too strong for us) and we can no longer hope that friends will see us to safety. So speak up, tell us your thoughts. I fear our deaths are close at hand.

AMPHITRYON: Daughter, it is no easy thing to advise lightly in such a case, showing enthusiasm but taking no trouble. We lack strength; let us not be too hasty.

90 MEGARA: Have you not sorrows enough? Is this how much you love life?

AMPHITRYON: I do take pleasure in this sunlight and I still cherish hope.

MEGARA: As do I; but we should not hope for what cannot happen, old man.

AMPHITRYON: There is comfort for the oppressed in deferring misfortune.

MEGARA: But the time that intervenes is so painful, so hard to bear!

AMPHITRYON: Daughter, a fair wind may yet arise to bring us both to land, free from these troubles that beset us. He may yet come, that son of mine and husband of yours. Calm yourself and banish those tears that spring so readily from your children's eyes. Soothe them with your words. Though the deceptions you utter may be wretched, you must use them none the less. Men's misfortunes diminish and stormy winds blow out at last; Fortune does not smile on her favourites for ever, for all things give place to something else. The true man is he who trusts in hope from first to last; to abandon hope is to be a coward.

[*The* CHORUS *enter slowly. They are elders of Thebes, once fine warriors but now decrepit old men.*]

CHORUS [Strophe]: *To the high-roofed palace I have come, to where old Amphitryon rests his limbs, my weight supported by this staff I pivot round. I am old,[12] a singer of sorrowful songs like a white-haired swan; mere words am I, no man but a ghost, the semblance of a dream in the night. These legs of mine shake but my spirit is strong, and my heart goes out to you, you children who have no father, and you, old sir, and you, unhappy lady, mourning for your husband in the halls of Hades.*

[Antistrophe:] *Onward, put your best foot forward, dragging those weary limbs, like a horse in harness that pulls the weight of a wheeled wagon up some steep and rocky slope. If any man's step falters through weakness, hold fast to your neighbour's arm or clothing. Let one old man support another, as once we fought beside each other, young warriors all with spears level as we entered the fray, bringing no disgrace to our glorious homeland.*

[Epode:] *Look at their flashing eyes, so like their father's, the stare of a Gorgon! His ill luck has not deserted his children nor his handsome bearing either. O Greece, if you lose such youngsters as these, what champions will be snatched from you!*

CHORUS-LEADER: Enough; I see Lycus, king of this land, approaching the palace.

[*Enter* LYCUS.]

LYCUS: Father of Heracles, and you, his wife, I have some questions for you, if I may; and, as your royal lord, I may ask what I please. How long do you seek to prolong your life?

What hope of help do you see that will stay your execution?
Do you believe these boys' father will return? He lies dead
with Hades! [*The two bow their heads in grief.*] Oh, you give way
to sorrow beyond your deserts, seeing that you have to die –
you, with your empty boasts[13] to every Greek that Zeus is your
partner as husband and father, and you, claiming to be a hero's

150   wife! Well, then, what is this splendid feat of your husband,[14]
if he destroyed the serpent of the swamp or the beast of Nemea
that he trapped in a snare and claims he strangled with his bare
hands? Are these the arguments you bring against me? Is this
why the sons of Heracles should be spared execution? His
reputation for bravery was won from battling with wild beasts
but in other matters he was no great warrior – he was nothing!
He never held a shield in his left arm or stood up to an enemy's

160   spear; he carried a bow, that weapon favoured by cowards, and
was poised to take to his heels. Archery is no test of a man's
courage;[15] courage is shown when a man stands his ground,
waiting in the battle, and stares unflinchingly at the enemy
ranks as they cut a swift furrow through his own.

What I do now, old man, shows careful planning, not a lack
of shame. I realize I killed this woman's father, Creon, and
now sit on his throne. I do not want to let these boys grow up
to become my executioners and take their revenge.

170 AMPHITRYON: Let Zeus protect that part of his son which comes
from Zeus. As for me, Heracles, it is for me to take your part
and show with words the folly of this man. This abuse of your
name is not to be tolerated.

First, then, with the gods as witnesses, I must defend him
against your unspeakable charges (unspeakable, Heracles, is
any charge that brands you a coward). I hereby call to witness
Zeus' thunderbolt and chariot in which Heracles rode to war
against the earth-born Giants,[16] lodging his winged arrows in

180   their ribs, and came back to dance and sing the song of victory
amidst the gods. Then go to Pholoe, most craven of kings, and
ask that violent race of four-legged Centaurs what man they
would judge to be the greatest of heroes. None but my own

son – the man you call a sham! Put the question to Dirphys, your home in Euboea – it would not praise you. Not a single place would you find in that island of your birth to testify to one brave deed of yours.

Then you criticize that ingenious discovery, the bow! Listen now to me and learn some sense. The infantryman is the slave   190
of his own weaponry: if he shatters his spear he cannot defend himself from death, as his only means of fighting is gone. Again, suppose the men on either side of him turn coward in battle, he gets killed himself because his comrades have lost their nerve. But not so the skilful archer: firstly – his chief advantage – he can launch hundreds of arrows and still he has others for defending himself; secondly, he engages the enemy from afar, wounding them with arrows they watch out for but fail to see, and so, from perfect safety, denying them the chance to strike   200
back at him. True skill in warfare lies in escaping the constraints of chance, and doing harm to the enemy at no risk to oneself. These arguments contradict your acceptance of traditional views.

Then there are these boys; why do you want to kill them? What have they done to you? Your attitude strikes me as shrewd in one point: as a coward yourself you fear the children of a great warrior. But it is a hard sentence for us to bear, that we shall lose our lives because you lack courage; if Zeus looked   210
on us with a just eye, this would be your own fate, to be killed by us, your betters. But if you simply wish to hold the Theban throne with no resistance from us, allow us to go into exile. Commit no violence or it will return on your own head, when the god's favour veers and blows against you.

Ah, land of Cadmus! Yes, I direct my words to you now and they are words of reproach. Is this the kind of protection you give to Heracles and his sons? Did he not, single-handed, confront all the Minyans and allow Thebans to gaze at the   220
world as free men? Greece, too, I criticize (and never shall I be silenced on this), for I have found her shamefully ungrateful to my son. She should have marched to help these little lads with

fire, with spears, with full armour, to pay him back for all his toil in purging land and sea. The truth is, children, you have no support, either from Thebes or from Greece. Your eyes are fixed on me but, though I love you, I cannot help you; I am nothing but a ranting tongue. The strength I once possessed is gone; shaking limbs and vigour without sap – these are the gifts for which I have to thank old age. But if I were young and sturdy still, I'd soon have seized my sword and made this man's blond hair run with blood. He'd run in terror from my spear, beyond the bounds of Atlas!

CHORUS-LEADER: A good man finds the words to make his case, even if they come slowly to him.

LYCUS: Yes, use your eloquence to abuse me in this arrogant fashion; I will let my actions serve to punish your insults! [*To his attendants*] Here, you men! Go some of you to Helicon, others to Parnassus' glens and tell the woodsmen to cut logs of oaks. Once they have been brought back to Thebes, pile them around the altar here and set them aflame. Reduce the five of them to ash! I want them to realize that I am the ruler of this land now, not that dead man. [*A number of his attendants leave the stage.*] As for you greybeards who oppose my will, you'll have more than Heracles' sons to weep for; there will be your homes as well, when they come to grief. Then you will be reminded that I am your king and you my slaves.[17]

CHORUS-LEADER: Offspring of the earth, you men whom Ares once sowed as the teeth he had ripped from a dragon's ravenous jaws, lift up the staffs[18] that support your right hands and dash them on this man's godless head, making it run with blood! He is a worthless upstart ruling over my people, foreigner though he is and no son of Cadmus! [*He rounds on* LYCUS.] You will never make me your slave without regretting it, or enjoy all that I laboured long and hard to win! Go back where you came from and show them your insolent ways! While I live you will never kill the sons of Heracles. He may have left his children behind but he is not buried so deep below the earth that we forget him. You now possess his land, which you have ruined, while he, its benefactor, does not get his just deserts. And am I now meddling in seeking to help a dead friend where he most needs that help?

O right hand of mine, how you long to hold a spear! But your strength is gone and you have lost your wish [*shaking his staff at* LYCUS]. Otherwise I would have stopped you calling me your slave and won honour by coming to the aid of this city of Thebes, where you now take your pleasure. Civil strife and foolish counsels have made us Thebans lose our senses. Were we sane, we would never have got you for a ruler. 270

MEGARA: Gentlemen, I thank you.[19] It is right that friends should feel a just anger on behalf of friends. But I do not want you to come to any harm on our account by venting your anger on your overlord. Listen, Amphitryon, to what I think; perhaps my words may strike you as worthwhile. I love my children. Of course I love them – did I not give them birth and work hard to rear them? And death to me is a fearful thing. But in my judgement the man who struggles against the ways of necessity is a fool. Now, since we must die, let us not die wasted by fire and so invite the mockery of our enemies; I count that a worse end than dying. We have received many noble gifts from the house and stand in its debt. You once enjoyed a famous name as a warrior. Will you now die a coward's death? That would be intolerable! As for my husband, he is glorious even without witnesses. If these children brought disgrace on their name, he would refuse to save them; men of noble birth are afflicted by their sons' dishonour. And I must not hesitate to follow my husband's example in this. 280 290

You must weigh this hope of yours in the light of my reasoning; do you really suppose that your son will return from the earth below? What man who has died has ever made the journey back from Hades' realm? Or do you imagine that this man will be softened by words? Far from it! You should keep clear of an enemy who lacks humanity but yield to one who is wise and well-bred; by submitting to his sense of honour you may more easily seal a pact of friendship with him. 300

I have already thought that we might beg him to sentence these children to exile rather than death. But what a miserable fate for them – to make their safety depend on humiliating poverty! As they say, an exile can count on a host's smile of welcome for only one day. Join us in facing death bravely; it waits for you anyway. You are nobly born, no less than we; we challenge you. When a man strives to get free of the fate the gods cast over him, his striving is folly. What will be will be; no man will ever change it.

CHORUS-LEADER: If anyone had tried to ill-treat you when these arms of mine still had their strength, I would easily have stopped him. As it is, I'm a spent force. It is now your task, Amphitryon, to think how to break through your fate.

AMPHITRYON: It is not cowardice or love of life that keeps me from dying; I want to save his children for my son. But it's useless; I seem to be crying for the moon. [*He moves away from the altar and the other suppliants follow.*] Look, here is my neck, ready for your sword: stab it, spill my blood and fling my head from a cliff. But I beg you, king, grant the pair of us one kindness: kill me and this wretched woman before the children. We wish to be spared the obscene sight of them dying, their cries of 'Mother! Grandpa!' As for the rest, do as you wish; we have no power to stave off death.

MEGARA: I too beg you to add another favour to the first; one man you may be, but still oblige the pair of us in two ways. Unbar the palace doors that now keep us out and let me fetch funeral garments to dress the children in. I want them at least to have this part of their family inheritance.

LYCUS: Very well. [*To attendants*] Unbar the doors, I say! [*To the suppliants*] Go inside and dress yourselves. I do not grudge you these garments. When you have dressed I will come to send you down to the nether world. [LYCUS *and attendants leave.*]

MEGARA: Come now, children, follow your poor mother into your father's house. Others now possess his property but his name is still ours. [*She enters the palace with the children.*]

AMPHITRYON: O Zeus, how worthless was my gaining you as

partner in my marriage, how worthless my hailing you as   340
partner in fatherhood![20] You were less a friend to me, it seems,
than I supposed. I have behaved more honourably than you,
though you are a great god and I a mere mortal, for I have not
betrayed the sons of Heracles. You knew how to steal into
another man's bed and enjoy his wife, though no invitation
was given, but you do not know how to protect your own
family from harm. Either you are a stupid sort of god or you
have no sense of justice. [AMPHITRYON *makes his way into the
palace.*]

CHORUS [Strophe]: *Phoebus can sing a lament after a song of good
fortune, when with golden plectrum he strikes his lovely sounding lyre.*   350
*And I wish to sing of the man who has passed into the gloom of the
world below, whether I should call him the son of Zeus or child of
Amphitryon, crowning him with a garland of song*[21] *in honour of his
labours. Valorous deeds nobly performed are what give glory to the
dead.*

[Mesode:] *First he cleared Zeus' grove of the lion, and, putting it*   360
*on his back, he covered his golden head with the fearsome beast's ruddy
jaws.*

[Antistrophe:] *Then with his deadly arrows he laid low in time
gone by the mountain-haunting breed of savage Centaurs, slaying
them with his winged shafts. Witnesses to this are Peneus of the lovely
stream, the plain with its acres of farmland bereft of crops, the settlements*   370
*of Pelion and dwellings on Homole's lush slopes, where they tore up
pines to serve as spears as they galloped in triumph through Thessaly.*

[Epode:] *Next, the golden-horned hind of dappled hide, ravager
of the countryside, he slew and dedicated the spoils to Oenoe's huntress
goddess.*

[Strophe:] *Then he mounted the chariot of Diomedes, and with*   380
*bit and bridle subdued the four mares whose jaws, with unbridled zest,
dispatched bloody food in their bloodstained stalls, as they fed joyously
on the flesh of men, savage feasters. And beyond the banks of silver-
flowing Hebrus did he range, in pursuit of his labours for Mycenae's
king.*

390 [Mesode:] *Then on to Malia's strand, along the waters of Anaurus, where he destroyed with his bow Cycnus the cleaver of strangers, who dwelt in solitude near Amphanae.*

[Antistrophe:] *Next to the west he went, where the Singing Maidens have their home, to pluck with his own hands the golden fruit from the leafy apple-boughs, and killed the serpent whose back gleamed*
400 *like fire, the sentinel that none dared approach, writhing in coils. He ventured into the deepest reaches of the sea, making safe passage for voyaging mortals.*

[Epode:] *Then to Atlas' home he went, and, thrusting his hands evenly beneath the dome of heaven, he supported with his great strength the starry mansions of the gods.*

410 [Strophe:] *Next he crossed the Great Sea that gives no welcome to strangers and entered the land around Maeotis with its many rivers, where the warrior Amazons ride. From all the land of Hellas he had raised a host of comrades to wrest the deadly prey of the gold-decked girdle from the tunic of Ares' daughter. Greece received the famous spoil of the Amazon maid and in Mycenae it is preserved.*

420 [Mesode:] *Then he burned to ashes the many-headed, murderous hound of Lerna, the hydra, and smeared its poison on the arrows with which he slew the three-bodied herdsman of Erytheia.*

[Antistrophe:] *Other trials he completed with glorious success, and then, as the last of his labours, he sailed to Hades, where tears abound.*
430 *There, after enduring so much, he brings his days to an end; he has not returned. His house is stripped of friends; life's journey for his children is god-forsaken and forsaken by justice; no home-coming for them as Charon's oar awaits them. Your house looks to you to save it, Heracles, but you are not here.*

[Epode:] *Oh, if I had the vigour of my youth and wielded my spear in battle, together with my fellow sons of Cadmus, I would have*
440 *championed these children with my might. But as it is, the fire that blessed my young limbs is spent.*

[AMPHITRYON, MEGARA *and the* SONS OF HERACLES *enter from the palace.*]

CHORUS-LEADER: But here I see them, wearing the garments

of the dead – the sons of the man who once was called 'Heracles the Mighty', his beloved wife, dragging them in tow, and Heracles' old father. Oh, what a wretch am I, no longer can I check the tears that well from my tired old eyes!   450

MEGARA: Very well; who will serve as priest,[22] who wield the knife that spills our unhappy blood? Here stand the beasts for slaughter, ready to be led off on the road to death. O children, we are led off under a yoke that offends decency, a procession of the dead – old, young, parents and children together. Oh, what a miserable fate has come upon me and these children, whom now I look at for the last time! I gave you birth, but I reared you for enemies to mock, maltreat and destroy!

Ah, it is hard! How fair were the hopes your father's words   460
once raised in me, how utterly false they have proved! [*She addresses the oldest boy.*] To you your dead father would assign Argos; you were going to have the palace of Eurystheus and rule over fertile Pelasgia. He used to drape over your head the savage lion's pelt that he wore as his own armour.

[*To the second son*] But you were king of Thebes, rich in chariots, possessing as your heritage the broad lands given to me. Oh, how you used to beg him to agree, your own dear   470
father, and he would put in your right hand, as if it was a present, his great fighting-club of carved wood!

[*To the third*] To you he promised the gift of Oechalia, sacked by him in the early days with his far-shooting arrows. In this way your father meant to exalt the three of you with three kingdoms, laying his plans with a proud and confident heart. My role was to select the choicest brides, contracting marriages from the land of Athens, of Sparta and of Thebes, to bind you fast by mooring-cables and so ensure you happy and prosperous   480
lives. This hope, too, has taken wing. Fortune changed and gave you fiends instead as your brides,[23] while to me in my misery she gave tears as the ritual water I must carry. Your father's father gives the wedding feast, acknowledging Hades as your father-in-law – joyless marriage tie.

O my little ones, which of you should I clasp to my heart

first, which last? Whom shall I kiss or hug? If only I could draw in all your laments, gathering them together like a buzzing bee, and shed them in a single burst of tears! O Heracles, beloved husband, if any mortal utterance reaches the ears of Hades' citizens,[24] on you I call now! Death hangs over your father and children; ruin has come upon me too, whom men once called blessed because of you. Come! Defend us! Appear to me, even as a phantom! Come, just come as a vision, and that will suffice! Cowards are killing your own children!

AMPHITRYON: Continue with your prayers to win over the dead, my daughter. [*Raising his arms*] I'll throw my hands to the sky and make my prayer, Zeus, to you: if you mean to help these children at all, defend them now, for it will soon be too late. And yet I have called on you many times. My effort is wasted; our death, it seems, is inescapable.

[*To the* CHORUS] Gentlemen, life is no great matter; pass through it as pleasantly as you can, avoiding pain from daybreak to nightfall. Time is not concerned with preserving our hopes but flies on his way, intent on his own business. Look at me: I did great deeds once, drew the eyes of all men, and in a single day Fortune has snatched it all from me, as a feather is blown to the sky. Great wealth, reputation – what man can possess these with confidence? I know of none. Farewell, my friends since the days of my youth; this is the last time you will set eyes on me.

MEGARA: Ah! Old man, can it be my dearest love I see?[25] What am I saying?

AMPHITRYON: I don't know, daughter; I, too, am lost for words!

MEGARA: It is he, the one we were told was below the earth, unless I see a dream by daylight! What am I saying? What kind of 'dreams' can I see in my mind's confusion? This is your son and no one else, old man! Come here, children, hurry, cling to your father's cloak and never let go – he is no less a saviour to you than Zeus the Deliverer!

[*Enter* HERACLES.]

HERACLES: Greetings, my house, and you portals to my hearth!

What joy to see you now I have returned to the daylight! Why, what's this I see – my children in front of the house, wearing funeral wreaths on their heads, a crowd of men – and there, my wife and my father! What has happened to make them weep like this? I must approach and find out. [*To* MEGARA] 530 What has happened here, dear wife?

MEGARA: O my dearest husband!

AMPHITRYON: O light that has returned to your father's eyes!

MEGARA: Are you here, have you come safe home to your family in their hour of need?

HERACLES: What are you saying? Father, what trouble do I find here?

MEGARA: We are being destroyed! [*To* AMPHITRYON] Do forgive me, sir, if I usurp your right of reply. We women are more emotional than men – my children were about to be killed, and so was I.

HERACLES: Apollo! What a way to start a reply!

MEGARA: My brothers are dead. So is my old father.

HERACLES: What? How did he provoke this? Or who struck 540 him down unprovoked?

MEGARA: Lycus, the new ruler of Thebes, killed him.

HERACLES: Did he make war on the city or was it suffering from faction?

MEGARA: The city was divided; mighty Thebes with its seven gates is in his power.

HERACLES: How, then, could terror have reached you?

MEGARA: He was going to kill your father, and me and our children.

HERACLES: What are you saying? My sons were without a father – what did he have to fear from them?

MEGARA: He was afraid they might one day avenge my father's death.

HERACLES: But why are the children dressed like this, in robes that suit the dead?

MEGARA: We have just now put on these burial clothes.

550　HERACLES: And he was going to use force on you, to kill you?
　　Oh, how can I bear this?

　　MEGARA: Yes; we had no friends. You were dead, so it was
　　reported.

　　HERACLES: What caused you to give up hope of me like this?

　　MEGARA: Eurystheus' heralds kept delivering this message.

　　HERACLES: Why had you left my house and hearth?

　　MEGARA: They used force; your father was thrown out of the
　　bed he lay in . . .

　　HERACLES: . . . What? Was he not ashamed to mistreat an old
　　man?

　　MEGARA: Ashamed? Shame is a goddess he does not care to
　　worship.

　　HERACLES: Were friends so few in my absence?

　　MEGARA: What friends does a man have when misfortune over-
　　takes him?

560　HERACLES: Did they so easily forget my battles with the
　　Minyans?

　　MEGARA: I tell you again, bad luck brings the end of friendship.

　　HERACLES: Then fling away[26] these hellish wreaths that bind
　　your hair and let the light of deliverance shine from your eyes!
　　Let them look no more on the nether darkness but see instead
　　the welcome light of day! The time has come: I must act now.
　　First I'll go and level the palace of this parvenu king; I'll cut off
　　his impious head and throw it out for dogs to tear at. As for
　　Cadmus' citizens, those I find guilty of disloyalty despite my
　　kindness will have this club to reckon with, architect of my
570　glorious victories; the rest I'll tear asunder with my feathered
　　arrows, filling all Ismenus with their gory corpses and making
　　the silvery waters of Dirce run with blood! Is there anyone I
　　have a greater duty to protect than my wife, my children, and
　　this old man? Farewell to my labours! How pointless they were
　　if I have failed to help my own family! These boys were to die
580　for their father's sake; I must die in their defence, if need be.
　　At Eurystheus' bidding I fought the hydra and lion: what
　　honour can I claim from that if I do not exert myself when my

own sons are in mortal peril? Then I will forfeit the title of Heracles the Triumphant.

CHORUS-LEADER: It is right that a father should help his children, and also his old father and spouse.

AMPHITRYON: It is typical of you, my son, to love your friends and hate your enemies. But do not act too hastily!

HERACLES: What do you find too hasty in what I intend, father?

AMPHITRYON: There are in Thebes many impoverished men[27] who live beyond their means and the king can count on their support. They have caused sedition and brought down the city to get their hands on their neighbours' goods, having squandered their own wealth and seen it slip away from their idle fingers. You were seen entering the city. Since this is the case, your enemies have had time to gather and you must guard against coming to unexpected grief.

HERACLES: I wouldn't care if the whole city saw me. But I saw an omen, a bird on an unpropitious perch, and so, realizing that my home was in danger, I showed foresight and entered by a secret route.

AMPHITRYON: Good. Now go inside and greet Hestia and let your ancestral home look on your face. The king will come in person to drag your wife and children off to their deaths and to slaughter me beside them. Stay inside and you will have all you need; you'll succeed at no risk to your safety. As for your fellow-citizens, my son, don't stir them up until you have settled this business well.

HERACLES: I agree; it's good advice. I shall enter the palace. Now that I have returned at last from the sunless caverns of Hades and the Maid below, I'll not neglect to pay my first respects to the gods who keep this house.

AMPHITRYON: Did you really enter the regions where Hades dwells, my boy?

HERACLES: Yes, and I brought up to the daylight the beast with three heads.

AMPHITRYON: Did you beat him in a fight or was he a gift of the goddess?

HERACLES: I fought him; I had witnessed the sacred rituals of the initiates and this gave me good fortune.[28]

AMPHITRYON: And the beast, is he now in Eurystheus' house?

HERACLES: Hermione is his home; he inhabits the grove of the Earth-Mother there.

AMPHITRYON: Is Eurystheus unaware of your return from the lower world?

HERACLES: He is; I wanted to come here first and discover how things stood.

AMPHITRYON: But why did you spend so long under the earth?

HERACLES: I delayed to bring Theseus[29] up from Hades' realm, Father.

620 AMPHITRYON: Where is he? Has he returned to the land of his forefathers?

HERACLES: He has gone to Athens, glad to have escaped the world below. But come, children, walk with your father into his house! You're happier entering it than you were coming out! Be brave, stop crying all these tears! And you, my wife, pull yourself together and stop trembling!

Let go my clothes! I'll not fly away or try to escape from you!

630 Ah, they are not letting go, but cling to my clothing all the more! Were you so close to death? [He takes them by the hand.] Well, I'll take them myself by the hand and lead them, like a ship towing little boats. I don't object to looking after children. In all respects men are the same: whether of noble or humble birth, they love their children; they may differ in wealth – some have it, some don't – but the whole race loves children.

[The whole family goes into the palace.]

CHORUS [Strophe]: Youth is what I love; old age ever rests on my
640 head as a burden weightier than Etna's crags, covering the light of my eyes so that they are dark. I would not desire the wealth of an Asiatic throne, or a palace filled with gold, in preference to youth, fairest of prizes in prosperity, fairest in poverty. But old age – dismal, bloody –
650 is what I hate. May it sink beneath the waves and never come to the

24

homes and cities of mortals! May it take wing and fly for ever through the air!

[Antistrophe:] *If the gods possessed understanding and wisdom such as men have, a second youth would be the prize for those whose lives bore clearly the stamp of virtue.*[30] *After death such men would return to the rays of the sun and run a second race, but ignoble spirits would know one life only. In this way good men and bad could be distinguished, even as the sailor makes out a constellation among clouds. As it is, we have no god-given means for telling good men from bad, and a man's life-span, as it rolls past, adds only to his wealth.*

660

670

[Strophe:] *I will not cease from joining the Graces with the Muses, a most delightful union. May I never live without the Muses' gifts but always wear my proper crown.*[31] *Aged singer though I be, still I loudly celebrate Memory, still I sing of Heracles' glorious victories, be it when the Roarer's gift of wine is poured, or when music sounds from the seven-toned tortoiseshell, or from the Libyan pipe. I am not yet too old to stop praising the Muses, who set my feet moving in the dance.*

680

[Antistrophe:] *The maidens of Delos sing their triumph-song outside the temple doors, as they praise Leto's son, blessed child, whirling round in their lovely dance; but I for my part shall sing your triumphs at your portals, an aged singer uttering praise, swan-like, from my grey old throat. Virtue is the theme of my song: he is the son of Zeus; excelling still more in greatness of heart than in birth, he has by his labours brought calm to man's sea of troubles, destroying fearsome beasts.*

690

700

[LYCUS *enters from the side of the stage, accompanied by servants, and* AMPHITRYON *comes out of the palace.*]

LYCUS: You're none too soon[32] in coming out of the palace, Amphitryon; you've taken a long time now, all of you, dressing yourselves up in funeral clothing. Get a move on, now, tell Heracles' wife and sons to show themselves outside the palace here. Those were the terms on which you agreed, voluntarily, to die.

AMPHITRYON: King, you persecute me, though my state is miserable, and heap insult on me in my bereavement. Your

eagerness should show some measure, for all your power. But
710   since you compel us to die, we must acquiesce; your will must
be enforced.

LYCUS: Where, then, is Megara? Where are the children of
Alcmena's son?

AMPHITRYON [*standing at the doors of the palace*]: To judge from
here, I think . . .

LYCUS: You think? And what is your conclusion?

AMPHITRYON: . . . she is sitting as a suppliant at Hestia's holy
altar-steps . . .

LYCUS: Well, there is a suppliant who wastes her breath; she
won't escape death!

AMPHITRYON: . . . and calling vainly on her dead husband.

LYCUS: He's not here; he'll never come back.

AMPHITRYON: No, not unless some god raises him from the
dead.

720   LYCUS: Go to her and fetch her from the palace.

AMPHITRYON: If I did that, I would be an accomplice in her
murder.

LYCUS: Then, as you have this scruple, I'll go myself and bring
them out, mother and children together; such qualms do not
bother me. Follow me inside, you men – I want to see an end
to this trouble and gladden my heart!

[*Exit* LYCUS *with attendants into the palace.*]

AMPHITRYON: Well, go on your way, go where fate calls you.
Someone else perhaps will see to the rest. Your actions were
brutal, so you may expect a brutal reception. [*To the* CHORUS]
730   Sirs, his leaving is timely; evil-hearted coward that he is, he
thinks he's going to kill his victims, but a net will catch him
up in its mesh and drop him on a sword-point! I will go to see
him fall in death; what pleasure it gives when an enemy dies
and pays the price for his misdeeds. [*Exit* AMPHITRYON *into
the palace.*]

CHORUS [Strophe]: *Suffering has now changed sides; in majesty the
former king has turned his horses and rides back from Hades to the*

path's end! Hail Justice! Hail the tide of fate that flows from heaven!

CHORUS-LEADER: At last you have come where death will seal   740
your punishment for trampling so insolently on your betters.

CHORUS: *Tears of happiness start from my eyes; he has come back,
Thebes' king has come back – never in my heart could I have hoped
to experience this!*

CHORUS-LEADER: Come, sirs, let us look inside the palace to
see if someone is suffering as I wish.

[*A scream of pain is heard from inside the palace.*[33]]

LYCUS [*within*]: Oh, help me!   750

CHORUS [Antistrophe]: *It begins in the house, the refrain I long to
hear! His death is near. In lamentation the king cries out this prelude
to the spilling of his blood.*

LYCUS [*within*]: O land of Cadmus, I am being murdered treach-
erously!

CHORUS-LEADER: Yes, for you are a murderer. Bear up as you
pay retribution in punishment for your actions!

CHORUS: *Who was he, that man of mortal flesh, who, polluting the
gods with the stain of lawlessness, launched his foolish calumny at the
blessed dwellers in heaven, claiming that they had no power?*[34]

CHORUS-LEADER: Sirs, the godless man's life is over. The palace   760
is silent. Let's turn to dancing!

CHORUS [Strophe]: *Dancing, dancing and feasting prevail throughout
Thebes' holy city. Tears of grief have turned to joy, this happy change
has given birth to new songs. Our new king has gone and the one of
earlier days holds sway, leaving Acheron's harbour behind! My hope
is fulfilled, exceeding all expectation!*   770

[Antistrophe:] *The gods, the gods concern themselves with men
unjust as well as pious, so that they take heed of them. Gold and good
fortune, dragging with them unjust power, lead men on, luring them
out of their minds. No one dares cast his eyes back on the track but,
passing by the law and giving rein to lawlessness, he smashes prosperity's dark chariot.*   780

[Strophe:] *Ismenus, put on garlands! And you, polished streets of
our seven-gated city, and fair-flowing Dirce, start up the dance!*[35] *You
maiden daughters of Asopus, come also, leaving your father's stream,*

and join us, Nymphs, in celebrating Heracles' fight and triumphant victory!

790   You wooded crags of Pytho's Lord and haunts of the Muses on Helicon, extol with echoing shouts of joy my city and my city's walls, where the stock of Sown Men appeared, the bronze-shielded company who pass this land in turn to their children's children, a sacred light to Thebes.

[Antistrophe:] O marriage bed that welcomed two loving husbands,
800   one of mortal birth, the other Zeus, who came to embrace the bride who was daughter to Perseus! How true it has long seemed to me, Zeus, your union with her, though it was hard at times to believe. Time has revealed the shining valour of Heracles, who came up from the earth's chambers, leaving behind the infernal dwelling of Pluto. In
810   my eyes you are a superior monarch to this ignoble king; all who observe your clashing swords can see whether the gods still approve of justice.

[IRIS and MADNESS appear above the palace.][36]
Ah, look! Are we all struck by the same quivering terror? What kind of vision do I see above the house?

      Run, move those tired old legs[37] and run! Get away from them! O
820   Healer King,[38] deliver me from harm!

IRIS: Take heart, old men! Do not tremble at the sight of Madness here, child of Night, and myself, Iris, who do the gods' bidding. We are not here to do any harm to Thebes but to attack the home of a single man, the son, they say, of Zeus and Alcmene. Before he had accomplished his terrible labours he was protected by Fate, and Zeus, his father, would not allow Hera or
830   me ever to do him harm. But now that he has performed Eurystheus' labours, Hera wishes to fasten on him the taint of kindred murder, by making him kill his children, and in this I am her willing partner.

      Come now, virgin daughter of black Night, summon up the cruelty in your heart – let frenzy loose on this man, twist his mind to long to kill his children, set his feet kicking in distraction! Loosen the mooring-rope of murder, that he may send

28

his lovely crown of sons, slaughtered by his own hands, across
Acheron's stream! Then he will know what kind of hatred   840
Hera feels for him[39] and learn my rancour too. Otherwise the
gods are worthless, if this man does not pay the penalty, and
mortal men are supreme.

MADNESS: Of a noble father I am born, and a noble mother,
from the blood of Uranus and Night. This office I hold is not
a source of delight to me, and I take no pleasure in visiting
those mortals I hold dear. Let me give advice to you and Hera
before I see her tumble into folly; perhaps you will do as I say.
This man whose house you send me to destroy is famous, on   850
earth as in heaven. He tamed lands untrodden by men and seas
infested by beasts; when impious men had trampled on the
worship due the gods, he alone restored it. I cannot, then,
approve your plans to do him harm.

IRIS: It isn't your place to criticize plans laid by Hera and me.

MADNESS: I'm trying to turn your steps from wrong and to set
you on a better path.

IRIS: It wasn't to exercise judgement that Zeus' consort sent you
here.

MADNESS: I make the Sun my witness[40] that I act against my
will. If it is indeed fated that I should help Hera and you, then
go I will. Neither the raging sea with its groaning waves, nor
earthquake, nor stabbing thunderbolt, breathing anguish, will
show such fury as I, in the race that I shall run against the breast
of Heracles. I will shatter his house and overthrow his palace,
having first killed his sons. The slayer will not know that he
has killed his own sons until he is free of my frenzy.

But look! Already he is tossing his head at the starting-
posts, silently rolling and distorting those fearsome eyes; no
longer can he master his breathing – he begins to roar terribly,   870
like a bull about to charge. I am the huntsman and I summon   860
the Fiends of Hell to come with clamorous baying to my
heels!

[To HERACLES] Oh, soon enough, I'll set you dancing, I'll
play my pipe and put panic in your steps!

[*To* IRIS] Wing your way to Olympus on those noble feet of yours, Iris. I will enter, unseen, the house of Heracles.

[*Exit* IRIS *above;* MADNESS *enters the palace.*]

CHORUS: *What woe is here, what sorrow! Make lamentation! O wretched Greece, the pride of your nation, Zeus' son, is cut down, and you will lose, will lose your benefactor, who has been set dancing to the manic strains of frenzy that ring in his ears.*

880   *Madness, mother of woe, has mounted her chariot. Bent on destruction, with eyes that turn to stone, she goads on her team, like a Gorgon-child of Night, bristling with the heads of a hundred hissing snakes.*

    Swiftly has fate overturned the man of success; swiftly will his children die at their father's hands.

AMPHITRYON [*from within*]: *O, pity! Pity!*

CHORUS: *O Zeus, soon your son, childless, will be destroyed most wretchedly by the Spirits of Vengeance – frenzied, feasting on raw flesh, enemies of what is just!*

AMPHITRYON: *O you palace walls!*

890 CHORUS: *The dance begins but no cymbals does it have, nor is it blessed by the staff of the Roaring One . . .*

AMPHITRYON: *O my home!*

CHORUS: . . . *but to blood it is directed, not to the pouring of Dionysus' libation of the grape.*

AMPHITRYON: *Run, children, make your escape!*

CHORUS: *Murderous, murderous is this song the pipe accompanies. He hunts down his children; they are his quarry. Never will Madness riot in the house and not achieve her goal!*

AMPHITRYON: *Oh, misery! What horror!*

900 CHORUS: *Ah, misery in truth! How I grieve for his aged father and for the woman who bore his sons and raised them, all for nothing!*

    Look! Look! A storm-blast shakes the palace! The roof is collapsing!

AMPHITRYON: *Ah, ah, what are you doing to the palace, daughter of Zeus?*[41] *It is a hellish confusion you are launching at these walls, Pallas, as once you assailed Enceladus!*

[Part of the palace collapses.[42] *A* MESSENGER *rushes out, mourning. The* CHORUS *engages in a lyric exchange with him.]*

MESSENGER: O sirs, pale with all your years . . .   910

CHORUS: *What is it you are trying to say? Why do you address me so loudly?*

MESSENGER: Inside the palace . . . it is abominable!

CHORUS: *So much I can well believe.*

MESSENGER: The children are dead!

CHORUS: *Oh, no, no!*

MESSENGER: You lament what is truly lamentable.

CHORUS: *O cruel and bloody deed! Cruelty unworthy of a father's hands!*

MESSENGER: What we have suffered is beyond any man's telling.

CHORUS: *Can you reveal the ruin, the woeful ruin the father brought on his children? Tell how this destruction from heaven swooped on the*   920
house! Make plain the sufferings and wretched fate of the children!

MESSENGER: The sacred victims for sacrifice to purify the house were standing in front of Zeus' altar, as Heracles had killed the king of Thebes and thrown his body out of the palace. There, too, stood the children – a handsome group they made – with their grandfather and Megara. The basket had already wound its way around the altar and we were keeping a reverent silence.[43] Alcmena's son stood, saying nothing, poised to lift   930
the torch in his right hand to dip it in the holy water. As their father hesitated, the boys stared at him. He was a different man; in his affliction he started rolling his eyes, where bloody veins had sprouted, and foam began to trickle down his bushy beard.

Then, with a manic outburst of laughter, he spoke: 'Father, why do I offer sacrifice and purifying fire, when I still have Eurystheus to kill? I'm doubling my labour! These hands of mine need only perform a single ceremony to settle this business well. Once I've brought Eurystheus' head here, I'll cleanse my   940
hands of the blood I've spilled – his and those men's I killed today. You there, pour out that water! Throw those baskets down! Give me my bow, one of you, and another, my

club! I'm off to Mycenae. I must take crowbars and pickaxes
to level that Cyclopean masonry; hooks of iron are needed for
that stonework ruled by red marker and fitted by chisels!'

Then he started to move. Thinking he had a chariot when
there was none, he tried to mount, clasped the rail and struck
950 out vigorously, like a man striking out with a goad. The
servants were confused, poised between amusement and terror,
and, as they looked at each other, one of them said, 'Is the
master playing a joke on us, or has he lost his wits?'

But he kept roving to and fro inside the palace. He burst
into the hall, claiming he had reached the town of Nisus, and
then, going further inside, he suddenly sprawled on the ground,
just as he was, and started preparing a meal. After a short while
only, he announced he was drawing near to the wooded plain
960 of the Isthmus, where he would stay. Next he unpinned his
cloak, stripped off and started competing against nobody. He
kept calling for silence from the crowd and proclaiming himself
the triumphant winner over no one. Then in his imagination
he was at Mycenae, shouting threats at Eurystheus.

But his father grasped his mighty hand and spoke these words
to him: 'My son, what is wrong with you? How is it you
behave in this extraordinary way? Surely the blood you have
just shed has not taken away your senses?' But Heracles, thinking this was Eurystheus' father clinging to his hand and trembling before him in humble entreaty, thrust him away and made
970 ready his bow and arrows to shoot his own sons, supposing it
was Eurystheus' children he was killing. Terrified, they began
running this way and that. One cowered in the folds of his
poor mother's dress, another in the shadow of a column, the
third, like a bird, behind the altar. Their mother shouted out:
'What are you doing? You're their father! Are you killing your
own children?' The old man and a crowd of servants echoed
her cries.

But Heracles, moving round the boy as he circled the pillar,
turned back with frightening speed and, facing the child, shot
980 him in the side. He fell back, gasping for life and spattering the

stone pillars with his blood. Heracles cried out in triumph, adding this boast: 'Here's one of Eurystheus' brood down and dead, paying for his father's hatred of me!' Now he was aiming his bow at another boy, who was crouching at the base of the altar, thinking he had escaped his father's eye. This poor wretch was quicker off the mark: ducking to clasp his father's knees, he reached out to touch his cheek and neck, and cried, 'Father, dear father, don't kill me! I'm your son, yours! You won't be killing one of Eurystheus'!' But Heracles' eyes were like a   990
Gorgon's[44] – savage, rolling. As the boy was too close for his deadly arrows, he swung his club above his head, like a blacksmith striking red-hot iron, and, bringing it down on the lad's golden head, he smashed the skull-bone. Having dispatched his second son, he now set about sacrificing the third victim to add to the others. But their mother, wretched woman, had anticipated him; she seized the child and, rushing into an inner room, barred the doors. Heracles thought he now faced the very walls built by the Cyclopes; he attacked the doors, heaving at them with pickaxe and crowbar, smashed in the door posts, and with a single arrow laid low wife and   1000
last son together.

Next he galloped off to murder his old father. But a phantom intervened, Pallas as it revealed itself to our eyes, brandishing her spear on the palace roof-top. She flung a rock at Heracles, which hit him in the chest, checking his furious lust for blood and knocking him senseless. He tumbled to the ground and struck his back against a pillar that was lying on its base, broken in two when the roof had collapsed. We who had taken to our   1010
heels came back and helped the old man tie him fast to the pillar with sturdy ropes, to stop him committing any further crimes when sleep left him. There he sleeps, but it is no enviable sleep, poor man, for he has murdered his wife and sons. Indeed, I know of no one on this earth more miserable. [*Exit* MESSENGER.]

CHORUS: *Most famous in its day in Greece, and past belief, was the*

slaughter of Danaus' sons,[45] *known to the rocks of Argos. But these*
1020 *woes surpass that day's, which have visited the wretched son of Zeus.*

I can tell of Procne's killing of her son, sacrifice of blood for the
Muses; but he was her only child, while you, violent man, were given
the lot of madness that made you destroy three sons of your own
begetting.

Ah, what lament, what dirge, what song for the dead shall I sing?
What dance of death shall my song describe?

[*The doors of the palace open to reveal the corpses of* MEGARA
and the THREE BOYS. *Nearby, asleep and bound to a pillar, is*
HERACLES.][46]

1030 *Oh, oh, look! The lofty palace doors are moving apart, swinging open!*
Ah, unbearable! See them where they lie, the wretched children at their
unhappy father's feet! After his children's slaughter he sleeps — a
dreadful sleep. Round him wind fetters and knotted ropes that support
his body and bind him tight to a stone pillar of the house.

[AMPHITRYON *enters from the palace behind.*]

1040 CHORUS-LEADER: And here is the old man — slow and painful
are the steps he takes — lamenting his precious grandchildren,
as a bird mourns for her young in the nest.

AMPHITRYON: *Be quiet, elders of Cadmus' town, be quiet![47] While*
he is relaxed in sleep, let him forget his woes!

CHORUS: *I weep tears of sorrow for you, old man, for the children, for*
the glorious conqueror!

AMPHITRYON: *Stand further away; no sound, no word! He lies in*
1050 *tranquil repose, bound in sleep; do not wake him from his rest!*

CHORUS: *Ah, the blood, all the blood . . .*

AMPHITRYON: *Enough! You will destroy me!*

CHORUS: *. . . though shed, it rises up!*

AMPHITRYON: *Sirs, not so loud in your laments! If he wakens he will*
break his fetters and destroy our city, murder his father and make havoc
of the palace!

CHORUS: *I cannot help it; I cannot!*

1060 AMPHITRYON: *Silence! Let me test his breathing. Come, let me put*
my ear close.

CHORUS: *Is he asleep?*

AMPHITRYON: *Yes, he is asleep – not a true sleep but an accursed one: he has killed his wife, killed his children, with twanging bow!*

CHORUS: *Then mourn . . .*

AMPHITRYON: *I do.*

CHORUS: *. . . for the children's death . . .*

AMPHITRYON: *Oh, the pain!*

CHORUS: *. . . for your son.*

AMPHITRYON: *Ah!*

CHORUS: *Old sir . . .*

AMPHITRYON [*bending over* HERACLES *again*]: *Be quiet, be quiet! He wakes; he turns and twists! Come, let me hide, conceal myself indoors!*   1070

CHORUS: *Have no fear; it is yet night with your son.*

AMPHITRYON: *Look out, look out! I am not afraid to die – I am a wretch, whose life has been miserable; I fear he will kill his father, piling suffering onto suffering, more blood of kin to add to this work of Furies.*

CHORUS: *Then was the time for you to die, when you returned after avenging for your wife the Taphians' murder of her brothers, by sacking*   1080 *their city surrounded by the sea!*[48]

AMPHITRYON: *Flee, sirs, flee away from the palace! Escape from the madman who now awakes; soon he'll rampage again through the Cadmeans' city, adding one murder to another!*

CHORUS-LEADER: O Zeus, why did you feel such strong hatred for your own son? Why did you launch him upon this sea of woes?

[AMPHITRYON *and the* CHORUS *withdraw some distance from the bound* HERACLES. *With a sudden cry he wakens.*]

HERACLES: Ah! Well, I'm alive, anyway.[49] I see all I should –   1090 the sky, the earth, these shafts of sunlight. And yet my state of mind is strange indeed – confused, tossing as if on a sea-swell – and my breath comes hot and shallow, not steady from the lungs. What's this? Why am I sitting here moored like a ship, my sturdy chest and arms bound by ropes, beside a column of chiselled stone that is broken in half,[50] with corpses to keep me

35

1100 company? And here, scattered on the ground, are my feathered arrows and the bow[51] that often in the past supported me in battle, preserving me from harm, as I have preserved them. Surely I haven't gone down once more to Hades, having just come from his kingdom on the return journey for Eurystheus? No; I see neither Sisyphus with his boulder, nor Pluto, nor yet the daughter of Demeter, sceptre in hand. I am dismayed, helpless. Wherever am I? Hey, there! Is there a friend near or far who can cure my ignorance? For I don't recognize clearly anything familiar.

AMPHITRYON: Sirs, should I approach my own calamity?

1110 CHORUS-LEADER: Yes, and I will be at your side; I will not betray you in adversity.

HERACLES: Father! Why do you weep and cover up your eyes? Why do you stand so far from the son you love well?

AMPHITRYON: O my son! For mine you are still, however stricken by fate!

HERACLES: Stricken? What affliction prompts this flood of tears?

AMPHITRYON: One that would cause a god himself to groan, if he heard of it.

HERACLES: That is no small claim to make; but you still have to tell me what has happened.

AMPHITRYON: You can see with your own eyes, if your senses have now returned.

HERACLES: Tell me if you are trying to shed some strange new light on my life.

AMPHITRYON: If your hellish antics are at an end, I will tell you.

1120 HERACLES: Oh, no! You frighten me with these riddles!

AMPHITRYON: I'm not sure if you are yet fully restored in mind.

HERACLES: My mind was deranged? I don't have any memory of that.

AMPHITRYON: Should I untie the ropes that bind my son, old friends? What is the alternative? [He frees HERACLES.]

HERACLES: And tell me who bound me. I am shocked.

AMPHITRYON: Be content to know this much of your sorrows; let the rest be.

36

HERACLES: Can silence satisfy me? I want to know!

AMPHITRYON: Zeus, do you see this[52] from where you sit on Hera's throne?

HERACLES: Hera? Have I suffered some hostile stroke at her hands?

AMPHITRYON: Leave the goddess out of it; see to your own burden of grief.

HERACLES: I'm ruined – you are about to devastate me with   1130
some awful news!

AMPHITRYON: Look, then; look at these children's bodies.

HERACLES: Oh, no! Pity me! What sight is this I see?

AMPHITRYON: You fought a war that was no war against these children, my son.

HERACLES: Why do you speak of a war? Who was their destroyer?

AMPHITRYON: You and your bow, whichever heavenly power was to blame.

HERACLES: What are you saying? What was the deed I committed? O Father, your news is dire!

AMPHITRYON: You were deranged. Oh, the pain it causes to answer your questions!

HERACLES: My wife, did I kill my wife too?

AMPHITRYON: All this is the work of your hand alone.

HERACLES: Ah, what anguish! A cloud of lamentation engulfs me!   1140

AMPHITRYON: That is why I grieve for your suffering.

HERACLES: Did my raving cause me to damage my own house?

AMPHITRYON: I know one thing only: your fall from happiness is total.

HERACLES: Where did the frenzy take hold of me? Where did it seal my ruin?

AMPHITRYON: It was at the altar, when you were purifying your hands with sacrifice.

HERACLES: Oh, no! Then why do I spare my own life,[53] I who became the murderer of my own precious sons? Will I not go and leap from some bare cliff, or aim a sword at my own heart   1150
and avenge my sons for their murder? Or shall I set fire to my

own flesh and stave off the life of infamy that awaits me? [*He catches sight of* THESEUS *approaching.*] But here comes Theseus,[54] my kinsman and friend, to thwart my designs on death. I shall be seen; the taint of child-murder shall light upon the dearest of my guest-friends. Ah, what shall I do? Where can I find a place beyond the panoply of my woes, taking to the skies or

1160 passing below? Come, let me veil my head with my cloak. My wicked deeds fill me with shame; I have no wish to cause injury to others, innocent though they are, by exposing them to my blood-guilt.[55]

[HERACLES *covers his head in his cloak.* THESEUS *enters with attendants.*]

THESEUS: I have come with others who wait by Asopus' stream, warriors of the Athenians' land, bringing help in war to your son, sir. For report has reached the city of Erechtheus' people that Lycus has seized the throne of Thebes and makes war on

1170 you and your family. I have come to pay back Heracles for his services in rescuing me from the underworld, if you and yours, old man, have any need of help in war, from me or from my allies. But what's this? Why is the ground strewn with these corpses? I haven't come too late, have I, arriving in the wake of crimes unforeseen? Who killed these children? Whose wife was the woman I see here? Children don't stand in the line of battle! No, this is surely some strange and wicked crime I've stumbled on!

[*In the lyric exchange that follows,* AMPHITRYON, *still overcome by grief, sings, while* THESEUS *speaks.*[56]]

AMPHITRYON: *O king of the hill where olives grow . . .*

THESEUS: Why do you address me so? You begin in sorrowful strain.

1180 AMPHITRYON: *. . . piteous are the sufferings we have endured at heaven's hands.*

THESEUS: These children you are weeping over – whose are they?

AMPHITRYON: *Their father is my own wretched son; he fathered them and he killed them, enduring the taint of their spilled blood.*

THESEUS: What are you saying? What was the deed he per-
petrated?

AMPHITRYON: *He was adrift on a tide of madness, and the arrows he
used were dipped in the hundred-headed hydra's blood.*

THESEUS: What monstrous news!

AMPHITRYON: *Our life is over, over, flown to the skies!*

THESEUS: No more – your words test the gods' patience!

AMPHITRYON: *I have no wish to disobey you.*

THESEUS: Hera was at work in this; but who is that man among
the dead, old man?

AMPHITRYON: *He's my son, my son, the man of many labours, who* 1190
*once marched to do battle with the Giants, standing at the side of the
gods on Phlegra's plain!*

THESEUS: Oh, this is hard to bear! What man was born to greater
sorrow than he?

AMPHITRYON: *No mortal has endured trials or travels greater than
his; not one would you find his equal.*

THESEUS: Why does he hide his poor head in his cloak?

AMPHITRYON: *He is ashamed to meet your eye, ashamed before your* 1200
love as his kinsman, and the blood of his own sons.

THESEUS: But what if I came to share his pain? Uncover him.

AMPHITRYON: *My son, take the cloak away from your eyes, throw it
down, reveal your face to the sun!* [AMPHITRYON *falls to the ground
beside* HERACLES *and grasps hold of him like a wrestler.*] *I lend my
weight to these tears I shed, as I struggle to convince you! I beg you,
by your chin, your knee, your hand, falling before you with an old
man's tears! O my son, curb that lion's wild spirit of yours! It leads* 1210
*you on to a trail of impious bloodshed, my child, when you would pile
one evil on another!*

THESEUS: Now then, you who sit there in misery, I bid you
reveal your face to a friend. No darkness has a cloud so black
as could conceal the depths of your misfortune. Why do you
shake your hand at me, showing fear? Are you afraid I may be
polluted[57] if I speak to you? It does not trouble me if your 1220
friendship brings me bad luck; there was a time it brought me

good. That happy hour came when you brought me safely into the light of day from the world of death.[58] I hate a friend whose gratitude fades with age, or one who wants to enjoy your success but not to share your voyage when storms arise. Stand up, uncover your wretched head and look at me! [HERACLES *rises from the ground and* THESEUS *unveils him.*] A noble heart endures what the gods send; it does not recoil.

HERACLES: Theseus, have you seen how I clashed with my sons here?

1230   THESEUS: I heard the woeful tale and now you show the facts to one who understands.

HERACLES: Then why did you uncover my head before the sun?

THESEUS: You ask that? You are mortal; you cannot pollute what is divine.

HERACLES: I am defiled, unholy – keep away, you wretch!

THESEUS: No avenging curse passes from friend to friend.

HERACLES: Thank you; because I befriended you, I do not refuse. [HERACLES *clasps* THESEUS' *hand.*]

THESEUS: I knew kindness from you then; I give you pity now.

HERACLES: I have your pity, though I killed my sons?

THESEUS: I weep for your kindness now that your fortune has changed.

HERACLES: Have you encountered other men in greater misery?

1240   THESEUS: Your misfortune reaches from earth to heaven.

HERACLES: Therefore I am determined to die.[59]

† *Two lines of text missing*†

THESEUS: Do you think the gods care at all for your threats?

HERACLES: The gods please themselves; I shall treat them likewise.

THESEUS: Watch what you say! Such boasting may earn you further suffering!

HERACLES: My hold is full of suffering; I have no room for further cargo.

THESEUS: What will you do? Where will such defiance sweep you?

HERACLES: I will die; I returned from beneath the earth and I shall go below again.

THESEUS: These are the words of an ordinary man.

HERACLES: And you, a stranger to my suffering, criticize me!

THESEUS: Are these the words of Heracles, the all-enduring?   1250

HERACLES: Never did I know sorrow such as this; there must be a limit to endurance.

THESEUS: The benefactor of mortal men, their great friend?

HERACLES: And what help are they to me? Power lies with Hera.

THESEUS: Greece would not tolerate a fool's death for you!

HERACLES: Then listen; for I want to match your words of advice with arguments of my own.[60] I will explain to you how my life, both now and before, should never have been. Firstly, I am this man's son; he married Alcmena, my mother, though   1260 he had killed her old father and was tainted by his blood. When a family's foundations are not soundly laid, misfortune must befall its sons.[61] Then Zeus, whoever Zeus is,[62] sired me to become the target of Hera's enmity (no, old man, don't be angry; I count you as my father, not Zeus). While I was still a baby at the breast, Zeus' consort put fierce-eyed serpents in my cradle to cause my death. Once the sturdy flesh of youth   1270 had clothed my limbs, need I tell of the labours I endured? What lions or triple-bodied Typhons or Giants did I not destroy? What battles with troops of four-legged Centaurs did I not win? The hydra too, hound with heads all round that grew afresh, I killed, and then, after performing a host of other toils past number, I went down among the dead, at Eurystheus' word, to bring up to the daylight the triple-headed dog that guards the gates of Hades.

Now here is the final labour of the steadfast Heracles – to   1280 crown the evils of his house with the murder of his sons! This is the hopeless position I have reached: piety forbids that I live in my beloved Thebes; if I do stay, what temple, what company of friends will admit me? The curse I bear hardly encourages men's greetings! Well then, should I go to Argos? How can I,

an exile from my city? Should I hurry to some other city? Am
I then to endure sidelong stares on being recognized, am I to
be tormented by the cruel barbs of men's tongues? – 'Isn't that
1290 the son of Zeus, who once killed his wife and children? We
don't want him in this land; to hell with him!'

I think my wretchedness will come to this: Earth herself will
cry out, 'Do not set foot on my soil!', sea and rushing rivers,
1300 'You must not cross!' I will resemble Ixion,[63] bound by chains
to the wheel that drives him.

Why then should I live? How will it profit me to have a life
that serves no purpose and offends heaven? Let the glorious
wife of Zeus now dance for joy and make Olympus shake with
her footsteps! She has achieved her will; she has cast down
from on high the foremost man of Greece, toppling him from
his very foundations! What man would utter prayers to such a
goddess? Because of jealousy of another woman's bed, to spite
1310 Zeus, she has destroyed the benefactor of Greece, though he
was innocent of wrong-doing!

CHORUS-LEADER: We see here the hand of none other than
Hera, wife of Zeus; you are quite right.

THESEUS: {If you were going to be the only person abused by
chance} I would advise you {to kill yourself}[64] rather than to
bear misfortune. But there is no mortal, no god, untouched by
fortune's blows, if poets' tales are true.[65] Have not the gods
engaged in lawless love with one another? Have they not
defiled their fathers by putting them in chains for the sake of
power? But still they live on Olympus and allow themselves to
be consoled for their offences.

1320 What defence will you make if you, a mortal, complain
unduly at the ways of chance, while gods do not?

Well then, do what the law requires and leave Thebes.
Come with me to Pallas' city. There I will cleanse your hands
of pollution and give you a home and a share of my wealth. I
will give you the gifts my fellow-citizens gave me when I had
killed the Minotaur and saved the fourteen youths.[66] Everywhere throughout my country plots of land have been assigned

to me. Henceforth these shall be named after you, and, while   1330
you live, men will celebrate them. When you die and pass to
Hades' realm, the whole Athenian state will revere you with
sacrifices and stone memorials. It will be a crown of honour to
my people that they are famed among Greeks for helping a
noble man. I too shall be showing my gratitude to you for
rescuing me; for you are now in need of friends.

HERACLES: Ah, these honours do not meet the severity of my   1340
woes. I do not believe that the gods indulge themselves in illicit
love or bind each other with chains. I have never thought such
things worthy of belief and I never will; nor that one god treats
another as his slave. A god, if he is truly a god, needs nothing;
these are the wicked tales of poets.[67]

For all my woes, I see that taking my life might seem an act
of cowardice.[68] If a man did not resist the blows of fortune, he   1350
could not face an enemy's spear. I shall stand fast and hold to
life; I will come to your city, and for your gifts you have my
warmest thanks.

But, as men know, I have tasted many a hard task. Never
have I refused one, or wept to see it through; nor would I have
thought I could ever reach the stage of shedding tears. Now,
it seems, I must be fortune's slave. So be it; old man, you see
me exiled, you see me the murderer of my own sons. Wrap   1360
their bodies for burial and place them in a tomb, and honour
them with your tears (the law does not allow me to do this).
Lay them on their mother's breast, in her arms' embrace,
unhappy union that I destroyed unwillingly. When you have
buried the dead, live on in this city, albeit in misery.

O children, I who gave you life and breath have taken
them from you. You gained no profit from my noble deeds,
undertaken for your sake, as I laboured to win for you a life   1370
of fair renown, a father's honourable bequest. And you, poor
woman, so faithful to the honour of my bed, so patient in
guarding our home all this time, how did I return your loving
kindness – I killed you! Oh, I weep for my wife and children,
I weep for myself! How wretched is my fate, my separation

from my children and my wife! What pain it is to kiss you, and yet what sweetness! What pain, again, these weapons give me, though they have been my constant companions! I am torn – should I keep them or throw them away? They will hang at my side as I kneel and speak like this: 'With us you killed your wife and children; if you keep us, you keep the killers of your sons!' Shall I then carry them in my hands? How can I justify it? But am I to strip myself of them, the weapons with which I performed the finest deeds that Greece has witnessed? Am I to submit to my enemies and die a shameful death? I must not part with them, but keep them, whatever misery they bring!

1380

Theseus, lend me your help in one task: come with me to Argos, and help me bring the savage dog there; I fear my grief for my sons may work against me if I lack company.[69]

1390

O land of Cadmus, and all you citizens of Thebes, come to the burial of my children, cut off your hair in their honour and share my mourning! You will be mourning us all by your tears, myself and my sons together. We are all ruined, struck down in anguish by a single stroke of fortune from Hera.

THESEUS: Stand up, my sorrowful friend; we have had enough tears.

HERACLES: I cannot; I am rooted to the ground.

THESEUS: Yes, even the strong can be overcome by fate.

HERACLES: Oh, agony! If only I could stay here, changed into a rock, oblivious to suffering!

THESEUS: Enough! I will help you; give your friend your hand.

HERACLES: No! I must not stain your clothes with blood!

1400

THESEUS: Wipe it off on me, to the last drop; I cannot refuse.[70]

HERACLES: I have sons no more but in you I have a son.

THESEUS: Put your arms round my neck; I will be your guide.

HERACLES: A yoke that binds friends, but one is no friend of fortune. [To Amphitryon] Father, this is the sort of man to have as a friend!

AMPHITRYON: Yes, the land that is his mother bears noble sons!

HERACLES: Theseus, let me turn back! I want to see my children!

THESEUS: What good will this do? Will they work some charm to ease your mind?

HERACLES: I long to; and I want to embrace my father.

AMPHITRYON: Here I am, my son; I share your wish. [*They embrace.*]

THESEUS: Have you quite forgotten the labours you under- 1410 went?

HERACLES: The horrors I faced then are as nothing compared with my present woes.[71]

THESEUS: This woman-like behaviour will win little praise from any man who sees you.

HERACLES: You think me base in this life I now live? It was not so, I think, in the past.

THESEUS: All too true; you are sick and not the famous Heracles.

HERACLES: What kind of man were you when you were hard-pressed in the underworld?

THESEUS: I was as weak in fighting-spirit as any man.

HERACLES: How then can you blame me, if I am reduced by my miseries?

THESEUS: Then lead on.

HERACLES: Farewell, Father!

AMPHITRYON: Farewell, my son!

HERACLES: Bury the children as I said.[72]

AMPHITRYON: Who shall bury me, my child?

HERACLES: I will. 1420

AMPHITRYON: When will you come?

HERACLES: When you die, father.

Now, take my children's bodies inside – a grievous burden, hard to bear. I, who have devastated my house with deeds of shame, will follow Theseus, utterly ruined, like a boat towed by a ship.[73] If any man desires the benefits of wealth or power more than those of worthwhile friends, he is a fool. [THESEUS *and* HERACLES *leave.*]

CHORUS: *With pity in our hearts and many tears we go, for we have lost our greatest friend.*[74]

[AMPHITRYON, *and servants take up the bodies and carry them into the palace. The* CHORUS *depart in the opposite direction from* THESEUS *and* HERACLES.]

IPHIGENIA AMONG
THE TAURIANS

PREFACE TO *IPHIGENIA*
AMONG THE TAURIANS[1]

The name of Iphigenia is absent from Homer. In one passage he mentions three daughters of Agamemnon as still alive and marriageable in the final phase of the Trojan war: Electra, Chrysothemis and Iphianassa. The last is sometimes identified with Iphigenia in later usage, but if that was Homer's understanding, either he must be unaware of the tale that Agamemnon sacrificed his daughter at Aulis to gain a fair wind for the fleet, or he is silently rejecting it. It has often been argued that certain tales were objectionable in Homer's eyes, and that he might have avoided stories involving kin-killing: in the *Odyssey* he does mention, but guardedly and in passing, the matricide of Orestes. Other poets, however, were less squeamish or more sensational: the sacrifice of Iphigenia figured in an early Greek epic poem known as the *Cypria*, and is mentioned frequently in Attic tragedy: it forms a sinister part of the past in Aeschylus' *Agamemnon*, is invoked as a major part of the indictment against Agamemnon by Clytemnestra in the *Electra* plays of both Sophocles and Euripides, and is dramatized at length in Euripides' posthumous *Iphigenia at Aulis*.

As early as the *Cypria*, there was a tradition that Iphigenia did not die at Aulis but was miraculously rescued by Artemis, to whom she was being offered in sacrifice. According to the surviving summary of the *Cypria*, Artemis carried her off to the land of the Tauri (the modern Crimea) and made her immortal. In some versions she is replaced by a deer or a bear, beasts associated with the goddess. But in Aeschylus it is taken for granted by all, including the audience, that she died at the altar; nor would the ferocity of Clytemnestra's vengeance be easy even for her to justify were this not believed to be the case. Similarly in this play, not even Iphigenia's surviving relations suppose that she is still alive. Since she is also misled by a dream about her brother, and does not know him when he arrives, the playwright has scope for many-sided ironies.

The most striking feature of the Euripidean version, indeed, is that Iphigenia has not been immortalized or translated forever to some remote land of the gods, but is still herself, a living woman, though forced to dwell in a savage land and act as priestess to a barbaric cult of Artemis, a fiercer version of the kindly Greek divinity; she is even obliged to preside over human sacrifices. But since she is still alive, and within the human sphere, the possibility exists of her being found and rescued; and who better to do so than her brother Orestes? The journey of Orestes to the land of the Tauri, and the bringing-home of Iphigenia to Greece, are probably though not certainly Euripides' own inventions. What can definitely be said is that this plot gave abundant opportunity for the type of scene which Euripides particularly favours: scenes in which people who are related or otherwise close to one another are brought together without knowing it; in which they misunderstand or misdirect each other through ambiguous remarks or efforts at self-concealment; and in which the seeming inevitability of recognition is constantly delayed, deflected, but eventually brought about, with the deferment adding to the joy of the participants and the relieved satisfaction of the audience. We meet with scenes of this kind in *Ion* and *Helen*, to look no further; but the long-drawn-out recognition sequence in this play best shows Euripides' total mastery of the technique.

Orestes is traditionally heir to the throne of Mycenae or Argos, but since Aeschylus' time the tragedians had also associated him with Athens. In Aeschylus' *Eumenides* he is given refuge from the Furies and tried for matricide in the Athenian court of the Areopagus; acquitted, he returns to claim his throne. Euripides presupposes the trial in Athens, which Orestes narrates to his sister in his speech at 939ff. But according to this speech that was not the whole story: some of the Furies were not satisfied with the verdict, and have continued to pursue him. Once again he took refuge at Delphi, and appealed to his protector Apollo, who declared that he must journey to the land of the Tauri to seize a statue, an image of Artemis, and bring it back to Athens. The same speech also gives considerable detail about his reception in Athens, and we can recognize allusions to the supposed origins of Athenian festivals and rituals. When at the end of the play Athena rather than Apollo appears in order to resolve the action, her own speech also prophesies aspects of the future cult of Artemis Tauropolos in Attica (1446–74). In this way Euripides uses aetiology (the tracing of the origins of a custom or cult) to link the mythic past with the historical period. He also brings Orestes more decisively within the sphere of Attic mythology and religion. Iphigenia too has an Athenian destiny: when Athena foretells that her duty is 'to keep the keys for this goddess in Brauron's holy meadows', this anticipates the cultic worship which later Athenians paid to Iphigenia herself, as a companion or indeed an aspect of the goddess Artemis. Although the main attraction of the play for modern audiences involves the ironies of identity and recognition, these other aspects show how important the religious and aetiological aspects of tragedy could still be, even late in the century.

The divinities of *Iphigenia* form a striking contrast with the malignant gods of *Heracles* or the more ambiguous role of Apollo in *Ion*. Although Orestes suffers exile and madness, he will finally return to rule in his native land; Iphigenia will come home; even the chorus of Greek women are allowed to return to Greece. The image of Artemis is to be conveyed to a place where it will, we are confident, receive more appropriate worship than in the wilds of the Taurians. Athenian rites will commemorate the hardships of Orestes. Even Thoas, king of the Tauric people, is appeased and accepts the divine will. Although Iphigenia had earlier expressed her revulsion at the notion that Artemis or any deity might welcome human sacrifice (380–91), that moment of criticism is isolated, and the issue of human sacrifice is not explored as a moral issue, but rather deployed as a source of tension and suspense: will Orestes' sister shed the blood of her brother? Here all concerned reach a happy outcome through the wisdom of the gods, whereas in *Hippolytus* or *Heracles* the gods bring suffering and destruction. Greek myths and Greek tragedy had room for both types of tale.

CHARACTERS

IPHIGENIA, *daughter of Agamemnon and priestess of Artemis*
ORESTES, *her brother*
PYLADES, *companion of Orestes*
CHORUS *of female Greek prisoners, attendants of Iphigenia*
COWHERD *of the Tauric Chersonese (Crimea)*
THOAS, *king of Tauric Chersonese*
MESSENGER *in the service of Thoas*
ATHENA

Orestes has been ordered by Apollo to bring
back to Greece Artemis' statue so that
he can be saved from the Furies that still
chase him

— This is a sequel to Oresteia

— Contrast between Electra and Iphigenia
　　　　　　　　　　－bitter　　　　－loyal to family
　　　　　　　　　　－spiteful　　　－good ending
　　　　　　　　　　－bad ending

— Romantic Tragedy along with Ion and Helen
　　　－Sacrifice
　　　－Illusion
— Questioning of Apollos' oracles
　　　－critique of the gods
— Brother-sister Doublet
　　Orestes gets back to Greece Iphig
　　Apollo　　"　　w. Artemis

[*The scene is set in front of the temple of Artemis in the region of the Chersonese inhabited by the Taurians.* IPHIGENIA *enters from the temple.*]

IPHIGENIA: Pelops,[2] son of Tantalus, came to Pisa with his swift horses and won the hand of Oenomaus' daughter. She became the mother of Atreus, and Atreus had as sons Menelaus and Agamemnon. I am Agamemnon's daughter, Iphigenia, the child he had by Tyndareus' daughter. By Euripus' banks, where the ceaseless gusts churn its waters and disturb the dark surface of the sea, my father sacrificed me, as he thought, for Helen's sake,[3] to honour Artemis in Aulis' famous bay.

For it was there he had assembled a Greek fleet of one 10
thousand ships, King Agamemnon, determined to win for the Greeks the crown of a glorious victory over Troy and to please Menelaus by avenging the insult to Helen's marriage. But when unfavourable winds struck, preventing the fleet from sailing, he turned to sacrifice to see what the flames could tell. These were the words of Calchas: 'King Agamemnon, who commands this Greek expedition, do not put your fleet to sea until your daughter Iphigenia has been offered in sacrifice to Artemis. For it was your vow to sacrifice to the goddess who brings light whatever fairest creature the year should bring 20
forth.[4] Well, your wife Clytemnestra gave birth to a child in your palace,' said Calchas, referring the title of 'fairest' to me, 'and it is this child you must sacrifice.'

Through the stratagems of Odysseus, the Greeks took me from my mother on the pretext of marriage to Achilles.[5] I came

53

to Aulis and there in my wretchedness they hoisted me above the pyre, intending to kill me with the sword. But Artemis stole me away, giving the Greeks a deer in my place, and conducted me through the bright air to this land of the Taurians where she gave me a home.

Thoas is king here, barbarian ruler of barbarians, whose wing-like speed of foot earned him this name in recognition of his nimble heels.[6] My lady Artemis has made me priestess in her temple and ever since that day, according to the ritual customs of the festival in which the goddess takes delight (only its name is honourable; as to the rest, my lips are sealed, for I fear the goddess), I consecrate the victim before the slaying; others have responsibility for the sacrifice itself.

A weird vision[7] has appeared to me, brought by the night just passed, and I mean to tell it to the sky; perhaps this will heal my troubled mind. I dreamt that I had left this land and was living in Argos, where I lay asleep in the seclusion of the women's quarters. The earth, it seemed, was suddenly shaken by convulsions. I rushed outside and, standing there, I saw the cornice of the house fall and the whole building from its high gables collapse in ruin to the ground. One solitary pillar, it seemed to me, was left from all my father's house. This sprouted forth from its capital golden hair and it assumed a human voice. Then, in due observance of this office I have of slaying strangers, I sprinkled water on him, with tears falling from my eyes, to mark him for the sacrificial blade.

Here is the way I interpret this dream: Orestes is dead, for it was he I consigned to death at the altar. The pillars of a home are its male offspring and death is the fate of all who are purified at my hands. So now I wish to offer funeral libations for my brother (that at least I can do), though we are not united here but far apart, I and my maidservants, the women of Greece given to me by the king. But some reason keeps them yet absent. I will go into the house where I dwell inside the goddess's precinct.

30

40

50

60

This seems to be a subtle allusion to the problematic nature of sacrifice

[IPHIGENIA *enters the shrine.* PYLADES *enters cautiously, followed by* ORESTES.]

ORESTES: Look out, mind that no one is in our path!

PYLADES: I'm looking, I'm keeping my eyes open, searching everywhere.

ORESTES: Pylades, do you think this is the temple of the goddess that we sailed the seas from Argos to find?

PYLADES: I do, Orestes; and you must share my view.

ORESTES: And the altar where the blood of Greeks drips from the sacrifice?

PYLADES: Well, the streams of blood have made the cornice bright.

ORESTES: And under the cornice itself do you see the severed heads that hang down?

PYLADES: Yes, trophies taken from the bodies of slaughtered strangers. But I must take a good look round and examine things carefully. [PYLADES *approaches the temple to inspect it.*]

ORESTES: O Phoebus,[8] what new trap is this you have led me into with your prophecies, since I avenged my father's murder by killing my mother? Furies in droves have hounded me on my exile's path, a stranger now to my homeland, and many a lap has this race seen me run. I came to you and put the question how I might end these sufferings, this madness that spins me ever onward. You told me to come to the borders of the Tauric land, where Artemis your sister has her altars, and to take from there the goddess's statue, which they say fell from heaven into this temple here. When I had done this, either by deceitful means or good fortune, and seen the dangerous task through, I was to present the statue to the land of the Athenians (beyond that there was no further instruction) and, this done, I would breathe free, my agony at an end. Your words have won me over, and here I stand in this unknown land where strangers find no welcome.

[PYLADES *returns and joins* ORESTES.]

I ask you, Pylades (you are my partner in this labour), how

70

80

90

should we proceed? You see how high the surrounding walls are. Shall we climb up a ladder and make our way inside? But how would we avoid being seen? Or shall we use crowbars to force the bronze bolts, so gaining access to the shrine? If we are caught opening the gates or devising some means of entry, it will be death for us. No, sooner than die, let's make a run for the ship that brought us here!

PYLADES: Making a run for it is out of the question; when has this been our way?[9] We must not disregard the oracle of the god. Let's get away from the temple and hide ourselves in the cave that the dark sea washes with its waves, away from the ship, in case anyone spies the hull and reports it to the rulers. Then we would find ourselves prisoners. When gloomy night's eye comes, we need to show our daring and try to take the statue of hewn stone from the temple, using all our ingenuity. Our best plan is to let ourselves down where there is an empty space between the triglyphs. Hardship brings out daring in men of true worth; cowards vanish from sight. We haven't voyaged all this way only to spread our sails for home again without reaching our goal.

ORESTES: Good advice and it shall be taken! We must find a place where we can hide without being seen. I will not be the cause of the god's holy word coming to nothing; we must brave it. Young men have no excuse for shunning any hard task.

[*Both men leave the stage.* IPHIGENIA *comes out of the shrine. At the same time the* CHORUS *enters from the right of the orchestra. They are Greek captive women who join with their mistress in singing a lament for her brother* ORESTES, *presumed dead.*]

IPHIGENIA: *Keep holy silence, you who dwell by the twin clashing rocks[10] that guard the inhospitable sea!*

CHORUS: *O Dictynna who haunts the mountains, daughter of Leto, to your courts, to your pillared temple with cornice of gold I come, waiting upon the holy steps of the holy maid I serve, the one who keeps the keys of your shrine. The towers of Greece, land of noble*

*horses, and its walled cities have I forsaken, an exile from the seat of
my ancestral home, and Europe's pasturelands, blessed with trees.*

[To IPHIGENIA *herself] I have come. What has happened?
What troubles you? Why have you brought me here, brought me to
the temple, daughter of Atreus' famous son, of him who came to the*   140
*towered walls of Troy with a glorious fleet of a thousand ships and a
host of ten thousand men?*

IPHIGENIA: *Ah, my serving-women,*[11] *how deep I am in lamentations
with mournful lamentation, in sorrowful songs unfit for the lyre, no
tunes to please the Muses' ears, oh, no, as I mourn a member of my
family! Disaster has come upon me, disaster, for it is my brother's life*   150
*I shed these tears for; such a vision of dreams have I seen in this night
whose darkness has just passed! I am ruined, ruined! The house of my
fathers is at an end! It is no more, my race, alas, no more! Oh, weep,
weep for the sufferings that Argos knows!*

*Ah, Fate, you have stolen from me my only brother and sent him
down to Hades! In his honour I mean to sprinkle these libations*[12] *on*   160
*the earth's surface, the bowl with which we honour the dead: milk from
mountain heifers, Bacchus' offerings of wine and the honey that
tawny bees labour to produce – these we offer to soothe the departed.*
[IPHIGENIA *turns to one of her attendants.] Now give me the bowl
of gold and its libation for honouring Hades.*

O scion of Agamemnon below the earth, to you as one dead I bring   170
*these offerings. Accept them; I cannot bring to your tomb my yellow
locks, or my tears. Far from your homeland I now dwell, far from my
own, where, as men suppose, I lie, the wretched victim of the sacrificial
knife.*

CHORUS: *My lady, I will utter an answering strain to you, a barbaric*   180
*song of Asiatic tunes, the music of lamentation that brings an empty
offering to the dead, melodies that Hades chants, not heard in songs of
victory. I weep for the house of Atreus and his sons. The light of your
ancestral home is quenched, the glory of the sceptre vanished, ah, the
pity of it! The beginning of the present ruin lay with the prosperous*   190
kings of Argos. Woe upon woe has fallen upon it,[13] *unceasing, since
the Sun in his holy radiance changed his accustomed course, drawn by
his whirling winged steeds. Diverse tribulation did the golden-fleeced*

200 lamb *bring upon the house, slaughter upon slaughter, woe upon*
woe. Vengeance for the offspring of Tantalus who came to grief in
earlier days is visited on the house; Fate leaps upon you, eager in
malignity.

IPHIGENIA: *From the beginning my life has been accursed, since my*
mother's bridal night and my conception; from the beginning the Fates,
goddesses who presided at my birth, have kept a hard hand upon me;
my schooling to the rein has been a harsh one. I was born as the
210 *first-begotten fruit in her chamber to Leda's wretched daughter; she*
raised me to become the victim of sacrifice outraged by my father, an
offering of little pleasure to the nostrils of the gods.[14] *In a chariot drawn*
by horses they brought me to Aulis' sands, a bride (though no true
bride) for the son of Nereus' daughter – it makes me weep!

Now I live, a stranger, in cheerless dwellings by the sea that is no
220 *friend to strangers, and no husband have I, no children, no fellow-*
citizens, no friends, I whose hand the men of Greece sued to win! No
hymns do I sing to honour Argive Hera,[15] *no likeness of Attic Pallas*
and the Titans do I embroider with shuttle as the loom hums sweetly;
my work is to make altars run red with the blood of slaughtered
strangers, harsh music to the ear, while pity resounds in their agonized
cries, pity in the tears they shed.

230 *But even this I can now forget, as I weep for my brother, dead in*
Argos, who was still a suckling babe when I left him, a youngster still,
an infant still, in his mother's arms and at her breast, my princely
Orestes.

[*A* COWHERD *enters from the sea-shore.*]

CHORUS-LEADER: But here comes a cowherd, leaving the sea-
shore to bring you some news.

COWHERD: Child of Agamemnon and Clytemnestra, listen to
the news I have to bring to your attention!

240 IPHIGENIA: What can there be in what you have to say to cause
such alarm?

COWHERD: Two young men have arrived in our land, after
braving the dark-blue Clashing Rocks in their ship and passing
safely through. Their blood will flow in welcome sacrifice

58

before the shrine of our goddess Artemis. You must lose no time in preparing the bowls and first offerings!

IPHIGENIA: Where are they from? What country does the strangers' clothing suggest?

COWHERD: They are Greeks; this is the one thing I know and nothing more.

IPHIGENIA: Did you not hear even the strangers' names? Do you not know this? Can you not tell me?

COWHERD: Pylades was the name that one of them called the other.

IPHIGENIA: What was the name of this one's partner?   250

COWHERD: Nobody knows; we didn't get to hear.

IPHIGENIA: Where did you see them? Where did you come across them and take them prisoner?

COWHERD: By the very edge of the Unfriendly Sea.

IPHIGENIA: And what do cowherds have to do with the sea?

COWHERD: We had come to wash our cattle down in sea-water.

IPHIGENIA: Go back to that question I asked earlier, how it was you made them your prisoners. That's what I want to hear about.[16]

COWHERD: When we had begun to drive our cattle that usually   260
graze in the woodlands into the sea that flows out through the Clashing Rocks, there was a broken cliff, shattered and worn hollow by the constant pounding of the waves, where purple-fishers[17] were accustomed to shelter. It was there that one of us cowherds caught sight of two young men and came straight back to tell us his news, making his way on tiptoe. 'Don't you see?' he said, 'Gods are sitting over there!'[18] One of us, a man who feared the gods, raised his hand at the sight and invited them: 'O son of sea-dwelling Leucothea, Lord Palaemon,   270
protector of ships, be gracious to us! Or if you are the Sons of Zeus who sit on the shore, or beloved offspring of Nereus, who fathered his noble band of fifty Nereids, give us your favour likewise!'

But another fellow, a scoffer whose irreverence made him bold, laughed at these prayers, saying that they were shipwrecked sailors sitting in the cave out of fear of our custom, since they had heard we sacrifice strangers in these parts. Now most of us reckoned that he was talking sense and so we decided to hunt down the victims for the goddess as custom prescribes.

During this time one of the strangers had left the cave in the cliff and stood outside, shaking his head up and down and groaning. He was trembling to the tips of his fingers and, as his wits wandered in madness, he cried out like a hunter: 'Do you see her, Pylades? Don't you see the hellish dragon there, how she means to kill me, her face fringed by fearful serpents to launch against me? She breathes murderous flames all around, she hovers on wings; she has my mother, that mass of rock, in her arms and is going to hurl her at me![19] Oh, no, no! She is going to kill me! Where can I run to?'

Now, no such forms or shapes as these were to be seen; he mistook the lowing of the cows and the barking of the dogs for the Furies' voices: they are said to utter sounds similar to those animals'. We shrank back from him, thinking his last moment was near, and huddled there in silence. He drew his sword and, leaping like a lion into the midst of the cows, he slashed at their flanks with the blade and pierced their ribs until the sea glowed blood red like a field of flowers. In this way, he imagined, he was defending himself against the divine Furies.

In the meantime, at the sight of our cattle falling to this wild butchery, each one of us started to arm himself and blew on conch-shells, rousing the countryfolk around; we thought that cowherds would be no match in a fight against strangers who were young and trained athletes. In no time our numbers had swelled considerably. Then the stranger lost the pulse of madness and collapsed, froth dripping from his chin. When we saw him fall, a ready victim, not one of us held back as we pelted and beat him. But the other stranger wiped the froth away and tended him, using his finely woven cloak to shield him, as he sought to protect his friend from the hail of blows and minister to him with loving attention.

The stranger returned to his senses. Leaping to his feet he

saw the wave of attackers threatening and, realizing the calamity
facing the two of them, he cried out in despair. We continued
our assault with stones as we pressed on them from all sides.
That was when we heard the shout of exhortation that made   320
us quake: 'Pylades, we are going to die, but make sure it is a
death for heroes! Draw your sword and follow me!'

Now, when we saw those two swords in our enemies' hands,
we fled, flocking into the woodland glens. But only some of
us fled, the rest kept up the attack, pelting the pair, and
whenever they drove off those opponents, the others returned
to the offensive with a volley of stones. It was beyond belief;
though stones were flung from countless hands, not a single
marksman succeeded in hitting those destined for the goddess's
altar. After a long struggle we gained the upper hand, but not   330
through any courage on our part; we formed a circle round
them, dashing the swords from their hands with our stones,
and they sank to the ground on their knees out of weariness.
Then we brought them before the ruler of this land. The
moment he set eyes on them, he sent them to you for the
lustral water and the bowls of sacrifice.

Maiden, you prayed to have such fine strangers grace your
altars hereafter. Slaughter some more strangers of this quality
and Greece will pay in full for shedding your own blood in
sacrifice at Aulis![20]

CHORUS-LEADER: This is a weird tale of madness, whoever the   340
man is who has come from Greece to the Unfriendly Sea!

IPHIGENIA: No matter; [to the COWHERD] Go and bring the
strangers, while I turn my mind to the rites I must perform
here. [He leaves and IPHIGENIA reflects.]

O my poor heart, before you were always gentle to strangers,
always disposed to pity, paying due measure of tears to victims
of your own race, whenever men of Greece came into your
power. But now these visitors will find no warmth in me,   350
whoever they are: my dreams have made me savage. Not a
breath of wind has ever come from Zeus, not a ship, that would
have brought Helen my destroyer here, through the Clashing

Rocks, and with her Menelaus, to let me take my revenge and pay them back – an Aulis here for the one I suffered there, when the sons of Greece trussed me like a young heifer and tried to slaughter me, and my own dear father was the wielder of the knife!

Ah (I cannot rid my mind of that day's horror[21]), how many times I clasped my father's chin and knees, clinging to them, as I spoke words like these: 'Father, you give me away in a marriage that brings you shame! While you are preparing to kill me, my mother and the women of Argos are singing marriage-songs, the whole palace resounds with flutes, and here am I, facing death at your hands! He is Hades, then, not the son of Peleus, this Achilles whom you pretended was to be my wedded lord;[22] you used deceit to bring me here by chariot to a marriage of blood!' A fine-spun veil was covering my eyes, and so I did not pick up in my arms my brother who is alive no more, and modesty kept me from kissing my sister. I thought I was going to the palace of Peleus, and so, supposing I would soon return to Argos, I saved for a later day all those loving greetings.

O poor boy, if dead you are! O my Orestes, what prosperity, what an enviable lot have you lost that your father now enjoys!

[IPHIGENIA *breaks out in anger.*] Oh, I cannot admire this equivocating of the goddess! She denies her altars to any man whose hand has shed blood or touched a woman due to give birth or a dead body, counting him unclean, but she herself delights in sacrifices where men's blood is spilled. Leto won the heart of Zeus;[23] never would she have brought such foolishness into the world, I cannot believe it. No, I think it incredible that Tantalus gave a banquet for the gods in which they feasted with pleasure on his son's flesh. It is the inhabitants of this land, I think, being themselves murderers, who attribute their vileness to the goddess. I cannot suppose any god capable of evil.[24] [IPHIGENIA *goes into the temple.*]

CHORUS [Strophe]: *O dark, dark meeting place of the seas, where the gadfly, winging its way from Argos, passed from Europe to the land*

of Asia, crossing the Inhospitable Gulf![25] Who are these men who
have come from reedy Eurotas' lovely stream, or from Dirce's holy   400
waters, come to this alien land, where the divine maiden is honoured
by the human blood that sprinkles her altars and pillared temples?

[Antistrophe:] Did they sail their vessel over the ocean's waves
with breezes wafting their sails, their pinewood oars churning the   410
water on either side, eagerly striving to increase wealth for their
homes? For hope is prized by mortals and, as they cannot have their
fill, it brings ruin upon them, when they strive to carry off the
burden of wealth, wandering over swelling seas and passing from city
to city in foreign lands, possessed all alike by the same expectation. To
some the thought of wealth comes ill-timed, but to others in proper   420
measure.

[Strophe:] How did they pass by the Clashing Rocks and Phineus'
coast that never slumbers?[26] Amid Amphitrite's surge where Nereus'
fifty daughters sing and circle in the dance, loveliest of sights, the two
did race along the cape with breezes filling their sails; at the stern the   430
rudder creaked in its rowlock, as the southerly winds or Zephyrus'
breath brought them over the Unfriendly Sea to the white isle, land
beloved of birds, land of Achilles, his glorious racecourse.[27]

[Antistrophe:] If only my lady's prayers were answered and Helen,   440
precious child of Leda, could leave Troy's city and come here to die by
my mistress' throat-slashing hand, the curls of her hair soaked with
the water that receives the blood – then would she pay full justice! And
how gladly would I hear the news, if some mariner came to bring me
release from this miserable servitude! Oh, how I long, even in dreams,   450
to be in my home again, in the city of my fathers, enjoying blissful
sleep and sharing in the pleasures of prosperity!

[IPHIGENIA comes out of the temple. ORESTES and PYLADES
are brought on from offstage by guards.]

CHORUS-LEADER: But here come the two of them, the latest
offering to be sacrificed to the goddess, their hands tightly
secured by cords. Silence, friends! These are the finest speci-   460
mens of Greek manhood who are approaching the temple; the
cowherd was no false messenger. [CHORUS raise their arms in

prayer to Artemis.] O my lady, if you are satisfied with the rites
of your people here, accept the sacrifice that we Greeks find
unholy but the custom of the land prescribes.[28]

IPHIGENIA: Very well; my first concern must be to see that my
duty to the goddess is properly fulfilled. [*To the guards*] Untie
the strangers' hands – they are consecrated to the goddess and
470   so must no longer be tethered. Go inside the temple and
make the preparations that are necessary and customary for the
present situation.

[IPHIGENIA *is struck by the sight of the two young men.*] Ah!
Who is she, the mother[29] who gave you birth? Who is your
father and, if you have one, your sister? No brothers will she
have soon, robbed of such a fine pair of men! Who knows on
whom such fates will fall? All the gods' dealings with us proceed
obscurely and no one knows the harm that is to come. Chance
leads us on to dark pathways.

480   Where have you come from, wretched strangers? It took
many a day for your ship to reach this land, and many a day
will you be parted from home in the world below!

ORESTES: Why do you shed these tears, lady, whoever you are,
and cause yourself pain over sufferings that affect us? I see no
sense in someone about to kill another seeking to use pity to
overcome the victim's fear of death nor in someone who
laments death's proximity when he has no hope of rescue. He
compounds two evils out of one; he shows himself to be a fool
and dies in any case. Fate must be allowed to run its course.
490   You should not lament us; we know the rites of sacrifice you
practise here, we realize their nature.

IPHIGENIA: Which one of you was called by the name Pylades
over there? This is what I wish to learn first.[30]

Stycho-
mithia   ORESTES: The man here, if you want to know.

IPHIGENIA: What Greek land claims him as a citizen?

ORESTES: How would you benefit from this knowledge, lady?

IPHIGENIA: Are you two brothers, born of one mother?

ORESTES: Our friendship makes us so, but we are not true
brothers.

IPHIGENIA: And you? What name did your own father give you?

ORESTES: The right name for me would be Unlucky. 500

IPHIGENIA: That is not my question; blame that on chance.

ORESTES: If I died without a name, I would escape mockery.

IPHIGENIA: Why do you grudge me this? Is your pride so great?

ORESTES: You can sacrifice my body, but not my name.

IPHIGENIA: Will you not even tell me the name of your city?

ORESTES: No; as I am about to die, your question brings me little gain.

IPHIGENIA: But what prevents you from doing me this kindness?

ORESTES: The land I call my own is Argos the renowned.

IPHIGENIA: Gods above, is that really where you come from, stranger?

ORESTES: From Mycenae the prosperous, as once it was. 510

IPHIGENIA: Well, if you came from Argos, someone longed for you to come!

ORESTES: I didn't; if you did, that's your affair!

IPHIGENIA: Did you leave your homeland as an exile, or how did it happen?

ORESTES: I am an exile in some sense – I fled willingly and yet against my will.

IPHIGENIA: Will you tell me something I want to know?

ORESTES: That is a trifle compared with my misfortune.

IPHIGENIA: I take it you know of Troy, as all the world does?

ORESTES: How I wish I did not, even in a dream!

IPHIGENIA: Men say it exists no more, levelled by the spear. 520

ORESTES: It is true; your ears have not been deceived.

IPHIGENIA: Did Helen return to Menelaus' house?

ORESTES: She did, and her coming brought ruin to one of my family.

IPHIGENIA: Where is she? I too have a debt to settle with her.

ORESTES: She lives in Sparta with her former bedfellow.

IPHIGENIA: O creature hated by all Greece, not me alone!

ORESTES: I too gained little joy from her marriage.

IPHIGENIA: Did the Greeks get safely home, as report tells?

ORESTES: How you ask me all your questions at once!

IPHIGENIA: Yes, for I want to ask you this before you die.

530 ORESTES: Ask away, as this is your desire; I will answer you.

IPHIGENIA: Did a man called Calchas,[31] a prophet, return from Troy?

ORESTES: He is dead, according to the people of Mycenae.

IPHIGENIA: O my Lady, good news! What of Laertes' son?

ORESTES: He has not yet returned to his home but he is alive, they say.

Odysseus

IPHIGENIA: I pray he never reaches his own land but dies first!

ORESTES: Spare your curses; all his world has been overturned.[32]

IPHIGENIA: What of the Nereid Thetis' son, is he still alive?

ORESTES: No; little good came to him from his marriage at Aulis.[33]

IPHIGENIA: Yes, it was a piece of trickery – those involved know this.

540 ORESTES: But who in the world are you? How well informed you are of matters in Greece!

IPHIGENIA: That is my homeland; when I was still a child I lost it.

ORESTES: Then I understand why you long to know the news from there, lady.

IPHIGENIA: What of the commander? They say he prospers.

ORESTES: Which man? The one I know is not to be numbered with the prosperous.

IPHIGENIA: He was, I believe, called Agamemnon, Atreus' son.

ORESTES: I do not know; leave this line of questioning, lady.

IPHIGENIA: In heaven's name, stranger, do not deny me! Tell me and make my heart glad!

ORESTES: He is dead, poor man, but he destroyed another besides.

IPHIGENIA: Dead? What happened to him? Oh, misery!

550 ORESTES: Why that cry of sorrow? You were not related to him, surely?

IPHIGENIA: I grieve to think of his former happiness.

ORESTES: Yes, it was a terrible end, slaughtered by a woman.

66

IPHIGENIA: Oh, how pitiful they both are, she who killed and he who died!

ORESTES: Stop now at last, no further questions!

IPHIGENIA: This only: is the wretched man's wife alive?

ORESTES: She is not; the child she bore, he killed her with his own hands.

IPHIGENIA: A ruined household! What on earth made him do this?

ORESTES: He was taking revenge on her for his father's murder.

IPHIGENIA: Ah, how well he exacted his wicked justice!

ORESTES: He may well be a just man but the gods do not make him prosper. 560

IPHIGENIA: Has Agamemnon another son left in his palace?

ORESTES: He left behind only Electra, a virgin child.

IPHIGENIA: Is there any word, tell me, of the daughter who was sacrificed?

ORESTES: None, except that she died and sees the sunlight no more.

IPHIGENIA: I pity her, and the father who killed her.

ORESTES: For a wicked woman's sake she was killed, a reason that was no reason!

IPHIGENIA: Is he living still in Argos, the son of the father who was killed?

ORESTES: He lives a life of misery, nowhere and everywhere.

IPHIGENIA: O dream that lied to me,[34] farewell! Now I know your worth!

ORESTES: Gods whom we credit with wisdom can mislead us 570 even more than winged dreams. In matters divine, as in human, much confusion reigns. But one thing brings pain above all: when a man comes to grief, not through folly but because a prophet's words have won him over, as one man fell – those who know him know how.[35]

CHORUS-LEADER: Oh, how this makes me weep! What of us and those who are our parents? Are they alive? Are they not? Who will say?

IPHIGENIA: Listen! I have formed a plan that furthers your

580 interests, strangers, and my own at the same time. It is our best
means of achieving success, provided we all agree on the same
course. [*To* ORESTES] Would you be willing, if I saved your
life, to go to Argos with a message from me to my friends
there? Would you take a letter that a prisoner of war wrote out
of pity for me, for he felt that my hand was not a murderer's
but he was dying because of the custom prescribed by the
590 goddess? I have had no one to take my message to Argos, no
one who could be saved to deliver my letter to any of my
family. But you, sir (it seems you are of noble birth, you know
Mycenae and my friends), save yourself and go there – it is no
shameful reward you will win, your life for carrying a letter!

This man must not share your journey, however; he must
be sacrificed to the goddess, as the Taurians require.

ORESTES: I approve of all you say, stranger, except for one point;
it would be a heavy burden for me to bear if this man were
sacrificed. I am the one who steered his course to disaster; he
600 has shared my voyage because of my troubles. Justice does not
allow that his death should be the price of earning your gratitude and escaping from ruin. I propose a different way. Give
your letter to this man; he will take it to Argos and your wish
will be fulfilled. As for me, let me be killed – it makes no
difference who wields the knife. It brings only shame if a man
secures his own safety by bringing ruin on his friends. This
man is my friend; I want him to live no less than myself.

610 IPHIGENIA: No common man could show such a spirit – you
are born of some noble stock and are a true friend to your
friends! If only I might have in any of my surviving family a
man of your stamp! For I do have a brother, strangers, it is just
that I do not see him. Since it is your wish, I shall send this
man with my letter and you shall be killed; you are truly
possessed by some great desire for death.

ORESTES: Who will sacrifice me and dare do the terrible deed?

IPHIGENIA: I shall; this service of the goddess is mine to perform.

ORESTES: Not one to be envied, young woman, or a happy one.

68

IPHIGENIA: Necessity constrains me and I cannot disobey.　620

ORESTES: You do the deed yourself, sword in hand, a woman sacrificing men?

IPHIGENIA: No, I will only sprinkle the holy water on your hair.

ORESTES: Who, then, will wield the blade – I must put the question?

IPHIGENIA: Inside the temple here are men whose task this is.

ORESTES: What kind of grave shall hold me when I die?

IPHIGENIA: A sacred fire inside and a wide, rocky chasm.

ORESTES: Oh, what an end! If only a sister's hands could shroud me!

IPHIGENIA: That's a foolish prayer to make, poor man, whoever you are; she lives far away from this barbarian land. All the　630 same, as you are a true citizen of Argos, I shall not leave undone any service I can render. I will dress you fully for the tomb, quench your ashes with yellow oil and pour on your pyre the gleaming labour of the nimble mountain bee, culled from flowers.

　Now I will go and fetch my letter from the goddess's temple. [*The attendants once more take* ORESTES *and* PYLADES *into custody.*] Lest you think it is *I* who bear you ill will, keep them under guard, you men, but unfettered! Perhaps I shall be　640 sending to Argos news that was never imagined by the member of my family I love best; by telling him that the one he thought dead still lives, the letter will bring a joy beyond belief.

　[IPHIGENIA *enters the shrine.*]

CHORUS: *We shed tears for you, the victim of the lustral bowl's bloody drops.*

ORESTES: My fate merits no pity, stranger women, but fare you well.

REST OF THE CHORUS: *We honour you, young man, for your blessed fortune in returning to your native land.*

PYLADES: No one is to be envied this, if it means the death of　650 his friend.

69

CHORUS: *O wretched homecoming — it racks my heart — you bring ruin upon two; ah, what sorrow! My wavering heart still debates two courses: should I wail in lamentation first for you or for you?*

ORESTES: Pylades, in the name of the gods, have you had the same thought as I?

PYLADES: I do not know; you ask me a question I cannot answer.

660 ORESTES: Who is the young woman? How like a Greek she questioned us — about the sufferings at Troy, the homecoming of the Greeks, Calchas skilled at reading omens, and the name of Achilles! How she showed pity for the wretched Agamemnon and kept asking me about his wife and children! This stranger must be from that part of the world, an Argive by birth. Otherwise she would never be sending a letter and questioning us like this, behaving as if the good fortune of Argos was hers as well.

PYLADES: You anticipated me a little; I would have said the same 670 as you except for one thought: the fate of kings is known to all men familiar with the world and its ways. But a second thought has occurred to me.

ORESTES: What is it? Share it with me and your thinking will become clearer.

PYLADES: It brings me no credit that you should die and I continue to live. I shared your voyage here and I should share your death as well. If not, I will be thought a coward and villain in Argos and the many glens of Phocis' land. Most people, being malicious themselves, will conclude that I betrayed you to save my own skin and returned home alone. They may even 680 suppose I murdered you, taking advantage of your stricken house to plot your death and seize your throne, calculating that I would gain your sister's inheritance as her husband.[36] I am afraid to incur such disgrace as this. There is no other way: I must breathe my last with you, face with you the sacrificial knife and the pyre that will consume our bones, for I am your true friend and fear for my good name.

ORESTES: In heaven's name, mind what you say! The woes that are mine to bear I must bear; I will not endure a double agony

when a single one is possible. What you say brings pain and   690
reproach on you wounds me no less, if I am to cause your
death, the man who has shared the burden of my tribulations.
As far as I am concerned, it is no great sorrow for me to lose
my life when the gods use me in this fashion. But Fortune
smiles on you, your house is pure, untainted by any curse,
while mine has offended the gods and earned her hatred. If
you survive, you will father children by my sister, the woman
I gave you as your wife, and my family name would remain;
my ancestral home would never fade from men's lips through
lack of progeny.

No, go your way and live! Make my father's house your   700
home. When you come to Greece, and Argos rich in horses, I
urge you to do this for me, by this right hand of yours: build a
tomb and lay on it some memento of mine. Let my sister grace
my grave with her tears and locks of hair. Tell how I died at
the hands of an Argive woman, ritually slaughtered over an
altar. Never betray my sister, though you witness the desolation
of my father's family that you have now joined by marriage.

[ORESTES *embraces* PYLADES.]

Fare you well! You have proved the truest of my friends,
my comrade in the hunt, my boyhood playmate! How you   710
have shouldered all my many woes!

I have been deceived by Phoebus,[37] prophet though he is;
he cunningly drove me as far from Greece as possible, ashamed
of his former prophecies. Entrusting all my fortune to him, I
killed my mother in obedience to his oracle and now in turn
my own life is forfeit.

PYLADES: You shall have your tomb, poor man, and I shall be
no traitor to your sister's bed; in death no less than in life you
may count on my love.

But the god's oracle has not destroyed you yet, though you   720
stand on the verge of death. It is possible there is yet a chance
that your dire ill fortune may swing round to the other extreme.

ORESTES: Speak no more; Phoebus' words are no help to me,

71

for here is the woman coming out of the temple. [IPHIGENIA *emerges*.]

IPHIGENIA [*to the guards*]: Away, go and prepare things inside for those who oversee the sacrifice! [*Guards enter the temple*.] Here it is ready, strangers, the letter with its folded tablets.[38]

730 Let me tell you the rest of my wishes. No man shows the same spirit in adversity and when his fear gives way to courage. I am afraid that the man who is going to take this message to Argos may think my letter of no importance once he has left these shores and reached his home.

ORESTES: What *do* you want? What is your difficulty?

IPHIGENIA: Let him give me his oath that he will take this letter to Argos and deliver it to the friends I wish.

ORESTES: And will you give him as good an oath in return?

IPHIGENIA: To do or not do what? Tell me.

ORESTES: To let him leave this barbarian land with his life.

740 IPHIGENIA: That is a fair request; how else would he act as my messenger?

ORESTES: And will the king agree to this?

IPHIGENIA: Yes; I will persuade him. And I will put your friend on board a ship myself.

ORESTES [*to* PYLADES]: Swear. [*To* IPHIGENIA] And you prescribe an oath that will be holy.

IPHIGENIA: 'I shall give this letter to your friends.' Say it!

PYLADES: I shall give this letter to your friends.

IPHIGENIA: And I shall send you safely beyond the Dark Rocks.

PYLADES: Which of the gods do you pray will witness this oath?

IPHIGENIA: Artemis, in whose dwelling I hold office.

PYLADES: And I invoke heaven's lord, venerated Zeus.

750 IPHIGENIA: And if you abandon your oath and do me wrong?

PYLADES: May I never reach home. And what should be your fate, if you fail to ensure my escape?

IPHIGENIA: Never to live to set foot again in Argos.

PYLADES: But let me tell you something we have not taken into account.

IPHIGENIA: Share it with me straight away, if it is a good idea.

PYLADES: Allow me to make this proviso: if anything happens to the ship, if the letter gets lost in the waves along with the rest of my belongings and I escape only with my life, grant that this oath between us should no longer be binding.

IPHIGENIA: Listen to what I shall do; it's as well to have more than one string to your bow. I will tell you in my own words 760 the contents that are written in the folds of the letter, so you can give your friends a full account. This will ensure the message does not perish. If you manage to save the letter, it will need no voice to convey its contents; but if it is swallowed up at sea, and you preserve your own life, you will preserve my words as well.

PYLADES: That is an excellent suggestion; it suits your interests and benefits me too. Now tell me to whom I am to take this letter in Argos and what I am to say in your name.

IPHIGENIA [*handing the letter to him and reciting from memory*]: Take this news to Orestes, son of Agamemnon: 'She who was 770 slaughtered at Aulis sends this message, Iphigenia who is alive, though in Argos they think her dead –'

PYLADES [*interrupting*]: Where is that lady? Has she come back from the dead?

IPHIGENIA [*impatiently*]: She is before your eyes – do not disturb my train of thought! 'Bring me back to Argos, brother, before I die! Take me away from this savage land, from the bloody service I render the goddess, murdering strangers in my holy office . . .'

ORESTES [*turning to Pylades*]: Pylades, what shall I say? Where do we find ourselves?

IPHIGENIA: '. . . or else I will become a curse to your house, Orestes', to make you hear the name a second time and note it well.

ORESTES: O you gods! 780

IPHIGENIA: What makes you call upon the gods in matters that are my business?

ORESTES: I have no reason. Continue; my thoughts were on something else.

IPHIGENIA: Perhaps when he questions you he will become sceptical. Say this: 'The goddess Artemis rescued me by substituting in my place a deer which my father sacrificed, thinking he was driving the sharp blade into me. She gave me a new home in this land.' This is the letter, these are the words written in the tablets.

PYLADES: It is an easy oath you require me to honour, yes, and an excellent guarantee you make. I will not waste a moment
790   in fulfilling the pledge I have given. Look, I bring you a letter, Orestes,[39] and duly deliver it, from your sister here.

ORESTES: I receive it. But I will not look at the folded tablet; first I will enjoy a pleasure no words can supply. [ORESTES *moves forward to embrace* IPHIGENIA.] O my darling sister, I am overwhelmed, but I will rush to seize my joy, clasping you in incredulous arms! This discovery fills me with wonder.

IPHIGENIA [*retreating in alarm*]: Sir, you offend justice in laying hands on the servant of the goddess, grasping her inviolable robe!

800   ORESTES: O my own sister, born of the same father, Agamemnon, do not reject me! You have the brother you thought you would never have!

IPHIGENIA: You – my brother? No more of your words! Argos and Nauplia are both full of his name.

ORESTES: Poor woman, your brother is not to be found there.

IPHIGENIA: Was your mother the Spartan woman, Tyndareus' daughter?

ORESTES: Yes, and my father was the grandson of Pelops, whose descendant I am.

IPHIGENIA: What are you saying? Can you show me any evidence for this?[40]

ORESTES: I can; ask some question about your father's house.

810   IPHIGENIA: Should you not be speaking and I drawing conclusions?

ORESTES: I will begin by saying what I have been told by Electra. You remember the dispute that took place between Atreus and Thyestes?[41]

74

IPHIGENIA: I have heard about it; they quarrelled over a golden lamb.

ORESTES: Do you remember weaving this subject on a fine web?

IPHIGENIA: O dearest, you strike a chord in my heart!

ORESTES: And a likeness of the sun turning back in its course?

IPHIGENIA: I did indeed weave that picture with fine threads!

ORESTES: And you know the holy water that your mother gave you for your wedding at Aulis?

IPHIGENIA: I remember; it was not so fine a wedding as to make me forget that.

ORESTES: Yes, and how you gave a lock of your hair to be taken to your mother?   820

IPHIGENIA: Yes, to serve as a memorial at my tomb, empty as it was of my body.

ORESTES: I will tell you what my own eyes have seen, to prove who I am: in our father's house lies the ancient spear of Pelops, which he brandished in his hand when he killed Oenomaus and won the maid of Pisa, Hippodameia; it was hidden away in the quarters where you women lived.

[*They embrace one another and* IPHIGENIA *sings in her happiness.*]

IPHIGENIA: *O my dearest, I can call you by no other name, for dearest you are, I hold you in my arms, Orestes, so far from your homeland*   830
of Argos, my love!

ORESTES: And I hold you, the one who was thought dead!

IPHIGENIA: *Tears moisten your eyes, as they do mine, and grief mingling with joy. You were a little baby when I left you in our home, a tender infant in the arms of your nurse. O my heart that knows a happiness words cannot express, what can I say? What has happened here is beyond wonder, far beyond imagining!*

ORESTES: I pray that all our days to come may know such happiness between us!

IPHIGENIA [*to the* CHORUS]: *This is a strange pleasure I feel, my friends; I am afraid he may escape my hands and fly up to the sky. O hearth of my city, raised by Cyclopes, o my country, beloved Mycenae,*

I thank you, thank you for letting him live, for rearing this brother of mine to be a beacon to his house!

850 ORESTES: We are fortunate in birth, sister, but our experience of life has not been a happy one.

IPHIGENIA: *I remember, ah, how bitterly I remember the time when my father with misery in his heart thrust his sword into my throat.*

ORESTES: Oh, terrible! I was not present but I fancy I see you there!

IPHIGENIA: *It was for no wedding, my brother, that I was taken to the*
860 *deceitful marriage-bed of Achilles; beside the altar there were tears and cries of mourning. Oh, the pain, the pain, when I think back to that washing of hands for purification!*

ORESTES: I too feel the pain at the thought of what our father steeled himself to do.

IPHIGENIA: *No father, no father could have treated me in such a fashion! Yet various are the fates that come upon us by heaven's will.*

ORESTES: At least you did not kill your own brother, my poor girl.

IPHIGENIA: *Oh, what a wretch I was to dare so terrible a deed! Terrible*
870 *was my resolve, terrible, my brother, ah, the pain of that thought! How close you were to an impious death, slaughtered by these hands of mine! But how will these misfortunes end? What will happen to me now? What way can I discover,⁴² what way to send you back to your*
880 *homeland of Argos, away from death, away from this land, before the sword threatens to spill your blood?*

Here, poor heart, here lies the problem you must solve. Should it be by land, not by ship but on swift feet? If so you will court death, passing through barbarous tribes over trackless land. And yet the way
890 *by the Dark Rocks that clash is long for escape by ship. Oh, pity me, pity me! What god, what mortal, what chance unlooked for, will find a way where no way there is and show the only two scions of Atreus' house a release from their troubles?*

900 CHORUS-LEADER: Wonderful is what I have seen here, and with my own eyes, not heard from messengers. Words cannot describe it.

PYLADES: When loved ones set eyes on loved ones, Orestes, it is natural for them to embrace one another. But now you must give up these tears for each other and face the question how we are to make good our escape, a glorious prize, and get clear of this barbarous land.

ORESTES: Well said; and I think fortune will aid our escape, if we help ourselves. The gods are more likely to support a man   910
if he puts his heart into the task.

IPHIGENIA: No, do not obstruct me or seek to divert me from learning what is Electra's lot in life. This is of close concern to me.

ORESTES: She lives as this man's wife and enjoys good fortune.

IPHIGENIA: And where does this man come from? Whose son is he?

ORESTES: Strophius of Phocis is his father.

IPHIGENIA: So he is the son of Atreus' daughter and a kinsman of mine?

ORESTES: Your cousin, and the only true friend I have.

IPHIGENIA: He was not living when my father tried to kill   920
me.[43]

ORESTES: He was not; for some time Strophius had no children.

IPHIGENIA: Welcome, husband of my sister!

ORESTES: Yes, and not just a relative but the man who saved my life.

IPHIGENIA: That terrible action you took over our mother, how did you find the nerve for it?

ORESTES: Let us not discuss it; I was avenging my father.

IPHIGENIA: What was her reason for killing her husband?

ORESTES: Say nothing about our mother's behaviour; it is not fitting for you to hear.[44]

IPHIGENIA: I will not ask. Does Argos look to you now?

ORESTES: Menelaus is king; I am banished from my father's land.

IPHIGENIA: Surely your uncle did not take advantage of our   930
stricken house?

ORESTES: No, panic caused by the Furies sent me into exile from my country.

IPHIGENIA: Oh, I understand; because of your mother the goddesses drove you onward.

ORESTES: Yes, thrusting their bridle into my mouth till it bled.

IPHIGENIA: So this was the madness you showed on the shore, as reported to us here?

ORESTES: This is not the first time my wretchedness has been observed.

IPHIGENIA: What on earth caused you to make the journey to this land?

ORESTES: I came here in obedience to the orders of Phoebus' oracle.

IPHIGENIA: What were you required to do? May it be spoken or is it not for other ears?

ORESTES: I will tell you; this was the beginning of much suffering
940   for me. When my mother's – when that monstrous act I will not speak of had been performed, I was hounded by the Furies and driven into exile. Next Loxias directed my steps to Athens[45] to stand trial there before the nameless goddesses. There is a holy tribunal that in days gone by Zeus established for Ares as the result of a crime that polluted that god's hands. When I reached this place, at first no host was willing to receive me as one hated by the gods. Some, however, felt shame at this and
950   provided me with a solitary table as hospitality, though we all shared the same roof, and by refusing to speak to me they denied me the chance to converse with them. Their intention was that I should enjoy their food and drink, but separately from them, and, serving the wine in individual cups, an equal measure for all, they made merry.

I did not think it right to question my hosts and so I suffered in silence, pretending not to have it on my conscience, despite my heavy sighs, that I was my mother's murderer. I hear that my unhappy experience has become a religious rite for the
960   Athenians, and that the custom still stands whereby Pallas' folk honour the six-pint pot.

When I came to Ares' hill, I stood trial, I mounting the defendant's plinth, and the eldest Fury the other one. After I

had given and heard the arguments about my mother's bloodshed, Phoebus saved me by his testimony, and Pallas' arm,
separating the votes for and against me, found them equal in
number. I came off the victor in my trial for murder.

Those Furies who were won over by the verdict settled
there, marking out for themselves a sanctuary beside the very   970
scene of the voting. But those who disagreed with the decision
have hounded me constantly, denying me a place to rest my
head as onward I fled, until I came again to Phoebus' sanctuary.
There I prostrated myself before the holy entrance, refusing all
food, and swore that there I would die and end my life unless
Phoebus, my destroyer, saved me.[46]

Then the voice of Phoebus rang out from his golden tripod;[47]
he sent me here to seize a statue fallen from Zeus and to set it
up in the land of Athens. Now help me achieve the deliverance   980
the god has appointed for me. If we get possession of the
goddess's image my madness will leave me, I will provide you
with a ship and crew and restore you to Mycenae once more!

O my precious girl, dear sister, preserve your father's house,
save my life! It is ruin for my fortunes, ruin for all of Pelops'
house if we fail to seize the goddess's image from heaven.

CHORUS-LEADER: The gods' anger seethes, strange and terrible,
against the seed of Tantalus and drives them from one tribulation to another.

IPHIGENIA: Before you came here my heart was set on being in   990
Argos and seeing you, brother. Your wishes are mine as well,
to free you from your troubles, to rescue our stricken house
and restore the fortunes of our ancestral home, bearing no
grudge against the man who tried to kill me. Thus I would
both keep my hands free from the stain of spilling your blood
and preserve my home. But I fear detection by the goddess –
will she not see me? I fear the action of the king when he finds
the stone pedestal empty, its statue gone. Then will I surely
die; there is no excuse I can make. But if we succeed in both
these plans together, if you carry off the statue and set me on   1000
board your fine ship, the prize is worth the risk. If you fail

to manage my escape, it is the end of my life but you would succeed in your aim and return home safely. I do not shrink from this, even if the cost of saving you is my own death; a man's death is a sore loss to a house, a <u>woman's counts for little</u>.[48]

ORESTES: I will not be *your* murderer as well as my mother's. Her blood is enough! We think alike: I would like to live with
1010   you or to die and share your lot. I will take you with me, if I can escape from here myself and make the voyage home, or else I will stay here and die with you. Listen to what is in my mind. If this was an action that offended Artemis, how would Loxias have ordered me in his oracle to bring the goddess's statue to the town of Pallas and seen to it that I set eyes on you here? When I draw together all these threads it gives me hope of winning my way home after all.

IPHIGENIA: How then are we to avoid death and achieve our end? This is where my homecoming falters; this is where we need to plan.

1020 ORESTES: Would we be able to kill the king?

IPHIGENIA: <u>What a monstrous idea – visitors kill their host?</u>

ORESTES: But if it means safety for you and me, we must take the risk.

IPHIGENIA: I could not do it – but I admire your boldness.

ORESTES: What if you were to hide me secretly in the temple here?

IPHIGENIA: There are guards inside the temple who will see us.

ORESTES: Ah, we are ruined! How can we be saved?

IPHIGENIA: I think I have a new kind of device.

1030 ORESTES: What kind of device? Let me share your thoughts, so that I too may know.

IPHIGENIA: I shall use your troubles as a trick.

ORESTES: Women are certainly adept at thinking up schemes.[49]

IPHIGENIA: I will say that you have been driven from Argos as your mother's murderer.

ORESTES: Make use of my misfortunes, if you can turn them to advantage.

IPHIGENIA: I shall say it is unlawful to offer you in sacrifice to the goddess.

ORESTES: What will be your pretext? I am beginning to understand . . .

IPHIGENIA: That you are an impure victim; I will sacrifice only what is unblemished.

ORESTES: How will it then be easier to seize the statue of the goddess?

IPHIGENIA: I shall say I want to purify you in sea-water.

ORESTES: But the statue for which we have come will still stand in the temple. 1040

IPHIGENIA: I will say I intend to wash it as well since your hands touched it.[50]

ORESTES: Where is this to happen? Is it an inlet of the sea, swept by the spray, you mean to visit?

IPHIGENIA: Yes, the place where your ship is anchored by hawsers of stout rope.

ORESTES: Will you or someone else carry the image in your arms?

IPHIGENIA: I shall; piety requires that I alone should touch it.

ORESTES: What role in this task shall we assign to Pylades here?

IPHIGENIA: I will say his hands are tainted with the same pollution as your own.

ORESTES: When you carry out this plan, will it be without the king's knowledge or not?

IPHIGENIA: I will win him round with my version of events; I could not keep him in the dark. Your task is to see that everything else goes well.

ORESTES: Well, my good ship's thrashing oars are ready for action. We need one thing only: these women must join us in keeping this a secret.[51] [ORESTES *gestures towards the* CHORUS.] Appeal to them, devise words to win them over; women have the power to arouse pity. As for the rest, no doubt all will turn out well. 1050

IPHIGENIA [*addressing the* CHORUS *directly*]: O my women, good friends all, I look to you. On you depend my fortunes, either

81

to find happiness or to lose everything, robbed of my homeland,
1060 my dear brother and my beloved sister. First of all let this
thought begin my appeal: we are women, naturally supportive
of one another, and steadfast in guarding our common interests.
Give us your guarantee of silence and help us in the task of
managing our escape! It is a fine thing when a person may be
relied upon not to betray confidences. You see how we three,
so close to one another, are subject to one fate, either returning
to our native land or dying. [*Addressing the* CHORUS-LEADER
first, then individual members of the CHORUS] Help us to escape
and, to make you also share our fortune, I will see you safe to
Greece. I beg you by your right hand, and you, and you, and
1070 you by your fair cheek, your knees and all your loved ones at
home! What do you say? Who among you agrees to this, who
does not – speak out! If my words fall on deaf ears, it is the end
for me and for my poor brother!

CHORUS-LEADER: Never fear, dear mistress, only save yourself.
As far as I am concerned, nothing will be said about all you bid
me keep hidden (great Zeus be my witness).

IPHIGENIA: Bless you for these words! May fortune smile on
you! [*Turning to* ORESTES *and* PYLADES] Now it is your task,
1080 and yours, to go inside the temple. The ruler of this land will
be here soon to ask if the strangers have been sacrificed.
[ORESTES *and* PYLADES *go into the temple.*]

O lady divine, who in the glens of Aulis saved me from the
terrible hands of a murderous father, save me now too, and
these men! Otherwise, thanks to you, the oracles of Loxias will
no longer ring true for mankind. Be gracious and consent to
leave this barbarous land for Athens; this is no fit dwelling-place
for you, when you might have as your home a city favoured
by the gods.[52] [IPHIGENIA *turns and enters the temple.*]

1090 CHORUS [Strophe]: *Halcyon,*[53] *bird that sings your fate as a dirge
along the rocky sea-cliffs, uttering to those who understand that familiar
cry, your constant lament in song for your husband, I also have
lamentations to rival yours, I a bird without wings, pining for the*

82

assembly-places of the Greeks, pining for Artemis, protectress of
mothers, in her dwelling by the hill of Cynthus, by the soft-leaved   1100
palm and the lovely bay and the holy shoots of the pale olive, welcome
shelter to Leto in the pangs of childbirth, by the lake whose waters
swirl in a circle, where the swan honours the Muses with his song.

[Antistrophe:] O the many fountains of tears that tumbled down
my cheeks on the day when our walls fell in ruin and I was brought to
the ships, amidst the oars and spears of the enemy! Bartered for much   1110
gold, I sailed to a barbarous land where I serve the daughter of
Agamemnon, herself the handmaiden of the deer-slaying goddess, at
altars where no sheep are sacrificed. I envy the man who has never
known happiness; necessity's yoke does not oppress him, for it is his
constant companion. Change of fortune is misery; to know hardship   1120
after experiencing happiness, that is an existence that weighs hard on
mortals. *Catastrophe is part of tragedy according to Aristotle*

[Strophe:] As for you, my lady, an Argive ship of fifty oars shall
bear you home. The piping of the wax-bound reeds, played by
mountain-dwelling Pan, will urge on the oarsmen, and prophetic
Phoebus, singing to the music of his seven-stringed lyre, will give you   1130
fair passage to the Athenians' gleaming land. But I shall be left here
when you set sail and the oars splash in the water; the breeze will
make the halyards and sheets stretch out the sails so they billow out
over the bows of the speeding vessel.

[Antistrophe:] If only I might follow the glittering course of the
Sun's chariot, where his bright fire leaps onward! Oh, to still the
fluttering wings on my back above the chambers of my own home! To   1140
take my place in the dancing bands, where once, a maiden marked out
for a splendid marriage, I left my loving mother's side to whirl with
friends in competitions of grace amidst the joyful ring, eager to vie with
them in luxuriant hair, tossing my gorgeous veils and the curls that   1150
darkly clustered round my cheeks!

[King THOAS enters with attendants. At the same time
IPHIGENIA emerges from the temple behind, carrying the sacred
image.]

THOAS [to the CHORUS]: Where is the Greek woman who

keeps watch over this temple? Has she already consecrated the strangers for sacrifice?

CHORUS-LEADER [*pointing to* IPHIGENIA *as she emerges*]: There, my lord, is the woman who will give you a clear account of everything.

THOAS: What's this? Why have you taken in your arms the image of the goddess, daughter of Agamemnon? Why have you lifted it from its inviolate pedestal?

IPHIGENIA: My lord, stay where you are in the vestibule.

1160 THOAS: What strange thing has happened in the temple, Iphigenia?

IPHIGENIA: It is revolting! I say this to honour Holiness.

THOAS: What news is prefaced by these words? Speak plainly!

IPHIGENIA: The victims you hunted down for me were not unblemished ones, my lord.

THOAS: What has convinced you of this? Or do you speak of surmise?

IPHIGENIA: The statue of the goddess turned backwards on its plinth.[54]

THOAS: Of its own accord, or did some earth tremor twist it round?

IPHIGENIA: Of its own accord; and the statue closed its eyes.

THOAS: What caused this? Was it pollution carried by the strangers?

IPHIGENIA: That and nothing else; they have done a terrible thing.

1170 THOAS: Did they kill one of my barbarian subjects on the sea-shore, then?

IPHIGENIA: They came here with the blood of kinship on their hands.

THOAS: Whose blood? I long to learn!

IPHIGENIA: They joined forces to dispatch their mother with a sword.

THOAS: Apollo! Not even barbarians would have had the heart for such a deed![55]

IPHIGENIA: They were pursued and driven from all of Greece.

THOAS: These, then, are your reasons for bringing the statue outside?

IPHIGENIA: Yes, under the holy sky, to expel the taint of murder.

THOAS: How did you discover the strangers' pollution?

IPHIGENIA: I questioned them when the goddess's statue turned backwards.

THOAS: You are a clever daughter of Greece to have such sharp sight! 1180

IPHIGENIA: And then they dangled a bait to ensnare my heart.

THOAS: Did they offer some news of events in Argos to charm you?

IPHIGENIA: They said that my brother, my one and only Orestes, was prospering.

THOAS: No doubt they hoped your delight at this report would make you save them.

IPHIGENIA: And that my father was alive and enjoyed good fortune.

THOAS: You then naturally took the side of the goddess.

IPHIGENIA: Yes, in my hatred for all Greece that destroyed me.

THOAS: What then should we do about the strangers? Tell me!

IPHIGENIA: We are bound to honour the appointed custom.

THOAS: Are they not ready for action, the lustral bowl and your 1190
sword?

IPHIGENIA: I wish first to cleanse them with purifying ablutions.

THOAS: In water from springs or from the sea?

IPHIGENIA: The sea purges all taint of human evil.

THOAS: They would certainly be the purer when they fell as victims to the goddess.

IPHIGENIA: Yes, and my duty would be better fulfilled.

THOAS [noticing that IPHIGENIA was not taking the direct route to the sea]: Surely the waves break right by the temple?

IPHIGENIA: I need to be alone; there are other rites I intend to perform.

THOAS: Take them where you wish; I do not wish to see what may not be spoken of.

IPHIGENIA: I must also sanctify the statue of the goddess.

1200 THOAS: Yes, in case it has become infected by the taint of matricide.

IPHIGENIA: Otherwise I would never have removed it from its pedestal.

THOAS: Your foresight and devotion to the gods are entirely proper.[56]

IPHIGENIA [*warming to her scheme*]: You know what you must do for me now.

THOAS: It is for you to instruct me.

IPHIGENIA: Put the strangers in fetters.

THOAS: But where would they run to, if they escaped from you?

IPHIGENIA: There is no trusting a Greek.

THOAS [*to his attendants*]: Go now, men, put on the fetters.

IPHIGENIA: Yes, and let them also bring the strangers out here.

THOAS: So be it.

IPHIGENIA: Let them cover the prisoners' heads with their cloaks.

THOAS: As a protection for the fiery sun.[57]

IPHIGENIA: Send some of your attendants to escort me.

THOAS: These men will accompany you.

IPHIGENIA: And send a man to tell the townsfolk . . .

THOAS: That what has happened?

1210 IPHIGENIA: . . . to stay every one of them indoors.

THOAS: To avoid coming into contact with murder?

IPHIGENIA: Yes, such things are an affront to decency.

THOAS [*to an attendant*]: Away with you now; give the instruction.

IPHIGENIA: No one is to come near the sight.

THOAS: Your concern for the people does you credit.

IPHIGENIA: And for friends to whom my duty is greatest.

THOAS: These words refer to me.[58] † † How right all my people are to admire you!

IPHIGENIA: You should stay here in front of the temple and serve the goddess.

THOAS: What am I to do?

IPHIGENIA: Cleanse her dwelling with torches.

THOAS: So that you may find it purified on your return.

IPHIGENIA: And when the strangers come out . . .

THOAS: What should I do?

IPHIGENIA: . . . pull your cloak over your eyes.

THOAS: I see, to avoid being tainted by the murder.

IPHIGENIA: And if you think my absence is too long . . .

THOAS: What limit should I set on this?

IPHIGENIA: . . . let nothing make you wonder.   1220

THOAS: Do not be hasty in satisfying the goddess's wishes; honour her well.

IPHIGENIA: I pray this purification may fall out as I wish!

THOAS: I echo that prayer.

[THOAS' *attendants appear at the door of the temple, leading* ORESTES *and* PYLADES *in chains. They are followed by servants carrying vessels for purification and leading animals for sacrifice. The procession moves off.*]

IPHIGENIA: Here are the strangers now, I see, leaving the temple, and with them the adornments of the goddess, and new-born lambs whose blood will let me wash away the taint of blood. Blazing torches, too, are here and all the other means of purification I prescribed for the strangers and goddess. [IPHIGENIA *joins the end of the procession.*] I warn all citizens to keep their distance from this pollution, whether they are temple servants purifying themselves for the gods, or approaching to ask for blessing before marriage or for aid in childbirth. Flee, stand aside, let none of you incur this taint!

Royal mistress, virgin child of Zeus and Leto, if I cleanse   1230
these men of blood guilt and offer sacrifice at the proper place, you will inhabit a dwelling that is pure and we shall know happiness. I shall not speak of the rest but show my heart to the gods who know more and to you, goddess.

[*The procession leaves and* THOAS *enters the temple.*]

CHORUS [Strophe]: *A lovely child was Leto's baby boy,*[59] *when she bore him in Delos' fertile vales. Golden-haired he was, and skilful with the lyre, and his joy is in true archery. Leaving the glorious*

1240   *birthplace, his mother brought her child from the sea-reef to Parnassus'*
summit with its bountiful springs where Dionysus leads the revel.
There the ruddy serpent with spotted back, a wondrous monster on the
earth, used to haunt the grove amid the dense shade of the leafy laurel,
infesting the oracle founded by Earth. That creature you slew, Phoebus,
1250   *though you were still a babe, still bouncing in your mother's arms, and*
you entered the holy oracle. At the tripod of gold you sit, on the throne
of truth, and from the depths of the holy chamber you issue to mortal
men your oracular decrees. Beside Castalia's waters you dwell in your
shrine at earth's centre.

1260   [Antistrophe:] *But Apollo had dispossessed Themis from Earth's*
holy oracle, and so Earth brought forth nocturnal visions, dreams that
revealed to many a mortal as he slumbered in darkness upon the
ground the past and the future, all that it held in store. Thus Earth,
jealous on her daughter's behalf, robbed Phoebus of his oracular
1270   *privileges. At this the king rushed on swift feet to Olympus, and,*
clasping the throne of Zeus in baby fingers, he entreated him to release
his Pythian home from the divine anger of Earth. The god laughed to
see his child come so quickly to claim the worship that brought in so
much wealth. Shaking his locks to give consent, he ordered that the
nocturnal voices should cease. He withdrew from mortals the prophetic
1280   *truth that came by night and restored his privileges to Loxias. And so*
he revived men's confidence in the verses of his oracles, chanted at his
throne where troops of visitors throng.

[*Enter a* MESSENGER *in haste.*]

MESSENGER: Temple guards, attendants at the altar, where has
Thoas gone, the ruler of this land? Open the bolted doors and
call the Taurians' king out of these halls!

CHORUS-LEADER: What is it, if I may speak without your
permission?

1290   MESSENGER: They've gone, the two young men, clean gone!
<u>Thanks to the planning of Agamemnon's daughter they've fled</u>
<u>from this land, taking the holy statue with them in the bowels</u>
<u>of their Greek ship!</u>

CHORUS-LEADER: I cannot believe your words! As for the

king of this land whom you wish to see, he has left the temple in some haste.[60]

MESSENGER: Where did he go? He must be told what is happening.

CHORUS-LEADER: We do not know. Go, hurry after him and, if you find him, tell your story!

MESSENGER: You see how little trust should be put in women! You, too, have some share in these events!

CHORUS-LEADER: You are mad! If the strangers have run away   1300
what fault is it of ours? Hurry off to the king's gates and don't waste more time!

MESSENGER: Not until a functionary tells me if the country's ruler is indoors or not! [*He hammers at the door.*] Hey there! Undo the bars, I say, you inside, and tell your master why I'm here at his gates, with a load of bad news to announce!

THOAS [*coming out of the temple*]: Who is raising a shout at the goddess's house here, hammering at the doors and deafening those inside?

MESSENGER: These women were misleading me and trying to keep me away from the temple, saying you were out; but you   1310
are at home after all, it seems.

THOAS: What did they hope to gain? What were they fishing for?

MESSENGER: I will explain their motives another time. Hear what trouble you are faced with right now. The young woman whose place was beside the altar here, Iphigenia, is gone, and the strangers with her. She has left this land, taking with her the holy statue of the goddess. The purification was a trick.

THOAS: What's that you say? What ill wind favoured her?

MESSENGER: Her plan was to save Orestes; that will surprise you!

THOAS: Orestes, you say? The son of Tyndareus' daughter?

MESSENGER: The man the goddess marked for dedication at this   1320
altar.

THOAS: It's beyond belief! What stronger words can I find for what has happened?

MESSENGER: Think no more of that and listen to me; pay close attention and, as you hear my words, consider what manner of pursuit will hunt the strangers down.

THOAS: Speak; your advice is sound. A long sea-voyage awaits them and they will not outdistance my ships.

MESSENGER: When we reached the sea-shore, where Orestes' ship was moored in secret, we whom you had sent as escorts for the strangers, with fetters, had our instructions from

1330 Agamemnon's daughter. She said that we should stand at some distance to let her carry out the secret rites of fire and cleansing for which she had come. She walked behind alone, holding the strangers' fetters in her hands. This did strike us as suspicious, my lord, but your servants let it pass.

Sometime later she raised a piercing cry, to make us think she was engaged in some momentous business. Then she began to chant in unintelligible strains as part of her magic ritual, as if she were washing away the taint of murder.

1340 When we have been sitting there for a long time, it occurred to us that the strangers, released from their fetters, might kill her and make their escape. Fear of seeing that which we should not kept us sitting there in silence, but in the end we all had the same thought, to go to the place where they were, though we were forbidden. And there we saw a Greek ship, a fine broadside of oars furnishing it with wings, and a crew of fifty men with oars in the rowlocks, and the young men standing

1350 at the ship's stern, freed of their fetters. Some of the seamen were steadying the prow with poles, others were hauling up the anchor to the cat-heads, while others again were hastily passing a ladder through, which they lowered from the stern into the sea for the stranger woman.

Now, when we saw this cunning piece of trickery, we lost all respect for the woman and grabbed hold of her and the hawsers as well, trying to pull the rudder-blades from their holes at the stern of the sturdy vessel. Then we called out: 'By what right do you descend on our shores and steal statues and

1360 priestesses? Who are you, whose son are you, to carry off this woman from our land?' Then came his reply: 'Orestes, her brother, let me tell you, and son of Agamemnon! This is my own sister I am taking away as my prize, the woman I lost from my home!'

But we kept our grip on the woman all the more determinedly, trying to force her to accompany us back to you. That was when our cheeks sustained some fearful blows. Like us they had no weapons to hand, but their fists kept dashing into us and both the young men together rained kicks against 1370 our ribs and stomachs, making us collapse stunned with the pain. They stamped us with their terrible signature until we started to run for the cliff, some with bloody wounds on our heads, others on our faces. We took our stand on the hill and put up a more cautious defence by pelting them with stones. But their archers, standing on the stern, kept us in check with their arrows and forced us to keep our distance.

At this point a fearful wave threatened to drive the ship onto 1380 land but the maiden was afraid to step into the water. Orestes hoisted his sister onto his left shoulder and, striding into the surf, he leapt onto the ladder and set her down inside the sturdy ship, along with the statue of Zeus' daughter that fell from the sky. A cry rang out from midship: 'Sailors of Greece, good lads, bend to your oars and send the white spray flying! We have it now, the prize we sailed to win, past the Clashing Rocks and into the Unfriendly Sea!'

Then the crew roared out a yell of joy and struck the brine 1390 with their oars. As long as the ship was inside the harbour, she made progress towards the entrance, but once past this she encountered a heavy sea and started to labour. An alarming gale had sprung up suddenly, forcing the sails aback. The crew worked manfully, struggling against the waves, but the surging undercurrent was driving the ship back to land. Then Agamemnon's daughter stood up and prayed: 'Maiden child of Leto, I am your priestess: bring me safe from this barbarous 1400 land to Greece and look kindly on my theft. You also, goddess, love your brother; consider that I too love my family.'

The sailors began to sing the paean[61] in response to the girl's prayer and with arms bared to the shoulder they swung their oars in time to the call. Closer and closer to the rocks moved the ship. Some of us rushed into the sea, others were making loops of rope fast on shore. I was dispatched here at once, my lord, to tell you what is happening there. Come now, bring fetters and ropes with you! Unless the sea calms down,[62] the strangers have no hope of being saved. The revered Poseidon, ocean's king, is no friend to Pelops' house and watches over Ilium. And so now, it seems, he will deliver into your hands and your people's the prize of Agamemnon's son and his sister, who is guilty of betraying the goddess, forgetting the bloodshed at Aulis.

1420 CHORUS-LEADER: Poor Iphigenia, you will fall under the power of your master once again and be killed, together with your brother!

THOAS: Come on, all you citizens of this barbarous land, fling bridles on your horses, race along the shore and capture the survivors of the Greek ship! Hurry with the goddess's help and hunt down these godless men! You others, drag my fast ships down into the sea! With them by sea and horsemen on land I mean to seize our quarry, then throw them from some craggy rock or impale their bodies on stakes! [*Turning to address the* CHORUS] As for you women who were a party to this plot, I will punish you later, when I have the time! For the moment we have this business in hand and must not stand idle.

[*The goddess* ATHENA *suddenly appears above the stage.*][63]

ATHENA: Where, oh where are you leading this chase, King Thoas? Hear my words, the words of Athena! Give up this pursuit! Stop inciting your men to stream out for battle! It was ordained by Loxias' oracles that Orestes should come here, seeking to escape the anger of the Furies,[64] and that he should escort his sister to Argos, bringing to my land the holy statue, and so find respite from the woes that haunt him now. These are my words to you. As for Orestes, whom you expect to seize on the swelling sea and kill, Poseidon for my sake is

1410

1430

1440

Deus ex machina

already calming the rough waters, so that his ship can voyage over the sea.

And you, Orestes, learn my commands (you are not here but can still hear the voice of the goddess): go on your way, taking the statue and your sister. When you come to Athens,[65] built by a god, there is a place on the furthest borders of Attica, close to the Carystian rock, a sacred place that my people now call by the name Halae. There you are to build a temple and set up the statue in it, and let it bear the name of the Taurian land and the tortured wanderings you endured as you journeyed throughout Greece, maddened by the Furies. In days to come mortals will honour her in hymns as Artemis who dwells among the Tauri. You are also to institute this custom: whenever the folk hold a festival in the goddess's honour, in requital for your blood not spilled in sacrifice, let them apply a sword-blade to the neck of a man and draw blood, to satisfy religion and so that the goddess may have her privileges.

Your duty, Iphigenia, is to keep the keys for this goddess in Brauron's holy meadows. There you shall die and have your grave. Garments of fine-spun web, such as women who die in childbirth leave in their homes, will be your offerings.

[ATHENA *gestures to the* CHORUS.] As for these women of Greece, in recognition of their virtue I order you to send them out of this land. I saved your life once before, Orestes, when I judged the votes equal on the hill of Ares. This shall stand as a custom: if the votes for a man are equal to those against, he shall be acquitted.[66] Take your sister away from this land, son of Agamemnon. And you, Thoas, forget your anger. *See Odyssey XXIV.*

THOAS: Queen Athena, the man who disobeys the gods when he has heard their wishes has taken leave of his senses. I will not be angry with Orestes for carrying off the goddess's image, or with his sister. What is the use? Let them go to your land with the goddess's statue and may they set up her image with good fortune! I will indeed give these women escort to blessed Greece, as your bidding requires. And I will stop the spearsmen

1450

1460

1470

1480

I launched against the strangers, together with the ships' crews, as this is your will, goddess.

ATHENA: Well said! The gods as well as you must bow to necessity. Come, you breezes, blow Agamemnon's son on his course to Athens! I will accompany his voyage and protect my sister's holy image. [ATHENA *disappears.*]

1490 CHORUS: *Go in good fortune, blessed in belonging to the number of the saved!*

Pallas Athena, revered among immortals as among mortals, we will carry out your command. Truly joyous and unexpected is this message my ears have heard!

[*The* CHORUS *exits.*]

ION

PREFACE TO *ION*

The play is set at Delphi, the most holy of Apollo's shrines and the centre of his worship in the Greek world. Its importance in Greek life was symbolized by its being regarded as the centre or 'navel' of the whole world, an idea mentioned several times in the play. Delphi was most famous for its oracle, at which Apollo was thought to give prophetic responses through his priestess, the Pythia (Pytho being another name for Delphi and 'Pythian' one of Apollo's titles). Although the oracle always spoke the truth, it did not always speak clearly or unambiguously: many stories in Greek literature hinge on the obscurity or double meaning of an oracular pronouncement. The legend of Oedipus, who was told that he would slay his father and marry his mother, is a case in point: this warning seemed clear to him, but he was misled by his ignorance of the true identity of his parents. *Ion* involves an ambiguity of a different kind: Xuthus, who greatly desires a son, is told that he must treat as his son the first person he meets on leaving the shrine. He takes this to mean that Ion is indeed his son, fathered in a youthful escapade; but the truth is otherwise. Apollo's truth can be misleading; the god's words, like his role in this play, are ambiguous.

To Delphi comes a group of Athenians, attending their queen Creusa and her foreign husband, Xuthus of Euboea. The contrast between Delphi and Athens is important in the play, and the presence of Athens offstage, a great city and a kingdom without an heir, is strongly felt. Creusa and Xuthus have no child, and seek the guidance of Apollo in the hope that their wish may be granted. The audience knows, but the characters do not, that the temple-servant Ion is in fact Creusa's child, whom she bore after having been raped by Apollo, and exposed in shame. She does not recognize her son, now a promising youth; he does not know his origins. The play develops this situation in the most ingenious ways, which it would be superfluous to summarize. Recognition and failed recognition are both key elements in Euripides' lighter dramas, and they are handled with the skill of a master of irony. Eventually Creusa and her son are reunited, but the twists and turns of the plot keep the audience guessing how this can possibly be achieved.

Recognition, and the failure or delay in reaching that goal, had since the *Odyssey* been a major source of literary and dramatic plots. In the second half of the *Odyssey* the hero moves in disguise within his own palace, testing the loyalty of his servants and his wife, observing the misdeeds of the suitors who have taken over his home. In both the Sophoclean and the Euripidean versions of the Electra myth, Orestes remains in disguise much longer than seems natural or necessary, but the suspense is intensely effective. In *Iphigenia among the Taurians*, Orestes and Iphigenia converse, and again and again it seems inevitable that they will realize each other's identity, but the poet continually defers the final moment of comprehension. Other examples are easily found. In the present play one influential element is the use of tokens to prove Ion's identity (again, this goes back to Homer, for Odysseus establishes his true identity by the evidence of the scar he bears from his youth). This type of plot often seems more suited to comedy, or at least to less serious forms of tragedy, for it normally involves the welcome reunion of those who belong together, whether husband and wife or other relations. As ancient critics already remarked, the line continues to the New Comedy of Menander and his Roman imitators; we can follow the tradition still further, to Shakespearian comedies such as *The Comedy of Errors* (itself based on a classical model) or *As You Like It*, and to the drawing-room recognitions of Oscar Wilde. The handbag of Miss Prism in *The Importance of Being Ernest* is the distant descendant of Ion's royal cradle!

As with other plays in this volume, we need to consider the significance of the Athenian dimension of the story. We immediately respond with sympathy to the story of Creusa's loss of her virginity, her agonized decision to expose her infant child, her subsequent regrets and her longing for a son to replace the one she lost; also attractive and appealing is the portrayal of Ion as a naïve, unworldly but polite and virtuous young man. The political dimension, however, means that this is more than just a personal drama. The throne of Athens needs an heir. By a procedure common in tragedy, contemporary laws and preoccupations are projected back on the mythical period, so that it is assumed that a true Athenian should be of Athenian birth on both sides (this was in fact required by legislation passed at Pericles' instigation in 451–450 BC). This means, as Ion hints in the play, that to be Xuthus' son is not as good as to have Athenian parents (at 670–75 he hopes that he may at least find that his mother is Athenian). In the end he discovers that he is the son of the god Apollo and a royal princess of Athens; the monarchic structure of myth is rather uneasily associated with democratic legal structures.

Ion himself is not a major figure of mythology, but does occupy a significant place in the heroic genealogies. The Greeks sometimes saw themselves as a unified nation: a famous passage in Herodotus refers to the bonds that unite them in the face of a foreign invader as shared blood, shared language, common sanctuaries and sacrifices, and similar customs. But in fact there were many divisions among the peoples we think of as Greek, not only the division into many different political communities, but ethnic or racial differences which were reflected in customs and dialect. One of the most prominent is the division into three peoples, the Ionians, the Dorians and the Achaeans. These divisions were given mythical justification, and Ion is the ancestor of the Ionian peoples; in other versions he has a brother Achaeus, who similarly gives his name to the Achaeans. For Hesiod, Xuthus is son of Hellen and brother of Dorus and Aeolus (again names associated with ethnic groups). The marriage of Xuthus to the Athenian Creusa reflects Athenian claims to be the leaders of the Ionian peoples, and the Euripidean version, making Ion son of Apollo, carries this further, eliminating non-Athenian ancestry and giving a higher status to Ion as opposed to the other sons of Xuthus, Dorus and Achaeus, who have no such divine blood. The passage in Athena's speech which looks forward to later generations is a conventional element at the end of most plays, but in this play more than most the aetiology has political resonances (1571–94).

What of Apollo? Many interpretations have seen the rape of Creusa as the central and horrific fact of the play, and have read *Ion* as a critique of divine immorality. This gains some support from the intensity of Creusa's distress, especially the powerful aria in which she breaks years of silence and cries out in angry accusation of the god (859ff.). It is also striking that the god does not appear in person to defend himself. Hermes represents him at the start of the play, Athena at the conclusion; nor does Apollo's plan work out precisely as Hermes predicts in the prologue. We must remember, however, that Creusa's outburst dwells chiefly on the loss of her child, a loss which will not be permanent. By the end of the play, mother and son are reunited. As Athena says and the mortals accept, 'All has been well managed by Apollo' (1595). It is typical of Euripides to raise questions about the ways of the gods, and he does so at several points in the play, especially through Ion's mouth (384–400, 1312–19, 1537). But it does not seem that these questions, however startling to those who share Ion's naïve piety, are intended to amount to a wholesale assault on Olympian religion. The gods of Greek myth are as they are: from the *Iliad* onwards, it was possible for mortals to denounce them and even to resist their will, but the better course is normally to accede to that will and hope to receive more good than bad at their hands. In the last book of the *Iliad*, Achilles comments that there are two jars which stand at Zeus' side, filled with good fortune and bad; to some he gives nothing but bad, to others a mixture of good and evil. But no mortal receives unmixed good fortune. This sombre but realistic outlook is also present in Greek tragedy. In the closing scene of this play Ion comments: 'It was the work of a god; but I pray that our fortune may be as good in days to come as it has proved bad in the past' (1456–7). Neither the play nor other myths involving Ion and Creusa give us reason to suppose that this prayer was disappointed.

CHARACTERS

HERMES
ION, *son of Creusa by Apollo*
CHORUS *of women, servants of Creusa*
CREUSA, *queen of Athens and wife of Xuthus*
XUTHUS, *king of Athens*
OLD MAN, *in service of Creusa*
SERVANT *of Creusa*
PROPHETESS *of Apollo*
ATHENA

- 'Romantic Tragedy' → happy ending
- Humor:
  - Hermes retreating to watch from the shrubbery
  - Kreousa relating her misfortunes as those "of a friend"
  - Gruff Xouthos embracing the boy who misunderstands his approach

- Gods fare badly:
  - Plot does not proceed as Hermes predicted in the prologue
  - Apollo gives a false oracle to Xouthos
  - Athene has to show up to 'cover' for her brother

- Patriotic propaganda — Ionians (Athenians) are descended from god Apollo while other Greeks have only human forebears.

[*The scene is Delphi, in front of the temple of Apollo, where* ION
is the young sacristan. HERMES *enters. The time is shortly before
sunrise.*]

HERMES: Atlas,[1] whose bronze shoulders support the weight of
the heavens, ancient home of the gods, was father of Maia by
one of the goddesses, and she bore me, Hermes, to mighty
Zeus, to run errands for the gods. To this land of Delphi I have
come, where Phoebus chants his oracles to men from his seat
at the earth's navel, giving them constant prophecy of things
that are and things that are to be.

    Now there is in Greece a city whose fame is well known
among Greeks, one that is named after Pallas of the gilded
spear. Here it was, under the hill of Pallas in the land of the
Athenians, where stand the northerly cliffs called by the lords
of Attic soil the Long Cliffs, that a child of Erechtheus,[2] Creusa,
fell victim to Phoebus' violent passion.[3] Without her father's
knowledge (for this was the god's wish) Creusa endured her
pregnancy to the end; but when her time came, she took the
baby boy she had borne in the palace to the very same cave
where the god had seduced her and there she exposed him to
die, so she thought,[4] inside the shelter of a round cradle. But
she showed regard for a custom established by her ancestors
and Erichthonius, who was born from the earth. To him the
daughter of Zeus had assigned as sentinels in his cradle a pair
of serpents[5] that kept him safe from harm, and she had entrusted
him to the care and protection of Aglaurus' maiden daughters.
From this derives the custom in Athens whereby Erechtheus'

people dress their infant young in serpent necklaces of beaten gold.[6] Creusa adorned her child with such finery as she had and left it to die.

Now, Phoebus, speaking to me as one brother to another, made this request: 'Go, brother, to famous Athens (you know the city of the goddess), to the people who are sprung from the land itself, and there take from a hollow rock a new-born baby, together with its cradle and the clothes it is wrapped in, and carry it to Delphi, to my oracle, putting it down at the very entrance to my temple. The rest will be my concern (the child, you should know, is mine).'

I obliged my brother Loxias. Taking up the wicker basket, I carried it off and here, at the top of the steps to his temple, I deposited the child, after first turning back the lid of its woven cradle so that he might be seen. This was done just before the sun's disk rose to start its race across the heavens, the time when the god's prophetess makes her way into his shrine. When she set eyes on the baby boy, she wondered if some Delphian girl could have dared to cast her love-child into the dwelling-place of the god, and her first thought was to get rid of it from the sanctuary. But pity made her abandon this cruel impulse, and the god was also working to prevent his son's ejection from the temple; she took up the child and gave it her loving care, not knowing that Phoebus was the father or who the mother was.

The lad shares this ignorance of his parents' identity. In his early days he would wander in play about the altars that gave him sustenance, but, when he came to manhood, the Delphians appointed him warden of the god's treasure and trusted steward of all, and to this very day he lives a life of holiness in the sanctuary of the god.

Creusa, the young man's mother, became the wife of Xuthus. This came about in the following way. War had engulfed Athens and Chalcodon's people, who occupy the land of Euboea. Because he had shared Athens' dangers in this war and had helped destroy her enemies by the service of his spear, Xuthus was granted the honour of marrying Creusa, though he was not of Athenian stock but an Achaean, from Phthia, and a son of Aeolus, whose father was Zeus. For many years he has tried to father children but he and Creusa have been denied offspring. This is the reason why they have come here to Apollo's oracle, to satisfy their desire for children.[7] Loxias is directing fortune to this end and he is not as forgetful as it seems. When Xuthus enters the shrine here, the god will give him his own son, declaring him to be the son of Xuthus, so that the boy may enter his mother's home and become known to Creusa.[8] It is also Loxias' wish that her union with himself should remain a secret, although his son will enjoy the honours that are his due. He shall cause him to be called throughout Greece by the name of Ion, the one who shall found cities in the land of Asia.[9]

Now I shall retire to the groves of laurels over there, to learn what happens to the boy. Here I see him making his way out, the son of Loxias, to make the portals before his temple bright with branches of laurel. I am the first of the gods to call him Ion, the name he is destined to bear.

[As HERMES *withdraws,* ION *enters from the interior of the temple and begins to sing.*]

ION: *See the sun's chariot and team of four, shining bright! Already his radiance lights up the earth, as his fiery strength makes the stars flee into sacred night. Parnassus' peaks, untrodden by men, catch the flames and, to bless mortals, receive the wheels of day. Fumes from the desert myrrh waft up to the roof of Phoebus' temple, while the Delphic mistress sits on her holy tripod, chanting to men of Greece all that Apollo's prophetic mouth declares.*

[*To the god's servants whom he has seen entering from the side*] *Come, you men of Delphi who serve Phoebus, go down to Castalia's silvery fountain and, when you have bathed in the pure dew of her waters, make your way into the temple. Avoid unseemly language! Keep guard on your tongues, revealing in your own speech fair words for those wishing to consult the god.*

And I will busy myself with the tasks that have been my constant occupation since boyhood, sweeping Phoebus' portals clean with laurel branches bound in holy wreaths and sprinkling the ground with drops of water. As for the flocks of birds that foul our sacred offerings, I'll use my bow and arrows to make them flee. Having no mother or father, I give my loving service to Phoebus' temple; it has been my nurse. 110

[Strophe:] *Come, servant broom,*[10] *offspring of the lovely bay, you that sweep the platform in the temple's shadow, grown from groves immortal where holy springs, pouring forth their everlasting stream, water the myrtle's sacred foliage! With you I sweep all day the god's* 120 *floor, performing this daily service from the time the sun's swift flight begins.*

O Healer, Healer, bless us, bless us, son of Leto!

[Antistrophe:] *Phoebus, it is a task that brings me honour, this service before your temple, as I show reverence to your oracular seat. A* 130 *glorious task for me, to serve a god as my master, no mortal man but an immortal god! How could I weary of the toil in so honourable a service? Phoebus is my sire and father;*[11] *he gives me nurture and so wins my praise; he it is, Phoebus, this temple's lord, who brings* 140 *blessings to me; he it is whom I call by the name of father.*

O Healer, Healer, bless us, bless us, son of Leto!

But now I will abandon my efforts at sweeping with this laurel-broom, and from this urn of gold I will fling fresh water that issues from Castalia's whirling spring. I cast these liquid drops myself, unsullied and pure as I am. Oh, may I never cease to serve Phoebus 150 *with such labour all my days, or, if I do, may it be with fortune's blessing!*

[ION *suddenly starts back at the sight of birds.*] *See, over there! The birds are stirring; already they've left their nests on Parnassus and have taken to the skies! I give you warning: stay away from the temple's eaves, and do not enter the golden house! You, too, will feel the force of my bowshot, herald of Zeus, though you subdue with your* 160 *talons the strongest birds that fly!*

Look! Another wings his way towards the sanctuary, a swan! Away with you and those crimson feet of yours, fly elsewhere! Apollo's lyre, your partner in song, will not save you from my bow. Continue on your flight! Come to rest on Delos' lake; do my bidding or you will change that lovely song of yours to a woeful lament!

170   Ah, look there! What strange bird is this coming towards us? Surely you don't mean to build your nest of straw for your young under our eaves? The twang of my bow will make you keep your distance! Take my advice: go to the waters of Alpheus or the Isthmian grove to raise your brood and leave undefiled the offerings and sacred dwelling of

180   Phoebus. And yet I hesitate to kill you who bring word to mortal men of heaven's will. But I will not shirk my allotted task; I will serve my master Phoebus and never cease to worship the one through whom I live.

[ION now withdraws into the temple. The CHORUS enter, female servants of CREUSA, and express their admiration of the sacred buildings. Individuals contribute their thoughts after each strophe is introduced by the leading singer.]

CHORUS [Strophe]: So not only in sacred Athens, then, are temple-courts with fine columns to be found, and pillars in honour of the god who protects streets. Here, too, at the shrine of Loxias, child of Leto, are a temple's twin façades, shining in fair-eyed beauty.[12]

190   See! Look there: the Hydra of Lerna being slain by Zeus' son with his scythe of gold! Oh, look, dear, look!

I see him! And at his side stands another who lifts up a blazing torch; can it be the one whose story I hear as I work at the loom, the

200   warrior Iolaus, who shared with Zeus' son the burden of his labours and endured them to the end?

Oh, here, look over here: the one who sits, mounted on his winged horse! He is killing the mighty fire-breathing monster with its three bodies!

[Antistrophe:] My eyes go everywhere, believe me! Look, there on the marble walls – the rout of the Giants!

We see it here, friends.

210   Then do you see her, shaking her shield with its Gorgon-face over Enceladus?

I see Pallas, my goddess!

What have we now? It is the mighty thunderbolt of Zeus, with both ends aflame, held in his powerful hands!

I see it; that is Mimas who battles with him and is burned black by his flame!

And Bromius, too, is slaying another of Earth's children, the revelling god who has as weapon a mere ivy-wand!

[ION *appears again at the temple entrance. One of the chorus addresses him.*]

CHORUS-MEMBER [Antistrophe]: *You, sir, standing at the way into the temple: are we permitted to enter the sanctuary, bare-footed?*   220

ION: *You are not, ladies.*

CHORUS-MEMBER: *Then might I ask you . . .*

ION: *Say what you wish.*

CHORUS-MEMBER: *. . . is it true that Phoebus' temple lies at the very mid-point of the earth?*

ION: *The naval-stone is here, wreathed with sacred garlands, and guarded by a pair of Gorgons.*

CHORUS-MEMBER: *So runs the tale we have heard.*

ION: *If you have made the offering of a cake in front of the temple and you wish to make some enquiry of Phoebus, you may enter the forecourt; the interior of the shrine is forbidden to you unless you have first sacrificed a sheep.*

CHORUS-MEMBER: *I understand; we have no wish to transgress the god's law and shall be more than happy to look at what may be seen outside.*   230

ION: *Enjoy the sight of all that it is lawful to view.*

CHORUS-MEMBER: *My master and mistress gave me leave to come here and look at the god's sanctuary.*

ION: *You are household servants? What family do you serve?*

CHORUS-MEMBER: *The palace where my mistress grew up is under one roof with the dwelling of Pallas.*[13] [CREUSA *enters with attendants.*] *But the lady you ask me about is here.*

ION: Lady, I welcome you to the shrine; for, whoever you are, there is nobility in your looks and your bearing gives proof of your good character. In most people nobility may be discerned   240 by outward appearance. But what's this? You surprise me now, shutting your eyes and letting tears moisten your noble cheeks at the sight of Loxias' holy oracle! Whatever has made you so anxious, lady? In this place, where all others rejoice at the sight of the god's sanctuary, do you weep?

CREUSA: It shows courtesy in you, sir, that my tears cause you surprise. The fact is, when I saw Apollo's temple here, it awakened an old, old memory in me; my thoughts were on that, though I stand here now. [Aside] Oh, what hardships women must endure![14] What may gods dare to do! I ask the question: to what authority shall we refer justice, if our masters' injustice is the cause of our ruin?

ION: What is this sadness that defies explanation, lady?

CREUSA: It is nothing; I have shot my bolt; for the rest, as I am silent, please give it no more thought.

ION: Who are you? Where have you come from? What country do you belong to? What name should we call you by?

CREUSA: Creusa is my name and Erechtheus my father; my homeland is the city of Athens.

ION: O my lady, how I honour you! The city you live in is a glorious one and your ancestors noble.

CREUSA: That is the extent of my good fortune, sir, that and no more.

ION: In heaven's name, is it true, as the story goes among men . . .

CREUSA: What is your question, sir? What do you want to learn?

ION: . . . that the father of your grandfather was born from the earth?[15]

CREUSA: Yes; this was the manner of Erichthonius' birth; little good has this lineage done me!

ION: And did Athena really take him up from Earth?

CREUSA: Into her arms, virgin though she was and not the child's mother.

ION: And then she gave it, as pictures always show . . .

CREUSA: . . . to Cecrops' daughters to keep safe but not to see.

ION: I heard the maidens opened the casket of the goddess.

CREUSA: And for this they died and made the cliff-face red with their blood.

ION: Ah! [*He pauses.*] But there is another story . . . is it true or false?

CREUSA: What is your question? I am not pressed for time.

ION: Your father Erechtheus, did he kill your sisters in sacrifice?[16]

CREUSA: For his country's sake he brought himself to spill their virgin blood at the altar.

ION: But what about you? How were you the only sister to escape with her life?

CREUSA: I was a new-born baby in my mother's arms. 280

ION: Is it true that your father was swallowed up in the yawning earth?[17]

CREUSA: The sea-god struck the ground with his trident and so my father perished.

ION: Have you a place there called the Long Cliffs?

CREUSA [*startled*]: Why do you ask this? Oh, you have brought back a memory!

ION: It is a place Apollo honours and sanctifies with the fire of his lightning.

CREUSA: *Honours*, you say? I wish I had never set eyes on it!

ION: I don't understand; you hate what the god holds most dear?

CREUSA: Never mind; we share a guilty secret, the caves and I.

ION: Is your husband an Athenian, lady?

CREUSA: He does not come from Athens but a different land. 290

ION: Who is he? He must be a man of good family.

CREUSA: Xuthus, of the line of Aeolus and of Zeus.

ION: How was it that a foreigner became your husband, when you are Athenian-born?

CREUSA: There is a land called Euboea that is a neighbour of Athens.

ION: They are separated by sea, I have heard.

CREUSA: He fought alongside the sons of Cecrops and helped them sack this place.

ION: He came to their assistance in war? And then he won your hand in marriage?

CREUSA: I was his battle-dowry, the prize won by his spear.

ION: Are you here at the oracle with your husband or have you come alone?

300 CREUSA: With my husband; he is detained at Trophonius' sacred cavern.[18]

ION: Did he go there merely to see it or to consult the oracle?

CREUSA: The answer he sought from him and from Phoebus was one and the same.

ION: Was it to ask for fertile crops he went or for the sake of children?

CREUSA: We remain childless after all our years of marriage.

ION: You have never to this day borne a child, never been a mother?

CREUSA: Phoebus knows the truth about my childlessness.[19]

ION: Poor lady, so blessed in the rest of your life and yet so cursed!

CREUSA: But what of you? Who are you? What a fortunate mother you have!

ION: They call me the servant of god, lady, and so I am.

310 CREUSA: Did some city give you as a dedication or did an owner sell you?[20]

ION: I only know one thing: I am called Loxias' boy.

CREUSA: Well then, you have my sympathy in turn, young man.

ION [bitterly]: For not knowing who my mother is or who my father.

CREUSA: Do you live in the temple here or in one of the houses?

ION: All the god's dwelling is my home, wherever sleep comes over me.

CREUSA: Did you come here as a boy or were you full-grown?

ION: I was a baby according to those who claim to know.

CREUSA: And who among the womenfolk of Delphi nurtured you?

ION: I never knew a nurse's breast; the woman who reared me . . .

320 CREUSA: Who was she, you poor boy? I have found a misery to match my own!

ION: Phoebus' prophetess is the one I think of as my mother.

CREUSA: How did you live from day to day as you grew to manhood?

ION: The altars and each new visitor gave me food.

CREUSA: Well, you are not without means; these are not shabby clothes you are wearing.

ION: I wear the livery of the god who is my master.

CREUSA: Have you made no effort to find out who your parents are?

ION: No, lady; I lack any evidence.

CREUSA: Then I pity your mother, whoever she is!

ION: Perhaps some woman was violated and I am her child.

CREUSA: Oh, that is sad! [*Pause*] Another woman shares your 330
mother's fate.

ION: Who? If only she would help me in my search, that would make me glad!

CREUSA: The woman for whose sake I came here before my husband.

ION: What is it that she wants? I will assist, lady.

CREUSA: She requires the counsel of Phoebus on a secret matter.

ION: Please tell me and I will set your enquiry in motion.

CREUSA: Listen, then, to her story; even though it makes *me* ashamed.

ION: That won't help you; shame's the enemy of action!

CREUSA: She says – this friend of mine – she lay with Phoebus.

ION: With Phoebus – a mortal woman? My lady, don't say such a thing!

CREUSA: Yes, and she bore the god a son, unknown to her 340
father.

ION: It cannot be! She was raped by some man and she is ashamed!

CREUSA: This is not what she says happened; and she had suffering yet to endure.

ION: In what way, if the god did lie with her?

CREUSA: The baby boy she bore she cast away.

ION: And where is he, this castaway child? Is he alive?

CREUSA: No one knows; this is my very reason for consulting the oracle.

ION: If he no longer lives, how did he die?

CREUSA: She imagines he was killed by wild beasts, poor creature.

ION: What kind of proof did she have for thinking so?

350 CREUSA: When she went to the spot where she had left him, he was nowhere to be found.

ION: Was there any trace of blood on the ground?

CREUSA: None, she said; and yet she scoured the area several times.

ION: How long is it since the child met its end?

CREUSA: If he were alive, he would be the same sort of age as you.

ION: What if Phoebus took up the child and raised it in secret?

CREUSA: Then he is acting unjustly in enjoying for himself what should be a pleasure shared![21]

ION: The god then wrongs her still; I pity the mother.

CREUSA: She had no other child after this one.

ION: Ah, this tale strikes a chord with my own case!

360 CREUSA: I imagine your own poor mother yearns to see you, too, young man!

ION: Ah, do not make me think of my own sorrows so long forgotten.

CREUSA: Forgive me; let us turn again to my own enquiry.

ION: Well, are you aware of the chief weakness in your case?

CREUSA: Is there anything that is not amiss in that poor woman's condition?

ION: There is little chance of the god revealing in his oracle what he wishes to keep secret.

CREUSA: He must, if the tripod where he sits serves all Greece!

ION: He feels shame at what happened; do not examine him further.

CREUSA: And she, his victim, feels pain at her suffering!

ION: There is not a man here will put this question on your
370 behalf. If he were shown here in his own temple to have

112

acted shamefully, Phoebus would justly punish the one who
performed such a task for you. You must abandon this request,
lady. It is wrong to consult the god on matters that go against
his will. When the gods answer our prayers unwillingly, we
win blessings that bring us no profit, lady; our benefit lies in
those blessings that they freely confer.   380

CHORUS-LEADER: The world is wide and wide is its breadth of
fortunes, with none of their manifestations the same; but
scarcely would you find a single human life blessed by
happiness.

CREUSA: O Phoebus, the woman whose cause I plead in her
absence has found you no friend of justice either in that land
or now in this; you did not save your son as you should have
done and, when his mother asks about him, though you are a
prophet, you will give her no reply. Thus you deny him a
burial mound if he no longer lives, and you take from her the
chance of ever seeing her son again if he still is alive.

[Enter XUTHUS *with servants and a number of Delphi's citizens.*]

But it is pointless to pursue this, if it is the god who prevents   390
me from learning what I want to know. I ask you, sir – for
here I see my noble husband Xuthus approaching, his business
at Trophonius' oracle over – not to mention to my lord the
conversation that we have had; I do not wish to be blamed for
meddling in so delicate a matter and one that may turn out
differently from the result we have been trying to achieve. We
women find men harsh judges; those of us who are honest are
lumped together with those who are not and tarred with the   400
same brush; this means we are born to a life of tears.

XUTHUS: First to the god I give my greetings – let him receive
the first fruits of my salutation – and then, my lady, to you.
[XUTHUS *notices that* CREUSA *is distressed.*] What's this? Has
my staying away so long upset you? Were you afraid?

CREUSA: No, no, but I had become anxious. Tell me, though,
what is the oracle you bring from Trophonius? How shall we
be blessed with children?

XUTHUS: He did not presume to anticipate the response of

Apollo. Only one thing did he say: I would not return home childless from the oracle, nor would you.

410 CREUSA: O blessed Lady, mother of Phoebus, may our coming here be propitious and the dealings we had before with your son change for the better!

XUTHUS: So they shall! But who is the god's spokesman?

ION: That is my responsibility, at least outside the temple; others have charge inside, sir, those who sit near the tripod, the nobility of Delphi, chosen by lot.[22]

XUTHUS: Thank you; I am entirely satisfied and now would like to go inside. I hear that a victim has been sacrificed before the
420 temple on behalf of all the visitors; on this day (as it is propitious) I wish to consult the god.

[*Turning to* CREUSA] You, my lady, with branches in your arms, go round the altars decked with bay, praying to the gods that the oracle I bring from Apollo's house gives promise of children.

CREUSA: So I shall! [XUTHUS *now enters the temple.*] If Loxias consents this day at last to rectify the wrong he did me once, he would still not be wholly my friend, but whatever he is willing to grant I will accept, since he is a god. [CREUSA *exits.*]

430 ION: Why does this lady speak in riddles to the god, constantly hiding the meaning of her words and taking him to task? Either it is out of friendship for the woman she seeks an answer for or she may even be concealing some unutterable secret. But what do I care for Erechtheus' daughter? She is no kin of mine. Time to take up the golden jug and put water in the sacred bowls.

And yet I should ask Phoebus to account for this behaviour of his;[23] can he have forced himself on an unmarried girl, then abandoned her? Fathered a child illicitly only to let it die without a thought? Never this, my lord! As you possess
440 strength, make it your aim to be virtuous! Wickedness in men is punished by the gods. How can it then be just for you, who prescribed the law for man, to be guilty of lawlessness? If you and Poseidon and Zeus[24] who rules the heavens are to answer to men for your predatory behaviour towards women (this is

impossible but I will put the case), then in paying fines for your
misdeeds you will empty your temples. You do wrong when
you go beyond caution in satisfying your desires. Who, then,
deserves the title 'wicked'? No longer mankind if we imitate   450
behaviour sanctioned by the gods, but the ones who teach us
these lessons! [*Exit* ION.]

CHORUS [Strophe]: *My own Athena, born without the pains of*
childbirth, delivered by the aid of Titan Prometheus from the crown of
Zeus' head,[25] *come, I entreat you, blessed Lady of Victory, to the*
Pythian dwelling; forsake your golden chambers and wing your way   460
down to these avenues, where, from the earth's centre, from his own
hearth and tripod, circled by dancing worshippers, Phoebus issues
oracles sure and true! Come, then, Athena, come, child of Leto's
womb,[26] *goddesses both, virgins both, revered sisters of Phoebus! Take*
to him our humble prayer, you maids divine; ask that Erechtheus'
ancient line may win by means of clear prophecy the long-awaited   470
blessing of offspring!

[Antistrophe:] *For mortals possess a sure and steadfast source of*
abundant happiness, when youngsters in their vigour, who promise
fruit hereafter, are a shining light in their fathers' halls, destined to
enjoy a wealth that can inherit from father to son through different   480
generations. This is a defence in times of trouble and a source of joy
when fortune shows favour; it brings saving strength to a man's
countrymen in battle. Before wealth and a king's palace may I have
the privilege of raising children of my own, true to their father's ways.
The life that admits no children repels me; the advocate of such a life
wins no praise from me. May I hold fast to a life blessed with children   490
and with modest means.

[Epode:] *O you rocks that border on the Long Cliffs with their*
many caves, where Pan has his seat, what have you seen? You saw
Aglaurus' daughters three treading in dance the green slopes before
Pallas' shrines, to the quivering sound of the pipe's music, when you   500
played your tunes, o Pan, in your sunless caves. You saw a wretched
maid[27] *bear a child to Phoebus and then cast it out for birds to feast*
upon and beasts to make their bloody prey, an outrage to her joyless

union. Neither at the loom's work nor in story have I heard of happiness coming to children borne by mortals to the gods.

[ION *enters from the precinct.*]

510   ION: You serving women,[28] who keep watch at the steps of this house of sacrifice and wait for your mistress, has Xuthus already left the sacred tripod and oracle or does his enquiry about childlessness still keep him in the temple?

CHORUS-LEADER: He is inside, sir; he has not yet come out through this entrance. But we hear a sound from the doors here, as if someone is about to emerge, and now you can see him, the master, coming out!

[*Enter* XUTHUS *from the temple. At the sight of* ION *he rushes to him and tries to clasp him in his arms.*]

XUTHUS: My child – I greet you! These are my first words and none could be more fitting!

ION [*shocked*]: And my greetings to you; only regain your senses and all will be well with both of us!

XUTHUS: Let me kiss your hand! Let me embrace you!

520   ION: Are you in your right mind? Has a god harmed your wits and made you mad?

XUTHUS: Am I not in my right mind when I have found my heart's desire and long to hold him close?

ION: Enough! Take your hands off the god's sacred bands – you will break them!

XUTHUS: I will not let go; I am no robber but have found what is my own!

ION: Get away from me before you feel my arrows in your ribs!

XUTHUS: What is it makes you refuse to recognize me, your dearest relative?

ION: I am not in the habit of enlightening boorish strangers who have lost their senses.

XUTHUS: Kill me and give me creation; you will be shedding your father's blood, if you do this!

ION: You, my father? How can this be? Are you mocking me in saying this?

XUTHUS: No; my meaning will become clear as my tale unfolds.

ION: And what are you going to tell me?   530

XUTHUS: I am your father and you are my son.

ION: Who says so?

XUTHUS: Loxias, who raised you when you were mine.

ION: There's only your own word for this!

XUTHUS: No, it's the god's oracle I have been told.

ION: He spoke in riddles and you mistook his meaning.

XUTHUS: Then my ears deceive me.

ION: What was it that Phoebus said?

XUTHUS: He said that the person who crossed my path . . .

ION: Crossed your path – in what way?

XUTHUS: . . . as I was coming out of the temple here, . . .

ION: What should happen to him?

XUTHUS: . . . he should be my son.

ION: The son born to you or a gift from other hands?

XUTHUS: A gift, but the child is mine.

ION: Then I was the first person to cross your path?

XUTHUS: No one else, my child!

ION: However has this happened?

XUTHUS: I'm as perplexed as you.

ION: What woman bore me to you?   540

XUTHUS: I cannot say.

ION: Did Phoebus not tell you?

XUTHUS: I failed to ask, such was my joy in his response.

ION: Is the Earth, then, my mother?

XUTHUS: Children are not born of the soil.[29]

ION: How, then, would I belong to you?

XUTHUS: I don't know; I can only refer this to the god.

ION: Come, let's examine this in a different way.

XUTHUS: That would be better, my child.

ION: Did you sleep with any woman before marriage?

XUTHUS: Yes, in the folly of youth.

ION: Before you took Erechtheus' daughter as your wife?

XUTHUS: And not at any time since then.

ION: Then it was on that occasion that you fathered me?

XUTHUS: It agrees with the time.

ION: How did I then end up in this place?

XUTHUS: Here I have no answer.

ION: To come so far!

XUTHUS: I'm baffled too.

550 ION: Have you visited rocky Delphi before now?

XUTHUS: Yes, when I attended Bacchus' torchlight mysteries.[30]

ION: Did you lodge with one of the welcoming officials?

XUTHUS: Thanks to him I made the acquaintance of some young women of Delphi.

ION: He introduced you to their company of worshippers, do you mean?

XUTHUS: I knew them when they were Maenads in the power of Bacchus.

ION: Were you in control of your faculties or drunk with wine?

XUTHUS: My thoughts were on the pleasures of Bacchus.

ION: Here's the answer to my question! That was how I was conceived!

XUTHUS: Fate has brought it to light, my child.

ION: How did I come to the temple?

XUTHUS: I suppose you were exposed by the girl.

ION [to himself]: I have escaped the taint of slavery.

XUTHUS [opening his arms]: Now accept me as your father, my child!

ION: It seems I cannot doubt the god.

XUTHUS: Now you are coming to your senses!

ION: And what better could I wish for . . .

XUTHUS: Now your eyes are truly open!

ION: . . . than to prove the son of a son of Zeus?[31]

XUTHUS: And so you are!

560 ION: May I, then, touch the one who fathered me?

XUTHUS: If you put your trust in the god!

ION [opening his own arms]: My father!

XUTHUS: What joy that name gives! What pleasures to hear it! [They embrace.]

ION: Let this day be blessed!

XUTHUS: It has blessed me indeed.

ION: O mother dear, when, oh when shall I see you also? Now more than ever I long to see you, whoever you are! But perhaps you are dead and even in dreams would escape me!

CHORUS-LEADER: We share the happiness that has blessed this household. And yet I could have wished that my mistress and Erechtheus' house were also blessed with children.

XUTHUS: My child, as to finding you the god has truly proved   570
his word; he has joined you to me and you in turn have discovered your own dear father, unknown to you before. Now, I too long for what you so properly desire, for you to find your mother, my boy, and I the woman who bore you to me. If we trust that time will solve this riddle, perhaps the answer will be revealed to us.

But now you must leave the god's shrine and this homeless existence you lead, and accompany your father back to Athens. Have you nothing to say?[32] Why do you keep your   [580]
eyes fixed upon the ground, absorbed in thought? What's become of the joy you felt just now? You are making your father afraid!

ION: When things are at a distance they strike the eye quite differently from when they are seen at close quarters. I welcome what has happened, now that I have found a father in you; but let me tell you, Father, what is on my mind. Illustrious Athens   590
they say, is sprung from the soil and her people wholly indigenous. I will intrude upon them labouring under two disadvantages, the foreign birth of my father and my own bastard status.[33]

With this reproach over my head I will never gain any influence and will have the name of a nobody. If I do aspire to the first rank of citizens and seek to make my mark, I will earn the hatred of those who lack influence in the State: superiority attracts envy. Then there are the worthy and capable men who, in their wisdom, keep their counsel and do not join the rush into public life;[34] these men will laugh at me and think me a   600
fool for not minding my own business in a city so prone to

apportioning blame. As for those who do take part in politics,
men who engage in public speaking, if I do succeed in gaining some repute, they will keep still closer watch over me
with their votes as weapons. This is what usually happens in
such cases, Father; men who hold positions of authority in
their cities wage ceaseless war against those who would take
their place.

Furthermore, I am to enter a house that is not mine, a
stranger, and be in the company of a childless woman who
610 used to share your former grief but now will bitterly resent
having to bear her own misfortune alone. Will she not have
every cause to hate me, when I stand beside your throne and
she, having no child, casts a jaundiced eye on your heart's
delight? If you show favour to your wife, you will be betraying
me; if you uphold my rights, that means the destruction of
your house for ever. How many times have women plotted to
destroy their husbands by the sword or with deadly poisons?
Besides, father, I feel sorry for your wife as she grows old
620 without children; she comes from a noble line of ancestors and
does not deserve to languish in childlessness.

As for kingship,[35] which men foolishly praise, it has an
attractive face but pain lurks within. What happiness, what
good fortune is there for a man who lives in constant fear,
looking round him for the assassin's knife? I would rather live
the life of an ordinary man who is happy than be a king, who
likes to have vicious men for friends and hates honest men for
fear they may kill him. You may say that gold outweighs such
630 misgivings, that wealth is a delightful thing. I have no desire to
clutch riches to my chest if I must listen to the voices of carping
criticism and be a prey to anxiety. No, modest means and a
carefree existence are what I pray to have.

Let me tell you of the blessings in my life here, Father. First
of all, I have enjoyed what men value most, leisure, and little
trouble, with no fellow of the lower sort jostling me off the
road.[36] It is intolerable when one has to give way on the road
to men of low birth. I spent my time praying to the gods or

talking to my fellow men and in serving them I found them
joyful, not sad. No sooner had I bidden some visitors farewell   640
than others would arrive, so that I was constantly in the agreeable position of meeting new people. Custom and nature alike
made me serve the god with a just heart, something that men
desire, even if they don't think they do. When I take this into
account, Father, I consider my life here superior to what awaits
me in Athens. Allow me to live here; to be content with little
can give as much pleasure as rejoicing in greatness.

CHORUS-LEADER: I applaud your words, if my dear mistress is
to prosper along with those you count as friends!

XUTHUS: You must stop talking like this and learn to enjoy your   650
good fortune. I want to inaugurate a public feast[37] in the place
I found you, my child, holding a banquet for all the people,
and to offer the sacrifice that was neglected at your birth.
Indeed, I'll offer you a delicious feast as if I'm bringing a friend
to my home, and in Athens itself I shall treat you as an admiring
visitor, not as my own flesh and blood. For I don't want this
good fortune of mine to be a cause of grief to my wife in her
childlessness. In time, when the moment is right, I will win   660
my lady's consent to your inheriting my throne.

As suits the lucky chance that brought us together as I came
out of the god's shrine, I give you the name 'Ion'.[38] Now
gather all your friends together and, when they are engaged in
the pleasure of feasting, bid them farewell on the eve of your
departure from this town of Delphi. [*Turning to address the*
CHORUS *directly*] And my orders to you, women of my house,
are to say nothing about this; one word to my lady and you
shall die for it![39]

ION: I will go. But in one respect my happiness is incomplete;
Father, if I fail to discover my mother, there is no life for me.   670
If I am to hope for more, I pray that the woman who bore me
may prove Athenian by birth, so entitling me to the right of
free speech on my mother's side.[40] For when a man seeks to
live in a city whose people are of unmixed blood, one that is
not his own, he may be a citizen in name but his speech is that

of a slave and he may not express his true thoughts. [ION *and*
XUTHUS *leave the stage.*]

CHORUS [Strophe]: *Tears and cries of sorrow I foresee, and transports*
680   *of grief, when my royal mistress discovers her husband is blessed with*
a son, while she is childless and alone, alone and childless!

O prophet son of Leto, what manner of oracle did you chant? Where
did he come from, this boy reared in your precinct? What woman gave
him birth? This response of yours makes me uneasy; it may harbour
some deception. I fear the outcome, whatever it might be.

690   *Strange are these tidings which the god's strange oracle delivers to*
me. A cunning web of trickery does he weave,[41] *this boy who has been*
raised of no Athenian blood. Who will not agree with us in this?

[Antistrophe:] *Friends, shall we let our mistress know this news,*
discreetly but in plain terms?[42] †   † *Now her fortunes decline,*
700   *while her husband's climb high; she is becoming old and grey-haired,*
while he shows no regard for his dear wife. Wretched man, he came, a
foreigner, into her home and into great wealth, but has not shared
her fortune.

I pray he meets his death, yes, death, for deceiving my royal lady,
and when he makes his offering to the gods, may they frustrate him
710   *and no bright flame leap up from the mixture! He shall know where*
my feelings lie and how much I love my queen! But they are now on
the threshold of horror, the pair of them, new-found father and
new-found son.

[Epode:] *O summit of Parnassus with your rocky cliffs and heaven-*
soaring uplands, where Bacchus with flaming torch raised high in either
hand leaps nimbly in company with his worshippers by night! May
720   *this boy never come to my city, but rather end his young life this very*
day! Our people would have every excuse for rejecting the unwelcome
arrival of a foreigner. It was by repelling the babbling throng of foreign
invaders that our one-time ruler, Erechtheus, kept Athens safe.[43]

[CREUSA *enters from the precinct, accompanied by an* OLD MAN
in her service.]

CREUSA: Come, old servant of mine, who once was tutor to my

father Erechtheus while he still lived; climb up to the god's oracle to share my happiness if Lord Loxias prophesies that I will have children! It is a joy to share in the good fortune of those we love; but, should any disaster happen, which heaven forbid, it is a joy no less to look into the eyes of a loyal friend! I care for you, though I am your mistress, as I would for my father, just as you once cared for him.

OLD MAN: Daughter, your nature is noble and worthy of your noble forebears; you bring no shame upon your family, descended as they are from the ancient sons of Earth. [*Stretching out his arms to* CREUSA] Pull me, pull me towards the temple! Help me on my way! Oracles are steep for me; give me your strength to stir myself and cure the frailty of my old age!

CREUSA [*taking hold of his arm*]: Come along with me, then; [*he nearly falls*] but watch where you put your step!

OLD MAN: Look, I may be slow on my feet but my mind is quick enough.

CREUSA: Use your walking stick to support you; it is a winding track.

OLD MAN: When my eyes let me down, my stick fails me too.

CREUSA: True enough; [*he nearly falls again*] oh, you're exhausted but don't give up!

OLD MAN: Not while I have the will; but if my strength is gone I do not control it. [*He finally succeeds in reaching a place to sit near* CREUSA.]

CREUSA [*turning to address the* CHORUS]: Now you women who serve me loyally at loom and shuttle, what luck regarding children has my husband received from here – for that was the reason for our visit? Speak out! Tell me good news and you will be warming the heart of a mistress who knows how to be grateful!

CHORUS-LEADER: O heavens above!

CREUSA: This is not a happy beginning to your tale!

CHORUS-LEADER: Oh, you poor woman!

CREUSA: Has the oracle given to your master something terrible?

CHORUS-LEADER [*to the rest of the* CHORUS]: Oh, no! What are we to do about this business with the threat of death over our heads?

CREUSA: What is this refrain? What is making you afraid?

CHORUS-LEADER [*still appealing to the other members of the* CHORUS]: Should we speak or stay silent? What shall we do?

CREUSA: Oh, speak! You have a tale of woe to tell and it points to me!

760   CHORUS-LEADER [*addressing* CREUSA *directly*]: Then it will be told, even if I am to die twice over for telling it. Never, my lady, will you take a child in your arms or lay it to your breast.

[CREUSA *sinks down beside the old man. In the lament that follows she sings throughout in contrast to the* OLD MAN *and* CHORUS-LEADER.]

CREUSA: *Oh, let me die!*

OLD MAN: O my dear child!

CREUSA: *Oh, pity me for my fate! My friends, this anguish that has come over me, this anguish I feel, it takes all the sweetness from life! I am ruined!*

OLD MAN [*still making no impression on her*]: Child . . .

CREUSA: *Oh no, oh no! The pain passes straight through me, it pierces to my heart!*

OLD MAN: Don't give way to tears yet . . .

CREUSA: *My grief is already here!*

770   OLD MAN: . . . until we learn . . .

CREUSA: *What news, I ask?*

OLD MAN: . . . if the master is in the same position and shares your misfortune or if this burden of sorrow is yours alone.

CHORUS-LEADER: Oh yes, Loxias has given him a son, old man, and now he is celebrating his luck in private, apart from this lady!

CREUSA: *Another misery for me to mourn, one that crowns the first!*

OLD MAN: And is this child you speak of yet to be born to some woman or did the oracle describe him as already born?

780   CHORUS-LEADER: Already born and a young man full-grown when he was given to him by Loxias; I saw him with my own eyes.

CREUSA: *What are you saying? What you tell me is unutterable, unspeakable!*

OLD MAN: Unspeakable indeed! But tell me more clearly how the oracle came to be fulfilled and who the son is.

CHORUS-LEADER [*to* CREUSA]: The god gave your husband as his son whichever man he met first on hurrying out of the temple.

CREUSA: Monstrous, and the house where I live shall be empty   790 and desolate! For me he has decreed a life, then, with no children, no children!

OLD MAN: Who was he, then, whom the oracle spoke of? Who was it crossed the path of this poor lady's husband? How did he set eyes on him and where?

CHORUS-LEADER: Dear mistress, do you know the young man who was sweeping this temple? He is the son.

CREUSA: *Oh, to fly away,*[44] *far from the land of Greece, up into the liquid air, towards the stars of the west, such is the misery I suffer, friends!*

OLD MAN [*continuing to question the* CHORUS]: And what was the   800 name his father gave him? Do you know, or does this remain unspoken yet and undecided?

CHORUS-LEADER: 'Ion', since he was the one who met his father first; who his mother is I cannot say. But, so you may know all I have to tell, he's gone, this lady's husband, to cheat her by holding a birth-feast for his son in a consecrated pavilion, offering sacrifice on his behalf as if he were a stranger but intending to honour his new-found son at a banquet for all.

OLD MAN: Mistress, we are betrayed by your husband, we, for I count your sufferings as mine! This is a plot to dishonour us   810 and banish us from the house of Erechtheus! I say this, not out of hatred for your husband, but because I love you better than him. Into Athens he came, no Athenian himself, and won your hand in marriage. He took over your palace and your inheritance[45] and now it appears he has been fathering children in secret by another woman! How much in secret I will now tell.

On learning you were childless,[46] he was not prepared to share your misfortune and shoulder his part of the burden; he took a slave-girl to his bed and, when he had fathered this boy
820   by her in secret, he sent the child away from Athens, entrusting it to some Delphian to bring up. And so it was he spent his boyhood days wandering free in the sanctuary of the god, so making it easy for him to escape detection.

When his father came to know that the boy had grown to manhood, he persuaded you to make the journey here because you had no children. And so it was not Phoebus who lied; it was *he* who lied; all this time he was bringing up the child. This was the web of deceit he was fashioning: if he was detected, he meant to throw the responsibility on to the god, and, once in Athens, wishing to guard against the onset of time, he intended to invest his son with sovereignty of that
[830]   city.

CHORUS-LEADER: Ah, how I have always detested unprincipled people who commit crimes and then use clever words to put them in a more favourable light! I'd rather have as a friend a simple fellow who is honest than a villain who is clever.

OLD MAN [*to* CREUSA]: And a disgrace that is worse than all of this will be reserved for you; he is bringing as a master into your home someone who has no mother and no standing in law, the son of a slave-woman! It would have been a less
840   embarrassing difficulty if he had fathered a child by a woman of good family, first gaining your consent by pleading your
[850]   lack of children, and then had introduced the boy into his family. If this notion was offensive to you, he should have taken a wife from the house of Aeolus. All this means that you must now perform a deed worthy of your sex![47]

CREUSA [*breaking into passionate song*][48]: *O my soul, how can I stay*
860   *silent? Yet how reveal that secret union and lose all modesty?*

Oh, what remains to hinder me now? Whose virtue is there for me
to emulate? Has my husband not been exposed as a traitor? I am cut
off from home, cut off from children; gone are the hopes I wished, in

vain, to realize with honour, by saying nothing of my ravishment,
nothing of that birth which broke my heart!

No, by the starry seat of Zeus I swear, by the goddess who dwells   870
on my city's rocky height and by the sacred shore of the Tritonian lake,
no longer shall I conceal my lover; once I have lifted this weight from
my breast, I shall be more at ease. My eyes are wet with tears, my
heart aches at such malice done to me by men and gods together; but I
will reveal their ingratitude and faithless treatment of my love!   880

[CREUSA turns to face the temple.] O you, who make music from
the seven-stringed lyre that rouses sweet echoes of the Muses' song from
the lifeless horns of beasts, I will proclaim your shameful act, son of
Leto, to the bright light of day! You came to me with gold shimmering
in your hair, that day when I was gathering in the folds of my dress
flowers whose saffron hue reflected the golden sunlight; you grasped   890
my white arms, like fruit on a tree, and dragged me, screaming
'Mother!' to lie with you, a god, in the cave, where you shamelessly
indulged your lust.

Wretch that I am, I bore you a baby boy, only to expose him,
through fear of my mother, in that cave of yours where you had ravished
me in my misery, finding no joy on that joyless bed. Oh, I cannot   900
bear it! Now he is gone, snatched up as a feast by birds of prey, my
little boy, and yours! And all the same – oh, your heart is hard! – you
sing songs of victory to the music of your lyre![49]

Ho, Leto's son, I call on you, who dispense your oracles from golden
throne in your shrine at earth's centre! I will proclaim my message to   910
the sunlight: 'Despicable seducer! To my husband who has done you
no previous service you give a son to inherit his house; but the child
born to me and to you, you heartless creature, is no more, carried off
by birds, snatched from the shawl his mother had wrapped him in!
You are hateful to your Delos and to the laurel saplings beside the   920
soft-leaved palm-tree, where in holy birth-pangs Leto bore you in the
bower of Zeus!'[50] *[CREUSA collapses.]*

CHORUS-LEADER: What woe is here! How vast a treasury of
suffering is now laid open! No one can fail to weep at this!
OLD MAN: Daughter, I look at your face and I am filled with

pity; my judgement has deserted me. As soon as I bale out one wave of trouble, your words cause a fresh one to raise me up astern, and, diverting them from the woes you had already, you have started on a different tack of sorrows! What are you saying? What is this charge you are bringing against Loxias? What do you mean by saying you gave birth to a son? Where in Athens did you say you left him out for beasts to make their welcome meal? Tell me again!

CREUSA: I am ashamed before you, old man, but none the less I'll speak.

OLD MAN: Yes, do; I know how to share a loved one's grief as finer feeling dictates.

CREUSA: Then listen: do you know the cave to the north of Cecrops' rocks, the ones we call the Long Cliffs?

OLD MAN: I do; it is where Pan has his shrine, and there is an altar nearby.

CREUSA: That was where I underwent a terrible trial.

OLD MAN: What trial? How your words make the tears start in my eyes!

CREUSA: Against my will – oh, what misery! – I lay with Phoebus.

OLD MAN: My daughter, was that, then, what I noticed about you?

CREUSA: I don't know; if you are right in what you say I'll tell you.

OLD MAN: I mean the time when a secret illness was causing you to suffer and keep away from prying eyes.

CREUSA: That was when it happened, the grim experience I am now revealing to you.

OLD MAN: But what happened next? How did you manage to conceal your liaison with Apollo?

CREUSA: I gave birth [the OLD MAN steps back, shocked]; wait, old man, hear what I have to say!

OLD MAN: Where? Who delivered you? Or were you alone when you went through this ordeal?

CREUSA: I was alone; it was in the same cave where I was ravished.

930

940

OLD MAN: And the boy, where is he, to bring *your* child-   950
less days to an end?

CREUSA: He is dead, old man; he was left out for the wild beasts.

OLD MAN: Dead? Apollo was so cruel? He gave him no help at
all?

CREUSA: No help; my son is being raised in Hades' halls.

OLD MAN: Who then left him out to die? It can't have been you,
surely?

CREUSA: I did, first wrapping him in my shawl under cover of
darkness.

OLD MAN: And no one shared with you the secret of the child's
exposure?

CREUSA: Only my sorrow and concealment.

OLD MAN: And how did you have the heart to abandon your
child in a cave?

CREUSA: How? I uttered many cries that would have stirred the
heart to pity, I . . . [CREUSA *breaks off, unable to continue.*]

OLD MAN: O my dear girl! Hard-hearted in what you dared to   960
do, but less so than the god!

CREUSA: Oh, if you had seen my little boy stretching his hands
out towards me!

OLD MAN: Searching for your breast or wanting to be laid in
your arms?

CREUSA: Yes, the very place I wrongly barred him from!

OLD MAN: What prompted the idea of leaving your child out to
die?

CREUSA: I thought the god would take steps to protect his own
son!

OLD MAN: Oh, what sorrow! How your prosperous house has
been ravaged by storm!

CREUSA: Why do cover your head and weep, old man?

OLD MAN: Because I see how you and your father are abused by
fortune!

CREUSA: Such is the life of man; nothing remains constant.

OLD MAN [*squaring his shoulders*]: Enough of this grieving now,   970
my daughter; we must not dwell on it.

CREUSA: What then should I do? Misery offers no solutions.

OLD MAN: Take revenge on the one who wronged you in the first place – the god!

CREUSA: And how am I to escape retribution, a mortal against a mightier power?

OLD MAN: Set fire to Loxias' holy oracle![51]

CREUSA: I am afraid; my cup of sorrows is already full.

OLD MAN: Then dare to do what *can* be done. Kill your husband!

CREUSA: He was once a good and loving husband. That compels my respect.

OLD MAN: Well, at least there is the boy who has risen up to do you harm – you must not let *him* live!

CREUSA: Yes, but how? If only I were able! How I would like to!

980 OLD MAN: Arm your serving-men with swords.

CREUSA: I will set about it; but where shall this take place?

OLD MAN: Inside the sacred pavilion where the father is giving a banquet for his friends.

CREUSA: Murder is easily detected and there is no strength in slaves.

OLD MAN [*losing his patience momentarily*]: This won't do, surely! You're losing your nerve! Come on, it's your turn now to think up a plan!

CREUSA: Well, I *do* have a scheme; it is clever and will work.

OLD MAN: I am your ready servant, with head and heart!

CREUSA: Then listen; you know about the Battle of the Giants?

OLD MAN: I do; it was when the Giants opposed the gods at Phlegra.

CREUSA: There, Earth gave birth to the Gorgon, a fearful monster.[52]

990 OLD MAN: To assist her own sons in battle and plague the gods?

CREUSA: Yes; it was slain by divine Pallas, child of Zeus.

OLD MAN: Is this the story I heard many years ago?

CREUSA: Yes; it is this creature's hide that Athena wears upon her breast.

OLD MAN: What they call the 'aegis', the armour of Pallas?

CREUSA: It received this name when she rushed into battle at the side of the gods.

OLD MAN: What form did its savage shape take?

CREUSA: It was a breastplate armed with coiling snakes.

OLD MAN: Just what harm might this bring to your enemies, Daughter?

CREUSA: Do you know of Erichthonius[53] or . . . but of course you must, old man.

OLD MAN: The ancestor of your family first spawned by Earth? 1000

CREUSA: When he was newly born, Pallas gave to him . . .

OLD MAN: What? You still have something to say.

CREUSA: . . . two drops from the Gorgon's blood.[54]

OLD MAN: What effect do they have on a man's constitution?

CREUSA: One causes death, the other cures diseases.

OLD MAN: What did she use to fasten them to his body and put them round the boy?

CREUSA: A golden chain; Erichthonius bequeathed the gift to my father.

OLD MAN: And when he died it passed to you?

CREUSA: Yes; I am the one who wears it, here on my wrist.

OLD MAN: How, then, is it constituted, this twofold gift of the 1010 goddess?

CREUSA: The blood that flows from the hollow vein . . .

OLD MAN: What must be done with it? What is its effect?

CREUSA: . . . it protects from disease and nurtures life.

OLD MAN: And what is the effect of the second one on your list?

CREUSA: It kills; it is venom from the Gorgon's snakes.

OLD MAN: Do you carry it mixed with the first one or separately?

CREUSA: Separately; good does not mix with bad.

OLD MAN: My dearest girl, you have all that you need!

CREUSA: This will bring about the boy's death; and the killer will be you.

OLD MAN: Where? What must I do? It is for you to say and me 1020 to dare.

CREUSA: In Athens, as soon as he comes to my home.

OLD MAN: That's not a good idea; after all, you found fault with my scheme.

CREUSA: Why? Are you worried by the same thing that strikes me?

OLD MAN: People will think that you killed the boy, even if you did not.

CREUSA: You are right; they say the stepmother has no love for the children.[55]

OLD MAN: Then kill him here, where you can deny the murder!

CREUSA: And at least I'll enjoy the taste of my revenge the sooner!

OLD MAN: And this way you will make your husband think you do not know the secret he is so eager to keep from you.

CREUSA: You know, then, what to do. Take from my hand this
1030   golden bracelet of Athena's, ancient piece of jewellery, and go to the place where this husband of mine is making his secret sacrifice. When they stop feasting and are about to pour libations in honour of the gods, take this poison you will have secreted under your robe and drop it in the young man's drinking-cup without being seen – not in everyone's, mind. You must keep his drink separate, for the one who intends to lord it over my house. And if he swallows it, he'll never reach Athens but remain here, a dead man!

1040   OLD MAN: Go now inside our lodgings. I will see to the task I have been assigned. [CREUSA withdraws.] Come, old feet of mine, find the spring of youth for this deed, in spite of your years. Assist your mistress, march out against her enemy. Give her your support in killing him and ridding her home of him. When Fortune smiles on a man, it is a good thing for him to honour piety; but when a man wants to do harm to his enemies, no law must stand in his way. [Exit OLD MAN.]

CHORUS [Strophe]: *Lady of the Cross-ways, daughter of Demeter,*[56]
1050   *who presides over visitations by night, at the noontide also guide the filling of the deadly bowl for those that my dear mistress intends, drawn from drops of gore from the Earth-born Gorgon's sundered neck; guide*

it to the lips of the one who seeks to lay his hands on the throne of Erechtheus! Never may any foreigner become our king, only someone from the noble house of Erechtheus!   1060

[Antistrophe:] *But if my lady's plot fails, if her efforts to kill him founder and she loses the opportunity for this act of daring that now seems so hopeful, she will end her life, either by means of a sharpened sword or by tightening a noose around her neck.*[57] *And so, by bringing her own wretchedness to a wretched end, she will enter a new phase of existence. Never would she tolerate, while yet she lived in the sun's bright light, the rule of another, not of Athenian stock, she the heir to*   1070 *a house of noble sires.*

[Strophe:] *I am ashamed to face the god praised in many a hymn,*[58] *if this youth shall be among the pilgrims by Callichorus' spring, keeping vigil to see the torches blaze forth on the night of the Twentieth, when the stars themselves in heaven's vault start up the dance, and the moon joins in, together with Nereus' fifty daughters in the sea and*   1080 *the nymphs of the immortal eddying streams, as they dance in honour of the Maid who wears the golden crown and her holy mother. And it is there he hopes to become king, seeking to profit by other men's labours, this homeless gypsy of Phoebus!*

[Antistrophe:] *All you poets, who float down music's stream,*   1090 *singing in slanderous strains of women's sinful loves and criminal passions, mark how much we surpass in virtue the lawless race of men!*[59] *Change your song and let your voices ring out against their lustful ways! Witness the ingratitude of the one who claims descent*   1100 *from Zeus. Not in union with my mistress did he father offspring to ensure the fortune of the house; he turned his loving attentions to another woman and got himself a bastard son!*

[*A* SERVANT *of* CREUSA *enters in some agitation.*]

SERVANT: Good women, where can I find Erechtheus' daughter, our royal mistress? I have searched the whole town through for her, running and changing tack in every direction, and yet I've had no luck!

CHORUS-LEADER: What's troubling you, fellow-slave? What makes you rush in so excitedly? What's the news you bring?   1110

SERVANT: They're after us! The local authorities of the region are trying to track her down. They mean to stone her to death!

CHORUS-LEADER: Oh, no, no! I can't believe it! They haven't found us out, surely, plotting the secret murder of the boy?

SERVANT: It's true; you will be among the first to suffer punishment.

CHORUS-LEADER: How was it detected, our hidden scheme?

SERVANT: The god exposed it; he wished to avoid pollution.

CHORUS-LEADER: But how? I beg you, for mercy's sake, tell
1120 me the story! Once I know, I will die the happier, if die I must, and so, too, if I'm spared!

SERVANT: When Creusa's husband had left the shrine, taking his new-found son with him, to attend the feast and sacrifices he was preparing for the gods, he went to the place where the Bacchic fire of the god leaps high so that he might make Dionysus' twin crags[60] run with sacrificial blood in recognition of his newly discovered child. These were his words: 'You stay here, my son, and supervise workmen in their efforts as they
1130 construct a spacious pavilion. If after sacrificing to the gods who preside over birth I should linger for any length of time, let the feast go forward for our gathered friends.' Then he took his victims and went on his way.[61]

With due attention to piety the young man erected on upright posts the framework of a pavilion, as yet lacking walls. He guarded well against the sun's shafts, so that it faced neither the noonday rays of his fire, nor yet his dying beams. For each side of his square he measured one hundred feet in length, so that the area inside came to ten thousand feet, so the experts
1140 say, his intention being to invite all the folk of Delphi to the feast.

Next he took from the treasury sacred tapestries and hung them as an awning, a marvel for people to see. First he spread[62] over the roof-tree a fold of drapery that Heracles, son of Zeus, had brought back as part of the spoils of the Amazons and had dedicated to the god. Among them were webs woven with figures of this kind: Uranus mustering his starry host in the

vault of heaven; Helios driving his steeds towards his flaming
goal and drawing behind him the radiant light of Hesperus;
Night, goddess in black robes, urging her chariot onward,   1150
drawn by two horses unassisted, while the stars made up her
escort; the Pleiad holding to her course in mid-heaven, with
Orion the swordsman beside her, while overhead the Bear was
lashing round his golden tail in the sky; Moon in full orb was
darting her beams upward, dividing the month in two, and
there were the Hyades, sign most sure to mariners, and Dawn,
bringer of light, chasing the stars. On the walls the young man
hung different tapestries, of oriental work: well-oared ships   1160
ranged against vessels of Greece, prow to prow, creatures half
man, half beast, the hunting of deer by mounted men, the
stalking of savage lions. At the entrance, with his daughters at
his side, was Cecrops coiling his serpent tail, the offering made
by some Athenian, and in the middle of the banqueting space
he had set mixing bowls of gold.

Then a herald, drawing himself up to his full height, proclaimed that any man of Delphi who wished might come to
the feast. When the pavilion was filled, the guests, with garlands
adorning their hair, eagerly started consuming the generous
quantities of food laid out before them. Once their appetites   1170
had been satisfied, an old man moved forward[63] and planted
himself in the middle of the floor-space, causing the banqueters
to laugh loud and long as he fussed over every detail. He passed
among them with ewers, pouring water from them for the
washing of hands, and went on to burn myrrh resin as incense,
presiding over the golden goblets all the while, a self-appointed
major-domo. When it came to the flute-playing as everyone
was to be served from the communal bowl, the old man spoke
up: 'Away with the small winecups, it's big ones we need to
bring, if these here gentlemen are to drown their sorrows in   1180
good time!' That gave the servants work to do, as they carried
round the goblets of gold and wrought silver.

Then he took in his hands a special cup and, as if paying a
compliment to his new master, he handed it to him full. But

first he had put in the wine the potent poison given him, they
say, by our mistress to bring an end to the youngster's life. No
one was aware of this but, as he was holding it in his hands,
preparing to offer libation with the other guests, the newly
1190   revealed son heard a slave let slip an unlucky word. Since he
had been reared in a holy place, among men skilled in divination, he took this as an omen and ordered another fresh bowl
to be filled.[64] The earlier drink offering to the god he poured
on the ground, telling everyone else to follow suit.

There followed silence, as we filled the sacred bowls with
wine of Byblus and with water. While we were engaged in
this, further guests arrived – a troop of doves that winged its
way into the pavilion (they live unafraid in Loxias' temple). In
their thirsty state the creatures dipped their beaks in the wine
1200   spilled by the guests and started drawing it down their pretty
throats.

The rest of the birds came to no harm from the god's libation
but the one that settled where the new young master had
poured no sooner tasted the drink than it went into violent
spasms throughout its downy frame and uttered an unintelligible shriek, a cry of anguish. We were amazed, every one of
the assembled throng, as we witnessed the bird's agony. At last
the crimson legs and claws relaxed, as death brought an end to
its gasping for breath.

Then the oracle's child bared his arms and thrust them across
1210   the table at the old man, shouting, 'Who's trying to kill me?
Out with it, old man! You were the one making such a fuss; it
was your hand I took the cup from!' Without delay he seized
him by his wrinkled arm and started to search the old fellow in
the hope of catching him red-handed, in possession of the
poison. He was found out and under pressure, reluctantly, he
revealed Creusa's crime and the device of the cup.

At once the young man whose birth Loxias' oracle had
disclosed ran outside with the guests at his heels and, taking his
1220   stand before the lords of Delphi, spoke these words: 'O sacred
Earth, Erechtheus' daughter, a stranger to us, is trying to end

my life with poison!' By many a vote Delphi's rulers determined
that my mistress should be executed by stoning for her attempt
to kill the temple boy and commit murder in the sanctuary.
All Delphi is hunting for the woman whose wretchedness set
her on this wretched course. It was desire for children that
brought her to Phoebus' door but now she has lost all hope
not just of children but of her own life. [*The* SERVANT *runs off
stage.*]

CHORUS: *Oh how miserable I am! I have no means, none, to escape* 1230
*from death! All is now clear; our plan stands revealed from the
libation of Dionysus' grape-clusters mixed murderously with the viper's
swift-working drops of blood. It is discovered, our sacrificial offering to
the powers below – disastrous for my life, but death by stoning for my
lady! Oh, how am I to escape the horror of those stones – should I fly* 1240
away on wings[65] *or journey below the earth and find refuge in its dark
recesses? Should I mount a chariot drawn by horses of swiftest hoof or
take to a speedy ship?*

CHORUS-LEADER: *There is no escape for us if it is not the god's will
to aid our concealment. O my lady, how I pity you! What pain yet
awaits your suffering heart? As it was our wish to do harm to our
neighbour, shall harm be done to us in turn, as justice requires?*

[CREUSA *rushes on stage, wearing a veil.*]

CREUSA: They are chasing me, good women, to kill me, to 1250
slaughter me! The Pythian vote seals my fate; I am betrayed!

CHORUS: We know of your plight, poor lady, we know the state
of your fortunes.

CREUSA: Where am I to take refuge? I barely got clear of my
house, running for my life, but I managed to give them the slip
and so am here.

CHORUS: Your only place of sanctuary is the altar.

CREUSA: And how can that do me any good?

CHORUS: It is not lawful to shed a suppliant's blood.

CREUSA: Yes, but it is the law that demands my life.

CHORUS: But first they have to catch you.

CREUSA: Look! Here they come, my adversaries, hurrying this
way with swords at the ready and anger in their eyes.

CHORUS: Sit down now at the altar![66] If they kill you when you
1260   are there, you will mark your killers with the stain of
blood-guilt. But you must endure your fate.

[CREUSA *takes her seat at the altar and holds fast to the statue
there.* ION *enters with armed followers.*]

ION: O father Cephisus, who took the form of a bull, what a
viper is this woman you have bred in your family! What a
dragon, with deadly fire blazing in her eyes! Nothing makes
her flinch; not even those drops of Gorgon's blood with which
she meant to kill me contain more poison than her heart! Seize
her! I want to see those lovely locks of hair being shredded
when we send her spinning down Parnassus' cliff to bound
from rock to rock!

It was lucky for me that this happened before I reached
1270   Athens and fell into the clutches of a stepmother. I still had
friends around me when I got the measure of your feelings and
learned how dangerous an enemy I had in you! Once you had
lured me into your home, the net would have been cast and
you would have sent me straight on my way to Hades' halls!

[ION *turns to his companions.*] Look at her, the woman who
will stop at nothing – what web on web of trickery has she
1280   woven; she crouches at the altar of the god, thinking she will
escape punishment for her crimes!

CREUSA [*as* ION*'s men move towards her*]: No, do not kill me! I
give you warning, in my own name and in the god's in whose
sanctuary we stand!

ION: You and Phoebus? What circumstances links the pair of
you?

CREUSA: My body is consecrated to the god and I have placed it
in his care.

ION: And yet you attempted to kill with poison one who
belonged to the god?

CREUSA: No, one who belonged to your father; you no longer
belonged to Loxias.

ION: I was indeed the god's – I speak of when my father was not here.

CREUSA: Then was the time when you were Apollo's; now you no longer are but I am his.

ION: But you are hardly innocent now; my life was one of innocence then.

CREUSA: I tried to kill you as an enemy to my house.

ION: I never tried to enter your country with weapons of war.

CREUSA: But with weapons of fire, to set alight the house of Erechtheus!

ION: Torches and firebrands? What fancy is this!

CREUSA: You intended to take by force the house and home that are mine!

ION: Then, because you feared what I 'intended', you sought to kill me?

CREUSA: Yes, to save my own life, in case you should succeed.

ION: Are you envious that my father found me, while you remain childless?

CREUSA: If I am childless, you will see fit to rob me of my home?

ION: The land was my father's, won by him and his to bestow.

CREUSA: And what claims do Aeolus' sons have on the land of Pallas?

ION: With weapons, not arguments, he delivered it from harm.

CREUSA: A mercenary could never make his home in Athens!

ION: Then could I have no share in that land, together with my father?

CREUSA: Only a shield and a spear – there is all your patrimony!

ION: Come away from the altar and its holy sanctuary!

CREUSA: Save your orders for your mother, wherever she is!

ION: And you, the one who tried to murder me, are you to escape punishment?

CREUSA: Not if you mean to cut my throat here in the sanctuary.

ION: Why do you want to die surrounded by the garlands of the god?

CREUSA: I will be giving pain in return for pain received.

ION: What a state of affairs![67] How terrible it is when the laws

1290

1300

1310

the gods have made for men are made neither well nor wisely! The criminal should be driven from the altar, not granted its protection. It is an offence that something holy should be touched by criminal hands; only the just have this right. It is the victim of wrongdoing who should receive the privilege of sanctuary; the good man and the bad when they seek refuge should not be given equal treatment by the gods.

[*Apollo's* PROPHETESS *enters from the temple. She carries in her arms a cradle decorated with woollen wreaths similar to those on the altar.*]

1320 PROPHETESS: Wait, my son! I have left my tripod of prophecy and step over this threshold, I, Phoebus' prophetess, chosen from all Delphi's womenfolk to preserve the time-honoured custom of the tripod.

ION: Greetings, Mother mine, though you did not give me birth.

PROPHETESS: Well, so I am called; the name is not unwelcome to me.

ION: Have you been told how this woman attempted to kill me by treachery?

PROPHETESS: I have; but this cruelty makes you guilty also.

ION: Is it not right that I should take her life when she tried to take mine?

PROPHETESS: Married women have never shown affection to stepsons.

1330 ION: And we have the same feelings for our stepmothers when they make us suffer!

PROPHETESS: Enough; leave the sanctuary and go to your own land . . .

ION: What is it I should do? Give me your advice.

PROPHETESS: Go to Athens with innocent hands and good omens.

ION: A man has innocent hands if he kills his enemies.

PROPHETESS: This is not for you. Listen to what I have to say.

ION: Then speak. Whatever you say will be well meant, I know.

PROPHETESS: Do you see this basket[68] I keep cradled in my arms?

ION: I see an ancient cradle with wreaths covering it.

PROPHETESS: You were placed in this when you came into my hands long ago, a new-born babe.

ION: What's that you say? This is a new detail in the story!　1340

PROPHETESS: Yes, I kept the facts concealed; but now I reveal them.

ION: How could you keep it from me all this time?

PROPHETESS: It was the god's wish that you should serve him in his temple.

ION: And now he no longer wants that? How can I be sure of this?

PROPHETESS: He has shown you your father and lets you take your leave of Delphi.

ION: Did you keep this basket safe at his order or was there some other reason?

PROPHETESS: Loxias inspired me then with the thought.

ION: To do what? Speak! Finish your story!

PROPHETESS: To keep this discovery safe until the present time.

ION: What does it hold in store for me? What profit or harm?　1350

PROPHETESS: In here is hidden the clothing in which you were wrapped.

ION: Are these clues you are producing that can help me find my mother?

PROPHETESS: Yes, for it is the god's will; until now he did not wish it.

ION [*raising his hands on high*]: How I bless this day for what it is revealing!

PROPHETESS [*giving him the cradle*]: Now take this and strive to find your mother.

ION: So I shall, if it means crossing all of Asia and Europe's boundaries!

PROPHETESS: This you must decide for yourself. To please the god I reared you, my child, and now hand over to you these things he wished me, uninstructed, to take and keep safe; his　1360 motive in this I cannot tell. Not a living soul knew that these articles were in my possession, or where they were hidden.

And now, farewell! [*The* PROPHETESS *embraces* ION.] I take
my leave of you as fondly as a mother! [*Exit.*]

ION: Oh, this is too much! How my eyes stream with tears as I
1370   think of that day when my mother, in her shame at being
seduced, tried to dispose of me, her unsuckled child, in secret!
A waif without a name, I lived a servant's life in the god's
temple. My holy master was kind but my lot a heavy one; all
the time I should have known the luxury of a mother's embrace
and taken delight in life, I was denied a loving mother's care
and nurture. I pity, too, the woman who gave me birth; her
own suffering is no less than mine, for she lost the joy of a
son.

1380   Now I will take this cradle and offer it in dedication to the
god; this will save me from making any discovery I may regret.[69]
If in fact some slave-woman gave me birth, it would be worse
to find my mother than to let the truth rest unspoken. [*Raising
the cradle in both hands and facing the temple*] To your shrine,
Phoebus, I here dedicate – no, what is wrong with me? Should
I try to thwart the god's purpose when he has preserved my
mother's tokens for me? I must not falter; I must open it; I
cannot cheat my destiny.

    [ION *lays the cradle down on the ground and begins to untie its
wrappings.* CREUSA *stares at him with rising excitement.*]

1390   O holy wreaths and fastenings that kept guard on my precious secret, what have you been concealing, I wonder? See
how by some miracle the rounded cradle's covering has not
aged and no mould has grown on the plaited work, though
many a year has passed since this was stored away!

CREUSA [*breaking her silence*]: Oh, what sight is this that I never
hoped to see!

ION: Hold your tongue! I have already had cause to know your
dangerous nature!

CREUSA: I have no reason for silence; do not criticize me! I see
the basket in which I exposed you all those years ago, my child,
when you were just a baby boy, laying you down inside the
1400   cave of Cecrops at the Long Cliffs with their roofs of rock.

[CREUSA *rises from her place of sanctuary and rushes to clasp* ION.]
I will leave this altar, even if I am to die for it!

ION [*to his men*]: Seize her! The god has made her mad; she has leapt up from the altar, leaving its images behind. Bind her arms!

CREUSA: Kill me! Show no mercy! But I will hold fast to this cradle, to you and to the things that are hidden inside it!

ION: Is this not outrageous – making me out to be her property by using deceit!

CREUSA: No, you are discovered as her own by one who loves you!

ION: You love me? And yet you tried to kill me by treachery?

CREUSA: You are my son – can a mother love anyone more than this?

ION: Stop spinning your cunning lies – I will catch you out!   1410

CREUSA: Oh, this is what I want, this is my aim, my child!

ION [*disengaging himself from* CREUSA]: Is it empty, this basket, or does it contain something?

CREUSA: The clothing I wrapped you in when I exposed you all those years ago.

ION: And will you name these articles before seeing them?

CREUSA: Yes, and if I fail, I agree to die.

ION: Then speak; there is something impressive in this confidence you show.

CREUSA [*to the* CHORUS *and* ION]: Look, all of you, at the cloth I wove all those years ago when I was a girl!

[*The* CHORUS *moves behind* ION *to gain a better view.*]

ION: What kind of cloth? Girls produce all sorts!

CREUSA: An unfinished piece, the sort of thing we are taught to weave as beginners.

ION: What design does it have on it? Don't expect to take me in   1420
like this!

CREUSA: There is a Gorgon in the middle of the cloth.

ION: O Zeus, what destiny is it that is hunting me down?

CREUSA: The Gorgon is fringed with snakes as is the aegis.[70]

ION: See! Here is the web, revealed to us just like an oracle!

CREUSA: O the work of my virgin youth, how long it is since I set eyes on you!

ION: Can you add any detail to this or were you just making a lucky guess?

CREUSA: A pair of serpents, gleaming with jaws all golden, the gift of Athena; for she bids us rear our young with serpents by them, imitating Erichthonius our ancestor.[71]

1430 ION: Tell me, what does she bid you do? What use should you make of the golden trinket?

CREUSA: It is for a new-born child to wear as a necklace, my son.

ION: Here it is! But I long to hear about the third thing here.

CREUSA: There was a wreath I placed on your head; it came from the olive-tree that Athena's rock first brought forth.[72] If that wreath is still there, its greenness will not have faded and it will continue to bloom, sprung as it is from an olive that is inviolate.

ION [embracing CREUSA, at last convinced]: O my darling mother, what a joy it is to see you! Let me hug you, blissful, my cheek against yours!

CREUSA: My child, light more precious to your mother than the
1440 sun (the god will forgive these words), I have you in my arms
. . . [CREUSA now breaks into song as her emotions overtake her] the treasure I never hoped to see, the one I thought was living with Persephone and the dead below the earth!

ION [showing more calm]: Dearest Mother, here you see me in your arms, the son who was dead and yet was alive.

CREUSA: O you expanse of glittering sky, what words should I utter or cry out? How did this unexpected delight come about? How has this joy become mine?

1450 ION: This is the last thing I would ever have imagined possible, Mother, that I should find myself your son.

CREUSA: I still tremble with fear!

ION: Fearing you do not hold me when you do?

CREUSA: Yes; I had cast my hopes far way. [Now addressing the PROPHETESS in her absence] Ah, lady, how did you come to take

*my baby in your arms? By what hand did he come to the dwelling of
Loxias?*

ION: It was the work of a god; but I pray that our fortune may
be as good in days to come as it has proved bad in the past.

CREUSA: *My child, tears in plenty accompanied your time of birth and
with cries of mourning were you separated from your mother's arms.
But now, when I have won this most blessed of joys, I breathe anew,* 1460
my cheek pressed close to yours.

ION: Your words equally describe my own happiness.

CREUSA: *No longer do I lack a son and heir! My house has its hearth,
my country a prince and Erechtheus is young once more! The palace of
the Earth-born looks no more upon the dark but gazes into the sun's
rays!*

ION: Mother, my father is here as well;[73] let him share in this joy
I have given to you!

CREUSA: *What are you saying, child? Oh, how my past is finding me* 1470
out!

ION: What do you mean?

CREUSA: *Your father is quite different, quite different!*

ION: Oh, no! Am I a bastard? You bore me out of wedlock?

CREUSA: *O my child, my darling boy, no torches or dances accompanied
the union that led to your birth!*

ION: Oh, this pains me! I am of low birth, Mother? By whom?

CREUSA: *The Gorgon-slayer be my witness . . .*

ION: Why did you say that?

CREUSA: *. . . she who has her seat on the hill of olives, on the* 1480
rock of Athens . . .

ION: I find your words obscure and far from clear.

CREUSA: *. . . by the rock where nightingales sing, with
Phoebus . . .*

ION: Why do you speak of Phoebus?

CREUSA: *. . . I lay in secret union.*

ION: Oh, say more! The news you bring me is good, is happy
news!

CREUSA: When nine months had completed their circle, I bore
you to Phoebus, and no one knew of it.

ION: Oh, what welcome news is this, if you speak the truth!

1490   CREUSA: I wrapped you in these baby-clothes, your maiden-mother's wayward efforts at weaving. I gave you no mother's nurture with the milk of my breasts, nor did I wash you with these hands; I left you to die in a lonely cave, offering you up to taloned birds to make their bloody feast.

ION: How could you bring yourself to do something so awful, Mother?

CREUSA: Fear had made me its prisoner, my child, and so I threw your life away. I did not want you dead.

1500   ION: And when I tried to kill you, was I not sinning also?

CREUSA: Ah, what we went through then was terrible, and terrible, too, is what we have just experienced! We are buffeted this way and that by fortune which is now good, now bad, as the winds change. Let our luck stay constant; our earlier sufferings were enough. My son, may a kindly breeze spring up now to blow us beyond our troubles!

1510   CHORUS-LEADER: Let no one think that anything in human affairs is beyond hope, in the light of what is happening here.

ION: O Fortune, whose shifting favours have sunk so many mortals in misery before now and raised them up again in joy, how close I came to killing my mother – monstrous fate! Ah, is it possible, wherever the sun enfolds us in his shining light, that we can learn so much each day? Precious indeed, Mother, is my discovery of you, and honourable, I would say, the parentage I have found.

1520   But there is something else I want to say to you alone. Come here! [ION *draws* CREUSA *towards him, away from the* CHORUS.] Let me whisper my words in your ear and veil the matter in darkness. Mother, I hope you are not showing the weakness that often affects young women betrayed into a secret love; you must not put the blame on the god and say you bore me to Phoebus, when my father was someone else, hoping to avoid the shame I would bring you.[74]

CREUSA: No! By our Lady of Victory, by Athena who marched once at the side of Zeus' chariot against the Earth's brood, no

mortal man is your father, my child, but the one who reared   1530
you, Loxias the King.

ION: How, then, did he come to give his own son to another
father and claim that I was born the son of Xuthus?

CREUSA: Not born to that man but presented as a gift to him,
though you were his own offspring. A friend may give his own
son to another friend for purposes of inheritance.[75]

ION: Does the god give true prophecy or false? This troubles my
mind, mother, and not without reason.

CREUSA: Listen to what has just occurred to me, my child. It   1540
was out of kindness to you that Loxias intended you to find a
noble home; if men spoke of you as son of the god, you would
never have won your royal inheritance or a father's name. This
would have been impossible when I myself was trying to
conceal the union and to kill you by stealth! The god has
assigned you to another father for your own benefit.

ION: My enquiry into this matter will not accept so weak an
explanation. I will go into the temple and ask Phoebus whether
I am born of a mortal father or of Loxias.

[*The goddess* ATHENA *appears*[76] *above the temple.*] Ah! What   1550
deity is this who rises up above the place of sacrifice, showing
a face as radiant as the sun? O Mother, let us flee in case we see
forbidden sights [ATHENA *motions them to stay*], unless the time
is right for us to see.

ATHENA: Do not flee! It is no enemy you seek to escape; I am
one who wishes you well, both here and in Athens. It is I,
Pallas Athena, who have come, the one whose name your
country bears. I have hastened here from Apollo, who has not
seen fit to appear before your eyes, in case blame for past
misfortunes should be aired in public.[77] He has dispatched me
to deliver to you this message: you are the child of this woman   1560
and Apollo is your father; when he gave you to the man he
did, it was not as a gift to a parent, but to bring you into a
noble house. When the true position was revealed, he feared
that you might be killed by your mother's plotting, or she by
you, and so devised this stratagem to save your lives. It was

King Apollo's intention to observe an interval of silence before making the facts known in Athens,[78] revealing that this woman is your mother and you the child born to her and your father, Phoebus.

But let me now complete my business; listen, both of you, 1570 to the god's oracle, the command I yoked my chariot to bring to you. Take this boy, Creusa, and return to Cecrops' land, and there establish him on a royal throne. As he is sprung from the sons of Erechtheus, he has the right to rule over my country, and great shall be his fame throughout Greece.[79] The sons he shall sire, four in number from a single root, shall give their names to the land and to its tribal people who inhabit my rock. 1580 Geleon shall be the first; then[80] †   † will come the Hopletes and Argades and the Aegicores, named after my aegis, will make up one tribe. The sons born to them shall in time be destined to settle the island cities of the Cyclades and the coastal lands, a source of strength to my own country. They will make their homes in the lands of two continents, on both sides of the straits, those of Asia and of Europe. In honour of his name they shall be called 'Ionians' and they will enjoy fame.

[To CREUSA] To you and Xuthus sons shall be born[81] – 1590 Dorus, from whom shall spring the Dorian state whose glories shall be sung throughout the land of Pelops; the second, Achaeus, shall rule over the coastal regions by Rhion, and its people shall be distinguished by being called by his name.

All has been well managed by Apollo. First he spared you the sickness of labour, to keep the truth from your family. Next, when you had given birth to this boy and wrapped him in his baby blankets, he ordered Hermes to snatch him up in 1600 his arms and convey the infant here. He nurtured him and did not allow him to expire. So say nothing about his child being your own, woman, so that Xuthus may find comfort in his illusion,[82] and you in turn may go on your way cherishing your blessings. I bid you farewell; now that you have found respite from suffering, I promise your fortune will be a happy one.

ION: O Pallas, daughter of mighty Zeus, we do believe the words you have spoken to us; I am persuaded that Loxias and this lady are my parents. Even before this I could have believed it.[83]

CREUSA: Now hear what I have to say. I praise Phoebus, though 1610
I did not do so before, for protecting his son and giving him back to me. These portals, this oracle of the god, now appear fair in my eyes, though they were hateful before. Gladly I now cling to the door-knocker and greet his portals.

ATHENA: I commend your praise of the god and your change of heart. The gods' purposes may be slow in coming to fruition but they are fulfilled without fail.

CREUSA: My child, let us go home.

ATHENA: Go on your way and I will share your journey.

ION: Worthy is the one who guides our path!

CREUSA: And the one who loves her city!

ATHENA: Assume your seat upon your ancient throne.

ION: A worthy prize for me to take!

[ATHENA *disappears from sight.* ION *and* CREUSA *leave together.*]

CHORUS: *Apollo, child of Zeus and Leto, farewell! The man whose house is troubled by misfortune should revere the gods and not lose* 1620 *heart; for at the end the good get their just reward, while the wicked, as their nature directs, shall never know happiness.*[84]

HELEN

PREFACE TO *HELEN*

Helen, the beautiful daughter of Zeus and the mortal woman Leda, was the cause of the Trojan war, according to the version of the myth presupposed by the *Iliad* and most later versions. The Trojan Paris, who judged Aphrodite the fairest of the goddesses competing for the title, was not an impartial judge, for Aphrodite had bribed him with the promise that she would reward him with the most beautiful of all mortal women. Since Helen was already the wife to the Greek Menelaus, the result was war between the Greeks and the Trojans. Ultimately Paris was killed, the Greeks won the war and Menelaus took Helen away with him back to Sparta, though they only reached home after lengthy wanderings. According to the fourth book of the *Odyssey*, those wanderings did involve journeyings almost as far as Egypt, and Menelaus had to consult Proteus, the old man of the sea, in order to find his way home again.

This is the familiar version, the version which with some variations is central to the Greek tradition. Among the variables is Helen's own personality: she could be presented as a victim of Aphrodite, constantly regretting her fate (as in the *Iliad*), or as a shallow, vain adulteress (as in Euripides' own *Trojan Women*). But a different tradition is attested in the poetry (now lost) of Stesichorus, a lyric poet of the sixth century BC. In a famous passage which survives in later quotations, Stesichorus addressed Helen saying, 'It is not true, the tale. You did not go in the well-benched ships; you did not come to Pergama of Troy.' According to these later sources, Stesichorus is the source from whom Euripides drew the tale that a phantom went to Troy in Helen's place. The historian Herodotus also discusses Helen, from the point of view of a sceptic who is reluctant to accept that a ten-year war was fought and a city destroyed for the sake of a woman. According to his account, Helen was detained in Egypt and the Trojans had no choice but to fight on, for they could not return the woman when the Greeks demanded her (Herodotus 2.112–20). This is a rationalizing version, eliminating the phantom but retaining the notion that Helen in fact did not go to Troy.

Euripides had alluded to the alternative tradition in passing, near the end of his *Electra* (1280–83), which is probably a few years earlier than *Helen*. In this play he adopts it whole-heartedly, and takes obvious pleasure in developing the paradoxes of the situation, as when Menelaus ponders in bewilderment whether there can be a man called Zeus in Egypt who could be father to a different Helen (483ff.). There are advantages of characterization: Helen makes a more intriguing central figure if she is no simple adulteress but a woman fraught with undeserved guilt and undesired responsibility for the futile war. Euripides had put Helen on stage before, but only in minor roles; here she is central, but a misunderstood and virtuous woman. There are advantages in the unfolding of the plot: before Helen and Menelaus can be reunited, he has to be freed from his delusion and induced to recognize her for who she really is. There is ingenious new use of familiar plot-motifs: the story of the woman imprisoned in a foreign land, longing for rescue but unable to return to Greece or to send a message there, closely resembles the plot of *Iphigenia among the Taurians*. Other elements of the play are also part of Euripides' stock in trade: the suppliant's refuge, the recognition duet, the plot to escape, the naïve barbarian. *Helen* shows a remarkable self-consciousness in its bold redeployment of literary devices which were already well known as typically Euripidean. It is not surprising that Aristophanes took the opportunity the following year to parody the play mercilessly in his own *Women at the Thesmophoria*. The Euripidean drama had already gone some way towards parodying a 'typical' Euripidean escape-plot: did Aristophanes feel that tragedy was beginning to poach on comedy's territory?

The alternative tradition raises worrying questions which may feed back into reflection on the more orthodox mythology of the war, and indeed on contemporary life. 'Then we sweated away for no reason to win a phantom?' asks Menelaus' subordinate in aggrieved incredulity at line 705 of this play. Why did the Greeks fight the Trojan war? What did they gain in the end? What indeed are the Greeks fighting for centuries later, in the Peloponnesian war which was still in progress when *Helen* was produced? These questions are implicit in the play, sometimes aired explicitly. They are not explored with the intensity that might have been expected, in this genre or from the poet of the *Trojan Women*; rather, they are presented through a witty and ingenious, innovative plot which charms and entertains the audience without entirely obscuring the darker implications of the dramatic situation.

Helen has often puzzled modern audiences and critics, poised as it is between the serious and the comical. Some have sought to solve the critical issue by labels: melodrama, tragi-comedy, escapist drama. But although *Helen* undoubtedly has many humorous touches (not least the confrontation of the self-important Menelaus, dressed in rags, with the bad-tempered door-keeper who sends him packing), it would be an unsatisfying reading that excluded the play's more serious aspects. Absurd the premises of the play may be, but it remains the case that many men have died and a whole society has been wiped out for no good reason; the discovery of the truth about the phantom cannot restore Teucer's brother or Helen's mother. The glamour of the war is reduced: Menelaus seems ridiculous in his boastfulness about his achievements on the Trojan plain. When the chorus, near the end of the play, lament the folly of warfare in general, this is suited to their character and situation, but it is difficult not to suppose that these lines spoke powerfully to a war-wearied generation (1151–64). Different members of the Athenian audience might enjoy the play as a delightful entertainment which offered a welcome distraction from their troubles, or they might ponder the serious point that seems to be hinted at in the myth of the phantom Helen – that all such goals are illusion, and that the profits of human ambition dissolve when gained. Euripides allows them, and us, to stress whichever side we find more congenial.

CHARACTERS

[The scene is an unspecific settlement in northern Egypt, near the mouth of the Nile. In front stand the palace of the king and, to the left of the central double-doors, the tomb of Proteus, where HELEN has taken sanctuary.]

HELEN: Here flow the lovely virgin streams of the Nile. When the white snows melt, he slakes the soil of Egypt's plain, bringing to the land the water that heaven's rain withholds.[1] While he lived, the king of this land was Proteus, who married one of the sea-nymphs, Psamathe, one-time bride of Aeacus. In this palace she gave birth to two children, a boy, Theoclymenus, and a noble maid, called Eido in her childhood, her mother's pride and joy. But when she grew to womanhood and was ripe for marriage, they gave her the name Theonoe, as she possessed divine knowledge of all things present and to come, a gift she inherited from her grandfather Nereus.[2]

My homeland, one of no less renown, is not here; it is Sparta, and my father was Tyndareus.[3] It is true there is a story that Zeus assumed the form of a swan and, being pursued by an eagle, flew for refuge into my mother Leda's lap, where he stole, together with her trust, her maidenhood. Such is my origin, if the tale be true. Helen is my name. I will now share with you the story of my misfortunes.

Rivals in beauty, they came to Ida's glen to the home of Paris, the three goddesses – Hera, the Cyprian and the maiden daughter of Zeus – each one wishing to be judged first in the contest.[4] The Cyprian won; she lured Paris with the bait of my beauty – if there is any beauty in misfortune – and the prospect

of my hand in marriage. And so Paris of Ida quit his cattle-shed[5]
and came to Sparta to claim me as his bride. But Hera was
vexed at not defeating the other goddesses. She turned my
marriage to Paris to thin air and presented to King Priam's son
not me but a living image she had made in my likeness,
fashioned from the air of heaven.[6] He idly fancied that he held
me in his arms, but he did not: what he held was an empty
illusion.

Again the plans of Zeus work to reinforce these sorrows.[7]
He caused the land of Greece to clash in war with the wretched
Trojans, to lighten Mother Earth's vast burden of mortals, and
to bring fame to the greatest warrior of Greece. When Trojans
laboured in the field of battle and Greeks competed for the
prize, it was not for me they fought, but my name alone.
Hermes took me up, wrapped in a cloud, and, transporting me
amid the hidden vaults of aether – Zeus had not forgotten me
– he set me down here in the palace of Proteus, judging him
to be the most virtuous of all mortals, so that I might keep my
honour as Menelaus' wife unsullied. Here, then, I have lived,
while my unfortunate husband mustered an army and sailed
off to Troy's walled town to hunt down his stolen wife. Many
a warrior met his end by Scamander's streams on my account;
and I, who have suffered so much, have curses heaped on me,
while men think I betrayed my husband and involved Greeks
in a costly war.

Why, then, am I still living? Because I have been given this
assurance by the god Hermes: once my husband learns that I
did not go to Troy, I will yet live at his side in Sparta's famous
land, provided that I do not take a lover. While Proteus saw
the sunlight, my honour was unsullied; but now that he lies
dead, wrapped in Earth's darkness, his son Theoclymenus
desires my hand in marriage with a hunter's passion. Because I
honour my husband of all these years, I lie here as a suppliant[8]
at the tomb of Proteus, asking that he keep me chaste for my
wedded lord; in Greece my name may be reviled but here I
will not have my body so disgraced.

[TEUCER *enters from the sea-coast to the spectator's right. At first he is unaware of* HELEN.]

TEUCER: This is an impressive palace – who is its master? That   70
royal circuit and corniced architecture make it a residence to
compare with Plutus' own!⁹

[*He sees* HELEN *at the tomb.*] Ah! You gods, what sight is
this? It is that loathsome woman, her very image, the murderous
creature who brought ruin on me and all the Greeks! How like
Helen you are – oh, may the gods detest you for it! If this were
not foreign soil I was standing on, this fine arrow of mine
would have taken your life in payment for your resemblance
to the daughter of Zeus!

HELEN: My misguided fellow, who are you? Why do you turn
away from me and hate me because of that woman's misfortunes?

TEUCER: I made a mistake; I should not have allowed my anger   80
to get the better of me like that. All Greece feels hatred for the
daughter of Zeus. Please excuse my words, lady.

HELEN: Who are you? What land have you left to voyage to this
country?

TEUCER: I am one of the wretched Greeks, lady . . .

HELEN: Ah, no wonder, then, that you hate Helen!

TEUCER: . . . and I am an exile, banished from my native soil.   90

HELEN: Poor man! Who has driven you from your country?

TEUCER: Telamon, my father; can any man be closer to me in
blood?

HELEN: What reason had he? Something terrible must lie behind
his action.

TEUCER: Ajax my brother died at Troy and so brought ruin on
me.

HELEN: How? It wasn't your sword, surely, that robbed him of
life?

TEUCER: It was his own sword and his own action that killed
him.

HELEN: Had he lost his senses? No sane man would have dared
such a deed!

TEUCER: You have heard of Achilles, Peleus' son?

HELEN: Yes; he came once as one of Helen's suitors, I am told.

100 TEUCER: He died and became the cause of a dispute between his fellow warriors over his armour.[10]

HELEN: And how did that prove harmful to Ajax?

TEUCER: Another man was awarded the armour, and so he ended his life.

HELEN: So your own troubles stem from his misfortune?

TEUCER: Yes; because I was not at his side to share his death.

HELEN: Then you too went to Troy's glorious city, stranger?

TEUCER: Yes, and I played my part in its sacking, though the price was my own ruin.

HELEN: Is it now burnt and levelled?

TEUCER: Aye; you cannot make out even a trace of where the walls stood.

HELEN: O Helen, you wretch, you are the cause of the Trojans' ruin!

110 TEUCER: And the Greeks' too; she is disaster's architect.

HELEN: How long is it since the city was laid waste?

TEUCER: Nearly seven years have come round and passed on their way.

HELEN: And before that how long did you spend at Troy?

TEUCER: Moon upon moon, ten long years in all.

HELEN: And did you capture her, the woman of Sparta?

TEUCER: Menelaus took her and dragged her off by the hair.

HELEN: Did you set eyes on the wretched woman or do you speak from hearsay?

TEUCER: I saw her as clearly as my eyes see you now.

HELEN: But consider: could she have been something that the gods made you all imagine?

120 TEUCER: Enough of her; talk on another subject.

HELEN: Is Menelaus now in his home, with his wife?

TEUCER: He is not in Argos or by Eurotas' stream.

HELEN: Ah, that is unwelcome news for those it affects.

TEUCER: In fact, he is reported as having vanished, and his wife with him.

HELEN: Not all the Greeks sailed home together, then?

TEUCER: They did, but a storm drove them all in different directions.[11]

HELEN: What waters were they sailing when it broke?

TEUCER: They were in mid-Aegean, halfway in their crossing.   130

HELEN: And since that time no one knows if Menelaus has made land?

TEUCER: No one; but the word throughout Greece is that he is dead.

HELEN [aside]: I am ruined! [To TEUCER again] And the daughter of Thestios, is she alive?

TEUCER: Leda, you mean? No, she is dead and gone.

HELEN: It wasn't Helen's infamy, was it, that drove her to death?

TEUCER: Yes; the story is that the noble lady hanged herself.

HELEN: And her sons by Tyndareus, are they alive or not?

TEUCER: They are dead and not dead; two accounts exist.[12]

HELEN: Which is the more reliable? [Aside] Oh, this tale of woe breaks my heart!

TEUCER: Men say they have been translated to the stars and are   140
gods.

HELEN: That is welcome news! But what is the other version?

TEUCER: That their sister's conduct made them end their lives with the sword. But enough of these stories; I have no wish to weep twice over. It was my desire to see the prophetess Theonoe that brought me to this royal dwelling. Will you act as my intermediary? I wish to gain her inspired guidance on how to steer a favourable course to the isle of Cyprus, for there, Apollo's oracle has said, I am to settle and give the name of Salamis to my new home, in remembrance of the island of my   150
birth.[13]

HELEN: The voyage will make this clear to you, sir, without help. But you must leave this land and take flight before its ruler, the son of Proteus, sees you. For the present he is away, hunting wild beasts with the help of his hounds, keen for blood. He executes any Greek stranger[14] who falls into his

hands. As to why he does this, do not try to find out; you will
hear nothing from my lips. What good would it do you?

TEUCER: Good advice, my lady, and thank you. I pray the gods
160   may reward you for your generous spirit. You may resemble
Helen in appearance but in heart you are not like her, indeed
very different. May she never reach the waters of Eurotas but
come to a foul end! But for you, my lady, my prayer is unending
prosperity!

> [TEUCER *exits in haste.* HELEN *now sings of her sorrow and is
> joined after the first stanza by the* CHORUS *in a lyric exchange.*[15]]

HELEN: *Oh, these are great sorrows I launch upon and great is the
pity they merit! What manner of lamentation should I utter, what
inspiration seek for my tears, my dirge, my anguish? Ah, me!*

[Strophe:] *Come, you Sirens,[16] winged maids, virgin daughters of*
170   *Earth, come, I pray, bearing the Libyan flute or pipes or lyres to blend
with my lament, with tears to suit my cries of sorrow, grief matching
grief, song matching song! Oh, send me your music to harmonize with
my laments, music of death, so that down in her palace of night
Persephone may receive from me as my tribute a tearful hymn for the
dead and departed!*

[*Enter* CHORUS.]

180 CHORUS [Antistrophe]: *By the pool's dark surface, on the curling
spring grass, it happened I was spreading[17] my crimson robes to dry
them in the warmth of the sun's golden rays, hard by the young reeds.
From there it was I heard a piteous sound, a song of sorrow not fit for
any lyre, a cry of grief and pain such as some river-nymph might utter
when, caught in the depths of a rocky cavern, she succumbs, screaming,
to the lust of Pan.*

190 HELEN [Strophe]: *Daughters of Greece, captives of a foreign fleet, a
Greek sailor has come, has come,[18] bringing with him tears to crown
my tears. Troy lies in ruins, consigned to enemy fire, and blame falls
on me, the death of warriors past number, and on my name, author of*
200   *untold woe. Leda is dead by her own hands; she hanged herself in
anguish at my shame. My husband, after all his wanderings on the
deep, has perished and is gone. Castor and his brother, twin glory of*

my homeland, have vanished, vanished, leaving the plain that echoed
to their horses' hoofs and the wrestling ground by reedy Eurotas where
their fellows exercised their young limbs.   210

CHORUS [Antistrophe]: Ah, lady, I pity you for your fate and woeful
destiny! A life not worth the living fell to you that day when, gleaming
through the aether, Zeus, clothed in the snow-white feathers of a swan,
cast his seed in your mother's womb! What misery has not afflicted
you? What have you not endured all through your life? Your mother
is no more; good fortune has deserted your two brothers, beloved children
of Zeus; the land of your birth is denied your sight; the talk of every
town is that you, my lady, have been given in marriage to a foreigner;
your own husband's life is lost at sea among the ocean waves, and
never again will you bring joy to your father's palace and the Lady of
the Bronze Temple.[19]

HELEN [Epode]: Ah, who on earth was he, Trojan or son of Greece,   230
whose hand felled the pine whose timbers would bring tears to Troy?[20]
From these was fashioned the accursed ship that Priam's son with his
eastern oarsmen sailed to my home, and sharing the voyage came the
Cyprian, murderous goddess, full of wiles, bringing death to the sons
of Danaus. Oh, how wretched, how unfortunate am I!

   Then Hera who sits on her throne of gold, august bedfellow of Zeus,
dispatched the swift-footed son of Maia,[21] who found me gathering
fresh rose petals in my dress to take as an offering to Athena of the
Bronze House in her temple. Seizing me, he carried me through the
air to this unhappy land, and so established discord, miserable discord,
between Greece and the sons of Priam. But my name, lingering by   250
Simois' water, is falsely slandered.

CHORUS-LEADER: Your lot is a miserable one, I know, but your
best course lies in bearing life's burdens as lightly as possible.

HELEN: Good women, friends, what fate am I chained to? Did
my mother bring me into the world for people to stare at as a
freak? My life has certainly been grotesque, and the troubles I   260
have, partly thanks to Hera, partly to my beauty. Oh, if only I
could be wiped out like a painted picture and start afresh with
a plainer look instead of this beauty! Then the Greeks could

forget the ill fate I now labour under and recall what does me credit, as they now remember what does not!

When you set your sights on one ambition and then are cheated of this by the gods, it is hard to bear but must be endured. Yet I am weighed down by sorrows in battalions.

270 Firstly, I have done nothing wrong and yet my name is reviled. When someone is punished though innocent of crime, it is a worse affliction than getting his just deserts. Then, the gods have transplanted me from my homeland to an exotic race, where I live bereft of friends, a free woman no longer but instead a slave; for in a land of this sort everyone is a slave apart from one man.[22] There was one anchor alone which secured my fortunes, the hope that my husband would one day return and free me from my troubles. But he is dead and so that hope

280 is no more. My mother has perished, and men say I am her murderer; this guilt does, however guiltlessly, belong to me. As for my daughter, the pride and joy of her home and her mother, she has no husband and grows grey in virginity.[23] The two Dioscuri, Zeus' sons, as men call them, are gone. Since my life is so utterly wretched, I am as good as dead, though I

[290] still live.

Why, then, should I continue with life? What fate remains for me? To exchange this misery for marriage and live with a man of foreign birth, sitting at a bountiful table? No; when a woman finds her husband offensive, her own looks offend her

[300] as well. This is how low I have sunk in my desperation: other women find their beauty a blessing, but mine has only brought ruin!

CHORUS-LEADER: Helen, it may be wrong to think that the stranger who has come, whoever he may be, has spoken the whole truth.

HELEN: Well, he was clear enough in saying my husband is dead.

CHORUS-LEADER: Many things could be expressed clearly and yet be false.

310 HELEN: Yes, and not so clearly and still be true.

CHORUS-LEADER: You have a fair prospect before you but veer off towards disaster.

HELEN: Fear has me in his net and drives me on to what I dread.

CHORUS-LEADER: Whose goodwill can you count on in the palace here?

HELEN: All of them are my friends, except the one who wants to ensnare me in marriage.

CHORUS-LEADER: This is what you must do: leave the sanctuary of the tomb . . .

HELEN: What are you going to say? What will you advise?

CHORUS-LEADER: . . . and go to the house of Theonoe the all-knowing, daughter of the ocean Nereid, and enquire of her whether your husband still lives or is no more; and when you have clear knowledge of this, then let your tears — of joy or sorrow — flow accordingly. Before you know anything for certain, what will you gain from grief? Do as I advise. I, too, wish to enter her house with you[24] and to learn the maid's holy words; women should support one another. 320

[HELEN *and the* CHORUS *now sing in a lyric dialogue that culminates in a monody from* HELEN, *lamenting Troy's fate and her own.*]

HELEN: *Friends, I accept your words of counsel; onward, on into the palace to learn what trials await me within.* 330

CHORUS: *I am ready to act; no need for further prompting.*

HELEN: *O wretched day! I shudder — whatever doleful answer will I hear?*

CHORUS: *Dear lady, do not prophesy sorrow yet nor weep too soon!*

HELEN: *My poor husband, what cruel fate has overtaken him? Do his eyes behold the sun's bright course through the heavens and the journeying stars, or does he dwell in endless exile below the earth, companioned by the dead?* 340

CHORUS: *Accept the future, whatever may befall, and turn it to your advantage.*

HELEN [*not heeding*]: *On you I call, Eurotas, swirling green between your reedy banks, by you I swear this oath, if report of my lord's death* 350 be true – what can they mean, these veiled tidings? – I will take my own life,[25] my neck in a choking noose, swinging high, or else I will drive a sword into myself, its murderous blade eager to make the blood leap forth in slaughter, a swift thrust through the flesh to offer myself as a sacrifice to the three goddesses, and to Priam's son who dwelt once in a cavern on Ida where he kept his cows.

360 CHORUS: May such horrors fall upon other heads and your own fortunes prosper!

HELEN: O Troy, city of sorrow, for deeds never committed you have perished and suffered a piteous end! I was the Cyprian's gift to you, a gift that engendered so much blood, so many tears, anguish and woe past telling, as mothers lost their sons and sisters unwed cut off their hair in honour of the dead, by Phrygian Scamander's stream.

370   Throughout the land of Hellas, too, the cry of grief rings loud and shrill, as hands descend on prostrate heads and soft-skinned cheeks grow bloody from raking nails.[26]

[The CHORUS by now has withdrawn into the palace.]

O blessed Callisto, Arcadian maid, who long ago was loved by Zeus, how much kinder was your fate than mine, though your two limbs became four![27] You took on the guise of a shaggy-limbed creature of the 380 wild, a fierce-eyed beast in shape, a lioness, and thus shed the burden of your grief. And blessed, too, in time gone by was the Titan maid, Merops' child, whose beauty made Artemis drive her from her company, transformed into a hind with horns of gold. But my beauty has brought ruin, ruin to the towers of Troy and the Greeks who perished there!

[HELEN, head bowed with anguish, enters the palace. MENELAUS enters in rags.]

MENELAUS: O Pelops,[28] who raced with Oenomaus once at Pisa in the famous chariot-race, I wish you had died that day, before 390 siring my father Atreus, who in turn sired by his wife Aerope Agamemnon and myself, Menelaus, famous pair! In my view – and I say this in no boastful vein[29] – I transported the greatest part of our troops in ships to Troy, no despot leading an army by force but a ruler commanding as his willing followers the young warriors of Greece.

Some of these men the roll-call can number as dead, others as having returned to their homes, happy survivors of the sea, whose loved ones had given them up for dead. But my case is different; ever since I sacked Troy's towered walls, I have wandered in misery over the grey sea's swollen depths, longing   400 to reach my homeland but deemed unworthy of this by the gods. Every desolate landfall, every inhospitable anchorage on Libya's coast has seen my vessel. And each time I draw near to my country's shores, strong winds drive me away; no favourable breeze ever swells my sails to bring me back to Greece.

And now I find myself driven on to this shore, a miserable castaway who has lost his friends, my ship shattered in a hundred   410 pieces on the rocks. Of all its sections so skilfully constructed only the keel survived, and on this, with much difficulty, and greatly to my surprise, I reached safety, and with me Helen, who is in my possession, after I dragged her out of Troy. I do not know the name of this land or of its inhabitants; it would have been embarrassing to meet ordinary people and so, out of respect for my own feelings, I am not revealing my predicament. When misfortune strikes a man in high position, its unfamiliarity hits him harder than one long accustomed to ill luck. My beggar's state drains me; I have neither food nor   420 clothes for my back; you could mistake these rags I'm wearing for remnants of my ship's canvas. The clothes I wore of old, splendid and costly robes, the ocean has plundered.[30] As for my wife, the source of all my woes, I hid her away in the depths of a cave before coming here, with strict instructions to my surviving friends to keep watch on her. I have come here on my own, looking for any provisions for them I may be able to get my hands on.

When I saw this building with its imposing entrance and   430 walls with surrounding cornices, indicating a man of means, I approached it; seafarers may hope to gain something from a wealthy house, but we could get nothing from those with nothing to live on, however willing they may be to help. [MENELAUS knocks hard on the central door.] Hey! Doorkeeper![31]

Come out here, will you? I want you to tell your master I need
his assistance.

[*An* OLD WOMAN *answers from inside, on a higher level.*]

OLD WOMAN: Who's at the door? Get away from the palace!
You'd better not stand there in the entrance, making trouble
for the master! Else it'll be death for you, Greek as you are; no
440   Greeks allowed in here!

MENELAUS: Old woman, I'm sure these words can be spoken
in a different tone; I won't be difficult; but not so angry,
please!

[*The* OLD WOMAN *opens the door and shows herself.*]

OLD WOMAN: Be off with you! It's my job, see, stranger, to
keep any Greeks away from these doors.

MENELAUS: Hang on! Don't wag your finger at me or try
pushing me away!

OLD WOMAN: It's your fault for not taking a blind bit of notice
of what I say!

MENELAUS: Then take this message inside to your master: . . .

OLD WOMAN: I don't think a message from you would do me
much good.

MENELAUS: . . . I've come to his land, a stranger and a castaway;
no one dares harm me.

450 OLD WOMAN: Then find another house to go to, not this one!

MENELAUS: I will not. I'm coming in. Don't try to stop me!

OLD WOMAN: You're a right nuisance, make no mistake! Any
minute now you'll find yourself out on your ear!

MENELAUS: Oh dear! Where is that glorious army of mine?

OLD WOMAN: You may have cut a fine figure in front of them,
but you don't in front of me!

MENELAUS: O you gods, what indignity to suffer!

OLD WOMAN: What's this? Tears in your eyes! Who's going to
feel sorry for you?

MENELAUS: The gods once looked on me with favour.

OLD WOMAN: Then go and cry in front of your friends.

MENELAUS: What country is this? Whose is this palace?

460 OLD WOMAN: This is Proteus' palace; the land is Egypt.

MENELAUS: Egypt? Heaven help me, what a place to have come to!

OLD WOMAN: And just what's wrong with the gleaming Nile, I'd like to know?

MENELAUS: I find nothing wrong; I was lamenting my own misfortunes.

OLD WOMAN: Bad luck comes to many people; you're not the only one.

MENELAUS: Is he at home, then, this king, whatever you called him?

OLD WOMAN: This is his tomb. His son is king now.

MENELAUS: And where would he be? Away from home or in the palace?

OLD WOMAN: He is not at home. And he really hates Greeks.

MENELAUS: Tell me so that I may benefit.

OLD WOMAN: Helen resides in this palace, the daughter of Zeus. 470

MENELAUS: What? What did you say? Tell me again!

OLD WOMAN: The child of Tyndareus, who once lived in Sparta.

MENELAUS: But where did she come from? This makes no sense!

OLD WOMAN: Why, she came here from Lacedaemon's land.

MENELAUS: When? [*Aside*] I haven't had my wife stolen from that cave, have I?

OLD WOMAN: It was before the Greeks went to Troy, stranger. Now be off, please. We've had a real to-do in here; it's turning the palace upside down. This is a very bad time for you to arrive; if the master catches you, you'll be killed – that's the 480 welcome he'd give! I quite like Greeks, you see, for all my harsh words earlier; it was because I'm afraid of the master. [*The* OLD WOMAN *goes back into the palace, shutting the door against* MENELAUS.]

MENELAUS: I don't understand. What am I to make of it? This new turn of events I'm hearing of makes things even more wretched than before. Can it be that I captured my wife in Troy, brought her here with me and put her in a cave for safe-keeping, and now I find another woman, with the same name as my wife, living in this palace? And, according to the

490 old woman, she is the daughter of Zeus! Can there be some
man with the name of Zeus living on the banks of the Nile?
There's only one Zeus, the one in heaven. And where on earth
does Sparta exist, if not where fair Eurotas' reed-fringed waters
flow? Are there two men called by the name of Tyndareus? Is
there another land called Lacedaemon, another Troy? I just
don't know what to say! Well, the world is a big place, after
all, and many men no doubt have the same names – many
women, too, and many cities. There's little to wonder at in this.

500 And I'm not going to be put off by a servant's scaremongering.
There's not a man so uncivilized as to refuse me food once he
has heard my name.[32] It was a famous fire that Troy saw and
famous too am I who kindled it, Menelaus, a name the world
knows well. I will wait for the king of this palace. There are
two ways I have of protecting myself: if he is a man of savage
temperament, I'll hide and make my way back to my wrecked
ship; if he shows any clemency, I'll ask for the sort of help my

510 present troubles require. This, then, is the final humiliation
waiting for me in my misery, that I, a king myself, should beg
a fellow king for bread to live by! But there is no alternative.
It is not my own saying, but a wise man's none the less, that
nothing is as strong as stern necessity.

[MENELAUS *withdraws into a temporary hiding place. The*
CHORUS *emerges from the palace.*]

CHORUS: *I heard the prophetic maid utter the response I went eagerly
to the royal palace to learn. She said that Menelaus has not yet passed
from sight to the gloomy shades of the nether world but continues to be*

520 *tossed on the high seas and has not yet made port in his native land.
He leads a wanderer's life, sick at heart, bereft of friends, and scarce a
land exists between here and Troy that has not seen his ship draw near
its coast.*

[HELEN *also comes out of the palace.*]

HELEN: Back I come again to my sanctuary at this tomb, after
hearing Theonoe's welcome words! [HELEN *starts back as*

MENELAUS *steps forward to intercept her.*] Ah! Who is this? Surely [530]
Proteus' godless son is not scheming to have me ambushed? [540]
I'll make a dash for the tomb like some filly at the gallop or
worshipper of Bacchus! Oh, he's a wild-looking sort of man,
this fellow bent on catching me!

MENELAUS: Why this desperate urge to get to the base of the
tomb with its smoke-blackened uprights? Wait! Why do you
run away from me? Oh, that face! You amaze me – I cannot
speak!

HELEN [*as* MENELAUS *continues to block her path*]: Good women,   550
this is an outrage! This fellow is keeping me from the tomb;
he means to catch me and deliver me to the king whose
marriage I shun!

MENELAUS [*stepping back indignantly*]: I am no criminal – no one
has pressed me into doing wrong!

HELEN: Well, that's hardly a gentleman's clothing you're
wearing.

MENELAUS: Don't be afraid, stop darting back and forth!

HELEN [*skipping past him at last*]: I'll stop all right, now I've got
my hands on this tomb!

MENELAUS: Who are you? That face of yours . . . who am I
looking at, lady?

HELEN: And who are you? I might well ask you the same
question!

MENELAUS: Never have I seen anyone so close in looks . . .

HELEN: O you gods! Yes, there is something godlike in recogniz-   560
ing loved ones.

MENELAUS: Are you Greek or a woman of this country?

HELEN: I am Greek; but I want to know your background
also.

MENELAUS: You look so like Helen, lady.

HELEN: And you so like Menelaus; I am lost for words.

MENELAUS: You have recognized me correctly, a man detested
by fortune.

HELEN [*trying to embrace him*]: Oh, how long it has been! Embrace
your wife!

MENELAUS [*shocked*]: What do you mean, *wife*? Hands off my clothes!

HELEN: I was given to you by my father Tyndareus.

MENELAUS: O torch-bearing Hecate,[33] send me no evil dreams!

570 HELEN: This is no ghostly night-vision you are looking at, sent by the Lady of the Cross-ways!

MENELAUS: But I can't be married to two wives!

HELEN: Another wife? No! Who is she?

MENELAUS: The one I left hidden in a cave after bringing her back from Troy.

HELEN: You have no other wife, just myself.

MENELAUS: Perhaps I have not lost my wits but my eyes are failing.

HELEN: When you look at me, don't you think I'm your wife?

MENELAUS: You have her appearance, certainly, but I am not yet sure.

HELEN: Look at me: what clearer proof do you need?

MENELAUS: You are like her; that I won't deny.

580 HELEN: What better instructor could you have than your own eyes?

MENELAUS: My difficulty is this: I already have a wife.

HELEN: I did not go to the land of Troy; it was my phantom.

MENELAUS: And who can create a living, breathing phantom?

HELEN: The gods; they fashioned a wife for you from the air itself!

MENELAUS: Which of the gods was her maker? What you say defies belief.

HELEN: Hera fashioned her as a substitute so that Paris would not get his hands on me.

MENELAUS: What? Then you were at one and the same time here and at Troy?

HELEN: A name might exist anywhere but its owner can only be in one place.

MENELAUS [*shaking his head*]: Let me go; I have come here with grief enough for cargo.

HELEN: What? You are going to leave me for a wife who does 590
not exist?

MENELAUS: I am, but you have my blessing for your resemblance
to Helen.

HELEN: This is the end! I win you back, my husband, only to
lose you again!

MENELAUS: You do not convince me as much as the thought of
all the sufferings I knew at Troy.

HELEN [*breaking down*]: Oh, how wretched I am! Was any woman
more to be pitied? The love of my life is leaving me and never
shall I live in my own land again, or see my fellow-Greeks!

[*As* MENELAUS *leaves, he is intercepted by an old* SERVANT,
one of his men.]

SERVANT: Menelaus, sir, I find you at last! I've wandered all over
this god-forsaken place in search of you, sent by the crew you
left behind.

MENELAUS: What's happened? You haven't been robbed by the 600
natives, I take it?

SERVANT: A miracle, though miracle doesn't do justice to what
happened.

MENELAUS: Speak up; this emphasis suggests strange news
indeed.

SERVANT: I say you went through all your sufferings to no
purpose.

MENELAUS: They are over now and in the past; what is your
news?

SERVANT: Your wife has gone, vanished into the air! Up she
went and disappeared from sight! The heavens opened and she
was gone; the haunted cave where we had kept our watch held
her no more, and this is what she said: 'You wretched men of
Troy, and all you poor Greeks, it was thanks to Hera and her 610
scheming that you met your deaths for my sake by Scamander's
banks; you thought that Paris possessed Helen but he did not!
Now that I have stayed for the appointed length of time and
obeyed the plan of destiny, I am returning to my father, the
sky. They were all undeserved, the foul words heaped on the

head of Tyndareus' miserable child; she was not to blame.' [*He suddenly sees* HELEN.] Ah, greetings, daughter of Leda! Here you were all along! There I was, making my report that you had vanished among the stars, and I never knew you had wings to make you airborne! [*He steps forward to grasp* HELEN *by the arm*.] Now I won't let you make fools of us like that again; you gave your husband quite enough trouble at Troy, him and the men who fought at his side!

MENELAUS [*raising his arm to forestall the* SERVANT]: I see it now; it's true, what she said earlier, true! [*Embracing Helen*] Oh, how I have longed for this day that lets me fold you in my arms!

[*Husband and wife now engage in a duet in which the former mainly speaks, the latter mainly sings.*[34]]

HELEN: *O Menelaus, dearest love, how slowly the years passed, but now what joy, for you are here!* [*To the* CHORUS] *See, ladies, I have my husband, after so many dawns lighting the sky with fire, I have my arms around his neck!*

MENELAUS: And you are in my arms. But so much has happened and there are so many things I want to know; I don't know where my questioning should begin!

HELEN: *Oh, what happiness! My hair shivers with joy* [*tossing her head*], *it has wings to make it fly! My eyes brim with tears as I discover anew, dear husband, the pleasure of holding you close!*

MENELAUS: No vision could please me more; all pain is cancelled. I hold my wife, the child of Zeus and Leda.

HELEN: *Whom her brothers, Heaven's Twins, once hailed as happy, happy, as, torches in hand, they rode their white horses . . .*

MENELAUS: Yes, in those days; and now the goddess who took you from my home steers us on a different course, better than this.

HELEN: *It was a happy misfortune that brought us together, you and me, my husband, apart for so long but together at last! May I live to enjoy what the gods have granted!*

MENELAUS: May you indeed; I join you in voicing the same prayer! Where we two are concerned, there is no unhappiness that is not shared.

HELEN [*to the* CHORUS]: *My friends, my friends, no longer do we grieve for sorrows past, or give way to anguish. I have him, my husband, my husband, the one for whom I waited, waited so many years, to return from Troy!* 650

MENELAUS: You have him, and I have you! So many days of hardship I endured, but now I understand the purpose of the goddess.

HELEN: *My joy makes these tears more happy than sorrowful.*

MENELAUS: What can I say? Who on earth could have hoped for this?

HELEN: *I clasp you to my heart, the person I never looked to see!*

MENELAUS: And I clasp you, the woman I thought had gone to Ida's town and Ilium's ill-fated towers! But in heaven's name 660 how did you make your escape from my home?

HELEN: *Ah, it is a painful beginning you seek to return to, a painful story you would have me narrate.*

MENELAUS: Speak, for I must hear it; all things are in the giving of the gods.

HELEN: *It disgusts me, the tale I shall be bound to tell!*

MENELAUS: Tell it just the same! Hearing of sufferings can bring pleasure.

HELEN: *Not to the beat of oars did the barbarian youth come, to win a bride, but to satisfy a beating heart's desire for a lawless marriage!*

MENELAUS: Which god or fate stole you from your home-land?

HELEN: *The son of Zeus, of Zeus and Maia, my husband, brought me* 670 *to the Nile.*

MENELAUS: Remarkable! Who sent you on your way? It is a strange tale.

HELEN: *I weep at the memory, my eyes grow wet with tears; the wife of Zeus was my destroyer.*

MENELAUS: Hera? What further harm did she want to heap on us?

HELEN: *Oh, the pain of remembering that spring, the bathing place where the goddesses shone in their beauty, that day they came to be judged!*

MENELAUS: Then did Hera punish you for the indignity of that judgement?

680 HELEN: *Her aim was to take me from Paris . . .*

MENELAUS: How? Tell me!

HELEN: *. . . to whom the Cyprian had promised me.*

MENELAUS: Oh, a cruel fate!

HELEN: *Cruel it was, cruel, when I was thus brought to Egypt.*

MENELAUS: Then, she substituted a phantom in your place, as you tell the story.

HELEN: *O my mother, what misery, what misery your house suffered!*

MENELAUS: What do you mean?

HELEN: *My mother is no more; she hanged herself in a swinging noose in shame at my infamous marriage.*

MENELAUS: Monstrous! What report is there of our daughter Hermione?

HELEN: *A stranger to marriage and to children herself, my husband, she*
690 *laments my shameful union, itself no true marriage.*

MENELAUS: O Paris, how utterly you have brought ruin on my house!

HELEN: *These things have destroyed not you alone but countless men of Greece in their armour of bronze. But I was driven by the goddess from my homeland, driven ill-fated and accursed from my city and from you, that day when I left behind – and yet did not – home and husband to make a marriage of shame!*

CHORUS-LEADER: Should good fortune come to you both from this day on, you would have recompense for your sufferings hitherto.

700 SERVANT: Menelaus, sir, give me, too, a share in your happiness; I can see it for myself but I'm still in the dark.

MENELAUS: Of course, old fellow, you also must share in our news.

SERVANT: Was this lady not the cause of everything we went through at Ilium?

MENELAUS: She was not; we were deceived by the gods.

SERVANT: Then we sweated away for no reason to win a phantom?

MENELAUS: This was the work of Hera, of the three goddesses who quarrelled.

SERVANT: Eh? This woman is really your wife?

MENELAUS: Yes, she is; trust me when I say it.   710

SERVANT [*turning to* HELEN *and raising his hands*]: Well, daughter, how intricate are the gods' ways, how hard to fathom,[35] but somehow they bring everything safely back on course, directing things now this way, now that. One man knows hardship, another avoids it, but still he comes to a sorry end; there is no security in the luck he enjoys from one day to the next. Now you and your husband had your share of suffering – you in the matter of your reputation, he in the unsparing test of war. How hard he laboured then, and for such a poor return, but now, without raising a finger, he has won the greatest of good fortune. So you did not bring shame on your old father   720 or the Dioscuri, you did none of the things that earned you a bad name!

Now I recall your wedding, now I remember the torches I held high as I ran alongside your team of four horses! There you stood in the chariot, at this man's side, as you left your wealthy home. After all, it's a poor kind of servant who doesn't respect his master's fortune, sharing his joys and sorrows alike. I may have been born a servant but I would have my place in the roll-call of noble slaves, having a mind, if not a name, that   730 is free.[36] This is a better state of affairs than being one person yet the victim of two evils: possessing a heart that is false and, as a slave, being at the beck and call of those near you.

MENELAUS: Come on, old fellow, you've known many hard-ships in the past, as you toiled away in battle with your shield next to mine, so now share in my good fortune; go and tell the friends you left behind how you've found matters here and what our situation is. Their orders are to stay on the shore in readiness for the trials which I expect await me if I am to   740 succeed in taking this woman away from here, and to watch for the opportunity for us to unite our fortunes and get safely away from this forsaken place, if we can.

SERVANT: I shall do this, my lord, but just consider how useless
and full of lies prophecy is! There is, it seems, no reliability in
divination by fire or the screaming of birds. Only a simpleton
thinks that men are benefited by birds! Calchas gave no word,
750   no indication to the army that he saw his countrymen dying
for a phantom's sake, no, nor did Helenus; we sacked that city
all for nothing! You may say the reason was the gods' reluctance
to let the truth be known. Why, then, do we seek to know
their minds through prophecy? When we ask for benefits, we
should sacrifice to the gods, but pay no heed to the trade of
prophecy. This was a barren invention, a bait to catch men's
minds; no one ever grew rich from being idle or putting his
faith in burnt sacrifices. Judgement and prudence are a man's
best means of divination.

CHORUS-LEADER: I share the old man's view of prophets; if a
760   man has the gods' goodwill, he has the best omen for his house.

HELEN: Very well; so far our situation continues fair. But I long
to know, my poor husband, how you came safe away from
Troy, though it would profit me little.

MENELAUS: How large a question put directly in so few words!
Why need I tell you of our losses in the Aegean, when Nauplius
lit his fires on Euboea's coast,[37] of the cities of Crete and Libya
that I visited, and the look-out where Perseus kept watch?[38]
770   My tale would not satisfy your curiosity, and, in telling you
how we suffered, my own sorrows would return.

HELEN: Your answer is wiser than my question. But pass over
the rest and tell me one thing: how long did you wander
exhausted over the ocean's briny depths?

MENELAUS: Seven circling years I spent on board ship, not
counting the ten I had to endure at Troy.

HELEN: Oh, how wretched! What a long time you tell of, my
poor dear! And now you have escaped that fate to meet the
sacrificial knife here!

MENELAUS: What's that? What are you telling me? This destroys
[780]   me, wife!

HELEN: The man who dwells in this palace is sure to kill you.

MENELAUS: And what have I done to merit this end?

HELEN: You have arrived without warning to thwart his marriage to me.

MENELAUS: What? Someone wants to marry my wife?

HELEN: An act of outrage against me, even if I submitted.

MENELAUS: Is he an ordinary citizen seeking to enforce his will, or does he rule the land?

HELEN: He is the son of Proteus and ruler of this land.

MENELAUS: That explains the servant's words that puzzled me so much.

HELEN: What gates did you stand at in this outlandish place?

MENELAUS: These ones, before they drove me away like some   790
mendicant.

HELEN: You weren't begging for bread, surely? Oh, what have I to endure next!

MENELAUS: That is what I was doing but I'm not happy with the description.

HELEN: It seems you know everything, then, about my marriage-to-be.

MENELAUS: I do; but what I don't know is, have you resisted his advances?

HELEN: Chaste I was as your wife and chaste I remain; be sure of that.

MENELAUS: How can I be sure if it? If true it would gladden my heart.

HELEN: Do you see this tomb where I have been sitting as a miserable suppliant?

MENELAUS: I see a mattress there, you wretched woman; what use did you put that to?

HELEN: That was my place of sanctuary in trying to escape this marriage!

MENELAUS: Had you no altar for this purpose, or were you   800
following a custom of the land?

HELEN: It gave me as much protection as a god's temple would.

MENELAUS: So is there no way for me to get you to a ship and safe home?

HELEN: You're more likely to feel the point of a sword than me in your arms.

MENELAUS: Then no man on earth is as wretched as I.

HELEN: Have no scruples now; make your own escape from here!

MENELAUS: And leave you behind? I sacked Troy for you!

HELEN: Better do as I say than let my marriage cause your death!

MENELAUS: That is cowardly talk, unsuited to the conqueror of Troy!

HELEN: You may be planning to kill the king but you would not succeed.

810 MENELAUS: Is his body so invulnerable to the sword?

HELEN: You will know soon; it is a fool who dares the impossible.

MENELAUS: Then am I to submit to having my wrists bound and utter not a word?

HELEN: You have reached an impasse; we need a clever plan.

MENELAUS: Yes, dying in action is the preferable course.

HELEN: There is one hope, one alone, that might enable us to escape.

MENELAUS: Does it call for bribery or daring or eloquence?

HELEN: If only the king could be prevented from learning of your arrival!

MENELAUS: He won't discover my identity, I know; who would tell him?

HELEN: Inside the palace he has an ally as potent as the gods.

820 MENELAUS: A private oracle in some secret recess of his home?

HELEN: No, his sister; they call her Theonoe.

MENELAUS: Her name is oracular;[39] tell me what she does.

HELEN: She is omniscient, and she will tell her brother that you are here.

MENELAUS: That's the end for me; I cannot keep a secret from her.

HELEN: Perhaps if we tried to win her over, throwing ourselves on her mercy . . .

MENELAUS: Asking her to do what? What hope are you offering me?

HELEN: . . . to refrain from telling her brother that you are here.

MENELAUS: Then, after persuading her, we would make our escape?

HELEN: Yes, without difficulty, if we have her help; if we try to delude her, it is impossible.

MENELAUS: I leave this to you; woman to woman is an appropri- 830
ate way to proceed.

HELEN: I'll clasp her knees like any suppliant, be sure of that!

MENELAUS: Yes, but what if she rejects our appeal?

HELEN: You will die and I will know the misery of submitting to a forced marriage.

MENELAUS: False woman! You use force as a pretext!

HELEN: No! I swear a sacred oath by your life . . .

MENELAUS: What oath – to die? Never to take another husband?

HELEN: To die, yes, and by the same sword; I will lie at your side.

MENELAUS: Then, to bind that oath, take my right hand.

HELEN [taking his hand]: And so I do; I swear to end my life if you are killed.

MENELAUS: And I swear to take my own life if I lose you. 840

HELEN: How, then, shall we die and keep our honour intact?

MENELAUS: I will kill you here on the tomb and then kill myself. But first I will mount a fierce challenge to win you. Approach, any man who dares! I shall not disgrace the glorious name I won at Troy or go back to Greece to face men's insults as the man who robbed Thetis of Achilles,[40] witnessed the corpse of Telamonian Ajax and Nestor childless, but refused to die him- 850
self for his own wife's sake! No, not I! If the gods have wisdom, the earth lies light on the tomb they give a brave man slain by his enemies; but the coward they cast up, unburied, on a hard reef.

CHORUS-LEADER: O you gods, grant happiness at last to the house of Tantalus, and bring them release from their woes!

[Voices are heard inside the palace.]

HELEN: Oh, help me! I am in such peril! Menelaus, we are ruined! She is coming out from the palace, the prophetess

181

860 Theonoe! The house resounds to the sound of bolts being
thrown back. Run! But there is no point – whether she sees
you or not, she'll know that you're here. Oh, what misery!
I'm finished! You escaped from Troy and its savagery only to
fall on savage swords here!

[THEONOE *enters from the palace, preceded by two female acolytes,
carrying an incense-burner and a torch.*][41]

THEONOE [*to first acolyte*]: Hold up the lamp in its radiance and
lead on! Fumigate in sacred ordinance every corner of the air,
so that I may breathe in heaven's pure breath! And you [*to
second acolyte*], purge with flame the path on which I am to
870 walk, lest any man has defiled it with unholy footprints, dashing
your torch on them before my feet, so I may proceed on my
way. Once you have paid my dues of service to the gods, return
the flares to their place in the hearth inside the palace. [*The
acolytes having performed this function go back into the palace.*]

Helen, have my predictions not come true? He has come,
your husband Menelaus, and there he stands before your eyes,
his ships lost, together with the phantom of yourself! Poor
man, what hardships you have overcome in getting to this
place, and still you do not know if you will return home, or if
you will remain here! For on this day there is to be a heated
debate about you among the gods, before the judgement seat
880 of Zeus. Hera, your enemy in the past, now looks on you with
favour. She wants to bring you and your wife safely to your
homeland, so that Greece may learn that Alexandros was
deceived in the Cyprian's gift of the bride he was to marry.
But the Cyprian wishes to thwart your homecoming; she has
no desire to be exposed as having bought the prize for beauty
with a marriage that, so far as Helen was concerned, was empty.
The decision rests with me, whether to oblige the Cyprian by
telling my brother you are here, so causing your death, or to
890 side in turn with Hera and save your life, deceiving my brother,
whose orders are that I tell him whenever your homeward
voyage brings you to this land.

HELEN: O maiden, I fall in supplication at your knees and entreat you in abject misery for myself and this man! I have only just found him after so long and it seems I now run every risk of seeing him dead. Please, do not tell your brother that my beloved husband has returned to my arms, but save him, I beg 900 you! Never sacrifice your own piety by purchasing tokens of his gratitude that debase your honour and justice itself! Heaven has no love of violence and would have us all possess property without recourse to robbery. My coming here was timely but it has proved no blessing to me. Hermes gave me to your father 910 to keep safe for my husband, who now stands beside me, wishing to receive his due. Would the god and your dead father want what belongs to another to be properly returned or would they not? I think they would. You should defer to a virtuous father rather than a foolish brother. You are a prophet-ess, a believer in the gods; will you taint your father's sense of 920 justice and indulge a brother who has none? Would it not shame you to know all the secrets of heaven, both past and present, but not the difference between right and wrong?

Consider my wretchedness, all the misery that is mine, and give us your protection, a step on the road to justice! Helen is a name reviled the world over. In Greece they say I betrayed my husband to live in a wealthy Trojan palace. But if I return to Greece, to a life in Sparta, and the people see and hear that 930 their ruin came from the gods' scheming, while I did not, after all, betray my loved ones, then they will once more consider me a virtuous woman; I will betroth my daughter, whom no man will have now; my life of bitter penury here will end and I shall enjoy the comfort and prosperity of my own home.

Had this man died at Troy and been cremated, I should have paid him the tribute of my tears, although he was far away; now that he is here, safe and well, shall he be taken away from me? Not that, maiden, not that! I ask this of you, in all humility: do me this kindness and imitate the nature of your just father; 940 no fairer renown can children have than to match in their characters the nobility of their parents.

CHORUS-LEADER: These words you offer for consideration

are pitiful indeed; pitiful, too, is your state. But I am eager to hear what plea Menelaus will enter for his life to be spared.

MENELAUS: I cannot bring myself to stoop before you or to let tears drop from my eyes; such lack of manliness would bring
950 much disgrace on Troy. And yet men say it is not beneath a man of noble birth to weep in adversity. But this honourable course, if honourable it be, I will not choose when I can show courage instead. No, if you decide to save a stranger's life, a man who quite properly seeks to reclaim his own wife, then give her back and save me too. If you decide otherwise, then once more I will know misery, my constant companion for many years, and you will reveal yourself as a woman of no principle.

[MENELAUS *moves towards the tomb of Proteus.*]

I will make the appeal we think we deserve and justice
960 demands, one that is most likely to touch your heart; I will fall at your father's tomb and speak these words: 'Aged spirit, who lives in this tomb of stone, give me back my wife, I beg you, whom Zeus sent here for safe-keeping. I know that you never will give her back to me, as you are dead; but your daughter will not tolerate her once glorious father being summoned from the world below to hear the curses of men. She now has the power to act.

[MENELAUS *turns from the tomb and stretches out his hands to the earth in prayer.*]

'And you, Hades, lord of the infernal regions, I call on you
970 also to be my ally. Many a warrior has my sword dispatched for Helen's sake to enrich your kingdom; you have your fee. You should either return those men now, alive once more, or at least compel this woman to show herself yet more pious than her pious sire by returning my wife to me.'

[MENELAUS *again addresses* THEONOE *directly.*]

But if you and your brother rob me of my wife, then I will tell you what she has declined to tell. You must know, maiden, that I am held fast by an oath, first of all to fight it out with
980 your brother, until he or I should die: there you have it. But if

he refuses to engage me in combat and chooses to starve us to death at the tomb we have made our sanctuary, I am resolved to kill my wife and then to thrust this two-edged sword into my own heart, here on the top of this tomb, so that streams of blood may drip down its sides; we shall lie, the two of us in death together, upon this polished sepulchre, to cause you anguish and stain your father's name for evermore. No one shall make Helen his wife, not your brother or any other man. I shall take her away myself, to my home, if I can; if not, then to join the dead! 990

CHORUS-LEADER: It is for you, maiden, to judge what each has said; make your decision one that will please all here.

THEONOE: Both nature and personal desire incline me towards piety. I am true to myself and will neither stain my father's glorious name nor render my brother a service that will bring 1000 me disgrace. There is in my heart a great shrine of Justice;[42] this is an inheritance I possess from Nereus, Menelaus, and I will try to preserve it. Since it is Hera's wish to help you, I will cast my vote with hers. As for the Cyprian, at the risk of incurring her displeasure, never have we had dealings with one another. I concur entirely with your words of reproach at my 1010 father's tomb: it would be a crime for me not to return your wife. Indeed, had he been alive, he would have given this lady to you to have and hold, and you to her. For not only are just and unjust acts rewarded among all the nations of the earth; the dead, too, observe this custom. When a man dies, his mind may cease to live but, through merging with the everlasting aether, it possesses everlasting consciousness.[43]

So, to keep my lecture brief, I will, as you have asked, say nothing; never will I be a party to my brother's foolishness. He 1020 may not realize it but I am doing him a service in turning his ungodly intentions to a proper respect for the gods.

It is for you to find an escape route for yourselves; my part will be to make myself scarce and hold my tongue. Begin with the gods; pray humbly that the Cyprian may allow your safe return to Greece and that Hera, who now wishes you and

your husband a fair voyage home, may not change her mind.
[THEONOE *turns to face the tomb*.] And this vow I make to you,
my dead father: as far as in me lies, I shall see that your holy
memory remains unsullied. [*She withdraws into the palace*.]

1030 CHORUS-LEADER: No man ever prospered through injustice,
but if his cause is just he has hope of salvation.

HELEN: Menelaus, the maid is no barrier to our escape; now we
must put our heads together and hatch a joint plan for our
route to safety.

MENELAUS: Then listen: you have lived in the palace for a long
time and have got to know the king's servants.

HELEN: Why do you say that? You give me hope! What plan do
you have in mind to help us both?

1040 MENELAUS: Could you persuade one of the men in charge of
the four-horse teams to give us a chariot?

HELEN: I could; but how shall we manage to escape when we
don't know the local terrain?

MENELAUS: There is no way – you are right. Well, what if I hid
in the palace and killed the king with my double-edged sword
here?

HELEN: His sister would not keep silent and let you carry out
her brother's murder.

MENELAUS: We don't even have a ship to escape in, once we've
made a run for it; my own is at the bottom of the sea.

HELEN [*struck by a new idea*]: Listen to this, if a woman, too, can
1050 make a clever suggestion:[44] are you willing to have a false report
spread that you are dead?

MENELAUS: It's a bad omen; still, if I profit from it, let's hear it.
I'm ready to die if it means I carry on living!

HELEN: Good; and then I would mourn your passing before the
ungodly king, cutting my hair and lamenting in woman's
fashion.

MENELAUS: How does this make it easier for us to escape? Your
plan is hardly very original.[45]

HELEN: I shall ask the king's permission to bury you in an empty
tomb as one who drowned at sea.

MENELAUS: Let's imagine he agrees. How are we then going to 1060
get safely away without a ship, for all this honouring me with
an empty tomb?

HELEN: I will put it to him that he provide a ship from which
we may drop your burial-offerings into the bosom of the deep.

MENELAUS: It's an excellent plan, except in one respect: if he
tells you to perform the burial on land, the scheme falls flat.

HELEN: Well, I'll tell him that it's against Greek custom to bury
on land those who died at sea.

MENELAUS: You meet my objection well; then I will go on
board with you to assist in the burial rites.

HELEN: Yes, it's essential for you to be on board with me, and 1070
those crewmen of yours, besides, who survived the shipwreck.

MENELAUS: Just get me a ship lying at anchor and I'll have my
men board her in proper army fashion!

HELEN: That's for you to take charge of; I only hope that
favourable winds swell our sails and bless our voyage!

MENELAUS: We *shall* have them; the gods are going to bring my
trials to an end. But who will you say gave you the news of my
death?

HELEN: You! You must stay that you are the only survivor of
those who sailed with Atreus' son and that you saw him die.

MENELAUS: Yes, and these rags I'm wearing will bear witness to 1080
your story of the shipwreck.

HELEN: They have come at a good time to cover your back,
though the loss of your proper clothes then must have seemed
far from timely. You are a pitiful sight, and this may prove our
deliverance.

MENELAUS: Should I accompany you into the palace or sit here
quietly by the tomb?

HELEN: Stay where you are; if he tries anything untoward against
you, this tomb will give you protection, and you have your
sword. I will go indoors, take the knife to my hair, change my
white clothes for black, and tear my cheeks with my nails until
they run with blood. [MENELAUS *begins to protest.*]

I must do this: no small issue is at stake and I see two ways 1090 the scales can tip: either I must die, if I am caught plotting, or else I am to return home and save your life.

[HELEN *raises her hands.*] O Lady Hera, who lies in the bed of Zeus, we beg you, stretching our arms up to the heavens tapestried with stars, where you have your dwelling, grant relief from suffering to two unhappy mortals! And you, Lady of Cyprus, Dione's child,[46] who won the prize of beauty with the promise of my hand in marriage, do not destroy me! I suffered enough cruelty before at your hands, when you degraded me – in name if not in the flesh – among the barbarians at Troy. Let me die, if it is this you want, in the land of my forefathers. Why do you never have your fill of human sorrow? Passion and deceit are what you foster, treacherous intrigues and potions that lead to death! Yet, if you knew moderation, there is no other god who brings more joy to mortal hearts.[47] I cannot deny it.

[HELEN *goes into the palace;* MENELAUS *conceals himself behind the tomb.*]

CHORUS [Strophe]: *On you let me call, who sit amidst the leafy coverts, turning your haunt into a chamber of song, melodious nightingale, sweetest of singers, bird of tuneful lamentation, come trilling through your russet throat to help me sing my dirge! Helen's piteous suffering is my theme, and the Trojan women's woeful fate as the Greeks' spears drove in, from the day when there sped on barbarian oar over the grey surge the man who came, came bringing from Sparta you, Helen, a bride to curse the sons of Priam with sorrow, Paris of deadly marriage, under Aphrodite's escort.*

[Antistrophe:] *And many a Greek met a pitiful end in Hades' embrace, slain by the spear or casting of a rock, causing wives to crop their hair in misery while their bedchambers are widowed. Many a Greek a solitary oarsman dispatched; lighting his fiery beacon on sea-girt Euboea, he dashed them on Caphereus' rocks and the headlands of the Aegean Sea by the light of his false star.[48] And inhospitable proved the wretched coastline to the man who then swept past it before the storm-blasts, away from his homeland, Menelaus, carrying on his ships the prize of a foreigner's visit that was no prize but the source of strife with Greeks, Hera's holy phantom.*

[Strophe:] *As for what is god, or not god, or something in between, what mortal having searched can say?*[49] *The distant end of this enquiry* 1140 *has been found by the man who sees the gods' fortunes leaping this way and that, and back again in twists of circumstance, contradictory and unforeseen. You, Helen, were born the daughter of Zeus; he assumed wings and fathered you in Leda's lap. And then your name was cursed by every Greek tongue as a traitor's, a breaker of faith, a breaker of laws of god and man! What tale of the gods among men is* 1150 *true and certain? I cannot tell.*

[Antistrophe:] *What fools you are, all who seek to gain honour in war and the clash of spear on spear, stupidly trying to solve men's troubles by death! If they are to be settled by contest of blood, never will strife end among the cities of men.*[50] *They received each one his portion of Trojan earth to slumber in, when reasoned argument might have solved the dispute you roused, Helen. Now they lie deep in* 1160 *Hades' lap, and Troy's walls, as if struck by Zeus' fiery thunderbolt, lie levelled; your heart, Helen, bears grief after grief; wretched and piteous are your misfortunes.*

[THEOCLYMENUS *enters with servants who carry hunting gear and hold hounds on the leash. He does not at first see* MENELAUS *as he honours his father's tomb.*]

THEOCLYMENUS: Greetings, Father! Here at the palace entrance I placed your tomb, Proteus, so that I might salute you; every time I leave or enter my house, I your son Theoclymenus pay you these respects, Father.

[*To the servants*] You men, take the hounds and hunting 1170 tackle into the palace! [*To the* CHORUS] I have been blaming myself as an utter fool; we don't use the death penalty nearly enough on criminals. It has just come to my notice that a Greek has landed on my shores in broad daylight, undetected by my scouts. Either he's a spy or he has Helen in his sights and plans to steal her. Well, he's a dead man, if only we can get our hands on him!

[THEOCLYMENUS *suddenly sees that* HELEN *is missing.*] Aha! Apparently it's all been accomplished, I find! Tyndareus' child has abandoned her seat of sanctuary at the tomb and taken ship 1180 from my land! [*He starts banging on the palace door.*] Hey there, you men, unfasten the bars, open up the stables, bring out the chariots! The woman I mean to marry is not going to be whisked away from these shores if I can help it. [*The door opens. The servants run to do his bidding when he suddenly sees* HELEN *coming to the entrance.*] Wait! I see her here, the lady I am after, inside the palace. She has not escaped.

[HELEN *emerges.*] What is this, lady? You have changed your white dress for a black one and taken a knife to your hair, 1190 marring that noble head! And you are weeping; your cheeks are wet with fresh tears! Has a dream in the night counselled you to sadness or have you heard some news from home that makes you ravage your mind with sorrow?

HELEN: O master – this is now the way I am to address you – I am ruined! What was mine is gone; my life is over!

THEOCLYMENUS: What has brought you to this? What is the matter?

HELEN: My Menelaus – ah, the pain! How can I find the words? – is dead!

THEOCLYMENUS: How do you know? Not from Theonoe's lips, surely?

HELEN: She has told me, as has the man who witnessed his end.

1200 THEOCLYMENUS: You mean someone has come and reported this as true?

HELEN: He has, and may he go off where I want him to!⁵¹

THEOCLYMENUS: Who is he? Where is he? I need to understand more clearly.

HELEN [*pointing to the figure of* MENELAUS]: There he sits, cowering at the tomb.

THEOCLYMENUS: Apollo, what a sight! How shabbily dressed!

HELEN: Oh! My poor husband was in no better state, I fancy!

THEOCLYMENUS: Where is the man from? From which port did he sail here?

HELEN: He is Greek, one of the men who shared my husband's voyage.

THEOCLYMENUS: What kind of death does he say Menelaus met?

HELEN: One most pitiful, amid the surging waves of the sea.

THEOCLYMENUS: In what foreign waters was he sailing then?　　1210

HELEN: Libya's rocky shores were where he was wrecked – no harbours there!

THEOCLYMENUS: How did this fellow escape death, if he was on the same ship?

HELEN: An ordinary man is sometimes luckier than one of royal birth.

THEOCLYMENUS: Where did he leave his wrecked vessel before coming here?

HELEN: Where I hope it perishes – except for Menelaus!

THEOCLYMENUS: He *has* perished! What sort of ship brought this fellow here?

HELEN: He says some sailors came across him and took him on board.

THEOCLYMENUS: And what about the phantom that was sent instead of you to curse Troy? Where is that?

HELEN: You mean the cloud-image? Vanished into air.

THEOCLYMENUS: O Priam and land of Troy, you were　　1220
destroyed for no reason!

HELEN: I too shared in the misfortunes of Priam's people.

THEOCLYMENUS: Did he leave your husband's body unburied or cover it with earth?

HELEN: He is unburied! Oh, pity me, pity me for the agonies I suffer!

THEOCLYMENUS: This made you cut off your locks of golden hair?

HELEN: Once he shared my life and still he has my love.

THEOCLYMENUS: You are right to weep at this calamity.[52]

† 　　†

HELEN: An easy task, to deceive your sister!

THEOCLYMENUS: Of course not. So, tell me, do you mean to continue making this tomb your home?

1230 HELEN: I do; in shunning you I keep faith with my wedded lord.

THEOCLYMENUS: Why do you tantalize me? Why not let the dead man go?

HELEN: I will tantalize you no more; you may begin the preparations for my marriage.

THEOCLYMENUS: Your agreement has come late but still I welcome it!

HELEN: Let me tell you what must be done; we should forget the past.

THEOCLYMENUS: What would you have me do? I must repay your kindness.

HELEN: Let us make peace and be reconciled.

THEOCLYMENUS: I renounce my quarrel with you; let it join the winds!

HELEN: Well, as we now are friends, I clasp your knees and beg you . . .

THEOCLYMENUS: Why do you stretch out your hands to me as a suppliant? What favour do you seek?

HELEN: . . . I wish to give my dead husband burial.

1240 THEOCLYMENUS: What, a grave without a body in it? Will you bury a ghost?

HELEN: It is a custom among Greeks, that if a man dies at sea . . .

THEOCLYMENUS: To do what? It's true, the Pelopid house has expertise in such matters.[53]

HELEN: . . . to give him burial rites in an empty shroud.

THEOCLYMENUS: Honour him as you see fit; raise a tomb wherever you wish in my land.

HELEN: This is not how we entomb those lost at sea.

THEOCLYMENUS: Then what *is* your practice? I am a stranger to the Greeks' customs.

HELEN: We take out to sea all the offerings that are due the dead.

THEOCLYMENUS: What would you have me provide for the dead man?

HELEN [*pointing to* MENELAUS]: This man knows. I do not have experience, as no such misfortune has afflicted me before now.

THEOCLYMENUS [*to* MENELAUS]: Fellow, you have brought 1250 welcome news.

MENELAUS: Not to myself or the one who has died.

THEOCLYMENUS: How do you Greeks bury those who died at sea?

MENELAUS: It depends on the dead man's means.

THEOCLYMENUS: For this lady's sake no expense will be spared. Tell me what I should do.

MENELAUS: First of all we make a blood sacrifice in honour of the dead.

THEOCLYMENUS: Which animal should be killed? Tell me and I will follow your instruction.

MENELAUS: You yourself should decide; any offering you make here will be acceptable.

THEOCLYMENUS: In this country the custom is to sacrifice a horse or bull.

MENELAUS: Do so but make sure the beast is unblemished.

THEOCLYMENUS: My herds are well stocked; such animals are 1260 mine in plenty.

MENELAUS: Then robes and a bier are brought out, even though there is no corpse.

THEOCLYMENUS: You shall have them; what else is usually provided?

MENELAUS: Weapons of bronze; he carried the spear with pride.

THEOCLYMENUS: The weapons I shall give will not disgrace a scion of Pelops.

MENELAUS: Finally, fruit and flowers – all the finest that your land produces.

THEOCLYMENUS: Agreed. But how do you lower these gifts into the sea?

MENELAUS: There must be a ship manned with oarsmen.

THEOCLYMENUS: And how far is this vessel to sail out from shore?

MENELAUS: So far that it is difficult to make out the white wake from land.

1270 THEOCLYMENUS: But why? What makes the Greeks observe this custom?

MENELAUS: It is to prevent any of the victim's blood from being washed back to the shore.

THEOCLYMENUS: You shall have a Phoenician galley that will not lack speed.

MENELAUS: That will do well; you are gracious to Menelaus.

THEOCLYMENUS: Are you not able to perform these rites alone, without this lady's assistance?

MENELAUS: The duty falls upon the mother or wife or children of the deceased.

THEOCLYMENUS: Then, from what you say, she has the task of supervising her husband's funeral.

MENELAUS: Well, piety demands that the dead are not cheated of their due.

THEOCLYMENUS: So be it; I would not have the wife in my home an enemy of piety. Go into my house, take what finery you require for the corpse, and, if your behaviour pleases this
1280 lady, I will not send you on your way empty-handed. You have brought me welcome news and so, to replace these rags, you shall be given clothes and provisions to see you to your homeland, since I see you now in such a wretched state. [*To* HELEN] And you, poor lady, must stop wearing yourself out in endless grief. Your grief is fresh, I realize; but Menelaus has met his fate and no amount of tears can make the dead come back to life.

MENELAUS: Now you know what you must do, young lady: you must be happy in the husband you have and bid farewell
1290 to the one you have no more. Given your situation, this is the best course for you to take. If I come safely to my Greek homeland, I will stop people cursing your name if you show yourself a fitting wife to the man whose bed you will now share.

HELEN: So I shall; my husband will never have cause to blame

me; you yourself will be there to witness this. Now go inside,
you wretched man, take a bath and change your clothing. I
will not keep you waiting for my reward. You will, I think, be   1300
readier to honour my beloved Menelaus as custom prescribes,
if you find me suitably grateful.

[THEOCLYMENUS *leads* HELEN *into the palace.* MENELAUS
follows them under escort.]

CHORUS [Strophe]: *In time gone by, the Mountain Mother[54] of the*
Gods rushed on swift feet through wooded glades, past swirling rivers
and the deep-voiced swell of ocean, longing to find her lost daughter
whose name men dread. And the thunderous cymbals rang out, raising
a piercing cry, when the goddess yoked her team of beasts behind her   1310
chariot to search for her child, stolen from the dancing ring of maidens.
At her side, with feet storm-swift, ranged goddesses – Artemis armed
with her arrows and, spear in hand, the Lady of the Gorgon Shield.
But Zeus, who sees all things, looked down from his heavenly throne
and decreed a different outcome.

[Antistrophe:] *But when the Mother, wearied by her rapid quest*
over many a land, had ceased in her labour to find the daughter stolen   1320
from her by stealth, she scaled the snow-bound heights of Ida, sacred
to its nymphs, and flung herself down in anguish on the rocky summit
where the trees are buried in snow. The spreading lands below she
turned from green to brown, frustrating mortal husbandry, and bringing
death to humankind. For the flocks she stopped the growth of fresh   1330
greenery to sustain them with leafy tendrils, and life began to ebb from
cities; of sacrifices to the gods or of burnt offerings at their altars there
were none. Gushing springs of bright water at her bidding ceased to
flow, as she mourned inconsolably for her child.

[Strophe:] *When the Mother had brought an end to feasting for*
mortals and gods, Zeus wished to appease her hateful anger and spoke   1340
to the Graces: 'Go forth, reverend ones, go to Demeter who is bitter
at the loss of her maiden child, and with loud music charm away her
sorrow. Let the Muses assist you with their skills of dance and song.'
Then first of the immortals came the beautiful Cyprian, and she took
up the rumbling voice of bronze and the drums stretched with hide.

1350   *The Goddess-Mother laughed and received in her hands the deep-
        sounding flute, delighted by the pulsating noise.*

        *[Antistrophe:] O princess, the love you kindled in your chamber
        offended purity and the eye of heaven; great is the Mother's anger at
        your neglect of Her ceremonies. There lies great power*[55] *in a dappled*
1360   *cloak of fawnskin, in the ivy-shoot wreathed round a holy fennel-stalk,
        in the spinning bull-roarer that is whirled round on high, in the wild
        tossing of hair in honour of Bacchus and the night-long vigil kept for
        the Mother. But you ignored all this and gloried only in beauty.*

        [HELEN *comes out from the palace.*]

        HELEN [*to the* CHORUS]: All goes well for us inside, my friends;
1370   Proteus' daughter who is helping to conceal my husband's
        presence was questioned about him but, to please me, she said
        he no longer lives. Then my husband brilliantly seized this
        chance: the weapons he was supposed to throw into the sea he
        took himself – shield with his left arm behind its band, spear
        held in his right hand – all to assist me, of course, in paying our
        respects to the dead man. He has put on defensive armour; he
1380   means to score a victory over any number of Egyptians once
        we board ship and get under way.

        I've given him a set of clothes to replace those rags from the
        wreck and a proper bath of fresh water for his skin after so long
        a time. But I must say no more; here he comes from the palace,
        the man who thinks my hand in marriage is his for the taking.
        I beg you to be loyal and guard your tongues. Perhaps, if we
        two escape, we may one day help you to do so too.[56]

        [THEOCLYMENUS *enters with attendants bearing gifts.*
        MENELAUS *follows in full battledress.*]

1390   THEOCLYMENUS: On your way, men, with these offerings
        consecrated to the sea; file off as the stranger instructed. And,
        Helen, if you agree, do as I ask and stay here. Whether you are
        on board or not, you will be rendering equal service to your
        husband. I fear that some longing may prompt you to jump
        into the sea, distraught by loving thoughts of your former lord.
        Your mourning for him is excessive, even though he is missing.

HELEN: O my new husband, I must honour my first marriage,   1400
when I was a virgin bride. Indeed, I love him so, I would even
share his death! But how would it gratify him that I should die
as he has died? Allow me to accompany his corpse in person
and give my gifts to the dead. And may the gods grant to you
all that I wish, and to the stranger here, for helping me in this
enterprise. You will find me the kind of wife you deserve to
have in your home, since you have been generous to me and
to Menelaus. All this conspires in our favour. Now, to crown
my obligation to you, give the order for a ship to be supplied   1410
for us to convey these offerings.

THEOCLYMENUS [to an attendant]: Go; give them a Sidonian
galley with fifty oars and crew to match.

HELEN: Shouldn't this man command the ship, as he is organizing
the funeral?

THEOCLYMENUS: Most certainly; my mariners are to take their
orders from him.

HELEN: Give that instruction again, so they may be in no doubt
as to your meaning.

THEOCLYMENUS [to his men]: I repeat the instruction! [To
HELEN] I'll give it a third time, if you like!

HELEN: Bless you! And bless my plans, too!

THEOCLYMENUS: Do not spoil your cheeks with all these tears!

HELEN: This day will make clear my gratitude to you.   1420

THEOCLYMENUS: These rites are a waste of effort; the dead are
nothing.

HELEN: My thoughts are with the dead as well as the living.

THEOCLYMENUS: You will find me just as good a husband as
Menelaus.

HELEN: I cannot fault you; I only need things to turn out well.

THEOCLYMENUS: That is for you to ensure; only be a loving
wife to me.

HELEN: I have not waited till now to learn to show love where
it belongs.

THEOCLYMENUS: Would you like me to participate in this
expedition myself?

HELEN: Oh, no! A king should not serve his own servants, my
lord!

THEOCLYMENUS: Let's proceed, then. I needn't concern myself
1430 any more with the customs of Pelops' people. Menelaus did
not give up the ghost here; my house has no such taint. [*To his
attendants*] One of you, on your way to tell my subjects they
may now bring their wedding presents to my palace. [*Exit one
of the attendants.*] The whole land must ring with their joyful
songs, so that men may envy my wedding with Helen! [*He
turns to address* MENELAUS.] You, stranger, go and consign
these offerings to the sea's embrace, honouring the man who
once was husband to this lady, and then hurry back home with
my wife. I want you to share my feast when I wed her; after
1440 that you can either sail for home or else stay here and be a
lucky man! [THEOCLYMENUS *goes into the palace.*]

MENELAUS: O Zeus, whom we call the Father and the god of
wisdom, look upon us in our troubles and grant us a change!
As we haul our fortunes up this steep hill, stretch out your
hand and send us to the top! A mere touch of your finger and
we shall reach the goal we desire. My former sufferings have
been enough. You gods, I have called upon you many times
with prayers that did me no good and gave offence; I deserve
to see an end to my misery; my path should now be a straight
1450 one. Grant me this one blessing and you will make me happy
for the rest of my days. [MENELAUS, HELEN *and attendants
move off in the direction of the shore.*]

CHORUS [Strophe]: *Hail! Swift Phoenician ship from Sidon, with
oars that beat so dear to Nereus' waves, dance-leader of the skilful
dolphins when the sea is windless and still and the grey-green goddess,
Calm, daughter of Ocean, speaks thus: 'Shake out your sails, you*
1460 *sailors, you sailors, bid farewell to sea-breezes and grip your pinewood
oars, as you escort Helen to the harbours of her native shores and the
city that Perseus raised.'*[57]

[Antistrophe:] *What will she find there?*[58] *Leucippus' maiden
daughters, perhaps, by the swirling river, or before Pallas' temple she*

may join at last in the ritual dance, or on the joyous night take part in 1470
the revelling for Hyacinthus, whom Phoebus challenged and killed
with the round discus. In his honour the son of Zeus proclaimed a holy
day for the land of Sparta to mark with sacrifice of bulls. Perhaps she
may see the daughter she left behind at home, flaxen-haired Hermione,
for whom the bridal torches have not yet burst into flame.

[Strophe:] If only we might find ourselves flying[59] through the air
where go the ranks of Libyan birds, leaving the winter storms behind, 1480
heeding their leader's piping cry, who shrills as he wings his way over
earth's plains, both waterless and fruitful. O feathered travellers with
your long necks, partners of the racing clouds, fly beneath the Pleiads
at mid-course and Orion in the night, and, as you come to rest on 1490
Eurotas, deliver the news that Menelaus who sacked Dardanus' town
will soon be coming home.

[Antistrophe:] And you, sons of Tyndareus,[60] come on your
steeds, I pray, galloping through the air, you whose dwelling is in
heaven under the whirling of the lustrous stars, come, you saviours of 1500
Helen, over the green salt depths, skimming the white-flecked ridges
that mark the sea's dark face, and bring the gentle breath of winds that
sailors welcome, the gift of Zeus. Vindicate your sister, branded as the
mistress of a foreign prince: remove the infamy she won in retribution
for the strife on Ida, though never did she go to Ilium's towers that 1510
Phoebus raised.

[THEOCLYMENUS *comes out of the palace, accompanied by*
servants. Before he can speak, the MESSENGER, *one of the servants*
he sent to accompany the procession, rushes in from the shore.]

MESSENGER: My royal lord, prepare yourself, for such is the
strange news you are soon to hear from me.

THEOCLYMENUS: What has happened?

MESSENGER: You must set about finding another woman to
woo; Helen has gone from this land.

THEOCLYMENUS: What? Did she soar into the air or escape on
foot?

MESSENGER: Menelaus has carried her off from Egypt by sea.
He was the man who came and reported his own death.

1520 THEOCLYMENUS: Oh, terrible news! But how could they sail away from this land? Your tale is beyond belief!

MESSENGER: In the ship that was your own gift to the stranger; in a word, he's gone, taking your sailors with him.

THEOCLYMENUS: But how? I must know how! A whole crew of men, yourself included – was I to imagine that a single man could overpower all that?

MESSENGER: When Zeus' daughter had left the palace here and come to the sea, stepping out with delicate tread she started like an expert on a lament for the husband who was there at her side and not dead at all.

1530 We reached the enclosure of your dockyard and started to launch a Sidonian galley on her maiden voyage, a vessel manned by fifty oarsmen. The various tasks were carried out in turn: one sailor was stepping the mast, another setting the oars in place, the white sails were folded and put in position, and ropes were used to lower the rudders by the stern.

While we were busy at this work, some Greek seamen, who had sailed with Menelaus and had doubtless been watching for 1540 this moment, approached us on the shore. They were handsome enough men but, dressed in rags from the shipwreck as they were, a picture of squalor. The son of Atreus, seeing them there, put on for us a crafty display of pity and spoke to them: 'You poor fellows, what brings you here? What Greek vessel were you on and how were you wrecked? Join us in giving burial to the fallen son of Atreus! This lady, Tyndareus' daughter, is going to perform the ceremony, though his body is lost.' So, with feigned tears in their eyes, these men began boarding the ship, bringing with them their sea-offerings in Menelaus' 1550 honour. Now this made us suspicious and we muttered to one another about the number of these extra passengers. However, we obeyed your instructions and held our tongues. For you had given the stranger command of the ship and that was what caused the whole fiasco.

Now most of the gear was manageably light and we had little trouble in loading it on board. But not the bull:[61] his

hoofs twisted and turned as he refused to mount the gangway;
he rolled his eyes and bellowed, humping his shoulders and
glaring along his horns, and let no one touch him. Then Helen's
husband called out, 'Come on, you men who sacked the town   1560
of Ilium,[62] lift up that bull the Greek way! Get your young
shoulders under him and heave him on board! Are we to deny
the dead man his sacrifice?' They moved to do his bidding,
and, hoisting up the bull, carried him and set him down on the
deck. The horse was easier to deal with; Menelaus patted his
neck and forehead and so enticed him on board.

In the end, when everything was loaded on deck, Helen
mounted the ladder, stepping with trim ankles up each rung,   1570
and took her seat alongside her supposedly dead husband, next
to the stern quarterdeck. The remaining Greeks sat equally to
port and starboard, man for man, each with a sword concealed
under his clothes. The churning waters were filled with our
shouting as we responded to the boatswain's cries.

When we were some distance from land, not too far but
not near either, the helmsman put this question to Menelaus:
'Full ahead still, sir, or is this far enough? You are our ship's   1580
captain.' And he replied, 'Far enough!' Then, taking his
sword in his right hand, he made his way forward to the prow.
There he stood to sacrifice the bull and, with no mention of
any dead man, he slit the beast's throat and uttered this prayer:
'Poseidon, Lord of the sea, your own domain, and you holy
daughters of Nereus, carry me and my wife safely away from
this land and set us on the shores of Nauplia!' The blood shot
out in a stream and poured into the sea – an omen favourable
to the stranger. Someone said, 'Treachery on board! Let's sail   1590
back! You, give the order for a starboard pull, you, get the
helm over!'

The son of Atreus stood fast[63] where he had slaughtered the
bull and shouted to his comrades: 'What are you waiting for?
Now show you mettle, sons of Greece! Cut these foreigners
to pieces and throw them into the briny!' At this our captain
shouted in reply to your own sailors: 'These strangers are our

enemies! Quick, pick up end spars, smash benches, rip out rowlocks and crack their skulls open!'

1600 Every man jumped to his feet; we had oars in our hands, but they had swords. Then the ship was awash with blood. A voice could be heard shouting encouragement from the stern – it was Helen's! 'Where is that fame you won at Troy? Show these barbarians!' At her eager cry, men fell down or kept their feet; some were to be seen lying still, dead. Menelaus, fully armed, was keeping an eye out for any signs of his men struggling in the fight, and that was where he was to be seen, sword in right hand, sending your crewmen tumbling off the ship like divers

1610 and clearing the benches of them. Then he went over to the helmsman and told him to set course for Greece. His men raised the sail and the breeze freshened in their favour. So they have put Egypt behind them.

I managed to escape the slaughter by lowering myself into the sea alongside the anchor. Fatigue was getting the better of me when I was picked up by a fisherman, who brought me back to shore to tell you this news.

To sum up,[64] there's nothing more useful in life than showing a healthy scepticism. [*Exit* MESSENGER.]

CHORUS-LEADER: My lord, I would never have believed that

1620 Menelaus could appear here among us, as he did, without being recognized by you or us![65]

THEOCLYMENUS: Oh, to have been caught out[66] so miserably by a woman's wiles! My marriage has slipped from my hands! If there was any chance of overtaking their ship, I'd cram on every stitch of canvas to catch them. But instead I'll be revenged on the woman who betrayed me, my sister, who saw Menelaus in the palace but kept me in the dark. Never again will she deceive a man with her prophecies!

[THEOCLYMENUS *turns angrily to enter the palace but his path is barred by a servant who steps between him and the door and clutches him by the arms.*]

SERVANT: Now, sir, where are you off to? Who do you mean to kill, master?

THEOCLYMENUS: I go where Justice prompts me; get out of my way!

SERVANT: I won't let go of your robe! You're planning to commit a terrible crime!

THEOCLYMENUS: Are you, a slave, going to give orders to your master? 1630

SERVANT: Yes; what I say is right.

THEOCLYMENUS: You are disloyal, if you do not let me . . .

SERVANT: No! I will not let you!

THEOCLYMENUS: . . . kill my traitorous sister . . .

SERVANT: No traitor but a most pious lady.

THEOCLYMENUS: . . . who has betrayed me . . .

SERVANT: An honourable betrayal, to act as justice dictated.

THEOCLYMENUS: . . . by offering my wife to another man.

SERVANT: A man who has a greater right to her than you.

THEOCLYMENUS: Who has a right to what is mine?

SERVANT: He received her from her father.

THEOCLYMENUS: But Fortune gave her to me!

SERVANT: And Destiny took her away.

THEOCLYMENUS: You have no right to interfere with my affairs.

SERVANT: I do, if I am talking better sense.

THEOCLYMENUS: Then I am the subject here and not the ruler!

SERVANT: You rule to do what is right, not what is wrong.

THEOCLYMENUS: It seems you are in love with death.

SERVANT: Then kill me; you will not kill your sister before me, 1640 if I can help it! There is no more glorious end for a true-hearted slave than dying for his master.[67]

[As THEOCLYMENUS *raises his hand to strike the servant the* DIOSCURI *appear above the palace.*[68]]

CASTOR: Curb the unjust anger that grips you, Theoclymenus, king of this land! That is our command. We are the Dioscuri, sons of Zeus, who call you, whom Leda once bore, brothers of Helen who has fled from your home. This marriage that rouses your anger is not yours to enjoy, nor are you wronged by your sister Theonoe, maiden daughter of Nereus' divine daughter. She was honouring the laws of heaven and her

[1650]   father's just precepts. No, keep that sword unstained by a sister's blood and think of her action as inspired by virtue. Long ago we would have taken our sister from your land to safety, since

1660   Zeus had made us gods. But we were subservient to fate and to the gods as well, whose will it was that these things should be.

These are my words to you, and now I address myself to my sister. Sail onward with your husband; you will have a favourable wind. We your two Saviour brothers shall ride our horses over the sea with you and give you escort to your homeland. When your race is run and your mortal years at an end, you will be called a goddess[69] and, together with us, you will receive from men a cult-feast. This is the will of Zeus. There is a

1670   straggling island that keeps watch over Acte's coast,[70] where Maia's son first set you down after taking wing on his heavenly course from Sparta, stealing you away so that you would not become Paris' bride. Henceforth it shall be called by mortals 'Helen's Isle', since it gave you welcome when you were stolen there from home.

To Menelaus the Wanderer the gods grant as his destined home a dwelling on the Isle of the Blessed.[71] Men of noble birth are not hated by the gods, but they have more trials to undergo than their ordinary fellows.

1680   THEOCLYMENUS: Sons of Leda and Zeus, I will forego my former quarrel with your sister! Let her return to her home, if it is the gods' will, and I will renounce my decision to kill my sister. You are brothers in blood to a most excellent and virtuous lady. Go on your way rejoicing in Helen's great nobility of heart, something lacking in all too many women.

CHORUS: *Many are the forms the plans of the gods take and many the*
1690   *things they accomplish beyond men's hopes. What men expect does not happen; for the unexpected heaven finds a way. And so it has turned out here today.*[72]

CYCLOPS

PREFACE TO *CYCLOPS*

Nineteen plays have come down to us from ancient times under the name of Euripides. Of these all but one are tragedies; the *Cyclops* is his only surviving satyr-play. Indeed, it is the only complete specimen of that genre that is available to us, though thanks to the discovery of papyri we have a good idea of the shape and plot of Sophocles' *Trackers* and of Aeschylus' *Fishermen*. As explained in the General Introduction, the satyr-play was a form closely associated with tragedy, and at the Great Dionysia each competing tragedian would put on one satyr-play along with three tragedies. Although the satyr-play may be lighter in tone and shorter than a tragedy, the form still merited respect: after all, it was in the most obvious sense a tribute to the god of drama, Dionysus himself, the master of the satyrs. Aristotle indeed claims that tragedy itself originated from the satyric form, and if some truth underlies this claim, it may explain why the satyr-play was preserved as an integral part of the major tragic festival, although in some respects it had clearly diminished in importance and was less highly regarded by later critics. Nevertheless, despite the crudity and rumbustiousness of the half-animal satyrs, the tone of satyric drama remained less coarse and the themes less grotesque than those of contemporary comedy; the mythical setting of the plays also brought them closer to the tragedies with which they were associated. In Roman times, the poet-critic Horace in his long poem on 'The Art of Poetry' described Tragedy as a dignified matron who does not descend to trivial verse even though she deigns to associate, though modestly, with the cavorting satyrs (*Ars Poetica* 231– 3). The Greek critic Demetrius put it more crisply: the satyric drama is 'tragedy at play' (*On Style* 169).

A few comments are probably needed about the satyrs. The most important point is that they are half human and half beast in form. In early vase-painting they are sometimes half horse, but as time went on goat-legs and tails became more consistently characteristic. This marginal status is reflected in their moral outlook, for they are wild and sensual beings, unrestrained by human laws or inhibitions, yet also in some way divine, attendants upon the god of wine and wildness, and sharing something of his divinity. Similarly the elderly Silenus, sometimes represented as the father of the satyrs, is both a drunken buffoon and the god's protector and mentor. Although in this play Silenus is a cowardly figure of fun, in other legends he is a more awesome figure and a source of divine wisdom. In all these respects we can see that the satyrs are suited to a genre that stands midway between tragic seriousness and comic frivolity.

Satyrs form the chorus, as far as we know, of all satyric dramas. Other conventional elements are discernible even in the slender remnants that survive. It seems that the plots were consistently drawn from myth, though the stories were often burlesqued. These often involved the imprisonment and escape of the satyrs from captivity; certain plots were particularly favoured, including those in which the satyrs took responsibility for or took care of some charge, such as a divine child. Another common motif was the discovery of a notable invention: fire, wine, musical instruments or other artefacts. Again the interest in the border-area between civilization and wildness is evident. Perhaps surprisingly, there seems to be no expectation that Dionysus himself will necessarily appear in the play: indeed, Euripides in the *Cyclops* makes much of the absence of the god and the satyrs' consequent servitude. As in tragedy – perhaps indeed under the influence of tragedy – the range of mythical plots used by the poets in satyr-plays may have been expanded far beyond an original Dionysiac core.

The *Cyclops* itself is not one of the plays which we can date firmly from external evidence, but its most recent editor has made a good case for placing it very late in the poet's career, probably after 411 BC, in the last few years of Euripides' life.[1] In that case it is probably later than the plays in this volume (of which the latest, *Helen*, belongs to 412), but its similar theme of escape from a savage captor makes it natural to group it with *Iphigenia among the Taurians* and *Helen*. No comments here are dependent on accepting this date.

Little need be said about the content of the play. It is obviously a creative adaptation, at times a parody, of the Cyclops story in the ninth book of Homer's *Odyssey*: the arrival of the hero in search of food or loot, his withholding of his identity, the use of wine to incapacitate the giant, the trick of the pseudonym 'Noman', the use of the stake, and the departure in which the hero taunts the blinded monster, are all motifs derived from Homer. The adjustments and elaborations are mostly the consequence either of transferring the tale from narrative epic to the stage, or of the new context in a satyr-drama. Particularly notable is the fact that Odysseus talks in the dignified manner (and metre) of a character from tragedy, and stands in contrast with the more light-hearted and colloquial, even occasionally obscene, conversation of the other characters, especially the chorus of satyrs.

The other main character, the Cyclops Polyphemus, is a conventional ogre, though with some amusingly human and even sophisticated touches (he lectures Odysseus on human life in the manner of a fifth-century intellectual, 316ff.). Even in Homer little is done to suggest that the monster deserves more than detestation and violence (though the gentle affection that the Cyclops expresses towards his ram strikes a more attractive note [*Odyssey* 9.447–60]). In the *Cyclops* Odysseus may be a braggart, but the Cyclops is a caricature whom we delight to see outwitted. It is instructive to see how the generic context of satyric drama – a drama celebrating drink, sex, self-indulgent hedonism – neutralizes moral qualms which we would feel in other contexts, and which indeed we do feel in parallel scenes in other Euripidean dramas (such as the blinding of Polymestor in *Hecabe*). Even the searching and subtle mind of Euripides accepts the good-humoured scurrility and the hedonistic violence that are traditional and essential to the satyric ethos.

1. See the commentary on the play by R. Seaford (Oxford 1984), pp. 48–51, summarizing his article in the *Journal of Hellenic Studies* 102 (1982), pp. 163–72. Much that I say here and in the notes to this play is indebted to Seaford's exemplary work.

CHARACTERS

SILENUS, *father of the satyrs*
CHORUS *of satyrs, prisoners of the*
Cyclops
ODYSSEUS
CYCLOPS, *called* POLYPHEMUS

[*The scene is outside the cave of* POLYPHEMUS *beneath Mount Etna in Sicily. Buckets of water and a cauldron stand in front of the entrance.* SILENUS *emerges from the cave, holding a rake.*]

SILENUS: O Bromius, on your account I've performed no end of mighty tasks, now and in the days when I was young and strong! First there was the time you upped and left behind your nurses, the mountain nymphs, when Hera had robbed you of your wits; then, in the battle with the Sons of Earth,[1] I stood with my shield, protecting your right flank, and, striking Enceladus in the middle of his shield with my spear, I killed him – hang on, let me see, is this a dream I'm describing? No, by Zeus, it's not; I even showed the spoils to Bacchus.

But this task that's draining me right now is even greater 10 than those. For when Hera roused the Tuscan pirates[2] against you to have you taken off to a far country, I got wind of it and put to sea with my sons to track you down. Taking hold of the rudder myself, right at the stern, I began steering the double-oared ship, while my sons, seated at their oars, continued the quest for you, my lord, turning the grey sea's surface to white with their splashing. But when we had almost rounded Malea an east wind blew down on our ship and drove us ashore 20 here under rocky Etna,[3] where the sea-god's one-eyed sons, the murderous Cyclopes, live in lonely caves. It is one of these who has captured us and made us slaves in his home; Polyphemus is the name they give to the master we serve. We used to shout Bacchus' praises as we danced in his honour but now we're shepherds, tending the flocks of a godless Cyclops!

My sons, young fellows themselves, herd the young sheep
on far-off hillsides, but my allotted task is to stay here, keeping
the drinking troughs full and sweeping out this home of his,
while I attend his one-eyed unholiness at his godless meals.
And now, orders are orders, I must sweep his house clean with
this rake – can't have my absent master, the Cyclops, and his
sheep coming back to a dirty cave!

[*Enter the* CHORUS *with attendants, driving sheep.*]

But now I see my lads approaching, driving their flocks
before them. What's this, though? It's a lively dance you're
treading there – can it have the same rhythm as the time you
went revelling at Bacchus' side to Althaea's palace,[4] sauntering
in with your songs sung to the lyre?

CHORUS [*addressing a ram that has strayed*]: *Son of a noble sire, yes,
and a noble mother, what pathway, tell me, are you following as you
make for the rocks? Is this not the way to breezes soft and gentle and
pastures green? Water from whirling streams lies in the drinking troughs
hard by the cave, where your bleating young are to be found.*

*Shoo! This way, I say, this way! Here's the place for you to feed,
along this dewy slope! Hey, I'll throw a stone at you in a moment!
Get along with you, on you go, you horned beast, to the minder of the
fold for the shepherd, the Cyclops who roves in the wild!*

[*Addressing a ewe in the flock*] *Unburden your swollen udders.
Give the welcome of your teats to the lambs you left behind in the
cave. Your little bleating children have slept all day and are missing
you. Won't you go into the field, leaving your grassy pastures behind,
and make your way inside Etna's rocky cavern?*

*No Bromius is here, no dancing bands, no Bacchants bearing the
thyrsus, no resounding drums, no wine dripping fresh by gushing
springs of water. I cannot join the nymphs on Nysa's slopes and sing
the song 'Iacchus, Iacchus'[5] to Aphrodite, whom I chased so swiftly
together with the white-footed Bacchants. O Bacchus, dear friend,
where are you going without followers, tossing your golden locks, while
I, your attendant, serve this Cyclops with his one eye, a slave in*

banishment, wearing for a cloak this miserable goatskin, and robbed of   80
your precious company?

SILENUS: No more words, my children! Order your attendants
to drive the sheep together inside the cave with its rocky roof!

CHORUS-LEADER [*to the attendants*]: Carry on! [*They make their
way into the cave with the flock.*] But what is it that so concerns
you, Father?

SILENUS: I see a Greek ship by the sea-shore and the masters of
the oars approaching this cave with a man who must command
them. They carry empty pots about their necks, since food is
what they need, and pails for water. O sirs, I pity you! Who   90
are they, I wonder? They do not know the nature of my master
Polyphemus or how inhospitable is this land they have set foot
on; they do not know their own misfortune in coming to land
in a Cyclops' man-eating jaws. But calm yourselves, so we may
learn where they have sailed from to Sicilian Etna's crag.

[ODYSSEUS *enters with members of his crew.*]

ODYSSEUS: Strangers, be so good as to tell me where we may
find a stream of water to cure our thirst, and if anyone is willing
to sell food to needy seafarers. [*Noticing that they are not normal
men*] But what's this? It looks as if we've marched into Bacchus'
town! I see a crowd of satyrs outside the cave! I'll pay my   100
respects to the eldest first: Greetings!

SILENUS: Greetings to you, sir! But say who you are and what
is your homeland.

ODYSSEUS: Odysseus of Ithaca, lord of the land of Cephallene.

SILENUS: I know of the man, a sharp-tongued chatterer,
Sisyphus' son.[6]

ODYSSEUS: That's me all right; but there's no need to be rude!

SILENUS: Where have you come from on this voyage that brings
you here to Sicily?

ODYSSEUS: From Ilium and the laborious war at Troy.

SILENUS: How? Did you not know the course to sail for home?

ODYSSEUS: Stormy winds drove me here against my will.

110   SILENUS: Oh dear! The fate that dogs you is the same as my own!

ODYSSEUS: Were you also forced to come to these shores?

SILENUS: Yes, as I chased pirates who had kidnapped Bromius.

ODYSSEUS: What is this country and who are its inhabitants?

SILENUS: This is Mount Etna, the highest mountain in Sicily.

ODYSSEUS: And where are the walls of the city and its fortifications?

SILENUS: There are none; no humans occupy these headlands, sir.

ODYSSEUS: Then who live in this country? Wild animals?

SILENUS: Cyclopes, who make caves, not houses, their homes.

ODYSSEUS: Who is their ruler? Or is it the people who govern?⁷

120   SILENUS: They live solitary lives; no one owes allegiance to anyone else.

ODYSSEUS: Do they sow the grain of Demeter? Or what do they live on?

SILENUS: On milk and cheese and the flesh of their sheep.

ODYSSEUS: Do they have the drink of Bromius, the juice of the vine?

SILENUS: Certainly not; and that is why their land has no dancing.

ODYSSEUS: Are they hospitable folk, respecting the gods in the way they treat strangers?

SILENUS: It's strangers' flesh that they say tastes sweetest.

ODYSSEUS: What are you saying? They kill men and make a feast of them?

SILENUS: Not a soul has come here without being slaughtered.

ODYSSEUS: And where is he, the Cyclops himself? In his house?

130   SILENUS: He's away, hunting beasts on Etna with his hounds.

ODYSSEUS: Then do you know what you must do if we are to get away from this land?

SILENUS: Odysseus, I do not; but I'll oblige you in any way I can.

ODYSSEUS: Sell us some bread; that's what we lack.

SILENUS: As I said, all we have is meat.

ODYSSEUS: Well, that too is an agreeable antidote to hunger.

SILENUS: There's curdled cheese as well, and cows' milk.

ODYSSEUS: Bring them out; daylight's the thing when there's buying and selling to be done.

SILENUS: And, on your side, tell me, how much gold will you give in return?

ODYSSEUS: It's not gold I carry but the drink of Dionysus.

SILENUS: Oh, that's excellent news! Just what we have been without for so long!   140

ODYSSEUS: Yes, I had the drink as a gift from Maron, the god's son.[8]

SILENUS: The boy I raised once in my own arms?

ODYSSEUS: The son of Bacchus, to make it clearer.

SILENUS: Is it stored on your ship, or do you have it with you?

ODYSSEUS [*producing a wineskin*]: Here's the wineskin that holds it, as you see, old fellow.

SILENUS: I wouldn't get even one mouthful out of that![9]

{ODYSSEUS: You couldn't drink this wineskin dry.

SILENUS: You mean it produces new wine by magic?}

ODYSSEUS: Yes; twice as much drink as flows from inside it.

SILENUS: What a splendid fountain you describe! I like the sound of that!

ODYSSEUS: Do you want me to give you a taste of it neat to start with?[10]

SILENUS [*grabbing hold of the wineskin*]: That's fair; tasting invites   150
buying, after all!

ODYSSEUS [*politely restraining him*]: I *have* brought along a cup with the wineskin, actually.

SILENUS: Well, splash some in, to bring the taste of drinking back to me!

ODYSSEUS [*pouring, but not yet offering, the wine*]: There we are.

SILENUS: Well I never! What a splendid bouquet it has!

ODYSSEUS: Saw it, did you?

SILENUS: Don't be daft, I'm smelling it!

ODYSSEUS [*giving him the cup*]: Taste it, then. Let's have more than just lip-service!

SILENUS [*taking a gulp*]: Oh, yes! [*Beginning to hop up and down*] Bacchus is inviting me to dance! Whahey!

ODYSSEUS: That sloshed nicely down your throat now, didn't it?

SILENUS: I'll say – all the way down to my toenails!

160 ODYSSEUS: Now, that's not all: we'll be giving you money as well.

SILENUS: Just keep the wine coming. Forget the gold!

ODYSSEUS: Then bring out your cheeses or lambs.

SILENUS: And so I shall! Who cares what the master thinks? Once I had downed a single cup of this, I'd go mad – giving away all the Cyclopes' flocks and flinging myself off the Leucadian rock into the sea, well and truly sozzled, with my eyes shut tight! Anyone who doesn't enjoy drinking is off his

170 head: when you drink you can make *this* stand to attention, grab a handful of breast, look forward to stroking her bush, having a ball and forgetting your troubles. Shall I not, then, kiss a drink like this and tell that fathead Cyclops – and the eye in the middle of his head – to take a running jump? [SILENUS *turns and goes into the cave, cup in hand.*]

CHORUS-LEADER: Listen, Odysseus; there's something we'd like to chat to you about.

ODYSSEUS: Of course; you are my friends, as I am yours.

CHORUS-LEADER: Did you Greeks capture Troy and make Helen your prisoner?

ODYSSEUS: We did – and we sacked the royal seat of Priam's sons – every stone of it!

CHORUS-LEADER: Once you had caught the woman,[11] didn't

180 you all take turns in banging her, since having many partners was what she enjoyed? The traitress! One look at the fancy-coloured trousers on the man's legs and the gold necklace he wore round his neck and she was all a-flutter, leaving Menelaus behind, that fine little fellow! Ah, how I wish the female sex were nowhere to be found, except in my bed!

[SILENUS *comes out of the cave.*]

SILENUS: Look! Here they are, Odysseus, my royal lord, the

216

flocks I promised you, nurslings of the bleating sheep, and no   190
shortage of cheeses, made from curdled milk. Take them.
Leave the cave straightaway, once you have given me the drink
of Bacchus' vine. [*Catching sight of* POLYPHEMUS] Oh, no!
Here comes the Cyclops! What are we going to do?

ODYSSEUS: Then we're done for, old man. Where should we
run to?

SILENUS: Here, inside the cave, you'll find a place to hide from
him in there.

ODYSSEUS: That's a risky idea, putting our heads in the trap!

SILENUS: No risk at all; there are many places to hide in the
cave.

ODYSSEUS: No, I'll not do it! Troy would grieve loud and long
if I now turn in flight from one man, I who stood my ground
so many times, shield in hand, against a countless host of   200
Trojans.[12] No, if die I must, nobly shall I die, or live on and
preserve my fame of old.

[POLYPHEMUS *enters, carrying a club.*]

CYCLOPS: Right then, hold up, come along now! What's going
on here? Why are you all being so slack? Having a holiday
for Bacchus, are we? There's no Dionysus here, no bronze
clappers or rattling drums. How are my new-born lambs surviving in the cave? Are they at the teats and running under their
mothers' sides? Has the milk for the cheeses been curdled and
put in rush baskets? Nothing to say for yourselves, eh? This   210
club will soon make one of you cry! Eyes up, not on the
ground!

CHORUS-LEADER [*craning his neck to look up at* POLYPHEMUS]:
There! I've raised my head to Zeus himself and the stars and I
see Orion!

CYCLOPS: Is my supper well prepared?

CHORUS-LEADER: It is; just make sure your gullet is ready.

CYCLOPS: And what about milk? Are the mixing bowls filled?

CHORUS-LEADER: Enough for you to drink up an entire storage
jar, if you want.

CYCLOPS: Is it sheep's milk or cows' or a mixture of the two?

CHORUS-LEADER: Whatever you wish; only mind you don't swallow *me* down!

220 CYCLOPS: Have no fear of that; you lot would be the death of me with your twists and turns, leaping around in the middle of my stomach. [*Suddenly catching sight of* ODYSSEUS *and his men*] Hey! What's this collection I see near my cave? Some pirates or thieves who have landed here? I certainly see lambs here from my cave, tied up tight together with twisted willow-twigs, and cheese-baskets all mixed up, and an old man with his bald head swollen from blows.[13]

SILENUS: Poor old me! Oh! Oh! What a beating I've had! My face is on fire!

CYCLOPS: Who did it? Who has been punching you on the head, old man?

230 SILENUS [*pointing to* ODYSSEUS *and his men*]: These fellows, Cyclops, because I wouldn't let them carry off your property.

CYCLOPS: Did they not know I am a god with gods as forefathers?

SILENUS: That's what I kept telling them, but they didn't stop plundering your goods, and then they started eating the cheese, though I tried to stop them, and carrying out the lambs. And then they said[14] they would put a king-size collar on you and pull out your innards by force, in full view of your central eye, and flay your back good and proper with a whip, before trussing you up and throwing you under their ship's benches, to be

240 sold to someone needing boulders shifted, or flung into a mine.

CYCLOPS: Is that a fact? [*Turning to one of his servants*] Off you go, double quick, and sharpen up my carving knives, then put a big bundle of wood on the hearth and start a fire! [*The servant hurries off into the cave.*] They will be slaughtered at once and fill my belly, providing the server with a banquet hot from the coals, and the rest boiled and tenderized from the cauldron. I've had a sufficient taste by now of mountain game: lions and deer have supplied my table quite enough, and a meal of human flesh is long overdue.

250 SILENUS: Some new items on the menu will give more pleasure,

master, after your customary fare. It's certainly a long time since you've had any other strangers coming to your cave.

ODYSSEUS: Cyclops, give us strangers a hearing too. We came from our ship to your cave because we wanted to buy food. The lambs were sold to us by this fellow, handed over for a cup of wine once he had sampled it, all fair and above board, with no coercion. But there's not a single honest word in this rogue's tale, as he's been caught selling your goods while your back was turned.

SILENUS: Who, *me*? I hope you rot in hell!

ODYSSEUS: Fine, if I'm lying.

SILENUS: In the name of Poseidon, your own father, Cyclops, and of the mighty Triton, in the name of Nereus, of Calypso and the daughters of Nereus, in the name of the sacred waves of the sea and all the brood of fishes, I swear – dear Cyclops, dear, handsome Cyclops, best of masters – I wasn't selling off your goods to strangers! If this is a lie, may my sons here be damned utterly,[15] these naughty lads their father dotes on!

CHORUS-LEADER: Wish that on yourself! I saw you selling the property to the strangers. [*Addressing* POLYPHEMUS *directly*] Now, if I'm telling a lie, I hope my father may be damned. But don't punish these strangers unjustly.

CYCLOPS [*replying to the* CHORUS-LEADER]: You're lying. I put more trust in this man than in Rhadamanthus, and I consider him more honest. [*Turning his attention to* ODYSSEUS *and his men*] But I wish to ask you a question. Where have you sailed from, strangers? What is your homeland? What city raised you?

ODYSSEUS: We are Ithacans by birth, and have come from Ilium. We sacked that city and then storms at sea forced us to land on your shores, Cyclops.

CYCLOPS: Are you the men who went to punish Ilium's city on the Scamander for the theft of that trollop Helen?

ODYSSEUS: We are, and what a fearful struggle it cost us all!

CYCLOPS: A shameful enterprise that was – sailing off to the land of the Trojans for the sake of one woman!

ODYSSEUS: A god prompted the business; don't put the blame on any mortal. But now, noble son of the ocean's god, we are your suppliants and will speak plainly with you. When men have come in friendship to your cave, do not have the heart to kill them and make them a godless meal for your jaws. We are the ones, my lord, who kept your father safe[16] to enjoy his temple-dwellings at the farthest points of Greece: holy Taenarum's harbour and Cape Malea's inlets remain unharmed; safe, too, is Sunium's rock, rich in silver and sacred to divine Athena, and safe Geraestus' refuge for ships in distress. We did not yield up to the Phrygians what belonged to Greece – an intolerable disgrace. You also share in the benefits of this, living as you do at the edge of the Greek world under Etna, whose rocky summit drips fire.

[POLYPHEMUS *starts to yawn.*] But if you have no interest in these considerations, there is a convention among men that one should welcome suppliants who have been exhausted by their sufferings at sea, giving them the presents that hospitality requires and furnishing them with clothes, not skewering their limbs on spits for roasting oxen and then filling your jaws and belly. The land of Priam has caused enough bereavement in Greece, drinking the blood of many a dead warrior slain by the spear, turning wives into wretched widows and robbing grey-haired old men and women of sons. Now, if you are going to cook and consume in some grisly banquet those of us who have survived, where is any man to turn? No, do what I ask, Cyclops: disappoint those greedy jaws of yours and choose to honour not to insult the gods; many a man in making sinful gains has earned the reward of punishment.

SILENUS [*to* POLYPHEMUS]: Let me give you some advice: do not leave a scrap of this man's flesh. And if you chew his tongue, you will become smart, too, Cyclops, and a regular talker.

CYCLOPS [*looking down at* ODYSSEUS]: Wealth, my mannikin, is what the wise think of as divine; everything else is idle chatter and high-sounding phrases. As for the promontories on which my father's temples stand, I care nothing for them. Why did you make an issue of them in your speech?

Zeus' thunderbolt[17] holds no terrors for *me*, stranger, and I am not aware of Zeus being a more powerful god than I. He causes me no concern for the future, and let me tell you why this is so. Whenever he sends down his rain from on high, I have my snug shelter here in my cave; I dine on roasted calf or some wild beast, then, lying on my back, I give my belly a good soaking, drinking down a jar of milk, and poking against my tunic as I make a noise to match the thunderclaps of Zeus. And when the north wind from Thrace drives down the snow, wrapping myself up in the hides of beasts, I light a fire and give no more thought to snow.

The Earth from necessity, whether she wills it or not, brings forth the grass to keep my flock fat. I sacrifice them to no one except myself, never to the gods, but to the greatest divinity there is, this stomach. Drinking and eating every day, and avoiding all pain to oneself – this is Zeus in the eyes of sensible men. As for those who passed laws, complicating the lives of men, they can go hang themselves! I will not stop gratifying my heart – by eating you up. As for gifts of hospitality, you'll get the following – I don't want to be thought mean – fire and this bronze pot, that will bring your flesh, torn in pieces, to the boil and give it a nice overcoat. Now off inside with you, so that you can stand around the altar of the god in the cave and provide for my great feast.

[POLYPHEMUS *lifts up the cauldron and starts herding the Greeks into the cave with his club, assisted by* SILENUS. *As they leave,* ODYSSEUS *lingers to make this speech.*]

ODYSSEUS: Oh, this is past endurance! I have won through hardships at Troy and on the sea only to make port now in a godless man's cruel and harbourless heart! O Pallas,[18] o Lady Divine, child of Zeus, *now* is the hour for you to help! The trouble I now face is worse than any at Troy; I stand on danger's very altar-base! And you, Zeus who champions guests, dwelling in the shining realm of the stars, look upon our treatment!

[POLYPHEMUS *appears threateningly at the mouth of the cave and gestures to* ODYSSEUS *with his club.*] If you have no regard for these things,[19] then men are fools to worship you as a god, Zeus, when you are worthless. [ODYSSEUS *enters the cave, followed by* POLYPHEMUS.]

CHORUS [Strophe]: *Draw back those lips, Cyclops, open wide your gaping throat; the limbs of your guests, boiled, roasted or hot from the*
360 *coals, are ready for you to gnaw, tear and gobble up as you lie at ease in your woolly goatskin.*

[Mesode:] *No share of this for me, please, none for me! Load your cargo into your ship's hold for yourself with no one else's help! Oh, I want nothing to do with this dwelling, nothing to do with this sacrifice that the Cyclops of Etna performs, remote from any altar, joyously consuming the flesh of his guests!*

370 [Antistrophe:] *A heartless wretch is he who sacrifices guests who have taken refuge as suppliants at the hearth of his home, feasting on their boiled flesh warm from the coals, as he rips and devours it with teeth defiled*[20] †   †

[ODYSSEUS *emerges from the cave. He still carries the wineskin.*]

ODYSSEUS: O Zeus, what should I say, now I've witnessed in the cave terrible things beyond belief, such as might be told in stories, not found in the acts of men?

CHORUS-LEADER: What is it, Odysseus? Surely your dear comrades have not made a feast for the godless Cyclops?

ODYSSEUS: Yes; he looked at them and chose two, running his
380 hands over them to check who were the fattest and best-nourished ones.

CHORUS-LEADER: Poor man, how did your comrades come to suffer this fate?

ODYSSEUS: When we entered this rocky dwelling of his, he first kindled a fire, piling onto the spacious hearth logs from a lofty oak, so heavy that three wagons would be needed to carry them, and he set a bronze cauldron to boil over the flames. Then he spread out on the ground next to the blaze a bed of fir branches. After he had milked his cows, he filled to the brim with white milk a mixing bowl – it could hold as much as ten jugs – and beside it he set a drinking cup of ivy wood, four and a half feet wide, and what looked like six feet deep from rim to base. Then he put down spits of buckthorn wood, their tips burnt in the fire, but the rest of them trimmed smooth with a scythe.[21] †   †   390

When that hellish cook, hated by the gods, had everything prepared, he snatched up two of my comrades. He slashed the throat of the first over the bronze cauldron with a sweeping motion, killing his victim, and then he grabbed the second by the tendon at the end of the foot and, striking him against the   400 sharp edge of a rock, he dashed out his brains. Then, cutting them up with a vicious knife, he began to roast their flesh over the fire, flinging the rest of them, their limbs, into the cauldron to boil. As for me in my misery, with tears welling from my eyes, I was close by the Cyclops' side, acting as his assistant. The others huddled in the recesses of the cave, cowering like birds, their faces quite drained of blood.

But when he had eaten his fill of my companions and had fallen on his back, belching a foul vapour from his throat, I was   410 suddenly inspired by a thought from the gods. [ODYSSEUS *holds up the wineskin.*] I filled his drinking cup with this wine of Maron's and offered it to him to drink, saying these words: 'Cyclops, son of the ocean's god, come and taste this gleaming draught of Dionysus; see what kind of heavenly drink this is that Greece supplies from its vines!' Though his stomach was crammed with that disgusting meal, he accepted and gulped it down in one continuous draught. Then he lifted up his hands and spoke these words of approval: 'Dearest of guests, you crown a splendid feast with a splendid drink!' When I realized   420 he had enjoyed it, I filled his cup a second time, knowing that the wine would do him harm and he would soon get his come-uppance. Sure enough, he proceeded to burst into song, while I kept providing him with cup after cup, making his insides glow with the drink. His tuneless singing is now

mingling with the weeping of my shipmates nearby and the
cave echoes with the noise. I have crept out here, intending to
save my skin, and yours, if you are willing. Now tell me: do
you or do you not want to escape from this barbarous man and
430   live with the water-haunting nymphs in the halls of Bacchus?
Your father inside did agree to this but his strength is gone and
he has been taking advantage of the wine too much; he's
attached to his cup like a bird trapped in birdlime and flapping
its wings in distraction. But you're a young fellow, come, join
me in escaping and get back your old friend Dionysus, someone
quite different from the Cyclops.

CHORUS-LEADER: O my dear friend, if only we could escape
the clutches of the Cyclops, that ungodly creature, and live to
440   see that day! My poor old siphon[22] here has been widowed for
ages now, and has no place to find relief.

ODYSSEUS: Then listen now as I tell you how to punish that
villainous beast and bring your days of slavery to an end.

CHORUS-LEADER: Speak on; the sound of the Asiatic lyre would
not please my ears more than the news of the Cyclops'
death!

ODYSSEUS: This drink of Bacchus has pleased him so much that
he wants to go and have a party with his brother Cyclopes.

CHORUS-LEADER: I get it; your plan is to ambush him, alone,
in woodland and slit his throat, or to shove him off some cliff.

ODYSSEUS: Nothing of the sort; it's cunning that inspires me.

450   CHORUS-LEADER: Well, what *is* your plan? We've long been
told how clever you are.

ODYSSEUS: To rid him of this idea of going to have a party by
telling him that he shouldn't share this drink with the Cyclopes
but rather have a happy time keeping it for himself. And
when he nods off, conquered by Bacchus, there's a branch of
olive-wood in his home that I mean to sharpen at one end
with this sword and then put into the fire. Then, when I see it
is glowing, I'm going to lift it, all hot, and ram it right into the
460   Cyclops' face, causing his eye to melt. And just as a carpenter
building a ship uses two leather thongs to spin his drill round

and round,[23] I'll whirl my firebrand round in the Cyclops' orb of sight until I scorch his eyeball out.

CHORUS-LEADER [*starting to dance*]: Yippee! I'm overjoyed, quite mad at your inventions!

ODYSSEUS: And then I'll bring you, your friends and the old man aboard my black ship, safely stowed, and with all hands to the oar I'll quit this land.

CHORUS-LEADER: Is it at all possible that I, too, could grasp the   470
firebrand as it blinds his eye, just as happens with a libation made to a god? I want to play a part in this task.

ODYSSEUS: Oh, yes, you have to; it's a big brand and you must help in holding it.

CHORUS-LEADER: I could lift the weight of a hundred waggons if we are going to smoke out the eye of that pernicious Cyclops like a wasps' nest!

ODYSSEUS: Now, no talking about this! You know the plan and when I give the order obey the master-builder. No running   [480]
off for me, leaving my friends behind in the cave and saving my own skin!

CHORUS-LEADER: Come, who will be first,[24] who second to take up his post and grip the firebrand's handle tight, then shove it under the Cyclops' brow and grind out his bright eye?

[POLYPHEMUS *is heard singing in the cave.*] Hush! Hush! Our friend is drunk. Here he comes now, making his way out of his rocky home, producing a hideous attempt at music, a dismal   490
singer who will answer for it. Come on, let's educate the ignoramus with our revelling songs! Whatever happens, he's going to lose his sight.

[POLYPHEMUS *enters slowly from the cave, winecup in hand. He is supported by* SILENUS.]

CHORUS [Strophe 1]: *Happy the man who cries out in honour of Bacchus, as the precious liquid of the vine sets him fair on course for the revel. He leans on his friend's arm and, waiting for him on her bed, he has his voluptuous mistress, with her shining, golden hair, as,*   500
with scented locks himself, he asks, 'Who will open the door for me?'

CYCLOPS [Strophe 2]: *Ho! Ho! Ho! I'm full of wine. My spirits soar with the joy of the feast! I'm like a freighter, with hull loaded right up to the deck at the top of my stomach. This merry cargo brings me out to revel in the springtime with my brother Cyclopes.* [*To* SILENUS]

510 *Come on, friend, come on, give me the wineskin, do.*

CHORUS [Strophe 3]: *With beautiful glance he steps forth in beauty from the house. But who loves us? The lamp is kindled and awaits you; a rosy-skinned, tender nymph is in your moist cave. But more than one colour will stain the garlands that will soon deck your head!*

520 ODYSSEUS: Cyclops, I'm well acquainted with this Bacchus[25] I gave you to drink.

CYCLOPS: Who is Bacchus? Do people worship him as a god?

ODYSSEUS: In bringing joy to men's hearts he has no equal.

CYCLOPS: Well, I certainly enjoy belching him out!

ODYSSEUS: That is the god's nature; he harms nobody at all.

CYCLOPS: But a god like him, how can he be happy living in a wineskin?

ODYSSEUS: He accommodates himself to wherever he is put.

CYCLOPS: Gods shouldn't wear animal skins.

ODYSSEUS: So what, if he gives you pleasure? Have you something against skin?

CYCLOPS: I'm not keen on the wineskin; but this here drink I do like.

530 ODYSSEUS: Stay here, then, and have a good time drinking, Cyclops!

CYCLOPS: Shouldn't I give my brothers a share in this drink?

ODYSSEUS: No, keep it for yourself and they'll think more highly of you.

CYCLOPS: But if I share it with my family I'll be more helpful to them.

ODYSSEUS: Revelling can often end in punches and heated words.

CYCLOPS: I may be drunk, but just the same no one will dare touch me!

ODYSSEUS: My dear fellow, when you've been drinking it's best not to leave your home.

CYCLOPS: Only a fool dislikes revelling after drinking.

ODYSSEUS: But the man who stays at home when he's the worse for drink is wise.

CYCLOPS: What should we do, Silenus?[26] Do you think we should stay?

SILENUS: I do; why do we need others to drink with us, Cyclops?   540

ODYSSEUS: Yes, and the ground is softly carpeted with flowers and grass.

SILENUS: Besides, it's nice drinking when the sun's warm. Lie down here, please, and stretch out on the ground.

[POLYPHEMUS *lies down with the help of* SILENUS, *who slides the mixing bowl behind him.*]

CYCLOPS: There we are! Hey, why have you put the bowl behind me?

SILENUS: In case someone knocks it over in passing.

CYCLOPS: Oh no, it's a drink on the sly that *you're* after! Put it down between us. [*Turning his attention to* ODYSSEUS] And you, stranger, tell me the name I should call you by.

ODYSSEUS: 'Noman'. But what gift have you for me in order to earn my gratitude?

CYCLOPS: I'll have all the rest of your company for dinner before   550
I eat you.

SILENUS: A generous gift to offer your guest, Cyclops! [*He surreptitiously helps himself to some wine.*]

CYCLOPS: Hey, you! What are you up to? Having a secret drink, are you?

SILENUS: No, the wine kissed me because I look so handsome.

CYCLOPS: You'll be sorry for taking a fancy to the wine when it doesn't fancy you!

SILENUS: It does, I tell you; it says it loves me for my good looks.

CYCLOPS: Here, pour away; don't give me the cup till it's filled to the brim.

SILENUS: Have I got the mixture right? [*Peering into the bowl*] Let me see.

CYCLOPS: You'll be the death of me! Give me that and no more nonsense!

SILENUS [*placing a garland on* POLYPHEMUS' *head*]: Oh no, not until I've seen you wearing a garland and I've had another taste.

560 CYCLOPS: What a twister of a wine-pourer!

SILENUS: No, I protest – mind you, it's delicious wine. But now you must wipe your mouth clean; here comes your next drink.

CYCLOPS: There, it's done; my lips are clean, and my beard.

SILENUS: Now lean on your elbow in a graceful way and then drink it down, just as you see me drinking – or can't see me, now! [SILENUS *has buried his head in the bowl.*]

CYCLOPS [*sitting up with an effort*]: Hey, there, what's the idea?

SILENUS [*raising his head slowly*]: Excellent! That's the end of that!

CYCLOPS [*throwing his bowl to* ODYSSEUS]: Here, stranger, catch! You'll be my wine-pourer from now on.

ODYSSEUS: Well, my hand is not unacquainted with the vine.

CYCLOPS: Come on, then, fill me up!

ODYSSEUS: I am pouring; just stop talking, will you?

CYCLOPS: That's a tall order for anyone who's had a lot to drink.

570 ODYSSEUS [*handing him the filled cup*]: There you are; now take it and down the lot – don't leave a drop! The tippler and the tipple should end together.

CYCLOPS: Oh, yes, yes! What a clever tree the vine is!

ODYSSEUS: And if you sink a lot of wine on top of a big meal, filling your belly till its thirst is quenched, it will send you to sleep. But if you leave any in the cup, Bacchus will make your throat unbearably dry.

CYCLOPS [*downing a lot of wine quickly*]: Yeehah! That was a narrow escape from drowning! What undiluted pleasure! I seem to see the sky and the earth floating along together; I see

580 the throne of Zeus and the gods in all their holy majesty. Shall I not kiss them? [*Looking at the* SATYRS] The Graces are giving me the eye. Enough! [*Turning to stare at* SILENUS] Ganymede here[27] will give me a nicer time than the Graces if I take *him*

to bed. Boys somehow give me greater pleasure than females.

SILENUS: Oh, help! I'm Zeus' boy Ganymede, am I, Cyclops?

CYCLOPS [*grabbing hold of him*]: You certainly are, and I'm carrying him off from Dardanus' land!

SILENUS: I'm done for, lads! A monstrous fate awaits me now!

CYCLOPS: Are you criticizing your lover? Getting fussy because
he's had a drink?

SILENUS: This is awful! That wine will soon be the bitterest
drink I've had!

[POLYPHEMUS *exits into the cave, with the reluctant* SILENUS
under his arm.]

ODYSSEUS: Come now, children of Dionysus, noble lads, the   590
fellow's gone inside, and soon, stretched out in sleep, he'll be
spewing flesh out of his shameless throat. The firebrand has
been prepared inside the cave, giving off its smoke, and all that
remains is to set the Cyclops' eye on fire. But now see that you
behave like men!

CHORUS-LEADER: We will show a spirit as hard as rock or steel!
But go into the cave before something awful happens to our
father; we have everything in hand here, don't worry.

ODYSSEUS [*raising his hands in prayer*]: Hephaestus, Etna's lord,
burn out the glittering eye of your wicked neighbour and then   600
have done with him once and for all! And you, Sleep, offspring
of black Night, with all your strength invade this beast detested
by the gods, and, after their illustrious efforts at Troy, do not
allow Odysseus, himself and his crew, to be destroyed by a
man who cares nothing for gods or mortals. Otherwise we
must regard chance as a god and its powers as greater than the
gods'. [ODYSSEUS *goes into the cave.*]

CHORUS: *He who feeds on his guests will have his throat firmly gripped
by the tongs; in no time the fire will make him lose his bright eye.*   610
*Already the brand, reduced to charcoal, is hidden in the ashes, that
huge offspring of oak. Let Maron's wine come now and do its work!
Let it take out the mad Cyclops' eye so he gets a hangover! Then I
want to leave the Cyclops' lonely home behind and to set eyes on*

620 *Bromius, my longed-for lord, who loves to wear ivy in his hair. Shall*
such joy ever be mine?

[ODYSSEUS *comes out from the cave, angry.*]

ODYSSEUS: In heaven's name stop your chanting,[28] you brutes,
button your lips and keep quiet! I forbid any one of you even
to breathe or blink or clear his throat, in case the vile Cyclops
wakes up before his eye has its contest with the fire.

CHORUS-LEADER: We're holding our mouths tight shut, saying
not a word!

630 ODYSSEUS: Come on, then, I want you to come inside[29] and
grab hold of the firebrand; it's glowing nicely now.

CHORUS-LEADER: We need instructions! Who should be the
first to seize the stake itself and to burn out the Cyclops' eye?
We must share in the same fate! [*The* CHORUS *now divide into
two groups, each with its spokesman.*]

FIRST SPOKESMAN: Oh, *we* are standing too far from the cave's
entrance to thrust the fire into his eye!

SECOND SPOKESMAN: And *we* have just become lame!

FIRST SPOKESMAN: That's just happened to me too; I was
standing here and suddenly got a sprain in my feet – no idea
how!

640 ODYSSEUS: A sprain, while you were standing?

FIRST SPOKESMAN: Yes, and something has made my eyes
full of dust or ashes.

ODYSSEUS: They're timid fellows, good-for-nothing, these
allies.

CHORUS-LEADER: Just because I'm sorry for my back and spine,
and don't want my teeth knocked out, does this make me
timid? But I know a really good spell of Orpheus[30] that will
make the firebrand march of its own volition right up to the
skull of the one-eyed son of Earth and set him on fire.

650 ODYSSEUS: I've long since known the stuff you are made of, but
now I know it even better. I must resort to my own friends for
help. If you are so feeble when it comes to lending a hand,
then at least give us your encouragement, so that we may find

our friends brave in heart thanks to your support. [ODYSSEUS
disappears into the cave.]

CHORUS-LEADER: I will do this and let others take the risk for
us. If cries of support can do any good, let the Cyclops sizzle!

CHORUS: *Ha, ha! Ha, ha! Shove bravely, don't be slow, burn out the
eyebrow of the brute who makes a meal of guests! Burn him, yes, singe
him, yes, the shepherd of Etna! Spin it round, pull it round, so he*   660
doesn't do you some terrible harm in his agony!

   [POLYPHEMUS *staggers out of the cave, his face streaming with
blood.*]

CYCLOPS: Aargh! My bright eye has been burnt to cinders!

CHORUS-LEADER: Now that's a victory-song that makes good
hearing! Sing me that one again, Cyclops!

CYCLOPS: Aargh, the pain! How I have been abused, how
ruined! But there is no way you will get away from this cave
to boast about it, you miserable little wretches! I'll take my
stand at the entrance to the cave here and stretch my arms
across it.

CHORUS-LEADER: Why all this shouting, Cyclops?

CYCLOPS: I'm destroyed!

CHORUS-LEADER: You certainly look ugly.   670

CYCLOPS: And wretched into the bargain!

CHORUS-LEADER: Did you fall into the middle of the coals
when you were drunk?

CYCLOPS: Noman was my destroyer.[31]

CHORUS-LEADER: Then no one has done you wrong!

CYCLOPS: Noman has blinded me in my eye.

CHORUS-LEADER: Then you are not blind!

CYCLOPS: How's that?

CHORUS-LEADER: How would no man make you blind?

CYCLOPS: You are making fun of me. But this Noman, where
is he?

CHORUS-LEADER: No where, Cyclops.

CYCLOPS: To make it plain to you, it was my guest who
destroyed me, that contemptible creature, who scuppered me
with the drink he gave me.

CHORUS-LEADER: It's a terrible thing, wine, a hard wrestler to throw.

CYCLOPS: In the name of the gods, have they run away or are they still inside the cave?

680 CHORUS-LEADER: They are standing here in silence, sheltering by the overhanging cliff.

CYCLOPS: On my left-hand side or my right?

CHORUS-LEADER: On your right.[32] [POLYPHEMUS *moves away from the entrance, so that* ODYSSEUS, *his men and* SILENUS *are able to slip out quietly.*]

CYCLOPS: Where?

CHORUS-LEADER: Right up against the cliff. Do you have them?

CYCLOPS [*bumping into the rocky cliff*]: What I have is one pain after another! I've bashed my skull and broken it!

CHORUS-LEADER: Yes, and they're getting away from you.

CYCLOPS [*still searching with his hands*]: Wasn't it somewhere here, you said, over here?

CHORUS-LEADER: No, it's over here I mean.

CYCLOPS: Where do you mean?

CHORUS-LEADER: Turn round that way, to your left.

CYCLOPS: Oh, no, I am being mocked! You are making fun of me in my affliction!

CHORUS-LEADER: I won't any longer; there he is in front of you.

CYCLOPS: You utter wretch, wherever are you?

690 ODYSSEUS: Some way from you, keeping watch over Odysseus' body here.

CYCLOPS: What did you say? That's a new name you're using; you've changed it.

ODYSSEUS: It's the one my father called me by: Odysseus. You were destined to pay the penalty for your sinful feast. With little credit would we have burnt Troy to the ground, if I had failed to punish you for murdering my comrades!

CYCLOPS: Oh, no, no! An ancient oracle is being fulfilled![33] It said that I would be blinded by you after you had sailed away

from Troy. But it also prophesied that you would be punished
for this act by having to drift on the sea for many a year.[34]   700

ODYSSEUS: Go hang yourself! And I'm not just saying it, I have
done what I promised! I shall go down to the shore and set sail
over the Sicilian sea to my native land.

[*Exit* ODYSSEUS *and his men.*]

CYCLOPS: No you won't! I'm going to break off part of this
rock, hurl it and crush you to bits, you and your shipmates.[35]
I'll go up to the hilltop, blind though I may be, climbing
through the cave's back entrance. [*Exit* POLYPHEMUS *into his
cave.*]

CHORUS-LEADER: But we will become shipmates of Odysseus
here and give our service to Bacchus for evermore.

[SILENUS *and the* CHORUS *hurry off to join* ODYSSEUS *and
his men.*]

NOTES

HERACLES

1. *suppliants at an altar*: The ritual act of supplication of a god or gods for aid is often dramatized in Greek tragedy. To throw oneself on the god's mercy, the suppliant naturally takes a position at the god's temple or in some other sacred space. To violate this sanctuary is to risk the god's anger. This procedure is probably treated with more respect in the world of tragedy than in contemporary life. See further J. Gould's detailed treatment in the *Journal of Hellenic Studies* 93 (1973), pp. 74–103.

2. *shared his wife's bed with Zeus*: The language is designedly startling. When a god seduces or rapes an unmarried mortal woman, the resulting child is unambiguously the son or daughter of a god, as Ion is son of Apollo in *Ion*. But when the mortal woman is married already the poets often treat the child as having double parentage: thus Helen is referred to as daughter of Zeus and also of the mortal husband of Leda, Tyndareus. So here Amphitryon calls himself 'father of Heracles' although well aware that his wife Alcmena bore the hero to Zeus (to make the situation more complicated still, some versions told of Zeus visiting Alcmena in disguise, taking the form of Amphitryon). The issue of fatherhood is important in this play, in which characters often ask how Zeus can neglect his paternal duty to Heracles.

3. *Sown Men*: According to the myth, Cadmus, founder of Thebes, was told to sow the teeth of the dragon he had slain in the ground, and there sprang forth a crop of fully armed warriors who immediately began fighting with each other; the survivors became the first citizens of Thebes. The story symbolizes. the warlike nature of the Thebans.

4. *Creon, son of Menoeceus*: Creon also figures in other tragedies, notably Sophocles' *Antigone*. Earlier poetry such as Pindar's odes had already told of his acceptance of Amphitryon and betrothal of Megara to Heracles.

5. *Argos*: The reference is to an ancient city of Mycenae, in ruins in the Argolid since the 460s. The vast stone walls were thought of as the work of giants or (as here) Cyclopes, builders of superhuman strength. Mycenae is close to the still-inhabited city of Argos, and Greek poets often conflated the two.

6. *after killing Electryon*: There is no fuller version recorded of Amphitryon's killing of Electryon, his father-in-law. Here it is merely a narrative convenience to explain why Amphitryon is in exile and why Heracles is in service to Eurystheus.

7. *no one knows*: Euripides is in fact very likely to be restructuring the myth here. In some versions, attested later than Euripides, the labours follow the madness and the child-killing, and may even have been thought of as atonement for the killings. Euripides' plot achieves a different kind of effect, with the killing as a horrifying catastrophe when it seems all Heracles' troubles are over.

8. *the triple-bodied hound*: Cerberus, the monstrous dog which guarded the entrance to the underworld.

9. *came to hold sway in Thebes*: The story referred to here was dramatized in Euripides' own *Antiope*, which survives only in fragments. Lycus seized power, treated Antiope, the rightful queen, cruelly, and was deposed and slain by her children, Amphion and Zethus. The younger Lycus, the villain of this play, is probably a Euripidean invention.

10. *sick with party conflict*: The description of Thebes as riven by factional division recurs at 542. This anxiety about civil conflict echoes concerns in many cities during the Peloponnesian war, in which civil war or *stasis* was a major political factor, often leading to extreme violence. The phenomenon is analysed by Thucydides in one of his most famous passages (iii.82–3, which follows a detailed account of civil strife in Corcyra).

11. *the city of the Taphians*: This exploit of Amphitryon as leader of the Theban armies on a campaign to avenge his wife's brothers is also referred to at 1078ff., where it marks the peak of his past achievements. The Taphians are a people in northwestern Greece.

12. *I am old*: The age of the chorus, like that of Amphitryon himself, is frequently emphasized, sometimes in explicit contrast with the youthful strength of Heracles. But his strength in the end proves destructive to those he loves most.

13. *your empty boasts*: Lycus accuses Amphitryon of lying about Zeus' fathering Heracles, just as in the *Bacchae* the sisters of Semele refused to believe that Semele's child Dionysus was the son of Zeus. But Lycus' scepticism is perverse, as it assumes that Amphitryon is lying about being a cuckold.

14. *what is this splendid feat of your husband*: This introduces a denunciation of Heracles as no true hero but a coward. The paradox of arguing that Heracles was not brave makes this a typical example of rhetorical ingenuity in putting forward arguments for a highly implausible position – 'making the worse cause appear the better', as contemporaries put it. This kind of counter-intuitive argument was associated with the sophists such as Gorgias. Other examples in Euripides are numerous: see esp. *Trojan Women* 365ff. (Cassandra argues that the defeated Trojans are luckier than the victorious Greeks). Here the questioning of Heracles' status of a hero is effectively rebutted by Amphitryon; but the later events of the play will pose a more difficult challenge to Heracles' traditional heroism.

15. *Archery is no test of a man's courage*: Lycus voices the traditional language of military solidarity, which sees hand-to-hand combat (as in the hoplite warfare of fifth-century Greece) as the true test of courage and strength. Amphitryon's response is less traditional. Bowmanship might be admired but was an ambiguous skill for the reasons Lycus implies. In the epic tradition the bow was the weapon of Paris, who used it to kill the heroic Achilles, for whom he would have been no match in combat; and Pandarus in Book 4 of the *Iliad* wounds Menelaus with a treacherous shot which violates a truce. The bow is also the weapon of the cunning Odysseus. Lycus' argument is weak, however, as there were many occasions when Heracles overcame formidable foes by his own strength, not with the bow.

16. *war against the earth-born Giants*: The war of the Gods against the barbarous Giants is a common theme in art, though less frequent in literature. The notion here seems to be that Heracles shares Zeus' chariot; he fires his arrows while Zeus hurls thunderbolts.

17. *I am your king and you my slaves*: This kind of talk would have immediately roused the antagonism of an Athenian audience, hostile to monarchy and above all to autocratic tyranny. Citizens would not tolerate the description of them as 'slaves' to a ruler: the elders are suitably outraged.

18. *lift up the staffs*: The efforts of the old men to match their strength against that of the tyrant swiftly subside into regret and acknowledgement of their own powerlessness. This kind of role for a chorus is common in tragedy (e.g. Aeschylus' *Agamemnon*). Often the chorus form a marginal group or are helpless spectators of a sequence of action in which they cannot assist, however strongly they may desire to do so. See further J. Gould, 'Tragedy and Collective Experience', in M. Silk (ed.), *Tragedy and the Tragic* (Oxford 1996), pp. 217–43.

19. *Gentlemen, I thank you*: The formal opening, and the cerebral quality of the whole speech, are surprising to our naturalistic taste, but not uncharacteristic of Greek tragedy in general and Euripides in particular. Were this a scene in 'real life', we would expect an angry riposte from Lycus to the chorus's aggressive remarks. Instead Euripides leaves Lycus silent for some time while Megara has her say. She restates heroic values in a woman's terms, but her resolution is for death rather than defiance. The emphasis is on the dignity of the sufferers rather than emotional realism.

20. *partner in fatherhood*: See note 2 above. In this speech Amphitryon goes so far as to rebuke Zeus for his conduct. For passages of this kind see M. Heath, *The Poetics of Greek Tragedy* (London 1987), p. 51. In Greek religion, for a mortal to question, criticize or even accuse a god is not automatically wrong or blasphemous, though it does risk incurring the god's anger. In some passages of tragedy reproaches of this type are unjustified, and the speaker comes in the end to realize that the gods were in the right all along. *Heracles* handles the motif differently: in the short term Zeus will seem to have ensured the wellbeing of Heracles' family, but by the end of the play there will be even stronger reasons for all concerned to reproach Zeus and the other gods.

21. *crowning him with a garland of song . . . .* : This long and elaborate ode in praise of Heracles' achievements is the most ornate lyric passage in the play and one of the longest odes in all of tragedy. It is a kind of mourning song, as the opening words suggest: the chorus have now concluded that Heracles is dead. The language of the song recalls Pindar's odes: celebratory, allusive, full of poetic adjectives. The tone is more religious than usual in Euripidean choruses: the ode is close in manner to a hymn that recounts the exploits of a god.

The subject of the ode is the twelve labours of Heracles. This is the earliest passage in surviving Greek poetry which lists them in full (the later versions vary considerably both in the order and in what they include). The temple of Zeus at Olympia (*c.* 460 BC) had representations of a rather different series of twelve on its metopes. In the fifth century it seems there was no fixed canon of labours.

Euripides refers to the following sequence of labours. (1) The killing of the Nemean lion (this seems regularly to have been represented as the first labour). (2) The killing of the Centaurs. (3) The killing of the hind of Artemis. (4) The taming of the man-eating mares of King Diomedes. (5) The killing of Cycnus, a marauder who persecuted those visiting Delphi. (6) The gathering of the apples of the Hesperides (the Singing Maidens) in the Far West; these apples were guarded by a huge serpent. This labour is closely associated with (7) the clearing of the sea of monsters and (8) the bearing of the sky for a brief time in place of Atlas, who normally supported it. (9) The taking of the girdle of Hippolyta, queen of the Amazons, after doing battle with the Amazon hordes at the head of an expedition of Greek warriors. (10) The killing of the many-headed hydra of Lerna; with the poison from its blood he anointed his arrows and (11) killed Geryon, a triple-bodied monstrous herdsman: in this case the actual labour was to bring back Geryon's cattle, which meant killing him first. (12) The descent to Hades to bring back Cerberus.

For other names of places and people see the Glossary; for sample illustrations of many of the labours, see T. H. Carpenter, *Art and Myth in Ancient Greece* (London 1991), ch. 6.

22. *who will serve as priest* . . . : In these words and what follows Megara treats their death as a perverse kind of sacrifice. The threat of human sacrifice is quite frequent in Greek myth (as in *Iphigenia among the Taurians*), and sacrificial imagery is often applied to other forms of death where there is a slayer and a victim (as in the destruction of Pentheus in the *Bacchae*). In a landmark paper, 'Greek Tragedy and Sacrificial Ritual' (*Greek, Roman and Byzantine Studies* 7 (1966), pp. 87–121), W. Burkert offers a bold and controversial theory connecting these points to the ancient religious origins of tragedy. See also P. E. Easterling, 'Tragedy and ritual', in R. Scodel (ed.), *Theater and Society in the Classical World* (Ann Arbor 1993), pp. 7–23.

23. *fiends . . . as your brides*: The word for 'fiends', *keres*, denotes sinister spirits of death, not unlike the Furies.

24. *if any mortal utterance reaches the ears of Hades' citizens*: In different contexts characters in tragedy and other genres will express belief and disbelief in the afterlife, and opposing views about whether the dead care about the living or can be reached by them. Uncertainty about these questions is natural and realistic, especially in a culture in which the answers were not laid down by dogma. See further K. J. Dover, *Greek Popular Morality in the Time of Plato and Aristotle* (Oxford 1974), pp. 261–8.

25. *can it be my dearest love I see?*: Because of the size of the theatre and the length of the entrance passages (*parodoi*), new arrivals would take some time to reach the central acting area, and would be visible to all or most of the spectators before they could join in normal exchange with the actors on stage. Hence the need on occasion for these 'filler' lines, which also mark the importance of the entrance and create tension.

26. *Then fling away* . . . : The speech of Heracles prepares us for the violence to come. Some have supposed that his enraged words here are the first signs of the madness which is coming, and that the insanity is thus partly rooted in his own passionate nature. This cannot be right: Lycus has shown himself a figure unworthy of any sympathy, and we must be meant to endorse and approve of Heracles' wish to protect his family. The speech does however illustrate the hero's assumption that violent action will solve all his problems: the latter part of the play will show him wrong.

27. *many impoverished men* . . . : The social analysis here develops earlier references to civil strife in Thebes (34, 542f.). Similarly Plato and Aristotle theorize about the causes of revolution in cities: in an oligarchy, according to Plato, men of good birth acquire many debts and remain in the state discontented and eager for revolution as a means of bettering themselves (*Republic* 555d). There may be no specific contemporary state in Euripides' mind, but the line of thought would be familiar to his audience.

28. *this gave me good fortune*: Those who had been initiated in the mysteries of Demeter and Persephone at Eleusis were believed to enjoy a blissful state after death, as proclaimed at the end of the Homeric Hymn to Demeter. There was a tradition that Heracles had undergone initiation before his descent to fetch Cerberus. It seems to be referred to in a fragment of Pindar, and may go back to the sixth century BC.

29. *Theseus*: This reference paves the way for Theseus' later appearance to give aid to Heracles in return for his release from captivity in Hades. Euripides does not mention the discreditable reason for Theseus' own descent – to help his friend Pirithous carry off Persephone as his bride! The hero of Athenian myth is generally cut free from these more dubious past exploits.

30. *the stamp of virtue*: This paradoxical notion, expressed in a puzzling way which implies the difficulty of comparison between human and divine standards, resembles some of the utopian wishes uttered by Euripidean characters (e.g. *Medea* 516ff., *Hippolytus* 616ff.). But this wish is especially bizarre, and it is hard to see how it would work in practice. The distinction of good and bad men is problematical, as the play shows: Lycus is bad, but will we in the end think Heracles good? The events will disrupt the chorus's expectations. The relevance to Heracles' own case seems clear, since we have just heard that he has himself in a sense returned from death.

31. *wear my proper crown*: Biographical criticism insists on reading this as a *cri de coeur* from the poet himself, at this date in his sixties, but this is quite unnecessary and is at most a secondary allusion. We have already heard much from the chorus about the burden of age, and the momentary euphoria of Heracles' return makes them sing with joy and feel renewed vitality. The triumphal celebration will be short-lived.

32. *You're none too soon . . .* : The scene which ensues, in which Amphitryon lulls Lycus into a sense of false security, is a typical 'entrapment' sequence, for which parallels can be found in Aeschylus' *Agamemnon* or the *Electra* plays by Sophocles and Euripides. As is common in scenes of this type, there are several lines (esp. 719) which have a double meaning for Amphitryon and the audience but which Lycus does not fully understand.

33. *from inside the palace*: The cry of the victim from within is another 'typical' feature of deception plots: the archetype in extant tragedy is the scene in which the chorus hear Agamemnon's death-cries (Aeschylus, *Agamemnon* 1343ff.). There, however, the chorus are themselves unsure what is happening; here, they know and rejoice.

34. *claiming that they had no power*: Lycus has denied that the gods care about human crimes: Heracles' retribution seems to prove him wrong. Many passages in Greek tragedy refer to or appeal to the gods as upholders of human justice; often as in this play, the wrongdoer is punished but the virtuous do not escape misfortune.

35. *Ismenus . . . start up the dance . . .* : The address to the river Ismenus and the city of Thebes itself, to the stream of Dirce and to the rocks of Delphi, inviting them to join in dance and celebration, seems bizarre to our ears. But the figure of personification of places and geographic features is common in Greek lyric poetry, and the extravagance of this passage suits the excited enthusiasm of the chorus.

36. *IRIS and MADNESS appear above the palace*: This is the boldest theatrical stroke in the play. The normal pattern in Euripides, if gods appear at all, is for them to do so only in prologue or at the very close of the action. Here the *deus ex machina* ('god appearing on the crane' – the phrase refers to the mechanical device sometimes used to hoist the divinity in as though flying) appears in mid-play, and brings not resolution but chaos. There may be some precedent in earlier drama (a similar scene seems to have figured in Sophocles' lost *Niobe*), but this moment is as dramatically extraordinary as it is theologically disturbing. Iris, messenger of the gods, is a familiar mythical figure, here given a crueller personality than in other sources. Madness is a personified abstraction, but is given a more sympathetic character, pleading to be spared the unsavoury task she has been assigned. Euripides seems to play on the paradox of Madness herself arguing for greater restraint (esp. 857).

37. *tired old legs*: The recurrence of reference to the chorus's old age is ominous, after their joyful dancing.

38. *Healer King*: The invocation is of Apollo.

39. *Hera feels for him*: Earlier tradition from Homer onwards emphasizes Hera's persecution of Heracles, mainly on account of his being Zeus' bastard child. The following lines possibly hint at a further notion, that Heracles has achieved too much and earned the jealous anger of the gods through his great success. This point is disputed, however: for a discussion see G. W. Bond's commentary (Oxford 1981), pp. xxiv–vi.

40. *I make the Sun my witness . . .* : The speech of Madness, with its vivid imagery and promises of violence, does much to help us visualize the scenes which the poet cannot present on stage. The vivid narrative of the messenger later in the play complements this. In the closing part of this scene (from Iris's line beginning 'It isn't your place . . .' [855]) the metre shifts from the normal iambic trimeters to trochaic tetrameters, a longer line which seems regularly to be used in passages of vigorous action or agitation.

41. *daughter of Zeus*: The cry of Amphitryon is puzzling to the chorus and audience. It will be explained by the messenger's account later (1001–8). We are to imagine a divine epiphany within the palace: Heracles' protector, Pallas Athena, appears and hurls a rock at Heracles, knocking him unconscious. His falling body strikes and shatters a supporting pillar, leading to the collapse of the building.

42. *Part of the palace collapses*: It is very unlikely that this would be represented on the Greek stage, although some form of thunderous musical accompaniment may have been used. Some references are made to the surrounding ruins later in the play, but the stage-building was presumably a fixture and could not be dismantled in mid-play. Similarly, when Dionysus in the *Bacchae* releases himself from captivity with an earthquake, the audience is meant to participate imaginatively.

43. *keeping a reverent silence*: The preceding lines allude to the rituals of sacrifice in order to purify from the pollution of bloodshed. A basket containing barley and a knife to be used in the killing of the victim is circulated; then a flaming torch is quenched in water, and the moisture on it is sprinkled over the participants. After these preliminaries there is a call for pious silence, which normally precedes the sacrifice. But Heracles' onset of madness disrupts the expected sequence.

44. *eyes were like a Gorgon's*: Compare the preceding choral song in which Madness herself is said to goad on her team 'like a Gorgon-child of Night'. Her qualities are transferred to her victim.

45. *slaughter of Danaus' sons . . .* : The chorus cite two horrific tales from earlier mythology, both of which pale in comparison to the terrible acts of Heracles. The first reference is to the disastrous union of the daughters of Danaus with their cousins, the sons of Aegyptus. All but one of the reluctant brides killed their husbands on their wedding night. The second refers to the grim tale of Philomela, Tereus and Procne. Tereus was married to Procne and had a child by her. Lusting after Philomela, his wife's sister, he raped her; his wife learned the truth and in revenge killed their son and served him up to her husband at a meal; only after he had unwittingly eaten did he discover the truth. The point of 'sacrifice of blood for the Muses' is obscure; possibly it refers to the preservation of the boy's story through song. Parallels and examples of this kind are commonly quoted by choruses, and often the point is to stress the uniqueness of the present disaster (as here and e.g. Aeschylus, *Libation-Bearers* 586ff., Euripides, *Hippolytus* 545ff.).

46. *The doors of the palace open . . .* : The conventions of Greek tragedy did not permit indoor scenes, but the compromise device of the *ekkuklema* ('rolling-out platform') provided a solution in scenes like this. The platform, on wheels, seems to have emerged from the stage-building through the central door,

and conveyed the stationary figures of those within. Often those revealed were dead, asleep or unconscious. The device was already used in Aeschylus and frequently thereafter. See O. Taplin, *The Stagecraft of Aeschylus* (1977), pp. 442–3 (his scepticism about Aeschylus' employment of the device is generally thought unjustified).

47. *Be quiet . . . be quiet!*: Other tragedies also use this technique to create tension, with one character anxiously warning others not to wake a sleeping figure. There are parallels in Sophocles' *Women at Trachis* and *Philoctetes*, as well as Euripides' own *Orestes*.

48. *surrounded by the sea*: For Amphitryon's campaign against the Taphians see note 11 above. The notion that a man would be happier in dying at the peak of his good fortune is common in classical literature (cf. Herodotus 1.30ff., and the Latin expression 'felix opportunitate mortis' [lucky in the timeliness of one's death]).

49. *Well, I'm alive, anyway*: Euripides is fond of these scenes in which calm follows storm, and a character who has been deranged fights his way back to rationality or calmness. Compare Orestes' recovery from his fit of madness in *Orestes* 277ff., and the 'psychotherapy' scene between Cadmus and Agave in the *Bacchae* 1217–96.

50. *that is broken in half*: Heracles' questioning reminds the audience what they are meant to be visualizing, a man slumped amid the ruins of the royal palace.

51. *arrows and the bow*: It is clear in this speech and what follows that the bow has a symbolic significance as the emblem of his own heroic past: note especially Heracles' hesitation as to whether to take his weapons with him into exile. The earlier debate between Lycus and Amphitryon over the merits of archery is to some degree retrospectively justified.

52. *Zeus, do you see this . . .* : It is common for those who feel that the gods are neglecting their interests to call out to them in prayer or appeal, asking whether they are looking on and allowing injustice to happen: see, for example, the passages gathered by J. Griffin, 'The Divine Audience and the Religion of the *Iliad*', *Classical Quarterly* 28 (1978), pp. 1–4. The phrase 'on Hera's throne' gives a sharper edge to the criticism, as if Zeus were merely the consort of Hera.

53. *why do I spare my own life?*: Heracles now contemplates suicide as an escape from his guilt. In making Heracles contemplate death, Euripides reworks the themes of the earlier half of the play, in which Amphitryon and Megara resolved to accept the inevitable.

54. *But here comes Theseus . . .* : In tragedy Theseus, the favourite hero of Athenian mythology, is normally an attractive and sympathetic figure. Here he offers his own personal friendship and also, on behalf of his city, the refuge and home which Heracles needs. The echoes of the Athenians' idealized self-image (as also in *The Children of Heracles* and the *Suppliant Women*) are clear. See further S. Mills, *Theseus, Tragedy and the Athenian Empire* (1998), esp. ch. 4, on *Heracles*, and, more broadly, C. Pelling's 'Conclusion' in Pelling (ed.) *Greek Tragedy and the Historian* (1997), pp. 213–35.

55. *exposing them to my blood-guilt*: Physical and even social contact with a killer, or one who has committed other acts of violence, can bring 'pollution' even upon the innocent. On the complex range of religious ideas involved here, see R. Parker, *Miasma: Pollution and Purification in Early Greek Religion* (1983), esp. ch. 4 'The Shedding of Blood' and ch. 11 'Some Scenes from Tragedy': he discusses this episode of the play on pp. 316–18. For the avoidance of pollution by raising a physical barrier, such as Heracles' cloak here, compare *Hippolytus* 946–7.

56. *sings, while Theseus speaks*: Song in tragedy signifies more intense emotion than spoken verse. Theseus is not directly involved in the catastrophe, and his role in the scene is that of the voice of reason, seeking to calm and console the sufferers.

57. *Are you afraid I may be polluted . . .* : For Theseus, the bond of friendship overrides fears of pollution. See Parker, *Miasma*, pp. 309–10.

58. *safely . . . from the world of death*: See note 29 above.

59. *Therefore I am determined to die*: As indicated in the translation, it seems likely that a pair of lines have been lost after this one. The run of thought would be something like:

> THESEUS: And what will you gain by dying?

> HERACLES: At least it will show up the cruelty of the gods.

60. *match your words of advice with arguments of my own*: The phrasing makes clear that the characters are embarking on an *agon* or formal exchange of opposing speeches, which are often marked off from the rest of the Euripidean play in this explicit way. The point in dispute is 'should Heracles kill himself or not?'. The formality of the arguments seems forced on the printed page, but the intensity of an actor's powerful delivery would do much to mitigate this. In any case, argumentation, though not always valid argument, is of the essence of an *agon*.

61. *When a family's foundations are not soundly laid, misfortune must befall its sons*: We have been given no hint earlier in the play that Heracles' misfortunes are the result of any crimes in earlier generations of his family, nor is the suggestion taken up. It seems to be a vain effort to find an explanation which will help make sense of the disaster. On these ideas see Parker, *Miasma*, pp. 198–202.

62. *whoever Zeus is*: This is a daring variation on a formula of prayer. In Greek hymns and prayers speakers often express uncertainty as to which of the god's names and titles to use (e.g. Aeschylus, *Agamemnon* 160). But here the tone is bitter and dismissive, a fitting preliminary to Heracles' rejection of Zeus as his father.

63. *Ixion*: He was one of the great sinners, perpetually punished in Hades by being bound to a wheel which never ceased revolving. His crime was the attempted rape of Hera, which may give an additional aptness in view of the source of Heracles' sufferings.

64. *{If you were going to . . . kill yourself}*: The bracketed phrases represent a possible reconstruction of a line or two which have been lost during the transmission of the text.

65. *if poets' tales are true*: The myths which Theseus mentions in general terms are familiar from Homer and Hesiod. Among the adulterous divinities would be Ares and Aphrodite, whose *amour* is discovered by Hephaestus, her husband (the tale is told in Book 8 of the *Odyssey* by the bard Demodocus). Cronos deposed and castrated his father Uranus, and then was overthrown in his turn by his son Zeus, who chained up the Titans in Tartarus (as narrated in Hesiod's *Theogony*). But the idea of poets' tales being unreliable or deceptive is also as old as Homer: see L. H. Pratt, *Lying and Poetry from Homer to Pindar* (Ann Arbor 1991). The argument of Theseus also depends on treating human and divine experience as analogous, a parallel questioned elsewhere and crucially at issue in this play.

66. *the fourteen youths*: Athens was obliged to send tribute of seven young men and seven maidens to Minos of Crete, who gave them to the Minotaur to devour. Theseus journeyed to Crete as one of the victims and slew the Minotaur. The following lines offer an aetiology or story about the origin of the plots of land in Attica named as belonging to or sacred to Heracles. Whether this story was Euripides' own creation or more widely current is unclear; given the likely innovations in the plot of this play in general, the former is probable.

67. *wicked tales of poets*: Theseus had mentioned the possibility that poetic tales might be false, and Heracles more decisively asserts it. His words seem to hint at a more idealized vision of divinity, remote from the world of this drama. Psychological criticism will see this as a symptom of his inability to face the truth of his situation; biographical criticism will see Euripides as thrusting his own philosophic concerns on the audience. Neither explanation satisfies, and this passage remains controversial. See General Introduction, p. xxxi.

68. *taking my life might seem an act of cowardice*: Theseus has already expressed disapproval at 1248. As is natural, Athenian and Greek attitudes to suicide were various (Dover, *Greek Popular Morality in the Time of Plato and Aristotle*, pp. 168–9), but it is not surprising that in a society which set a high value on the citizen's military service to his community the decision to abandon life could be seen as ignoble. It is telling that when Plato's Socrates criticizes suicide in the *Phaedo*, he speaks in terms of a mortal deserting the post which has been assigned to him by God – again a military conception.

69. *work against me if I lack company*: He means that if left alone he may revert to despair and kill himself.

70. *I cannot refuse*: Again the magnanimity of Theseus is emphasized by his willingness to share in Heracles' sufferings, even to the extent of contact with the blood and potential pollution.

71. *compared with my present woes*: The contrast between his former labours, conquering the Hydra and the like, and his present suffering is a powerful one – physical versus mental, active versus passive. The Greek verb *etlēn*, translated here as 'I faced', can cover both resolute action and endurance.

72. *Bury the children as I said*: See 1389–92. Heracles as the killer cannot participate in the funeral rites; see further, Parker, *Miasma*, pp. 121–3.

73. *like a boat towed by a ship*: The image recalls the scene halfway through the play in which Heracles led his family indoors (line 631, where Heracles was also the speaker). The contrast between his role there as an apparently all-powerful protector and his present misery is brought out by the verbal reminiscence.

74. *our greatest friend*: The stress on friendship at the end of the play is both positive and negative. Theseus' support and sympathy for Heracles have been crucial in persuading him to go on with life, but the final note is of separation, as the hero leaves behind his father and the old men of the chorus.

IPHIGENIA AMONG THE TAURIANS

1. *Iphigenia among the Taurians*: This, not *Iphigenia in Tauris*, is the correct form of the title in English. This is the meaning of the Greek title, and also of the Latin form *in Tauris* (among the Tauri). The Latinate title has become current in English by false analogy with the title of the *Iphigenia at Aulis*.

2. *Pelops . . .* : The prologue, as so often in Euripides, begins with a fairly detailed account of past action by an individual alone on stage; often, as for example in *Hippolytus*, the *Bacchae* and others, the speaker is a god. This résumé may form the whole of the prologue, as in the *Bacchae*, or a second part, more lively and varied, may intervene before the entrance of the chorus (as here and e.g. in *Electra* or *Ion*). It became a Euripidean convention to have this first speaker trace his or her ancestry (and often to outline the remote origins of the present crisis): the tendency is mocked in Aristophanes' *Frogs*. Sophocles, who normally opens his plays with dialogue, seems to have been more alert to the dangers of monotony.

3. *for Helen's sake*: The post-Homeric Greek tradition is generally harsh on

Helen, treating her as a selfish adulteress. In Euripides' own *Trojan Women* and *Orestes* the portrayal is unsympathetic; his different approach in *Helen* represents a deliberate choice of a variant legend. In the account of the war's origins in Aeschylus' *Agamemnon*, Helen the 'much-married' is contrasted with the virginal Iphigenia.

4. *the fairest creature . . . bring forth*: The goddess who brings light is Artemis, who presides over the moon, while her brother Apollo is associated with the sun. Agamemnon's rash vow here is one among a number of versions which describe how the king was compelled to sacrifice his daughter. In another, used by Sophocles, he foolishly boasted that he was a better hunter than Artemis, and was punished for this offence.

5. *marriage to Achilles*: The story is dramatized in Euripides' later *Iphigenia at Aulis*. She is lured to her death on the assumption that she is coming to be married to the greatest hero of the Greeks. In Euripides' other play, Clytemnestra unexpectedly accompanies her daughter, to the dismay of Agamemnon.

6. *Thoas . . . nimble heels*: The sentence refers to the etymology of his name, from the Greek word *thoos*, 'swift'. His speed plays no part in the drama. For more telling uses of etymology see *Helen* 13–14 (Theonoe, 'divine in knowledge'); *Bacchae* 367, 508 (Pentheus, 'sorrow'), *Phoenician Women* 636 (Polyneices, 'much strife').

7. *A weird vision . . . .* : As in many cultures, the belief that dreams were supernatural in origin was common in Greek society, and is naturally reflected in literature. See further E. R. Dodds, *The Greeks and the Irrational* (1951), ch. 4, and 'Supernormal phenomena in classical antiquity', in Dodds, *The Ancient Concept of Progress and Other Essays* (Oxford 1973), ch. 10, esp. pp. 168–85. In *Iphigenia* the dream is misunderstood: although it predicts that Orestes is in danger, it does not foretell his death; and Iphigenia takes the sacrificial act as merely a general indication that death has come to Orestes, not as a premonition that he will come into her power.

8. *O Phoebus*: By making Orestes address the god, the playwright provides the audience with essential background information. The Greek dramatists tend to use devices of this kind rather than the full-fledged soliloquy familiar to us from later writers like Shakespeare.

9. *when has this been our way?*: Pylades strengthens Orestes' resolve at a crucial moment, just as in Aeschylus' *Libation-Bearers* he reminded him of his duty and of the god's command when he faltered at the point of killing his mother. Here too he reminds him of the oracle of Apollo. Pylades himself came from Phocis, near to Delphi.

10. *the twin clashing rocks*: The Clashing Rocks or Symplegades were a mythological obstacle associated with the passage into the Black Sea. Jason was traditionally supposed to have been the first to pass through them successfully, on his journey to Colchis. After that the moving rocks were said to have remained stationary, but they still presented a threatening natural feature for those venturing into the sea which the Greeks called 'the Euxine' ('kind to strangers' – a euphemism, intended to placate or pacify the threat the sea posed), or more bluntly 'the inhospitable sea', as here.

11. *Ah, my serving-women . . .* : Iphigenia sings here in response to the lyrics of the chorus; as is normal, song is used for more emotional utterances such as lamentation. In this passage she recapitulates much of the material covered in her speech in the prologue; the language is more allusive, the style more passionate.

12. *sprinkle these libations*: Libation, or pouring of liquid offerings, is one of the commonest ritual acts in homage to a supernatural power: see W. Burkert, *Greek Religion* (1985), pp. 70–73. As this passage shows, the appropriate offering may vary according to the power being invoked: honey, wine and milk are offered to the dead and to gods who dwell in the earth.

13. *Woe upon woe has fallen upon it . . .* : The text here is seriously corrupt and some phrases are far from certain, but the chorus are referring to the grim history of the house of Atreus, Agamemnon's father. A golden lamb, a divine artefact, gave its possessor the right to the throne of Argos. The two brothers Atreus and Thyestes both desired the kingship. Thyestes seduced Aerope, his brother's wife, and thus gained possession of the lamb; in the most common version, this was followed by the horrific revenge of Atreus, who killed Thyestes' sons and served them up, disguised under other meat, to their father at dinner. This hideous crime was marked by a momentous omen: Zeus caused the sun to reverse its course (see also *Electra* 737–42). Tantalus, father of Pelops and grandfather of Atreus and Thyestes, was the founder of this doom-laden house. There were further crimes in those earlier generations, but 'the offspring of Tantalus' in this passage probably refers only to the children of Thyestes. On the notion of inherited guilt which afflicts successive generations, see Parker, *Miasma*, ch. 6, and M. L. West, 'Ancestral Curses', in J. Griffin (ed.), *Sophocles Revisited* (Oxford 1999), pp. 31–45.

14. *to the nostrils of the gods*: Mankind offers sacrifice to the gods, who are thought to take pleasure and sustenance from the meaty odours that rise to their home on Olympus. In his comedy *Birds*, Aristophanes develops the absurd notion that the gods can be starved into submission by preventing the sacrificial smells from reaching them, thus cutting off their food supplies.

15. *to honour Argive Hera . . .* : Hera is the protective deity of Argos, and is naturally mentioned by Iphigenia. The rest of the sentence is better suited to the Athenian audience: the women of Athens wove a robe representing Athena

engaged in warfare with the Titans, as part of the worship of Athena at her major festival, the Great Panathenaea (cf. *Hecabe* 466–74).

16. *That's what I want to hear about*: The enquiry introduces the first messenger-speech of the play: the second, at 1327–1419, describes the escape of Iphigenia, Orestes and Pylades. Most Euripidean plays have at least one messenger-speech, several have two, and the *Phoenician Women* has four! A technique which no doubt originates as a means of narrating events that cannot be represented on stage has evidently developed into a form of vivid and exciting narrative performed and enjoyed for its own sake. For a study of the form as used by Euripides, see I. J. F. de Jong, *Narrative in Drama: The Art of the Euripidean Messenger-speech* (Leiden 1991).

17. *purple-fishers*: This refers to the fishermen who gather molluscs in order to extract dyes for fabric; the purple-crimson dye was made in Tyre, hence 'Tyrian purple'.

18. *Gods are sitting over there!*: The naïve countrymen take the foreign strangers to be gods, and invoke them accordingly. This is quite a common occurrence in mythical or semi-mythical stories: Alcinous wonders if Odysseus may be a god in the *Odyssey*, and the hero's son Telemachus has the same suspicion. When Paul and Barnabas visit the Roman colony of Lystra and heal a cripple, the crowd acclaim them as gods who have come down to earth in the likeness of men (Acts 14:8ff.).

The first invocation alludes to a strange myth of sea deities. The king of Thessaly, Athamas, killed his son in a fit of madness, whereupon his wife Ino fled into the sea with their surviving child Melicertes. Poseidon took pity on them and turned both Ino and Melicertes into sea-gods, who were subsequently worshipped as Leucothea and Palaemon. The 'Sons of Zeus' means Castor and Pollux, the Heavenly Twins. Nereus is a sea-god subordinate to Poseidon; one of his Nereid daughters was Thetis, mother of Achilles.

19. *my mother, that mass of rock . . . hurl her at me*: The transformation of Clytemnestra into stone is not a part of any regular version of the story, and must be seen as the product of Orestes' crazed imagination.

20. *in sacrifice at Aulis*: The cowherd, with rustic (or barbarian) naïvety, encourages Iphigenia to perform her bloody duty as a form of retribution for what Greeks did to her. Since her blood was in fact not shed, there is a paradox. In the prologue Iphigenia has already hinted that she did not favour the custom of human sacrifice, and in her next speech she is more explicit.

21. *I cannot rid my mind of that day's horror*: Iphigenia's recollections are made more vivid by the introduction of direct speech, recalling the words of her original appeal. The effect here is comparable to that of a 'flashback' in modern cinema. The detail also suggests the psychological trauma that still affects her.

22. *Hades . . . was to be my wedded lord*: The macabre idea of 'marriage' to Hades is quite frequent in tragedy, especially in the context of virgin sacrifice or execution. See further R. Seaford, 'The Tragic Wedding', *Journal of Hellenic Studies* 107 (1987), pp. 106–30.

23. *Leto won the heart of Zeus*: The point is that Leto was the mother of Artemis.

24. *I cannot suppose any god capable of evil*: The line makes a powerful conclusion to a striking passage. Euripidean characters frequently question received opinion about the gods and their motives (cf. General Introduction, pp. xxviii–xxxiii). In the same way Pindar expressed disbelief in tales which reflect discredit on the god: among the stories he rejects is the one which Iphigenia alludes to here, according to which Tantalus entertained the gods but served them human flesh; Demeter, distracted by her anxiety about her lost daughter, ate it unawares. See Pindar, *Olympian* 1.37–52. Sometimes human scepticism stands in conflict with the actions of the gods in the play, but here Iphigenia's distress is eventually shown to be shared by the goddess: Orestes will carry away Artemis' image and in future she will be honoured in a more wholesome fashion (1450–61).

25. *. . . crossing the Inhospitable Gulf*: As in earlier passages, this refers to the Pontus Euxeinos, the Black Sea. The 'dark meeting place of the seas' refers to the Thracian Bosporus which joins the Propontis and the Euxine. The name Bosporus ('cow's crossing') was thought to refer to the mythical Io, who was beloved of Zeus and then turned into a cow by the jealous Hera, who persecuted her further by sending a gadfly to torment her. Fleeing from the gadfly Io journeyed across the world, travelling through Asia and finally reaching Egypt. The myth is of marginal relevance here: the point is simply that the foreign visitors to the Taurians have followed the same route as Io and the gadfly.

26. *Phineus' coast that never slumbers*: Phineus is a figure in the Argonautic legends, a king persecuted by the Harpies. The meaning is apparently that the stormy weather never ceases on the coastline of Salmydessus, his kingdom on the shores of Thrace.

27. *the white isle . . . glorious racecourse*: 'Leuke' (White) was the name of a small island in the Black Sea, near the mouth of the Danube; traditionally the ghost of Achilles dwelt there (cf. also *Andromache* 1260–62), and in some versions other heroes lived with him after their deaths. Racing is a suitable pursuit for swift-footed Achilles even after death.

28. *the custom of the land prescribes*: The chorus, like Iphigenia herself, express misgivings about the sacrificial rites; but as one would expect, they do so less emphatically than the heroine of the play. Choral comment is characteristically cautious and moderate.

29. *Ah! Who is she, the mother . . .* : If Orestes answered this question at once, brother and sister would immediately know each other. Instead, Euripides

embarks on a remarkable scene in which recognition constantly seems about to take place but is continually delayed: not until line 777 does Orestes realize the truth, and Iphigenia's subsequent doubts prolong the tension still further. Scenes of this type are common in tragedy, especially in dramas of intrigue involving deception and plans for escape or revenge: thus Orestes returns in disguise to Argos in each of the plays dramatizing his revenge, and Helen and Menelaus in *Helen* do not at first recognize or believe in each other's identity. The Greeks obviously enjoyed delayed recognition-scenes of this kind: the tradition has its roots in Homer's *Odyssey*.

30. *what I wish to learn first*: This enquiry by Iphigenia occupies two verses; thereafter each question and answer is a single line in the Greek until Orestes speaks at greater length at 570. This device is known as 'stichomythia' (line-by-line speech), and is often used by the tragedians in contexts like these, where information is being sought or exchanged. The fast-moving dialogue encourages a sense of urgency and excitement: the audience awaits a crucial line of revelation on one side or the other, but it does not come. On stichomythia in general, see C. Collard, 'On Stychomythia', *Liverpool Classical Monthly* 5 (1980), pp. 77–85.

31. *a man called Calchas . . .* : On Calchas' role, see Iphigenia's narrative in the prologue, lines 15–24; on that of Odysseus ('Laertes' son') see lines 24–5. Iphigenia asks after the fates of each of the crucial agents in her death, coming to her father last. This type of scene, in which mythical detail familiar to the audience is 'filled in' for a character on stage, is paralleled in Helen's meeting with Teucer in *Helen*, and e.g. in Sophocles' *Philoctetes* 410–52.

32. *has been overturned*: Probably this refers only to Odysseus' hapless wanderings, but the audience may be meant also to think of the crowd of suitors besieging his wife Penelope and consuming Odysseus' property, as described in the *Odyssey*.

33. *Nereid Thetis' son . . . his marriage at Aulis*: The son of Thetis is Achilles, to whom Iphigenia supposed she would be married at Aulis, when in fact this was a trick to bring her there to be sacrificed. See her account of these events in the prologue.

34. *O dream that lied to me . . .* : Iphigenia reacts to the word 'lives', rather than to the 'life of misery.' She realizes she misinterpreted the dream narrated in the prologue (lines 42–55). This is in part an aside, and obviously Orestes cannot know her full meaning, but he does take up the matter of dreams.

35. *when a man comes to grief . . . those who know him know how*: Orestes refers to his own misfortune, since he is suffering the consequences of obeying the command of the prophetic god Apollo to kill his own mother.

36. *gain your sister's inheritance as her husband*: As we see in Euripides' *Electra* and elsewhere, it was a traditional element of the story that Pylades married Electra, the reward for his loyalty to Orestes. Here the mythical fact is given an ingenious negative twist. In the next speech by Orestes, 'my sister' again refers to Electra.

37. *I have been deceived by Phoebus*: Doubts about the wisdom or truth of Apollo's prophecies are frequently expressed in tragedy: cf. *Electra* 971, 1246; Sophocles, *Oedipus the King* 946–7. See further, J. Mikalson, *Honor Thy Gods: Popular Religion in Greek Tragedy* (1991), pp. 136–9. In most instances the mortal doubts are shown to be unfounded, and this is the case in this play. Pylades' pious confidence that all will finally work out well proves justified.

38. *the letter with its folded tablets*: The reference is to a kind of wooden note-pad in which a message would be written, often on wax, which would be protected by the wooden exterior. The idea of such implements being used in the heroic age is anachronistic, but this anticipation of later customs is common in tragedy.

39. *I bring you a letter, Orestes*: The stage business involved in the handling of the letter can readily be reconstructed from the text. It is typical of Greek tragedy that there are relatively few props and physical objects on stage, but those which are used carry considerable symbolic or emotional weight. A still more significant case is the bow in Sophocles' *Philoctetes*.

40. *evidence for this*: As in *Ion*, proof is necessary before the seemingly impossible can be believed. On tokens of childhood, etc., see *Ion*, note 68.

41. *between Atreus and Thyestes*: For the story of the dispute over the golden lamb, and of how the sun changed its course, see note 13 above.

42. *What way can I discover . . .* : The question, like Pylades' next speech, marks the transition from recognition-scene to a scene in which the reunited characters plan their escape; the same sequence is found in *Helen*, and the plotting scene in *Electra* is also closely comparable. The evidence suggests that this is a conventional pattern in Euripidean drama, and the parody of this kind of plot in Aristophanes' *Women at the Thesmophoria* supports this.

43. *He was not living when my father tried to kill me*: A slightly awkward detail, which makes Pylades somewhat younger than Orestes. Chronologically it remains possible, if we accept that the Trojan war lasted ten years, and that Clytemnestra and Aegisthus ruled in Argos for a further period of seven or eight years before the two men arrived to overthrow them.

44. *not fitting for you to hear*: The implication is that Clytemnestra's motive was merely lust for her lover. In other plays, including Aeschylus' *Agamemnon*, anger at the killing of Iphigenia plays a prominent role (cf. Pindar, *Pythian* 11.22–8), but in view of the fact that her daughter has in fact survived, this would complicate the moral issues too much: Euripides prefers simply to make Clytemnestra a 'bad woman'.

45. *Next Loxias directed my steps to Athens . . .* : Loxias is another name for

Apollo (see Glossary of Names). In the speech which follows, Orestes describes how he stood trial for matricide in Athens before the court of the Areopagus, the court which in historical times dealt with homicide cases. It had special prestige, and was said to have been formed to judge Ares after he had slain a son of Poseidon (cf. Euripides' *Electra* 1258ff.). This part of his speech is close to the plot of Aeschylus' *Eumenides*, which dramatizes the trial of Orestes in Athens, and in which Apollo appears as defender, the Furies as prosecutors and Athena oversees the court. When the human jurors are evenly divided, Athena declares that the verdict must be one of acquittal (the precise nature of Athena's intervention is disrupted, but it is clear in Euripides that she has the casting vote for mercy). In Aeschylus, Orestes returns to rule his father's kingdom in Argos, while Athena placates the Furies and offers them an honoured place in Athens. See also Athena's speech at 1469–72.

Euripides modifies the legend in two main respects. First, not all the Furies accept the verdict at Athens: this is patently a device to explain why Orestes is still a wanderer and still subject to fits of insanity. Second, Orestes is not tried at once in Athens, but first has to suffer a period of exclusion and of grim, reluctant hospitality in the households of some of the citizens. As Orestes' words at 958–60 make clear, this is an aetiology, a story told to explain the origin of a religious rite: in this case, the practice of separating those who participated in the festival of the Choes, on the second day of the Anthesteria: each of those present had a separate table and a separate pot of wine. On the nature of this festival, see H. W. Parke, *Festivals of the Athenians* (London 1977), pp. 107–20, Burkert, *Greek Religion*, pp. 237–42. The connection of Orestes with this practice is mentioned in a number of sources, and is unlikely to be Euripides' own invention.

46. *unless Phoebus, my destroyer, saved me*: There is a play on the resemblance between the name Apollo and the verb *apolesen*, from *apollumi*, 'destroy' (as also in Aeschylus, *Agamemnon* 1081 and elsewhere). Orestes' threat to die on sacred ground would expose the god and his shrine to pollution from his corpse. Compare Iphigenia's reference in lines 380–84 to Artemis' inconsistency in barring those who have touched the dead from her altar, while also demanding human sacrifice. See further, Parker, *Miasma*, ch. 2, esp. pp. 32–40.

47. *tripod*: Apollo's prophecies were delivered through a medium who sat on a tripod in a sacred vault of the god's temple.

48. *a woman's counts for little*: This view is still more emphatically stated by Iphigenia herself in Euripides' later play, *Iphigenia at Aulis* 1394. Offensive to modern taste, it would probably have been met with assent by many Athenian males in the audience, but there is no justification for ascribing this opinion to the dramatist.

49. *thinking up schemes*: In Greek literature women are often seen as more cunning and devious than men, who rely more readily on brute force: compare, for example, *Hippolytus* 480–81, *Andromache* 85. The whole plot of *Medea* relies on Medea's capacity to outwit men.

50. *since your hands touched it*: The image is unclean because of Orestes' pollution from his crime. See Parker, *Miasma*, pp. 52–3.

51. *must join us in keeping this a secret*: In realistic terms, Orestes' sudden anxiety about the chorus's discretion is long overdue. But for the chorus to swear itself to secrecy out of loyalty to the main characters is a convention of the genre (necessary because of their continuous presence) and, although Iphigenia makes an unusually full appeal, the audience will have already taken their consent for granted.

52. *a city favoured by the gods*: This is an incidental note of patriotic praise for Athens. More important, Iphigenia's prayer here reverses and supersedes her earlier indignant reproach of Artemis. The goddess is not after all content with the barbarous cult she receives; she, with her priestess, will soon be removed to a civilized land. The hope for fulfilment of Apollo's oracles also paves the way for a happy resolution, in contrast with Orestes' former pessimism.

53. *Halcyon*: The halcyon was a mythical bird identified with the kingfisher, who had been transformed from a woman's form and still lamented the loss of her young husband Keyx. Similarly, the chorus long for the prosperity they have lost and for their homes far away. The highly emotional and poetically ornate ode is typical of Euripides' late period: we find the same style exaggerated and parodied in Aristophanes' *Frogs* (1309ff., a passage which begins by invoking the halcyons).

54. *turned backwards on its plinth*: Iphigenia describes a prodigy, an unnatural and ominous event; Thoas' reply hints at a possible rational explanation for such a phenomenon.

55. *the heart for such a deed*: This is obviously a mischievous touch by the playwright. A real-life Thoas would be unlikely to refer to himself or his people as barbarians. Whereas up to this point the picture of the Taurians in the play has been of a savage people, we are now shown how Orestes' deed might look in the eyes of a naïvely virtuous figure, almost a 'noble savage'. That Greeks too are capable of 'barbarous' deeds is a recurring theme in Euripides.

56. *entirely proper*: After this line the metre changes to trochaic tetrameters for the remainder of the scene. Euripides regularly uses this metre for scenes of excitement and rapid activity.

57. *for the fiery sun*: Again the meaning is that the gods (and the sun is conceived as a divine power) must not be polluted by contact with a sinner. Humans must also take care, see 1218 below. Cf. *Heracles* 1214ff. See Parker, *Miasma*, pp. 310, 316ff., 371.

58. *refer to me*: Metrical analysis shows that a short reply from Iphigenia has been lost after these words. It probably amounted to no more than 'Exactly'.

59. *A lovely child was Leto's baby boy . . .* : The ode recounts the birth of Apollo, son of Leto, on Delos and his coming to Delphi, where he slew the monstrous Pytho, the snake which guarded the sanctuary (hence his title of Pythian Apollo). The achievement is made still more miraculous by the claim that he did so while still a child (*Wunderkind*). Dionysus is mentioned because of the Bacchic festival and revelry in the region of Delphi, and because of the special relationship between Apollo and Dionysus: see *Ion*, note 30.

Already in 1249 there is a reference to the personified Earth itself, a hazy figure of early mythic times, as the first owner of the oracle at Delphi; her successor was Themis, one of the wives of Zeus, whose name means 'Order'. The serpent Pytho was also a child of Earth, and guarded the shrine for his mother and sister. The story told in the antistrophe describes a divine contest for the first place among oracular guides to mankind, which Apollo wins. The colourful yet sometimes humorous narrative is reminiscent of the early poetry known as the Homeric Hymns.

See further, C. Sourvinou-Inwood, 'Myth as history: the previous owners of the Delphic Oracle', in J. Bremmer (ed.), *Interpretations of Greek Mythology* (London and Sydney 1987), pp. 215–41.

60. *he has left the temple in some haste*: It is unusual but not unparalleled for the chorus to lie to particular actors (they take steps to deceive Aegisthus in Aeschylus' *Libation-Bearers*); here it arises from their previous promise to help Iphigenia.

61. *sing the paean*: A paean is a song of praise, prayer or thanks to Apollo.

62. *Unless the sea calms down . . .* : It is a bold and unusual stroke for the messenger to bring a report of an *incomplete* action, where intervention may yet make a difference. In most cases they describe an event or series of events that have already reached a conclusion or at least come to a halt. In realistic terms, if there is such urgency it makes no sense for him to have gone on at such length; but the dramatic convention of the long messenger-speech overrides such considerations.

63. *The goddess* ATHENA *suddenly appears above the stage*: This is the device of the *deus ex machina*. Divine epiphanies of this kind figure at the end of many Euripidean tragedies: in this volume, in both *Ion* and *Helen*. It is usually a god who has some direct concern with the action: we might have expected Apollo or Artemis, but the Athenian aspects of the play and the speech make it appropriate for it to be delivered by the protecting goddess of Athens.

64. *the anger of the Furies*: See Orestes' speech at 939–86 and note 45 above.

65. *When you come to Athens . . .* : The next section of the speech, like Orestes' earlier narrative, is closely linked with the religious cults of Athens. As is normal in the speeches of a god at the end of a play, aetiological links are made explicit, tracing the customs of the Athenian present to their origins in the mythical past. Halae is in the east of Attica, facing the hill here called the Carystian rock, in southern Euboea. Athena predicts a cult of Tauric Artemis which still existed in classical times. The ritual will involve a shedding of blood which replaces but symbolically mimics the bloody human sacrifices among the Tauri. Similar rites seem to have been performed at Brauron, a few miles south of Halae. Euripides traces both to the same origin, sending the image of Artemis to Halae and Iphigenia as priestess to Brauron. In some contexts Artemis and Iphigenia seem to be identified; at the very least they are closely associated, with Iphigenia receiving heroic cult after death. Much is obscure about the nature of the rites at Brauron, but they seem to have been connected with preparing young girls for marriage and child-bearing.

66. *he shall be acquitted*: See note 45 on Orestes' earlier narrative of his trial in the court of Areopagus ('the hill of Ares'). The practice reflects Athenian legal convention: see Aristotle, *Constitution of the Athenians* 69.1.

ION

1. *Atlas . . .* : For the Euripidean practice of having the prologue spoken by a character alone on stage, who traces the action back to its origins, see note 2 to *Iphigenia*. Here Hermes is a detached observer of the action, whereas Iphigenia was deeply involved with the misfortunes of her family and the consequences of the past.

2. *a child of Erechtheus*: Erechtheus was one of the mythical early kings of Athens, and the Athenian people could be described as the 'sons of Erechtheus' (Erechtheidae). Euripides wrote another play, now surviving only in fragments, which dramatized the dilemma Erechtheus faced when it proved necessary to sacrifice his daughter or daughters if the city was to be saved: this terrible decision is referred to at 277–80, where Creusa is said to have been spared, being still only an infant. See note 16 below.

The relation between Erechtheus and Erichthonius, another figure prominent in the mythical royal house, is uncertain. According to 267ff., Erichthonius was Creusa's great-grandfather, Erechtheus her father; but the distinction of the two figures is probably a late development; these may originally be two names for the same mythical character. See further, R. Parker, 'Myths of early

Athens', in *Interpretations of Greek Mythology*, ed. J. Bremmer (London and Sydney 1987), pp. 193ff. and 200ff. [henceforth cited as Parker, 'Myths']; for more detail, see E. Kearns, *The Heroes of Attica* (*BICS* Supplement 57, 1989), pp. 110–15, 160–61.

3. *violent passion*: Greek gods often had their way with mortal women; Zeus himself recites a catalogue of his conquests, like Don Giovanni, in the *Iliad*. (Goddesses were sometimes as forward in satisfying their desire for mortal men, e.g. Aphrodite with Anchises). It seems to be the rule that even a single encounter with a god leads to pregnancy: Poseidon in the *Odyssey* (11.249–50) declares that 'the beds of the immortals are not without fruit'. In earlier literature, divine love-making is taken more or less for granted, but the emphasis on the violence of Apollo in this play (rape rather than seduction), and on Creusa's consequent suffering, makes the god's action much more problematic.

4. *exposed him to die, so she thought*: Exposure of unwanted children was common in ancient Greece, as in many poor societies: see, for example, R. Sallares, *The Ecology of the Ancient Greek World* (London 1991), pp. 151–7. In real life the parents may have hoped the child might be looked after by others, but in myth the normal pattern is that death is assumed to have occurred, while in fact the child has been saved by others and is brought up without knowing its true identity, which is eventually revealed. The story is a recurring one, found also in the myths of Paris, Oedipus, Romulus and Remus, and Moses, among others. To an audience accustomed to such tales, Ion's survival is no surprise.

5. *pair of serpents*: Snakes, dwelling partly above and partly below the earth, are ambiguous in other ways, capable of helping and harming. Their earth-born quality connects them with the claim of the Athenians to be 'autochthonous' (i.e. always to have lived on the same territory, and so to be native to Attica in a more intimate way than other peoples to their lands): see also 265–7 below, where Erichthonius is said to have been born of the earth itself, a symbol of this Athenian claim. See Parker, 'Myths', p. 195. Snakes play a prominent part in Erichthonius' tale too, as the next lines indicate.

6. *the custom in Athens . . . beaten gold*: This is an aetiology. Greek literature is rich in aetiological tales, and Euripides often brings them in at the end of his plays, especially in the speech of a god. *Ion*, like *Iphigenia among the Taurians*, has a number of explanations scattered through the play, mainly because it is concerned more than most of the dramas with Athenian myth.

7. *Apollo's oracle . . . desire for children*: In general, on the place of the Delphic oracle in Greek life, see H. W. Parke, *Greek Oracles* (London 1967), esp. chs. 6–8, and S. Price, 'Delphi and divination', in *Greek Religion and Society*, ed. P. E. Easterling and J. V. Muir (Cambridge 1985), pp. 128–54. In myth we tend to hear about abnormal or major consultations by rulers or exceptional people, but many consultations by private individuals must have been more humdrum. Even in tragedy, desire for children also prompts the visit of Aegeus to Delphi in *Medea* (667ff.). The question is of course of special importance when a ruler lacks an heir.

8. *become known to Creusa . . .* : This sentence and the next reveal Apollo's idea of how the action should unfold; the plot of the play will be very different. The god, it seems, is not omniscient. Misdirection of this kind is found also in the prologues of *Hippolytus* and the *Bacchae*. It would of course be duller for the audience if the action were entirely predicted at the start of the play.

9. *Ion . . . found cities in the land of Asia*: The Athenians claimed special status as the leaders of the Ionian cities of Asia Minor, who were united after the Persian wars in the so-called Delian League, a confederacy which began as a continued defensive alliance against Persia but developed into an Athenian empire. By making the Athenian Ion the founder of the Ionian cities, Euripides makes clear the subordination of these cities to their 'mother-city' Athens. See further the Preface to this play.

For Ion's name see 661ff. (and note 38 below), where Xuthus gives him the name. It seems he is to be thought of as nameless before. This is one way in which the play enacts his progress into full adulthood.

10. *Come, servant broom*: The monody of Ion began with the dignity of a hymn, and is throughout concerned with honouring Apollo, but the references to the birds' droppings, and still more the invocation of the broom and the indignant cries to the birds later in the song, strike a rather comic note. Euripides charmingly portrays Ion's naïvety, making him use high-flown style and language to describe very down-to-earth chores. This is the kind of passage which Aristophanes satirizes in the parodies of Euripidean lyrics in *Frogs* (esp. 1308–63): see also General Introduction, p. xxvi.

11. *Phoebus is my sire and father*: The Greek is equally explicit, and the irony is typical of the play.

12. *So not only in sacred Athens . . . shining in fair-eyed beauty*: There are several places in Euripides in which works of art are described and admired, usually by the chorus: for example, Achilles' shield, described at *Electra* 452–86. In this play, there is the account, by the messenger, of the embroideries on the magnificent tent erected for the banquet (1141ff.). There is a discussion of these passages by F. Zeitlin, 'The artful eye: vision, ecphrasis and spectacle in Euripidean theatre', in *Art and Text in Ancient Greek Culture* ed. S. Goldhill and R. Osborne (Cambridge 1994), pp. 138–96.

The opening of the choral entrance-song reminds the audience of the great buildings of Athens' Acropolis, such as the Parthenon (most of them built in the lifetime of Euripides). The patriotic note is evident: Delphi too can match the wonders of our own city!

The myths described in the next few lines are well known: Heracles' slaying of the monstrous hydra with the aid of his nephew Iolaus; Bellerophon on his winged horse Pegasus, killing the terrible Chimaera ('three-bodied' in that it was part lion, part goat, part snake); the battle between the Giants and the Olympian gods, in which Athena and Zeus naturally play prominent parts. (The Gorgon's head was a decoration on Athena's shield; Enceladus and Mimas are both giants.) Bromius the revelling god is of course Bacchus, wielding his ivy-wand or thyrsus as a weapon. It cannot be shown that all these scenes were visible at Delphi, but the war of Giants and gods certainly was. For more detailed discussion see Lee's commentary (1997), pp. 177–9.

13. *under one roof with the dwelling of Pallas*: She means the Erechtheion, which is under the same roof as the shrine of Athene Polias. The fifth-century Erechtheion, remains of which survive today, was built on the site of an older temple. But the old and the contemporary would no doubt merge in the Athenian audience's minds: anachronism of this kind is common in tragedy.

14. *Oh, what hardships women must endure!*: These words and the rest of Creusa's speech constitute an aside; in the Greek theatre, as in Shakespeare, comments of this kind are used to give some insight into the character's mind. The others on stage either do not hear her words or do not understand them. The convention is unrealistic but dramatically effective: Creusa is made to seem a more intriguing and sympathetic figure because she cannot reveal the cause of her grief except through these cryptic outbursts. See further D. Bain, *Actors and Audiences* (Oxford 1977), ch. 2, who discusses this passage on pp. 36–7.

15. *born from the earth*: On the importance of autochthony in Athenian myth see note 5 above. The story of Erichthonius (sometimes told of Erechtheus: see Parker, 'Myths', pp. 193–7) is a strange one. Hephaestus tried to rape Athena, but the virgin goddess escaped; his seed fell on the ground, and from that spot emerged their 'son' Erichthonius. The early king of Athens was thus under the protection of both deities, but the central fact about Athena, her virginity, was unaltered. Athena then hid the child in a chest with snakes to guard him, and entrusted it to the daughters of Cecrops to guard, warning them on no account to open it. Despite the warnings they did so, and went mad at the sight of what was inside, throwing themselves off the Acropolis to their deaths. Even in historic times, a sacred snake was kept on the Acropolis, in the precinct of Erichthonius.

16. *did he kill your sisters in sacrifice*: For the story see note 2 above, and Parker, 'Myths', pp. 202–4. The motif of human sacrifice is common in tragedy, and the plot involving sacrifice to save the State is found in several Euripidean plays, especially *The Children of Heracles* and the *Phoenician Women*; a variant is the sacrifice of Iphigenia to make possible a patriotic expedition against Troy (*Iphigenia at Aulis*). The *Erechtheus* of Euripides, which told of that king's difficult decision, was probably close to *Ion* in date, perhaps somewhat earlier, and may well have been produced during the building programme of the Erechtheum, begun in the last quarter of the fifth century BC.

17. *swallowed up in the yawning earth*: Erechtheus won a war against the Eleusinian king Eumolpus, but Poseidon caused an earthquake and Erechtheus disappeared in a chasm which opened up in the earth; this too was described in the lost play *Erechtheus*.

18. *Trophonius' sacred cavern*: Trophonius was a Boeotian seer with associations with Delphi; he had an oracular shrine of his own, on the slopes of Mount Helicon, about 15 miles from Delphi. There was an elaborate procedure of consultation; hence the delay.

19. *Phoebus knows the truth about my childlessness*: We have heard Creusa make her obscure asides; a similar purpose is served by ambiguous replies like these. The double meaning is clear to the audience but missed by Ion.

20. *dedication . . . sell you*: A state might offer a slave or a number of slaves as a gift to the shrine; or he might be sold into the service of the temple by an individual.

21. *a pleasure shared*: This way of viewing the situation highlights the moral issue, and is not adequately met by the resolution of the play, which does not restore the years of happy motherhood which Creusa has lost. That point is not emphasized at the end of the play, however.

22. *the nobility of Delphi, chosen by lot*: The priestess, inspired by the god, utters the prophecy, usually in verse; but the priests convey the words to the questioner and if necessary help to interpret the god's obscurities. On the procedures of Delphic enquiry, see Parke, *Greek Oracles*, ch. 7.

23. *And yet I should ask Phoebus to account for this behaviour of his*: The opening of Ion's speech expresses his sense of easy familiarity with the god, with whose shrine and worship he is familiar. His criticism of the god is again naïve yet his anxieties are likely to be shared by at least some of the audience. Greek mythology presented the gods as anthropomorphic, like men in their emotions and impulses, though far greater than men in strength and knowledge. But well before Euripides' time, Xenophanes and others had questioned whether this was an adequate conception of god. Ion insists that the gods lay down moral rules for men and ought themselves to obey those rules. But the point could be turned the other way: if gods are above humanity and make the laws, can they be judged by the same moral criteria? Ion's criticisms do not strike very deep, but they hint at larger philosophic issues.

24. *Poseidon and Zeus*: Both gods were said to have treated mortal women as Apollo has Creusa, Poseidon with Melanippe and Tyro, Zeus with (among others) Semele and Europa. The idea of the gods paying compensation in fines reflects Athenian law (and perhaps therefore strikes a comical note). The wealth of the temples comes from dedications of gifts and treasure by worshippers, individuals and states; the wealth of Delphi in particular was proverbial.

25. *from the crown of Zeus' head*: See Hesiod, *Theogony* 886ff., Pindar, *Olympian* 7.35ff. Zeus was said to have swallowed his first wife, Metis (whose name means intelligence), when she was pregnant with a child. When the time came for the birth he was stricken with agonizing headaches; Prometheus discerned the remedy, splitting Zeus' head with an axe and releasing, fully grown and armed, the goddess Athena, who is thus not only a virgin herself but born without the normal indignities. The surreal quality of the tale, like that of the birth of Erichthonius, is characteristic of the myths of very early times, before the Olympians were fully established as a more orderly 'royal family'. See also Parker, 'Myths', pp. 190–92.

26. *child of Leto's womb*: Artemis was the full sister of Apollo. Both she and Athena are virgins, but Artemis is regularly the protectress of women in childbirth; here both goddesses are ascribed power in this sphere.

27. *a wretched maid*: The chorus, we must remember, still think of this as the experience of a 'friend' of Creusa. Their distress will be still greater when they hear the truth.

28. *You serving women*: From this point on, through the dialogue between Ion and Xuthus and up to the next intervention by the chorus at 566, the metre is not the iambic trimeter normally used in spoken verse, but the longer trochaic tetrameter, often including, as here, a series of lines divided between two speakers who keep interrupting one another. It recurs for a brief passage at 1250–60 when Creusa rushes on and seeks refuge at the altar, and (for reasons which are harder to determine) at the very end of the play.

The mood of the scene which follows is hard to determine. The misunderstanding and muddle seem to have a comic aspect, and this is brought out, perhaps to excess, in the translation and interpretation by B. M. W. Knox, 'Euripidean Comedy', in *Word and Action: Essays on the Ancient Theater* (1979), pp. 260–2. Knox argues that Xuthus' overtures are misread as the eager advances of a would-be lover, and that this explains Ion's adverse reaction. Even if Knox's case is overstated, the scene certainly shows Xuthus as over-hasty and somewhat blundering. It is Ion who swiftly begins to reflect on the significance of this new discovery, and who finds reason to doubt that all is rosy. Further, Xuthus' relative indifference to Creusa and willingness to deceive her must offend an audience to whom she has been presented so clearly as a sympathetic victim.

29. *Children are not born of the soil*: These are the words of a Euboean who has married into the Athenian royal house; a true Athenian, proud of his mythic ancestry, would know better. See note 5 above on autochthony.

30. *Bacchus' torchlight mysteries*: Delphi is Apollo's domain, but according to Greek belief he absented himself in the winter months and Dionysus took his place. Thebes, birthplace of Dionysus, is not far from Delphi, and there was a festival of Dionysus at Delphi every second year. Dionysus is also associated with inspiration and divine possession: in myth the Maenads, women inspired by the god, run wild over the hills, and even in historical times this behaviour, more rigorously controlled through ritual, was part of the celebrations at Dionysiac festivals. Illicit liaisons between men and women were easier to manage (or to fall into) at festival times, when women had more freedom of action.

31. *a son of Zeus*: This is loosely expressed, as Ion would be son of a grandson of Zeus, Xuthus being son of Aeolus.

32. *Have you nothing to say?*: Ion's silence indicates that he is having misgivings, which he goes on to express. The play is much concerned with the inexperienced boy's growth to manhood; part of this is not just finding his parents but also learning to confront the world outside the safety of Delphi. His status as an 'innocent' allows him to comment critically on what he has heard about Athenian society. Although much of the play celebrates the myths and character of Athens, this scene offers a more oblique and negative perspective.

33. *foreign birth of my father . . . my own bastard status*: Ion views the prospect of being an outsider in Athens with unease. See the Preface to this play for discussion of the relevance of Pericles' 'citizenship law'. See also D. Ogden, *Greek Bastardy* (Oxford 1996), chs. 5–6, esp. pp. 166–73, 197–8. In this respect and in much of this speech the picture given of Athens is much more 'modern', more like the society of Euripides' own time, than an attempt at authentic reconstruction of an early phase of Athenian history. Anachronistic treatment of Athenian politics is found in most of the tragedies in which Athens figures, from Aeschylus' *Eumenides* to Sophocles' *Oedipus at Colonus*.

34. *do not join the rush into public life*: The politically inactive were exceptional in Athens, and treated with disdain by those who were at the heart of the political life (see esp. Pericles in Thucydides ii.40.2). See further, J. B. Carter, *The Quiet Athenian* (Oxford 1985), and for a full study of Athenian democracy and ideological clashes within it, see R. K. Sinclair, *Democracy and Participation in Classical Athens* (Cambridge 1988). On the political involvement of tragedy itself, see P. Cartledge in P. E. Easterling (ed.), *The Cambridge Companion to Greek Tragedy* (1997), pp. 3–35.

35. *As for kingship . . .* : The word in Greek is *turannis*, from which our 'tyranny' derives. Here the modern portrayal of Athenian politics gives way to a mythical perspective, in which it is natural for a city to be ruled by a king. Again Ion provides an 'innocent' commentary, but here one more attuned to Athenian anti-monarchical sentiment. Speeches recounting the unattractive aspects of kingship are common enough in tragedy for us to suspect that the arguments were commonplaces of rhetoric (cf. Creon in Sophocles' *Oedipus the King* 584ff. and Hippolytus in Euripides' *Hippolytus* 1013ff.).

36. *jostling me off the road . . .* : Ion's tone here has more of an aristocratic disdain. The comment recalls the remarks of an anonymous anti-democratic pamphleteer, usually referred to as the Old Oligarch ('pseudo-Xenophon', *Constitution of the Athenians* 1.10), a work probably contemporary with Euripides. See also Plato, *Republic* 563c, where Socrates says sardonically that the spirit of freedom in a democracy is such that it infects even the animals, and *they* refuse to get out of people's way in the streets.

37. *public feast*: Xuthus' proposal seems to combine several ideas. Athenians would celebrate the birth of a child with presents, a meal and a sacrifice, normally on the fifth or seventh day after the birth. Ion's birth has not been honoured in this way, so the lack should be remedied. A feast to celebrate a new guest-friend ('as if I'm bringing a friend to my home') is a completely different occasion. Thirdly, the reference to the name of Ion later in the speech suggests the *dekate* or ten-days-old banquet at which a child was named.

38. *I give you the name 'Ion'*: Cf. note 9 above. The point here is that 'Ion' can be taken to mean 'going' or 'coming', the present participle of a common Greek verb of motion. Xuthus met the boy as he was 'coming' from the shrine, and chooses this name to commemorate that moment of meeting. At this date of mythic time neither character can know what Hermes has already foretold, that Ion will be the founder of the Ionian cities. Significant names are common in mythology, for example Pentheus (connected twice in the *Bacchae* with *penthos*, 'sorrow').

39. *and you shall die for it*: It is a common motif in tragedy for the chorus to be sworn to secrecy; it happens in more than half of Euripides' plays. This arises from the fact that they are normally on stage throughout the main action and hence often overhear secrets. Normally their assent is immediate, but here they make no reply, significantly; for their loyalty is to Creusa and not to Xuthus. Their dismay at the turn events have taken is revealed immediately in the ode which follows.

40. *I pray that . . . on my mother's side*: This speech even more explicitly takes for granted the relevance of Pericles' law restricting citizenship: see Preface.

41. *A cunning web of trickery does he weave*: The chorus misread the situation, for the trickery is that of Xuthus, unprompted by Ion. This demonizing of Ion as the villain of the plot will go further in the dialogue between Creusa and her old servant.

42. *in plain terms*: The daggers after these words indicate a gap in the translation where the Greek text is incurably corrupt. Two lines are omitted: the broad sense may have been something like: 'Until now, she and her husband shared their sorrow.'

43. *by repelling . . . kept Athens safe*: Athenian hostility to foreigners is exaggerated to a xenophobic extent here. The lines must allude to Erechtheus' war against the Eleusinians under Eumolpus, a Thracian leader: hence the reference to the 'babbling throng', an allusion to the foreign quality of their speech. (This phrase, however, represents a conjecture by Diggle, and the exact wording remains uncertain.)

44. *Oh to fly away . . .* : Euripidean characters often express agonized wishes to escape from their present location and so win some freedom from the calamity that affects them. Cf. *Medea* 440, *Hippolytus* 742 and *Heracles* 1157ff.

45. *your palace and your inheritance*: The old man's concerns reinforce Creusa's natural distress. She grieves because of her own childless state and her husband's deception; he is furious about the intrusion of a foreigner's bastard into the royal house of Athens. Since Ion will be the heir to the throne, though apparently Athenian on neither side, the genuine royal line will, it seems, be at an end.

46. *learning you were childless . . .* : Given Ion's age, it seems hard to credit that even the old man can really believe that Xuthus has been planning this scheme since before the boy's birth. In his loyalty to his mistress and to Athens, the old man's imagination runs riot. Yet his fantasy is plausible enough to convince Creusa. The chorus, who should be intervening to reduce the tension, instead join in the blackening of both Ion and Xuthus.

47. *you must now perform a deed worthy of your sex*: The closing words are somewhat out of keeping with the positive portrait of Creusa so far; but Euripides frequently exploits the stereotype of women as cunning schemers, and the old man's encouragement paves the way for the plotting sequence to come, in which Creusa shows a different side of her personality. Before we embark on the plot, however, the aria of Creusa dramatically introduces the theme of her child by Apollo, previously unknown to all on stage.

48. *breaking into passionate song*: Creusa here breaks silence after a considerable interval – her last words were at 799 (though some of the intervening passage is omitted here as spurious). On significant silences in tragedy, see O. Taplin, *Greek Tragedy in Action* (1978), ch. 7. Her outburst is all the more powerful because it is sung, not spoken: as usual, the aria form expresses intense emotion. Even when she begins to speak, her first words are of doubt as to whether she should reveal the truth. On the qualities of this song, see Lee's commentary, pp. 256–8, and other works cited there.

49. *sing songs . . . to the music of your lyre*: Creusa describes the characteristic activity of the god, a timeless picture of his life of ease. Here and in the preceding passage his life is contrasted with her suffering, first through the rape itself and then from her abandonment of the child.

50. *. . . in the bower of Zeus*: Here 'bower' is metaphorical. The birth of Apollo was on Delos, where his mother Leto found refuge: the episode is narrated in the Homeric Hymn to Apollo. She gave birth to Apollo and his sister Artemis while leaning her body against a palm-tree which was subsequently held sacred. The divine experience of childbirth is contrasted with the human.

51. *Set fire to Loxias' holy oracle!*: The suggestion is blasphemous, and by this point in the scene the audience may be starting to feel less sure that they are altogether on Creusa's side, especially as she and the old man are working from false premises. But although the atmosphere is grim, there is some humour in the swift dismissal of the old man's wild suggestions; Creusa is the one who produces a plan that can work. See *Helen* note 44, a parallel case of a Euripidean 'clever woman' out-thinking a male. There too Menelaus makes two useless suggestions and then Helen offers a better one.

52. *the Gorgon, a fearful monster*: The Gorgon is here a child of Earth (in Hesiod she is daughter of Phorcys and Ceto, sea-deities); perhaps this suits the autochthonous Athenians and Erechtheus' family in particular. The more familiar legend tells how the Gorgon Medusa was killed by Perseus with Athena's aid, and in some versions it is her visage that adorns Athena's shield; but Perseus would be an irrelevancy here. What counts is the goddess of Athens slaying a threatening being and supplying the means for the queen of Athens to destroy her enemy. There were in any case several Gorgons, and Euripides avoids using the name Medusa.

53. *Erichthonius*: See note 15 above.

54. *two drops from the Gorgon's blood*: We may safely judge this particular gift to the child a Euripidean invention.

55. *the stepmother has no love for the children*: In ancient as in modern times stepmothers had a bad reputation. The evidence is assembled in a monograph by L. Watson, *Ancient Stepmothers* (Leiden 1994).

56. *Lady of the Cross-ways, daughter of Demeter*: The invocation is of Hecate, a goddess of night and with many sinister associations; here she is identified with Persephone, Demeter's daughter, with whom she was often associated. Her image sometimes stood at crossroads.

57. *by means of a sharpened sword or . . . a noose around her neck*: Tragic characters often contemplate various means by which to kill themselves (here, ways in which another may do so). On the implications of different types of suicide, see N. Loraux, *Tragic Ways of Killing a Woman* (Eng. tr., Cambridge, Mass. 1987).

58. *the god praised in many a hymn . . .* : Iacchus (a god often assimilated to Dionysus/Bacchus) is meant, as the reference to the torchlit festival of the 'Twentieth' below confirms. Iacchus was the son of Zeus by Persephone, and the twentieth day of the Attic month Boedromion was sacred to him: on that day his statue was conveyed in a procession from Athens to Eleusis. These lines refer more widely to the Eleusinia, celebrated for several days of that month. Callichorus is one of the sacred springs of Eleusis: Demeter was said to have rested there during her search for Persephone. Persephone is 'the Maid' referred to later in the strophe; Demeter is 'her holy mother'.

59. *All you poets . . . the lawless race of men*: Poets in antiquity were mostly men, and so the chorus, like the women in *Medea* 410ff., declare that poetry misrepresents female virtue and glosses over the crimes of men. Passages such as these make it hard to accept the distorted notion of Euripides as a misogynist. But the poet will not be simply endorsing the chorus's words: after all, Creusa herself has devised murderous plans on false premises.

60. *twin crags*: This refers to the double peak of Mount Parnassus.

61. *went on his way*: Xuthus' departure from the play is dramatically necessary in order that he may not witness the recognition between mother and son and the revelation of Creusa's having given birth. On a more mundane level, his absence is essential because tragedy is restricted to three actors: all three will be needed in the scenes which follow (playing Ion, Creusa and first the prophetess, then Athena).

62. *First he spread . . .* : This passage is an 'ecphrasis', an extended description of a work of art. Euripides enjoyed composing passages of this kind: see note 12 above. For detailed and perhaps over-ingenious readings of this passage, seeking thematic links with the rest of the play, see B. Goff, 'Euripides' *Ion* 1132–1165: the Tent', *Proceedings of the Cambridge Philological Society* 34 (1988), pp. 42–54, and F. Zeitlin, 'Mysteries of identity and the design of the self in Euripides' *Ion*', *Proceedings of the Cambridge Philological Society* 35 (1989), pp. 144–97; the latter is reprinted in F. Zeitlin, *Playing the Other* (Chicago 1996), pp. 285–338.

63. *an old man moved forward*: This is of course Creusa's servant; the description and scene setting are over, the plot resumes. His comical bustling makes him appear a harmless figure to the onlookers.

64. *another fresh bowl to be filled*: Normal practice is to pour a small portion of the wine as a libation, an offering to the appropriate god, and then drink. But in a ritual, any false move or inauspicious words invalidate the procedure, and Ion punctiliously begins again. His upbringing in pious ways saves his life. On another level, Apollo himself is at work: the doves that dwell in the temple precincts intervene to reveal the plot. It is a pleasant irony that these birds, which Ion tried to drive away in the opening scene of the play, now prove his salvation.

65. *should I fly away on wings . . .* : For conventional wishes of this kind, see note 44 above.

66. *Sit down now at the altar! . . .* : Taking refuge at an altar is a common motif in tragedy; see *Heracles* note 1. On 'blood-guilt' as a result of violating this kind of religious prohibition, see Parker, *Miasma*, p. 146. For a parallel situation see *Heracles* 240ff., 284ff.

67. *What a state of affairs!*: Again we see Ion giving vent to sententious moralizing. It is a Euripidean motif for characters to complain that the world is not well-organized: cf. *Hippolytus* 616–24, 925–31, and other examples in F. Solmsen, *Intellectual Experiments of the Greek Enlightenment* (Princeton 1975), ch. 3. But Ion's complaint here is misconceived: the rules he finds fault with are stopping him from committing matricide.

68. *Do you see this basket . . . ?*: The evidence by which Ion will be recognized as Creusa's son is brought on stage. The identification of unrecognized strangers through some physical sign or object is a recurrent motif in Greek literature: thus in the *Odyssey* the hero is identified by the scar on his leg, and in Aeschylus' *Libation-Bearers* Electra knows that her brother has come home because of the tokens she finds by Agamemnon's tomb. There are other cases in both tragedy and comedy, and Aristotle's *Poetics* (ch. 16) makes clear that the device was widespread in lost plays as well.

69. *making any discovery I may regret*: As often, the plot of the drama seems to be going off course; if Ion dedicates the cradle unopened, recognition cannot occur. His change of mind dispels the tension.

70. *as is the aegis*: The aegis is a magical object borne by Zeus and Athena, usually represented as a goatskin-covered shield, fringed with snakes and with a Gorgon's head in the centre; cf. 989ff.

71. *imitating Erichthonius our ancestor*: As Hermes already explained in the prologue, lines 20ff.

72. *Athena's rock first brought forth*: Athena's rock is the Acropolis of Athens. The olive was Athena's gift to the Athenians when she and Poseidon contended for the privilege of becoming the city's presiding deity (Parker, 'Myths', pp. 198–200). The olive tree on the Acropolis was thought to have almost miraculous properties: it was said to have survived the sack of the city by the Persians (see Herodotus 8.55). See also *Trojan Women* 801ff.

73. *my father is here as well* . . . : A second phase of the revelation begins. Ion now knows that Creusa is his mother, but still supposes Xuthus to be his father. Once again Creusa must confess her secret.

74. *hoping to avoid the shame I would bring you*: This suggestion is close to the situation described in the prologue of Euripides' *Bacchae*: Semele's child was by Zeus, but her sisters would not believe this, and supposed her to be lying and concealing the identity of a human lover.

75. *for purposes of inheritance*: The idea is that a male heir may be adopted from another's family, to prevent the dispersal of property. The provision is that of Athenian law: see, for example, W. K. Lacey, *The Family in Classical Greece* (London 1968), pp. 145ff.

76. *The goddess* ATHENA *appears*: On the *deus ex machina* as a recurring feature of Greek tragedy see *Iphigenia* note 63. Sometimes, as here, the epiphany enables the gods, and the poet, to steer the action back on course, not necessarily removing all doubts and unease.

77. *aired in public*: Apollo's concern to avoid public discussion of his behaviour is a particularly unsettling feature of the ending. It is unlikely that we are meant to think that Apollo is ashamed or embarrassed; rather, perhaps, he does not see the action as a mortal does, and having reunited Ion and Creusa, sees no point in prolonging distress over what is now in the past. But the whole presentation of Apollo is hard to interpret – harder still as he does not appear in the play. See also the Preface.

78. *before making the facts known in Athens*: This is not wholly consistent with Hermes' account of Apollo's intentions in the prologue, lines 72–3. But the audience will not recall that speech in so much detail, and a plan which does not now apply does not require further attention.

79. *great shall be his fame throughout Greece*: On the genealogical and political importance of Ion see note 9 above and the Preface; he is the ancestor of the Ionians, one of the key ethnic divisions in Greece and the one to which the Athenians belonged. See also Kearns, *The Heroes of Attica*, pp. 108–10, 174–5. Besides the national legacy, there is also the more specifically Athenian aspect of Ion. In early Athens the citizens were divided into four tribes, and Euripides makes a son of Ion the founder of each.

80. *Geleon shall be the first*: Here there is a gap in the text indicated by daggers. Presumably all four sons were named, then each of the tribes. The names

Hopletes, Argades and Aegicores seem to mean 'warriors', 'workers' and 'goatherds'.

81. *sons shall be born*: The sons of Creusa and Xuthus are naturally inferior to the son of Creusa and Apollo, so that the Dorian and Achaean races are inferior to the Ionians. The political implications are striking: in particular, Sparta, currently at war with Athens, was a Dorian state. Yet glory is allowed to attach to these races too.

82. *Xuthus may find comfort in his illusion*: Since the original plan of Apollo seems to have involved making Ion's parentage known, it is not altogether clear why this should not be done now. But we are probably not meant to feel too much anxiety about Xuthus being deceived: this is tit for tat, as he intended to trick his own wife in the same way. For a different emphasis, see Knox, 'Euripidean Comedy', in *Word and Action*, pp. 267–8: Knox sees Xuthus as the cuckold or dupe, who will become a stock character in later comic drama.

83. *Even before this I could have believed it*: Some editors find this remark surprising, but in what precedes Athena's appearance, Ion has veered from belief to doubt, so there is nothing unreasonable in his now emphasizing the former.

84. *Apollo . . . happiness*: As usual, the chorus have the last word. Their moralizing is commonplace, but readily applicable to the action: the first sentence to the house of the Erechtheids, which now beyond all hope has a true heir; the second to the eventual ('at the end') reuniting of mother and son. The reference to 'the wicked' is not relevant, but moral thinking often works by balance and polarity: the allusion to 'the good' gives rise to a comment on their opposites.

HELEN

1. *Here flow . . . the water that heaven's rain withholds*: The lines allude to Greek controversy over the sources of the Nile and the cause of its flooding; these disputes are tackled by Herodotus in his long account of Egypt in Book 2 of his great *History* (chs. 19–28). As is clear from Herodotus and other texts, the Greeks were fascinated by Egypt, especially because of its antiquity and the strangeness of its landscape and climate. Its customs too were found exotic: Herodotus goes so far as to describe it as a topsy-turvy society, where they do everything the other way round from Greece (2.35).

2. *Proteus . . . Nereus*: Helen's explanation of the background involves much embroidery and rationalizing of the story told in Book 4 of the *Odyssey*, in which Menelaus, returning from Troy, is driven off course to Egypt and has to consult Proteus, the old man of the sea. Here Proteus is a human being, though with a sea-nymph as bride. Theoclymenus and Theonoe seem to have been invented by Euripides. The latter's name means 'Divine in knowledge'. In mythology Nereus was another sea-god, similar to Proteus; here they are father and son.

3. *Tyndareus*: Helen is the daughter of Leda, who was married to Tyndareus, but she is normally said to be the child of Zeus, who seduced or raped Leda in the form of a swan. As in the case of Heracles, who can be described as the son of Zeus or of Amphitryon, she has two fathers. But in this passage she adopts a sceptical attitude to the myth of her own birth. In the late fifth century BC, rationalizing or demystifying mythology was a common practice among intellectuals (cf., e.g., *Trojan Women* 988–90 and Plato, *Phaedrus* 229c–30a).

4. *judged first in the contest*: This passage refers to the 'Judgement of Paris'. Paris, while minding herds on Mount Ida near Troy, was visited by the three goddesses, Hera, Aphrodite ('the Cyprian'; born in Cyprus) and Athena (the maiden daughter of Zeus), escorted by the messenger-god Hermes. Paris was asked to decide which of them was the most beautiful; each goddess promised different rewards. He chose Aphrodite as the winner, and his reward was the beautiful Helen. The hatred of Athena and Hera for Troy originated with this episode. Euripides often refers to the occasion as the fateful origin of the Trojan war. For a full study, see T. C. W. Stinton, *Collected Papers on Greek Tragedy* (1990), pp. 17–75.

5. *Paris . . . quit his cattle-shed*: The myth described Paris as living on the hillside tending herds. At some stage it was evidently felt that this was an unworthy occupation for a Trojan prince, and an elaborate story was devised in which Paris was exposed at birth, grew up as a shepherd, and only in adulthood came to be recognized as a son of Priam. The story was dramatized by Euripides in the *Alexandros* (see the Preface to *Trojan Women* in *Electra and Other Plays*, p. 177).

6. *fashioned from the air of heaven*: This notion of an illusory image of a human being can be found in Homer, in whose *Iliad* the gods sometimes create illusions to mislead men on the battlefield. But the main plot of *Helen* derives from Stesichorus: see the Preface. It is given a thin top-dressing of pseudo-science by the use of some contemporary 'buzz-words' such as 'aether' (a region of the sky) and by repeated references to the difference between illusion and reality. For more detailed discussions of this theme, see F. Solmsen, '*Onoma* and *Pragma* in Euripides' *Helen*', *Classical Review* 48 (1934), pp. 119–21 and J. G. Griffith, 'Some Thoughts on the *Helena* of Euripides', *Journal of Hellenic Studies* 73 (1953), pp. 36–41.

7. *the plans of Zeus . . . sorrows*: This motivation for the Trojan war was already found in the early epic poem known as the *Cypria*. It seems here to reinforce the impression we receive elsewhere in the play of divinities that care little for human suffering as a consequence of their decisions.

8. *as a suppliant*: The family of Heracles is in the same position at the start of *Heracles* (and indeed *The Children of Heracles*). On supplication, see *Heracles* note 1. In this play, however, the motif is handled with a light touch: no one is keeping watch on Helen, her captor feels free to leave her alone, and she is herself content to leave her refuge and go into the palace later in this prologue.

9. *to compare with Plutus' own*: Plutus, a god who is closer to being a personification than most, represents wealth and prosperity. He is not to be confused with Plouton (Latinized as Pluto), another name for Hades.

10. *dispute . . . over his armour*: The story is briefly alluded to in Book 11 of the *Odyssey*, and would have been narrated at greater length in other early epics. Ajax believed himself to be the worthy heir of the divinely forged armour after Achilles' death, but the verdict of the Greek judges gave it to Odysseus. In Sophocles' version Ajax goes mad with rage and eventually, after an abortive attempt to slaughter his successful opponent and others, kills himself in humiliation.

11. *a storm drove them all in different directions*: This is another traditional element; cf. Homer, *Odyssey* 3.173–85 and Aeschylus, *Agamemnon* 646–80.

12. *two accounts exist*: The sons of Tyndareus and Leda were Castor and Pollux, but again, as with Helen, the tradition was that one of them (Pollux) was son of Zeus. When that brother died, he was offered immortality, but chose to remain with his human brother. Zeus decreed a compromise, that they should live half the time on Olympus and half in Hades. The story is memorably told in Pindar, *Nemean Odes* 10. Here Teucer gives a gloomier version.

13. *island of my birth*: Teucer was banished from his home in Attic Salamis and founded a new city by the same name in Cyprus.

14. *He executes any Greek stranger*: The ferocity of Theoclymenus is analogous with the antagonism of the Taurians to foreigners in the parallel plot of *Iphigenia*. Since Theoclymenus is generally portrayed as virtuous, the characterization is somewhat inconsistent. The threat to visitors must be ascribed to his determination to keep Helen.

15. *lyric exchange*: The normal pattern of a choral entry-song is replaced (as, e.g., in *Electra*) by lyric dialogue between an actor who remains on stage and the arriving chorus. The technique helps to emphasize the closeness between Helen and the Greek women.

16. *Sirens*: In the *Odyssey* the Sirens are menacing figures with beautiful voices which they use to lure passing sailors to their doom. Here the singing and not the danger is relevant. On the portrayal of Sirens in poetry and art, see

E. Vermeule, *Aspects of Death in Early Greek Art and Poetry* (Berkeley 1979), ch. 6.

17. *it happened I was spreading . . .* : The domestic details recall the entry-song of the chorus in *Hippolytus* and contribute to the intimate atmosphere of the scene. Helen's personal grief is central rather than the public aspect of Teucer's news.

18. *has come, has come*: Euripides, especially in his later dramas, is fond of this kind of emotional repetition in lyrics, though they often seem unnatural in a prose version. The tendency was noted and mercilessly parodied by Aristophanes in the lyrics ascribed to Euripides in the *Frogs* (esp. lines 1137, 1352–5).

19. *the Lady of the Bronze Temple*: Athena was worshipped at Sparta under this cult title.

20. *who on earth was he . . . ?*: The *Iliad* (5.61) supplies the answer: the shipbuilder's name there is Phereklos. As in the opening lines of *Medea*, Euripides takes us back to the first beginnings of misfortune.

21. *swift-footed son of Maia*: This is Hermes.

22. *a slave apart from one man*: This ringing self-contained line would win applause in anti-monarchical Athens. Contrast line 395, where Menelaus declares that he was 'no despot leading an army by force'.

23. *my daughter . . . grows grey in virginity*: Teucer has in fact said nothing of Helen's daughter Hermione, but Helen's concern is a natural one and the deduction of her further misfortunes admissible.

24. *enter her house with you*: These words prepare for the departure of the chorus into the palace with Helen, so as to clear the stage for the entry of Menelaus. For the chorus once it has entered to leave the stage is unusual but not unique in tragedy: another case is in Sophocles' *Ajax*, where their absence is necessary if Ajax is to commit suicide, and their departure adds to his complete isolation. See further, Taplin, *Stagecraft of Aeschylus*, pp. 375–6.

25. *I will take my own life . . .* : The contemplation of the proper means to commit suicide is a recurring motif in scenes of tragic despair. See E. Fraenkel, *Kleine Beiträge* (Rome 1964), vol. 1, pp. 465–7, and Loraux, *Tragic Ways of Killing a Woman*.

26. *Throughout the land of Hellas . . . bloody from raking nails*: In ancient and in modern Greece, the rituals of grief and lamentation are more demonstrative than in the inhibited north. See M. Alexiou, *The Ritual Lament in Greek Tradition* (Cambridge 1974).

27. *two limbs became four . . .* : As elsewhere (see *Heracles* note 45) the tragic event is set in relief by use of comparison with other mythological catastrophes which are normally judged inferior to the present misfortune. Here Helen carries her rhetoric to extremes by calling Callisto 'blessed'. Callisto was changed to a bear, either by Zeus to allow her to evade Hera's jealousy, or by Hera as a punishment. In the end her son slew her while out hunting. 'Merops' child' is a story which seems to be unattested elsewhere, but Helen's words explain enough: she was one of the companions of Artemis until that goddess grew jealous of her beauty and turned her into a deer. The metamorphoses seem grotesque to modern taste, but Euripides cannot have intended humour. It is notable, however, that the allusions are kept brief.

28. *O Pelops . . .* : Menelaus' entrance initiates something like a second prologue. As Helen began the play proper by recalling her background and experiences, so her husband does the same here. In his opening lines he refers to his ancestor Pelops, who won his bride Hippodameia by competing in a chariot-race against her father Oenomaus (in most versions Pelops cheated and brought about her father's death).

29. *in no boastful vein*: In general Menelaus is a self-important character, very sure of his own achievements and concerned for his reputation. This is effectively ironic since he is so radically mistaken about the prize he has won in the Trojan war; he is also ill-suited to the unfamiliar land of Egypt, and is swiftly at a loss there.

30. *costly robes, the ocean has plundered*: The loss of the robes he used to wear is symbolic of his change of fortune and imminent loss of both dignity and illusions. Euripides, following Homer's *Odyssey*, likes to portray royal figures in rags, whether in disguise or in adversity: cf. the downtrodden Electra in the play of that name, and more generally Aristophanes, *Acharnians* 410–79 and *Frogs* 842, 846, 1063.

31. *Hey! Doorkeeper!*: Menelaus knocks at the door and enters a hostile world with which he is ill-equipped to deal. There is an amusing clash between the proud hero of serious drama and the bad-tempered old woman who seems to have emerged from the coarser and more realistic world of comedy. Impatient old crones are common in Aristophanes and his successors.

32. *once he has heard my name*: The following lines, down to 'my present troubles require', are bracketed as spurious by Diggle in the Oxford text, but this is one of the cases where we are hesitant about accepting his decision. Menelaus' self-important ponderings in this passage suit his demeanour in the scene as a whole, and the lines seem to raise no very difficult linguistic problems.

33. *Hecate . . .* : She is a goddess of the night, often associated with the moon, and attendant on Persephone, queen of the underworld; she is also the Lady of the Cross-ways (next line). Night brings ghosts, dreams and visions: several superstitious fears are mentioned at once. Torches were regularly part of her representation in art and played a part in her cult.

34. *the latter mainly sings*: As usual, song indicates a more intense and passionate emotional level than spoken verse. The distinction is related to gender contrasts in tragedy: men sing more rarely and more moderately than women. This does not necessarily mean that Helen cares for Menelaus more than he does for her, but it does imply that he can control his joy more readily. On Greek attitudes to the difference between the sexes, see Dover, *Greek Popular Morality in the Time of Plato and Aristotle*, pp. 95–102; for a more detailed discussion of song and speech in tragedy, see E. Hall, 'Actor's song in tragedy', in S. Goldhill and R. Osborne (eds.), *Performance Culture and Athenian Democracy* (Cambridge 1999), pp. 96–122.

35. *how intricate . . . how hard to fathom . . .* : The servant here is an interesting minor character. His naïve reflections in a way cut through the issues more searchingly than his social superiors (cf. the handling of the Fool and similar types in Shakespeare). But his observations fall short of the full examination of the logical and theological implications of the situation; they may, however, prompt further reflection on these in the audience.

There is some disagreement about how far these reflections are the authentic work of Euripides, and if authentic whether they belong to this play. Diggle in his text excises 713–19 (from 'directing things now this way, now that' to 'won the greatest of good fortune') and also 728–33 (from 'I may have been born a servant' to the end of the speech). He also deletes two sections of the servant's next speech, 746–8 ('There is, it seems, no' down to 'benefited by birds!') and 752–6 ('You may say' down to the end of that speech). These cuts have the effect of reducing the generalizing tendency of the speeches and making them more relevant to the action. But the moralizing slave is a common figure in tragedy, and although we are not convinced of the genuineness of these portions, we think them defensible and sufficiently interesting to retain in the text.

36. *having a mind . . . that is free*: Euripides often characterizes slaves as independent or intelligent human beings; compare the nurse in *Hippolytus* or Creusa's old servant in *Ion*. Contemporary sophistic thought went so far as to question the basis of distinctions between freedom and slavery (e.g. Alcidamas' saying 'God has left all men free; Nature has made none a slave'), and Euripidean characters sometimes echo these controversial views. See further W. K. C. Guthrie, *History of Greek Philosophy*, vol. 3 (Cambridge 1969), pp. 155–60, and K. Synodinou, *On the Concept of Slavery in Euripides* (Ioannina 1977).

37. *when Nauplius lit his fires on Euboea's coast*: The Greek intellectual Palamedes, one of the wisest of those involved in the Trojan war, aroused the jealousy of Odysseus, who in some versions incriminated him and brought about his execution, but in others actually murdered him. All three of the tragedians dramatized his story. Nauplius was Palamedes' father; enraged by the news he received of his son's treatment, he lit deceptive beacons on the rocky coast of his kingdom Euboea, and lured many of the returning Greek fleet on to the rocks. See lines 1126ff. and *Trojan Women* 90–91 for other references.

38. *the look-out where Perseus kept watch*: This is placed by Herodotus (2.15) at the westernmost point of the Nile Delta. There Andromeda was chained to a rock in order to appease a sea-monster sent by Poseidon; the hero Perseus arrived in time to save her, and 'kept watch' for the monster, whom he slew. Euripides' version of the story, *Andromeda*, was produced at the same festival as *Helen*, this reference can therefore be seen as either a 'trailer' or a reminder (we do not know the order of the plays on this occasion). It has no direct link with Menelaus' own story; the assumption is simply that he passed by this landmark.

39. *oracular*: This alludes to the etymology of the name (see note 2 above).

40. *the man who robbed Thetis of Achilles . . .* : These lines allude to various casualties of the Trojan war, for which Menelaus bears responsibility. Achilles son of Thetis was fated to die young, and perished in the last year of the war: Thetis' grief in anticipation of this event is a prominent motif in the *Iliad*. The death by suicide of Ajax, son of Telamon, is explained above in note 10. Nestor was the elderly counsellor of the Greeks, greatly respected by all; his favourite son Antilochus died in battle against the Ethiopian prince Memnon, ally of the Trojans. Although not literally childless, Nestor still grieves for Antilochus' death ten years on in the *Odyssey* (3.111–12).

41. *THEONOE . . . and a torch*: The sacred status of the priestess Theonoe, and her importance to the plot, are emphasized not only by the flurry of anxiety prior to her entrance, but also by its ceremonial quality. This is scarcely a normal Greek religious procedure; the scene is meant to seem unfamiliar and vaguely foreign. Theonoe's own role in the play is most unusual: the position she outlines in her first speech, whereby rival divinities are at loggerheads and the final decision rests with a mortal, is virtually unparalleled in Greek literature. Ironically, the closest analogy may well be the episode which began the Trojan war: the goddesses' inability to settle the dispute as to which of them was most beautiful, with the result that they appealed to Paris for a verdict (see note 4).

The subsequent *agon* or rhetorical contest is of a curious type: Theonoe requires her suppliants to speak, but they plead the same case rather than opposing each other, and in her own response it becomes clear that she is on their side anyway. The distortion of the usual antagonistic form of debate suits the bizarre plot and setting of *Helen* as a whole.

42. *There is in my heart a great shrine of Justice*: This is a striking way of saying 'I am much concerned with justice', associating the moral imperative with religious devotion, but internalizing this devotion. The idea of Justice as a goddess is found in Aeschylus, but the stress here on Theonoe's inner integrity suits a play in which the gods are for the most part regarded as frivolous and immoral.

43. *possesses everlasting consciousness*: A 'piece of high-toned but vague mysticism appropriate to Theonoe', comments A. M. Dale (see Bibliography). The ideas bear some similarity to views held by some of the Presocratic philosophers and developed later by Plato.

44. *if a woman . . . can make a clever suggestion*: Helen's wording is tactful, reflecting the common Greek view of women as inferior to men. But in this play, and in Euripides' work generally, women often surpass the male sex in intelligence and virtue. Here, Menelaus has just made two unhelpful suggestions, and it is Helen's proposal that will offer hope of escape.

45. *Your plan is hardly very original*: There seems to be a sly joke on Euripides' part here. The audience is meant to take the point that this is a standard motif in tragedy, which can be paralleled, for example, in Sophocles' *Electra* (not certainly datable, but probably earlier), and Euripides' own *Iphigenia among the Taurians* (almost certainly earlier).

46. *Lady of Cyprus, Dione's child*: The invocation is to Aphrodite, balancing the previous prayer to her enemy Hera. Aphrodite was often said to have been born from the sea off Cyprus (as in Botticelli's painting), but there was also a version which gave her an immortal mother, Dione (the name is a feminine form of Zeus). Although much less conspicuous in literature than Zeus' main consort Hera, Dione appears in the *Iliad*.

47. *. . . more joy to mortal hearts*: In Greek thought the gods often have this ambivalent quality: they can do great harm as well as great good, kill as well as cure. Compare Euripides' treatment of Dionysus in the *Bacchae*, esp. line 861, where the god describes himself as 'most terrible, yet most gentle towards mortals'. Greek religion laid more emphasis on the power of the gods than on their goodness.

48. *many a Greek . . . by the light of his false star*: This elaborate sentence refers to the vengeance of Nauplius, king of Euboea, the father of Palamedes; for this story, see note 37 above.

49. *what mortal having searched can say?*: The Greeks often comment on the impenetrability of divine purpose (e.g. Aeschylus, *Suppliants* 87–90), and in the late fifth century BC some thinkers went further and questioned the very possibility of saying anything about divinity (e.g. Protagoras, fragment B4). Euripides is perhaps influenced by the earlier thinker Xenophanes, who questioned the anthropomorphic assumptions of Greek mythology in a famous passage (fragment B34, cf. B10–16, 23–6).

50. *never will strife end among the cities of men*: It is hard not to feel that audiences in Euripides' Athens would have seen in these lines some relevance to their own wartime misfortunes. But it seems wrong to exaggerate the significance of the lines: though powerful in themselves, they do not constitute the moral or meaning of the whole play.

51. *and may he go off where I want him to*: Here and at numerous points in the following dialogue, Euripides uses the familiar techniques of double meaning and dramatic irony. Helen and Menelaus share full knowledge with the audience of what is really happening, and the spectators consequently enjoy a feeling of superiority to the duped Theoclymenus.

52. *at this calamity*: There seems little doubt that something has dropped out of the text at this point, since Helen's response must be to some momentary suspicion on Theoclymenus' part. A. M. Dale in her commentary suggests that the missing section ran along the lines:

HELEN: With such feelings as I shall never forget.

THEOCLYMENUS: How am I to know this man's tale is true?

53. *has expertise in such matters*: There is no clear explanation of this line. Possibly it alludes to a myth of which we lack evidence. R. Kannicht in his commentary (1969) appears to connect it with the major losses suffered at sea by the Greek forces under the Pelopids, Agamemnon and Menelaus: but can Theoclymenus know of these losses, and would he in these circumstances make so tactless a remark?

54. *In time gone by, the Mountain Mother . . .* : Normally this title refers to the mother of the gods, Rhea or Cybele, but here she is assimilated to the goddess Demeter, who ranged across the earth in quest of her daughter Persephone, whom Hades had carried off to the underworld to be his bride. In anger and grief she withheld the fruits of the earth and made gods and men suffer. The story is told in full in the Homeric Hymn to Demeter. In this version she is more easily appeased, through music and celebration. The cymbals, drums stretched with hide, and so forth are instruments used in the rites of the Great Mother, especially as practised in Asia Minor. Like Dionysus, whose rites have some of the same wild and ecstatic quality, Rhea was associated with the East.

The ode is unquestionably fine poetry, but its relation to the play around it is hard to determine. It introduces a more awesome and numinous conception of divinity, remote from the squabbling goddesses involved in the Judgement of Paris. But what have Demeter and Persephone to do with Helen? The last stanza of the ode offers an unexpected clue: that Helen has done something to offend Demeter, neglecting her ceremonies and exulting only in her beauty. This notion is not referred to either before or after this ode, and does not suit the plot of the play as a whole. The ode seems to present a different perspective on the action, an alternative reading which gives more dignity and magnificence to the gods, more guilt to Helen. There are puzzles here which critics have not yet solved.

55. *There lies great power* . . . : The fawnskin cloak and other objects mentioned are associated with the cult of Dionysus, here closely associated with that of the Mother. The 'bull-roarer' is a kind of whirling instrument, a rattle or tambourine. See M. L. West, *Ancient Greek Music* (Oxford 1992), p. 122.

56. *we may one day help you to do so too*: The chorus are not even given the opportunity to reply. Their willingness to keep the secret, a recurring motif in tragedy, is taken for granted. In general the treatment of the chorus in this play is somewhat perfunctory: it is never explained how Helen had this entourage of Greek women (they could hardly all have been brought here by Hermes), and despite these lines, nothing is said to ensure their homecoming (contrast the divine command issued by Athena at the end of *Iphigenia*, lines 1467ff., and Thoas' reply, 1482ff.). Euripides' priorities lie elsewhere.

57. *the city that Perseus raised*: Perseus was the original founder of Mycenae. The couple are returning to Sparta, but the close association between Agamemnon and Menelaus, kings of Mycenae and Sparta, make the reference natural enough. The sense is little more than 'back to Greece'.

58. *What will she find there?* . . . : The antistrophe alludes to various festivals and cults of Sparta. Leucippus' daughters were the wives of Castor and Pollux, Helen's deified brothers: in historic times they too were worshipped as goddesses at Sparta. 'Pallas' temple' refers to the temple of Athena of the Bronze House (see note 19). Hyacinthus was a beautiful Spartan youth beloved by Apollo, who accidentally slew him with a thrown discus. He was commemorated in the Hyacinthia, one of the chief festivals of Sparta. The chorus anticipate that Helen will be reintegrated into her community through participation in its central rituals. The new optimistic note is continued in the more positive hopes for Hermione; earlier in the play Helen had lamented that she would never find a husband (282–3), but here it is implied ('not yet') that this remains a possibility.

59. *If only we might find ourselves flying* . . . : It is common for Euripidean choruses to wish themselves miraculously transported from present circumstances to some safer or more delightful realm. Compare *Hippolytus* 732–51, *Bacchae* 402–16. The situation here is less extreme than in the parallels, as the main characters are already on their way to salvation.

60. *sons of Tyndareus*: Castor and Pollux, Helen's brothers. Here it is taken for granted that they are now among the gods, with a special concern for the fortunes of seafarers: the uncertainty about their fate voiced by Teucer is forgotten (137–41). The stanza paves the way for their appearance at the end of the play.

61. *But not the bull*: The animal's discontent is ominous. In Greek sacrificial ritual the beast should go willingly to the place of execution.

62. *Come on, you men who sacked the town of Ilium . . .* : We can compare the cries of encouragement that Helen gives once the battle on board the ship begins; she too refers to the successes at Troy as a source of pride. Whereas in Egypt Menelaus' repeated references to his victory seemed hollow, with the beginning of the journey home old values are reasserted. The anti-barbarian feeling is another indication that 'normality' is being restored.

63. *The son of Atreus stood fast . . .* : The warrior Menelaus is in his element once more. The influence of the *Odyssey*, strong in this play generally, is prominent in this climax, with revelation of identity followed by slaughter. Helen's exhortation can be compared with the encouragement of Odysseus by Athena in *Odyssey* 22.224–35.

64. *To sum up . . .* : Messengers often end their accounts with a moralizing conclusion based on the events described. This example is a naïve truism, in keeping with the lighter tone of the play. Contrast, for example, *Bacchae* 1150–52, much more integral with the themes of that drama.

65. *by you or us*: This is a self-defensive deception by the chorus, who have of course been well aware of Menelaus' identity. But their dishonesty is not developed: contrast the corresponding scene in *Iphigenia among the Taurians* 1431–3, where Thoas declares that the chorus's treachery will be punished. Here Theoclymenus' wrath is concentrated on his sister.

66. *Oh, to have been caught out . . .* : This speech, and the argument between king and servant which follows, are in a different metre, trochaic tetrameters, used frequently by Euripides in scenes which involve excitement and agitated conflict of views. Most of the lines prior to the appearance of Castor and Pollux are divided between Theoclymenus and the servant: in each case the king speaks first and the servant answers or interrupts him. The divine epiphany marks the point at which the play reverts to the normal trimeters.

67. *There is no more glorious end . . . than dying for his master*: The virtuous slave is a recurrent figure in Euripides, see note 36 above.

68. *above the palace*: Many of Euripides' plays end with a divine epiphany, and *Electra* also involves the appearance of Castor and Pollux. In both cases this arises from their brotherly concern with the action: they are brothers to Helen and Clytemnestra. Euripedes introduces more dignified representatives of the divine than the goddesses who have caused so much strife and bloodshed. Their declaration that they are subservient to fate and the gods' collective will preserve the mystery of the gods' purposes and also serve to evade responsibility for the action. The manuscripts do not make clear whether it is Castor or Pollux who speaks on their behalf, but Castor is explicitly the spokesman in *Electra*, and consistency seems a simple principle on which to decide. The staging is hard to be sure of. The two brothers may have appeared at the highest point of the stage-building, on the so-called 'divine platform', or they may have entered more dramatically on the *mechane* or crane-machine which represented divine beings in flight. See *Heracles* note 36. For a detailed discussion of these issues see D. Mastronarde, 'Actors on High: the Skene Roof, the Crane, and the Gods in Attic Drama', *Classical Antiquity* 9 (1990), pp. 247–94.

69. *you will be called a goddess*: Cult-worship of Helen in Sparta is attested in both literary and archaeological evidence. It is also predicted in the closing scene of *Orestes*. Helen's future divinity may even be presupposed by the *Odyssey*, in which Menelaus is told that he will enjoy special status after death because he is husband of Helen (4.563–9, referring to the 'Elysian plain'). On the whole the poets prefer to treat the living Helen as a human being, tragic, wicked or guilt-ridden, but the speeches of gods at the end of plays often extend the perspective, bringing in references to religious traditions of the poet's own time.

70. *Acte's coast*: Acte is an old form of Attica, and the island meant is Makronnisi, off Cape Sounium. This would be an odd route for Hermes to take from Sparta to Egypt, and it is clear that Euripides mentions it in order to bring in a further aetiological explanation, this time for the name or nickname of the island. There is a wordplay on 'Helen', which can be linked with the verb-root *hel-*, meaning 'take or steal away'.

71. *Isle of the Blessed*: This promise echoes that made to Menelaus in the *Odyssey* (see note 69 above). Post-Homeric poets took up that passage and brought a number of other heroes, including Achilles, to dwell after death in this fortunate land.

72. *And so it has turned out here today*: These closing choral lines also appear in identical or closely similar form at the end of *Alcestis*, *Medea*, *Andromache* and *Bacchae*. It has often been suggested that they are editorial insertions in some places, but a choral comment is normal at the end of a Greek tragedy, and the sentiments, though conventional, are appropriate enough in each case. For discussion, see D. H. Roberts, 'Parting words: final lines in Sophocles and Euripides', *Classical Quarterly* 37 (1987), pp. 51–64.

CYCLOPS

1. *in the battle with the Sons of Earth* . . . : Mythology told of several occasions on which the Olympian gods had to defend their sovereignty against older and monstrous powers. The battle between Gods and Giants was one such conflict.

Dionysus' involvement was traditional, but Silenus and the satyrs would have had little to offer in this cosmic combat. These lines probably allude to a more light-hearted version in earlier satyr-drama. Vase-paintings also show the satyrs armed for combat. Enceladus is one of the giants, sometimes their leader; he is usually said to have been defeated by either Athena or Zeus.

2. *when Hera roused the Tuscan pirates*: Hera's enmity (cf. already the opening lines above) is due to her antagonism to Zeus' bastard offspring (as with Heracles in Euripides' play and elsewhere). The story of Dionysus' abduction by pirates is told in the Homeric Hymn to Dionysus: in that poem the god's captors are transformed into dolphins. Again the variant involving the satyrs is probably derived from an earlier satyr drama.

3. *Etna*: The wanderings of Odysseus in Homer take place in a fantasy land with no clear geographical location, but by the fifth century BC the Mediterranean was much better explored and his adventures were placed on the map by tidy-minded scholars, whom the poets sometimes follow. Thucydides refers to the location of the Cyclopes in Sicily (6.2).

4. *revelling at Bacchus' side to Althaea's palace*: Dionysus once visited the court of Oeneus, king of Calydon, and fell in love with his wife Althaea. Oeneus prudently withdrew from the palace for a time, leaving the god a free hand, and the queen eventually bore Dionysus a child, Deianeira. The king was rewarded with the gift of the vine. This positive, celebratory sequence is contrasted with the miserable imprisonment of the present.

5. *'Iacchus, Iacchus'* . . . : A cult cry, an invocation of the god. Aphrodite, goddess of love and sex, is closely associated with Dionysus, as the lustful nature of the satyrs demonstrates.

6. *Sisyphus' son*: In the *Odyssey* and most other sources, Odysseus is the son of Laertes, but there was an alternative tradition that Laertes' wife Anticleia was already pregnant by the crafty Corinthian Sisyphus when he married her. In tragedy this accusation often goes with a negative portrayal of Odysseus as a villain; here the effect is milder, but Odysseus is naturally embarrassed.

7. *the people who govern*: The interest in constitutional forms is typical of democratic Athens. Silenus' reply continues the traditional presentation of the Cyclopes as uncivilized beings without a real community (*Odyssey* 9.112–15).

8. *Maron, the god's son*: In the *Odyssey* too, Odysseus brings this gift of strong wine which he has received from the Thracian Maron; but the idea of Maron being the son of Dionysus is novel and suits the atmosphere of a satyr-play.

9. *one mouthful out of that*: The next two lines are supplied by editors and translators; the manuscripts go straight on to Odysseus' line, 'Yes; twice as much . . .' Since the transition is impossibly abrupt, it is clear that something has been lost from the text.

10. *neat to start with*: The Greeks normally avoided drinking undiluted wine, and associated that practice with barbarians. Cleomenes, king of Sparta, was said to have learned this practice from visiting Scythians, and it was one of the reasons given for his going mad (Herodotus 6.84)! But it may have been acceptable to sample the wine neat before mixing it with water. Both Silenus and the Cyclops are soon the worse for their over-eager tippling.

11. *Once you had caught the woman . . .* : Condemnation of the adulteress Helen is common in tragedy too, but the outrageous coarseness of the satyrs' comment here is typical of their earthy, sensual attitude to the world; such obscenity would have no place in tragedy. Odysseus in this play has to struggle to retain his heroic dignity amid such company and in these unfamiliar surroundings. The jibe at the fancy-coloured trousers (Greeks did not wear such garments, and associated them with the East) and the gold necklace on a man suggests that Paris, Helen's abductor, is an effeminate barbarian, no proper man. This image of Paris has some background in Homer, but fifth-century authors tend to emphasize it more, no doubt partly influenced by their perception of the East after the Persian wars.

12. *a countless host of Trojans*: Odysseus' grandiose self-assertion may be compared with the bragging of Menelaus in *Helen*. In both plays the warrior has to learn to adapt to new kinds of problem, in which heroic braggadocio is not sufficient.

13. *bald head swollen from blows*: The old man is Silenus, but his flushed and swollen face is due to an excess of wine, not the result of a beating. Silenus seizes the opportunity to blame others and escape the Cyclops' anger himself.

14. *And then they said . . .* : The catalogue of varied threats is humorously extended, though some at least of these are things which might be done to a slave in ancient Greece. The notion of Polyphemus' eye witnessing his own disembowelment is particularly bizarre. But there is also irony, as Silenus does not mention the one thing that does in fact happen to the Cyclops, the blinding of his precious eye.

15. *may my sons here be damned utterly*: Silenus' cowardly self-protection becomes ever more outrageous. He wishes ill on the chorus of satyrs if he is lying; normally, in swearing such an oath one would wish ill on oneself. The satyrs indignantly reciprocate in their response: their version is the truth, but the Cyclops is foolish enough to trust Silenus more.

16. *who kept your father safe*: This takes up the reference above to Poseidon as Polyphemus' father ('noble son of the ocean's god'). But although Odysseus does his best, he cannot show any service they have rendered Polyphemus himself that should prompt his gratitude. The type of argument used here is often employed in an appeal to a god ('I have done you this service/paid you

these honours, therefore you should help me'), but it is highly artificial for Odysseus to claim that the conquest of Troy kept Poseidon's cult-sites in Greece free from Phrygian (Trojan) marauding. In any case, the Cyclops shows himself indifferent to his father's temples (318–19).

17. *Zeus' thunderbolt . . .* : The Cyclops utters similar sentiments, blasphemously declaring indifference to Zeus' authority, in Homer's treatment of the story (*Odyssey* 9.273–8).

18. *O Pallas*: Already in Homer, Pallas Athena is Odysseus' special protector and patroness.

19. *If you have no regard for these things . . .* : Appeals of this kind for a god to prove his concern for human misfortune or misdeeds are common in tragedy and especially characteristic of Euripides, in which such passages often, as here, involve a reproachful address or challenge to the god in question (cf. A. M. Dale, *Collected Papers* (Cambridge 1969), p. 182).

20. *with teeth defiled*: There is a short passage lost from the text at the conclusion of this ode.

21. *with a scythe*: The next line, omitted in the translation, is hard to interpret and is generally supposed corrupt; there may also be something lost in the text here.

22. *poor old siphon*: Obviously he means his penis. Actors in comedy often wore grotesquely exaggerated phalli as part of their costume, and the evidence of vase-paintings confirms that this was also the case with satyrs, whose phalli are frequently shown erect.

23. *carpenter . . . spin his drill round and round*: These lines are among the clearest reminiscences of the Homeric model. Homer uses this simile in narrating the act of blinding, *Odyssey* 9.383–6.

24. *Come, who will be first*: The metre shifts at this point from the customary iambics of regular dialogue to anapaestic rhythms, associated with marching and perhaps with military activity. But the 'revelling songs' which follow strike a different note, their style and metre being suited to drinking and celebrations, in particular wedding-songs. This paves the way for the rich comedy of the Cyclops treating Silenus as his beloved (this homosexual element was completely lacking in Homer).

25. *with this Bacchus*: By a common figure of speech Dionysus and wine are identified; similarly, classical poets speak of 'Hephaestus' when they refer to fire, and 'Ceres' meaning bread. But here the conflation is treated with comic literal-mindedness.

26. *What should we do, Silenus?*: Previously the Cyclops has been merely tolerant of the old man; here a note of flirtation enters, as the poet represents the two as behaving like lovers relaxing in a country spot. This parody of homosexual courtship reaches grotesque heights later when the Cyclops starts to carry Silenus inside to treat him as his Ganymede (see following note).

27. *Ganymede here* . . . : The beautiful Trojan youth Ganymede was abducted by Zeus and conveyed to Olympus, where he was to serve the king of the gods with nectar by day and join him in bed by night. The absurdity of the present parodic situation is obvious. Silenus is an old man and ugly, completely unlike Ganymede, but the Cyclops is too intoxicated to see the difference. The prospect of being ravished by Polyphemus sobers Silenus up at once!

28. *stop your chanting*: In Greek drama the choral songs are normally set somewhat apart from the action, and it is unusual for the actors to comment on or take up what has just been sung by the chorus. But a number of the exceptions involve a character urging the chorus to keep quiet lest a sleeping figure awaken (there are examples in Euripides' *Heracles* and *Orestes*, and Sophocles' *Trachiniae*).

29. *I want you to come inside* . . . : Here and elsewhere in the play Odysseus' surviving companions, who assist him in the Homeric version, are ignored (though a few lines further on he will resolve to make use of them instead). Here the aim is clearly to give an opportunity for the satyrs to show their cowardice, a traditional feature. This reluctance to aid Odysseus is also dramatically desirable: the chorus need to remain outside or the stage will be deserted.

30. *a really good spell of Orpheus*: Orpheus, son of Apollo, was a mythical singer and musician whose skill was so great that wild animals would listen tamely to his playing, and even inanimate objects might move in dance or in response to his summons. Naturally, the satyrs have no such spell, and Odysseus recognizes this at once.

31. *Noman was my destroyer*: The trick of the pseudonym used by Odysseus is handled differently and more functionally in the *Odyssey* (9.399–414). There, the agonized screams of the blinded Polyphemus attract the attention of his fellow-Cyclopes, who come asking him what is wrong. When he declares that 'Noman is killing me by trickery and force' they assume that he has nothing to complain about and depart. Here, of course, the chorus know perfectly well that Odysseus is Noman, but choose to conceal their knowledge in order to mock the Cyclops.

32. *On your right*: Again Euripides diverges from the *Odyssey*, this time out of dramatic convenience. In Homer, Odysseus and his men have to wait until the Cyclops moves the great rock that blocks the cave's entrance, then escape concealed beneath the ram and the flock of sheep which he allows to go forth to their grazing. The scene is effective in narrative (and was clearly admired and imitated: see Aristophanes, *Wasps* 177–96), but would be hard to stage convincingly. Euripides resorts to the simpler method of making the Cyclops leave the cave entrance unguarded.

33. *An ancient oracle is being fulfilled!*: In the *Odyssey* (9.506–21), Polyphemus describes what the prophecy predicted in more detail. This kind of ironic fulfilment of a prophecy, the true meaning of which is discovered too late, is very common in Greek mythology and especially in tragedy (e.g. Sophocles, *Oedipus the King*).

34. *drift . . . for many a year*: In Homer, Odysseus' wanderings last ten years before he finally reaches Ithaca; the adventure with the Cyclops is one of the earliest in the sequence of adventures.

35. *crush you to bits, you and your shipmates*: This is a forlorn hope when the monster is blind. Nevertheless, the threat is treated with surprising indifference, and the play ends without its being put into effect. Probably the audience is meant to supply what is lacking from their knowledge of the *Odyssey*, in which the Cyclops hurls great boulders but fails to strike Odysseus' ship.

BIBLIOGRAPHY

Texts

The standard Greek text, which forms the basis for this translation, is the new Oxford Classical Text edited by J. Diggle (3 volumes, 1984–94); this supersedes the much-used edition by G. Murray in the same series. The edition is arranged chronologically. *Heracles*, *Ion* and *Iphigenia in Tauris* are printed in volume 2, *Helen* in volume 3; the satyric *Cyclops* is set apart as the first play in volume 1 of Diggle's text, although it is probably a play close to *Helen* in date.

Those wishing to consult the plays in Greek will find the best guidance in the following annotated editions:

Heracles: G. W. Bond (Oxford 1981); S. Barlow (Warminster 1998).

Iphigenia among the Taurians: M. Platnauer (Oxford 1938); M. J. Cropp (Warminster 2001) [this edition unfortunately appeared too late to be used in the preparation of the present volume].

Ion: A. S. Owen (Oxford 1939); K. Lee (Warminster 1997).

Helen: A. M. Dale (Oxford 1967); R. Kannicht (German; 2 volumes, Heidelberg 1969).

Cyclops: R. Seaford (Oxford 1984).

Other translations

The Loeb Classical Library, which publishes bilingual editions of most classical authors, is currently bringing out an edition of Euripides by David Kovacs, arranged chronologically: at the time of writing four volumes have appeared, taking the sequence as far as *Iphigenia among the Taurians*. This edition replaces an older and wholly unsatisfactory edition by A. S. Way. Those who need to consider the detail of the Greek text should note that Kovacs presents his own text, which often differs from Diggle's.

286

Other translations available include those by various hands in the series edited by D. Grene and R. Lattimore, *The Complete Greek Tragedies* (Chicago 1941–58). Otherwise, complete versions of Euripides are hard to find, though the major plays are often translated individually or in smaller selections. A parallel enterprise to our own is the series published by Oxford University Press, with (prose) translations by James Morwood and introductions by Edith Hall: two volumes have appeared. These are grouped thematically rather than chronologically; the emphasis in the introductions is on reception and performance history.

General works on Greek tragedy

Goldhill, S., *Reading Greek Tragedy* (Cambridge 1986).

Hall, E., *Inventing the Barbarian: Greek Self-definition through Tragedy* (Oxford 1989).

Heath, M., *The Poetics of Greek Tragedy* (London 1987).

Jones, J., *On Aristotle and Greek Tragedy* (London 1962).

Knox, B. M. W., *Word and Action: Essays on the Ancient Theater* (Baltimore and London 1979).

Lesky, A., *Greek Tragedy* (English translation; London 1954).

Taplin, O., *Greek Tragedy in Action* (London 1978).

Taplin, O., *The Stagecraft of Aeschylus* (Oxford 1977): despite the title, relevant to all the tragedians.

Vernant, J.-P. and Vidal-Naquet, P., *Myth and Tragedy in Ancient Greece* (New York 1988; amalgamates two earlier collections of essays).

Vickers, B., *Towards Greek Tragedy* (London 1973).

Easterling, P. E. and Knox, B. M. W. (eds.), *The Cambridge History of Classical Literature*, vol. 1 (Cambridge 1985), includes expert essays on the Greek theatre and on each of the three tragedians (Knox covers Euripides); these chapters, together with those on satyric drama and comedy, were reissued in paperback as *Greek Drama*, eds. Easterling and Knox (Cambridge 1989).

Useful collections of work include:

Easterling, P. E. (ed.), *The Cambridge Companion to Greek Tragedy* (Cambridge 1997).

McAuslan, I. and Walcot, P. (eds.), *Greek Tragedy* (*Greece & Rome Studies* 2, Oxford 1993).

Pelling, C. B. R. (ed.), *Greek Tragedy and the Historian* (Oxford 1997).

Segal, E. (ed.), *Oxford Readings in Greek Tragedy* (Oxford 1983).
Silk, M. (ed.), *Tragedy and the Tragic* (Oxford 1996).

The Greek theatre

Csapo, E. and Slater, W. J., *The Context of Ancient Drama* (Michigan 1995): this excellent source-book translates and discusses many ancient texts relevant to theatrical conditions in the Greek and Roman world.
Green, J. R., *Theatre in Ancient Greek Society* (London 1994).
Green, R. and Handley, E., *Images of the Greek Theatre* (London 1995).
Pickard-Cambridge, A. W., *The Dramatic Festivals of Athens* (2nd edition revised by J. Gould and D. M. Lewis, Oxford 1968; reissued 1988): a standard work, but requires considerable knowledge of Greek.
Simon, E., *The Ancient Theatre* (English translation; Methuen, London and New York 1982).

Historical and cultural background

Andrewes, A., *Greek Society* (London 1971); originally published as *The Greeks* (London 1967).
Davies, J. K., *Democracy and Classical Greece* (London 1978; revised and expanded 1993).

Religion and thought

Bremmer, J. N., *Greek Religion* (*Greece & Rome New Surveys* 24, Oxford 1994).
Burkert, W., *Greek Religion* (English translation; Oxford 1985).
Dodds, E. R., *The Greeks and the Irrational* (Berkeley 1951).
Mikalson, J., *Athenian Popular Religion* (Chapel Hill 1983).
Mikalson, J., *Honor thy Gods: Popular Religion in Greek Tragedy* (Chapel Hill and London 1991): helpful, but perhaps emphasizes too strongly the gap between literature and the realities of cult and worship.
Parker, R., *Miasma: Pollution and Purification in Early Greek Religion* (Oxford 1983).

Studies of Euripides in general

Barlow, S. A., *The Imagery of Euripides* (London 1971).

Collard, C., *Euripides* (*Greece & Rome New Surveys* 14, Oxford 1981): an excellent short account with many examples and full bibliographical guidance.

Conacher, D. J., *Euripidean Drama: Myth, Theme and Structure* (Toronto and London 1967).

Michelini, A. N., *Euripides and the Tragic Tradition* (Madison, Wisconsin and London 1987): valuable chapters on the history of interpretation; also contains detailed 'readings' of four plays, including *Heracles*.

Murray, G., *Euripides and his Age* (London 1913); influential but out-dated.

Discussions of plays in this volume

HERACLES

Barlow, S., 'Structure and Dramatic Realism in Euripides' *Heracles*', *Greece & Rome* 29 (1982), pp. 115–24.

Mills, S., *Theseus, Tragedy and the Athenian Empire* (Oxford 1998), ch. 4.

Porter, D., *Only Connect* (Pennsylvania 1987), pp. 85–112.

Silk, M. S., 'Heracles and Greek Tragedy', *Greece & Rome* 32 (1985), pp. 1–22; reprinted in McAuslan and Walcot (eds.) *Greek Tragedy* [see above], pp. 116–37.

IPHIGENIA AMONG THE TAURIANS

Hall, E., *Inventing the Barbarian* (Oxford 1989), ch. 3: 'The barbarian enters myth'.

Sourvinou-Inwood, C., 'Tragedy and religion', in Pelling (ed.), *Greek Tragedy and the Historian* [see above], pp. 161–86, esp. 170–75.

Wolff, C., 'Euripides' *Iphigenia among the Taurians*: Aetiology, Ritual and Myth', *Classical Antiquity* 11 (1992), pp. 308–34.

ION

Knox, B., 'Euripidean comedy', in Knox, *Word and Action* [see above], pp. 250–74.

Loraux, N., *The Children of Athena* (English translation; Princeton 1993), ch. 5: 'Autochthonous Kreousa: Euripides, *Ion*' [also in J. Winkler and F. Zeitlin (eds.), *Nothing to do with Dionysus?* (Princeton 1990), pp. 184–236].

Zeitlin, F., *Playing the Other* (Chicago 1996), ch. 7: 'Mysteries of Identity and designs of the self in Euripides' *Ion*'.

HELEN

Burnett, A., *Catastrophe Survived* (Oxford 1973), ch. 4.

Segal, C., 'The two worlds of Euripides' *Helen*', in C. Segal, *Interpreting Greek Tragedy* (Princeton 1987), pp. 222–67.

CYCLOPS

Hall, E., 'Ithyphallic males behaving badly; or, Satyr Drama as Gendered Tragic Ending', in *Parchments of Gender: Deciphering the Body in Antiquity*, ed. M. Wyke (Oxford 1998), pp. 13–37.

Sutton, D. F., *The Greek Satyr Play* (Meisenheim am Glan 1980).

Special aspects

de Jong, I. J. F., *Narrative in Drama: The Art of the Euripidean Messenger-speech* (*Mnemosyne Supplement* 116, Leiden 1991).

Diggle, J., *Studies in the Text of Euripides* (Oxford 1982) and *Euripidea* (Oxford 1994): detailed discussions of many textual problems by the editor of the standard text.

Halleran, M. R., *Stagecraft in Euripides* (London and Sydney 1985).

Kovacs, D., *Euripidea* (*Mnemosyne Supplement* 132, Leiden 1994): includes detailed catalogue of ancient texts which refer to Euripides, and discusses problems of the text of the first few plays.

Kovacs, D., *Euripidea altera* (*Mnemosyne Supplement* 161, Leiden 1996): continues the textual discussions where the previous item left off.

Lloyd, M., *The Agon in Euripides* (Oxford 1992).

Stinton, T. C. W., 'Euripides and the Judgement of Paris', *Journal of Hellenic Studies: Supplementary Paper* 11 (1965); reprinted in Stinton, *Collected Papers on Greek Tragedy* (Oxford 1990), pp. 17–75.

General reference works

Hornblower, S. and Spawforth, A. (eds.), *The Oxford Classical Dictionary* (3rd edition, Oxford 1996): detailed and authoritative. For some readers the

BIBLIOGRAPHY

abridged and illustrated version, *The Oxford Companion to Classical Civilization* (1998) will be more suitable.

Howatson, M., *The Oxford Companion to Classical Literature* (Oxford 1989): useful particularly for summaries of myths.

GLOSSARY OF MYTHOLOGICAL
AND GEOGRAPHICAL NAMES

Information given here is not normally reproduced in the notes on particular passages.

ACHAEA a region in the N Peloponnese, south of the Corinthian Gulf.

ACHAEAN one of the racial sub-groups of the Greeks, particularly those resident in the N Peloponnese.

ACHAEUS according to Euripides, son of Creusa and Xuthus, and brother of Dorus; ancestor of the Achaean peoples.

ACHERON one of the rivers of the underworld. Its name signifies grief and lamentation.

ACHILLES son of the hero Peleus and the sea-nymph Thetis; greatest of the Greek heroes who fought at Troy; clad in armour forged by Hephaestus, he killed the Trojan champion Hector, but died in battle later, slain by Paris' arrow.

ACTE an old name for Attica, the area of Greece surrounding and controlled by Athens.

AEACUS grandfather of Theoclymenus in *Helen*. This may well be a Euripidean invention. There was a better-known Aeacus, grandfather of Achilles.

AEGEAN the part of the Mediterranean Sea separating Greece from Asia Minor.

AEOLUS father of Xuthus in *Ion*.

AEROPE wife of Atreus, seduced by his brother Thyestes.

AGAMEMNON king of Argos and Mycenae, leader of the Greek expedition against Troy. Father of Iphigenia, Orestes and Electra (also, in some versions, of Chrysothemis). Killed by his wife Clytemnestra.

AGLAURUS normally daughter of Cecrops, one of the earliest kings of Athens, and one of three sisters to whom the infant Erichthonius was entrusted;

according to Euripides in *Ion*, however, Aglaurus is the mother of the three girls.

AJAX there were two heroes of this name, both of whom fought at Troy. The one mentioned in this volume is the 'greater' Ajax, son of Telamon, second only to Achilles among the Greek warriors at Troy. After Achilles' death he was denied the armour of the dead hero, and went mad with rage and disappointment, finally killing himself.

ALCAEUS son of Perseus, father of Amphitryon, and grandfather of Heracles.

ALCMENA wife of Amphitryon and mother (by Zeus) of Heracles, mightiest of the Greek heroes.

ALEXANDROS see 'Paris'.

ALPHEUS a river originating in Arcadia in the Peloponnese and passing by the great cult-site of Zeus at Olympia; flows into the Ionian Sea.

ALTHAEA wife of Oeneus, a king of Calydon. She was successfully wooed by Dionysus, while her husband tactfully turned a blind eye.

AMAZONS a race of warrior women, who hunted, fought and governed themselves like men; usually located in remote Asia. Various Greek heroes, including Heracles, challenged them, sometimes celebrating victory by sleeping with their queen.

AMPHANAE a town NE of Thebes, near the Gulf of Pagasai.

AMPHION son of Zeus and Antiope; a marvellous singer and player of music, whose songs enchanted wild beasts and even moved the stones forming the walls of Thebes, which he ruled jointly with his twin brother Zethus.

AMPHITRITE one of the sea-nymphs known as Nereids; wife of Poseidon, god of the sea.

AMPHITRYON mortal father of Heracles, who was in fact the son of Zeus, who slept with Amphitryon's wife Alcmena.

ANAURUS a river that rises on Mount Pelion in NE Greece.

APHRODITE daughter of Zeus; goddess of love and desire.

APOLLO son of Zeus and Leto, brother of Artemis; one of the most powerful and dignified of the Olympian gods. He was famous for his good looks, his prowess as an archer, his musical gifts, and above all his power of prophesying the future through his oracles, of which that at Delphi was the most famous.

ARCADIA a mountainous region in the central Peloponnese.

ARCTUS the constellation Ursa Major or the Great Bear.

ARES god of war, usually regarded as a cruel and threatening figure.

ARGOLIS or ARGOLID region in the NE Peloponnese dominated by Argos.

ARGOS city in the N Peloponnese, often conflated in tragedy with the older site nearby, Mycenae.

ARTEMIS daughter of Zeus and Leto; sister of Apollo, and like him an archer; virgin goddess, associated with hunting and wild animals.

ASIA in Euripides a fairly vague term for the lands east of Greece, from the Hellespont as far as India. More specifically, Asia Minor, what is now mostly Turkey.

ASOPUS a river near the border between Attica and Boeotia, running south of Thebes.

ATHENA daughter of Zeus; virginal goddess of wisdom and patroness of Athens.

ATHENS the main settlement in Attica, in central Greece. See further, General Introduction and Preface to *Ion*.

ATLAS a gigantic figure or Titan, who was thought to have been punished by Zeus with the perpetual task of holding up the sky. He was located in the far west, at the Pillars of Heracles.

ATREUS former king of Argos and Mycenae, father of Agamemnon and Menelaus.

ATTICA the country around Athens and controlled by her, in central Greece.

AULIS a Greek town in Boeotia, opposite Euboea; the place where the great fleet of Greek forces assembled to set out for Troy. Because of unfavourable winds, Agamemnon was forced to sacrifice his daughter Iphigenia before they could leave there.

BACCHANT(E) a follower (usually female) of Bacchus, inspired with irrational ecstasy, often wild and violent in action.

BACCHUS another name for Dionysus, god of wine and associated with other wild and sensuous pleasures.

BRAURON (modern Vraona), in E Attica, one of the twelve ancient Attic townships united by Theseus into the Athenian state. Artemis had a particularly important temple and festival there.

BROMIUS a cult title of Dionysus, meaning 'the roaring one'.

BYBLUS a town in Phoenicia, north of Tyre and Sidon; famous for its wine.

CADMEANS the Thebans, so called because Cadmus founded Thebes and brought their race into being.

CADMUS son of Agenor from Tyre; founder of Thebes after he had slain a monstrous dragon guarding the site. He sowed the dragon's teeth, from which sprang forth warriors, the Sown Men, the first men of Thebes.

CALCHAS the prophet and adviser of the Greek army during the Trojan war. Although sympathetically presented in Homer, he gains a more sinister reputation in later times.

CALLICHORUS one of the sacred springs of Eleusis in Attica.

CALLISTO a nymph in the service of Artemis, who was loved by Zeus and seduced by him. She was changed into a bear, either by Hera or Artemis as a punishment, or as a disguise to protect her from Hera. Eventually she was placed among the stars.

CALYPSO a beautiful nymph who fell in love with Odysseus and tried to make him stay with her forever. She inhabited an idyllic island called Ogygia, far from Greece.

CAPHEREUS (or CAPHAREUS) a promontory to the SE end of Euboea.

CARYSTIAN associated with Carystus, a town in southern Euboea.

CASTALIA a sacred spring on Mount Parnassus, near Delphi. Those who wished to consult the Delphic oracle were required to purify themselves in this spring first.

CASTOR like his brother Pollux (or Polydeuces), a son of Zeus by Leda; brother of Helen and Clytemnestra. In some stories only one of them was immortal, but they are normally paired as the Dioscuri or Heavenly Twins, elevated after death to divine status and placed among the stars (the constellation Gemini, 'the Twins'). They were thought to watch over sailors at sea.

CECROPS early mythical king of Athens, allegedly half man, half snake, and said to have been born from the earth itself.

CENTAURS mythical creatures, half horse, half man. They were ambiguous in other ways: some (particularly the wise Chiron, tutor of Achilles) were kind and benevolent to men, while others were dangerous or potentially violent. This violent side was notoriously revealed when the Centaurs got drunk at the marriage of Pirithous and Hippodamia; a pitched battle ensued (the battle of the Lapiths and Centaurs).

CEPHALLENE one of the islands ruled by Odysseus, near Ithaca off the mainland of NW Greece.

CEPHISUS the main river of the plain of Athens. Like many rivers, he is sometimes invoked as a god.

CHALCODON an early ruler of the Abantes, on the island of Euboea, who gave his name to a town or region here.

CHARON the sinister ferryman who, in mythology, transported the dead across the river Styx to their eternal abode in the underworld.

CLASHING ROCKS one of the supernatural obstacles faced by travellers to the Black Sea, notably Jason on his quest for the Golden Fleece – massive rocks which moved in the water to smash any ship passing between them. They were vaguely located in the Bosphorus area.

CLYTEMNESTRA wife of Agamemnon, whom she murdered on his return from Troy, partly because of his treatment of Iphigenia, her daughter. Also mother of Orestes and Electra.

CREON one of the royal family of Thebes, brother of Jocasta. After the deaths of Oedipus' sons, he assumed the kingship.

CRETE large Mediterranean island to the SE of Greece.

CREUSA daughter of Erechtheus, an early king of Athens, and mother of Ion by Apollo; married to the Euboean Xuthus.

CYCLADES a group of islands in the SE part of the Mediterranean; the most important in mythological terms is Delos, birthplace of Apollo and Artemis.

CYCLOPS (plural Cyclopes) a one-eyed giant, hostile to men. The most famous Cyclops was Polyphemus in Homer's *Odyssey*, who trapped Odysseus and his men on their wanderings, and ate many of them before the hero managed to devise an escape. Cyclopes were thought to have helped in the building of some of the most ancient Greek cities, including Mycenae and Tiryns.

CYNTHUS a mountain on the island of Delos; hence associated with Apollo and Artemis, who were born there. Sometimes they are given the title 'Cynthian'.

CYPRIAN, THE Aphrodite, who was born from the sea off Cyprus, and who was held in special honour there.

CYPRUS large island in the eastern Mediterranean.

DANAUS father of the fifty girls known as the Danaids, and more generally conceived as the ancestor of the Danaans (which is sometimes a general title for Greeks but often more specifically means Argives).

DARDANUS first founder and king of Troy; hence the Trojans are sometimes called 'Dardanians'.

DELOS an island (one of the Cyclades), in the middle of the Aegean sea; birthplace of Apollo and Artemis and a major cult-centre.

DELPHI a town in the mountainous region of Phocis, location of the temple and oracular shrine of Apollo.

DEMETER goddess of fertility in nature, presiding over the crops and other products of the earth; mother of Persephone.

DICTYNNA ('lady of the net') a title of Artemis the huntress.

DIOMEDES a Thracian king, son of Ares, and king of the Bistonians. His man-eating horses were captured by Heracles as one of his labours. He should be distinguished from Diomedes, son of Tydeus, one of the Greek heroes at Troy.

DIONE one of the senior goddesses on Olympus and in some contexts treated as wife of Zeus; mother of Aphrodite.

DIONYSUS son of Zeus by Semele; god of wine and other natural forces; often seen as a wild and irrational deity, bringer of madness.

DIOSCURI ('sons of Zeus') Castor and Pollux, the Heavenly Twins; see 'Castor'.

DIRCE a wicked queen of Thebes, killed by Amphion and Zethus. After her death her name was associated with a stream near Thebes.

DIRPHYS a mountain in Euboea, origin of the tyrannical Lycus.

DORIANS one of the sub-groups of Greeks, often contrasted with the Ionians. Sparta and Argos were Dorian states, Athens Ionian.

DORUS according to the genealogy given in Euripides' *Ion*, son of Xuthus and Creusa, brother of Achaeus, and ancestor of the Dorians.

EARTH-MOTHER, THE a title for Demeter, who is linked to the earth through her concern with crops and fertility.

EIDO According to Euripides' *Helen*, the original name of the prophetess Theonoe (whose name means 'knowing the divine'). Her new name was given to her when her gifts as a seer were discovered.

ELECTRA daughter of Agamemnon and Clytemnestra; sister of Orestes, whom she supports in the murder of their mother. She subsequently married Orestes' friend Pylades.

ELECTRYON a king of Mycenae, father of Alcmena and consequently grand-father of Heracles.

ENCELADUS one of the Giants who in early mythical times staged a rebellion against Zeus and were defeated in battle by the united forces of Olympus, assisted by Heracles.

ERECHTHEUS an early king of Athens, father of Creusa. Hence the Athenians are sometimes called Erechtheids or 'sons of Erechtheus'.

ERICHTHONIUS son of Athena by supernatural means, and a figure in the early royal line of Athens; sometimes identified with Erechtheus, though Euripides distinguishes them.

ERYTHEIA an island in the great Ocean beyond the Pillars of Heracles (for us, the Atlantic), inhabited by the monstrous herdsman Geryon. One of Her-acles' labours was to travel there and take the cattle from Geryon.

ETNA volcanic mountain in Sicily.

EUBOEA a large island off the coast of Attica and Boeotia.

EURIPUS the narrow strait separating Euboea from Boeotia.

EUROTAS a major river in the southern Peloponnese, running through Spartan territory.

EURYSTHEUS son of Sthenelus; tyrannical king of Argos, persecutor of Her-acles and his family. He was responsible for setting Heracles his twelve labours.

FURY a daemonic and dangerous creature who was thought to persecute evil-doers in life and after death; hence any horrific and avenging figure, especially female. The Furies' most famous role in mythology is as pursuers of Orestes, whom they hounded after he had killed his mother.

GANYMEDE a beautiful Trojan boy who was carried away by Zeus because of his beauty; he became the cup-bearer of Zeus on Olympus as well as sharing his bed.

GELEON son of Ion; founder-member of one of the ancient tribes of Athens.

GERAESTUS a promontory at the southern tip of the island of Euboea.

GORGON a type of hideous female monster with snakes for hair, so horrible that to look at one outright would turn a man to stone. The most famous Gorgon, Medusa, was slain by Perseus who chopped off her head by looking not at her, but at her reflection in his shield. A Gorgon's head adorned the shield of Athena.

GRACES minor goddesses who embody the graceful beauty and pleasure of life, often associated with the Muses and represented singing or dancing.

HADES (a) one of the three most powerful Olympians, the others being Zeus and Poseidon; they divided up the universe, and Hades drew the underworld as his domain; (b) the underworld itself.

HALAE a small village on the E coast of Attica, on the Euboeic Gulf.

HEBRUS a river in eastern Thrace, flowing into the northernmost Aegean.

HECATE a sinister goddess associated with darkness, witchcraft and ghosts. Sometimes, however, she is identified with Artemis and viewed more positively.

HELEN daughter of Zeus and the mortal woman Leda; wife of Menelaus and mother of Hermione. According to the usual legend (deliberately avoided by Euripides in his *Helen*), she was carried away or seduced by the Trojan Paris. The Trojan war was fought to get her back. She eventually returned to Sparta and lived with her husband.

HELENUS son of Priam and Hecabe; a prince of Troy who had prophetic powers. He survived the Trojan war and eventually married Andromache and became king in part of Epirus.

HELICON mountain in Boeotia, thought to be a favourite place of the Muses.

HELIOS the sun, personified as a god. He is sometimes associated with or even identified with Apollo, who was also often regarded as a god of light (and whose sister Artemis presided over the moon).

HELLAS (a) a small area of southern Thessaly; (b) in classical times, often used to denote the Greek nation as a whole.

HEPHAESTUS son of Zeus and Hera; god of fire and of the arts of craftsmanship, especially metalwork, but lame and often treated disparagingly by his fellow divinities. His forges were thought to be located under Mount Etna.

HERA queen of the gods and consort of Zeus; presides over marriage; often associated with Argos, one of her favourite cities. Her jealousy of Zeus' love-affairs motivates many vengeful acts, especially against Heracles.

HERACLES son of Zeus and Alcmene; greatest of the Greek heroes, famous for his many victories over monsters and barbaric peoples; enslaved by Eurystheus and compelled to perform twelve labours.

HERMES son of Zeus and the nymph Maia; messenger of the gods.

HERMIONE daughter of Helen and Menelaus; she remained in Sparta while Helen went with Paris to Troy.

HERMIONE town in the SE Argolid.

HESPERUS the Evening Star.

HESTIA goddess of the hearth and hence almost a symbol of the home. Most Greek houses would have an altar to Hestia.

HIPPODAMEIA daughter of Oenomaus, who organized contests for her hand and slew her unsuccessful suitors, until Pelops was victorious and killed him.

HOMOLE, MOUNT a mountain in Thessaly, in N Greece.

HYACINTHUS a handsome Spartan youth beloved by Apollo, who accidentally killed him as they played with a discus. A cult was instituted in his memory.

HYADES ('the rainy ones') nymphs associated with water and rain. Like the Pleiades, they were imagined as goddesses enshrined in the stars and influencing the earth's weather.

HYDRA a monstrous and many-headed creature that appeared indestructible, as a new head grew whenever one was chopped off. Heracles eventually killed it by burning away the stumps of the heads with torches.

IACCHUS sometimes a title of Dionysus, sometimes a god distinct from him. He was closely associated with Demeter and Persephone, and was invoked in the festivities surrounding the Eleusinian mysteries.

IDA A mountain in Asia Minor, near Troy, where according to legend Paris was brought up as a shepherd.

ILIUM another name for Troy.

IOLAUS nephew of Heracles; he assisted him in some of his labours.

IONIANS descendants of Ion; one of the major ethnic divisions among the Greeks. The Athenians were Ionian, and in classical times claimed an ascendancy over other Ionian states.

IPHIGENIA daughter of Agamemnon and Clytemnestra. Her father was forced to sacrifice her in order to gain favourable winds for the Greek fleet; according to the version followed in *Iphigenia among the Taurians*, she was rescued by Artemis and carried off to the remote land of the Tauri.

IRIS a minor goddess who is often represented as messenger of the gods, especially of Hera. She was the personification of the rainbow, and a rainbow in the sky was thought to mean that Iris was descending to earth.

ISMENUS a river in Theban territory.

ISTHMIAN GROVE a grove of pines which grew by the temple of Poseidon on the Isthmus.

ISTHMUS the narrow stretch of land connecting central Greece with the Peloponnese. The Isthmian Games were celebrated here.

ITHACA an island off western Greece, part of the kingdom of Odysseus.

IXION king of the Lapiths; one of the great sinners of myth, traditionally the first Greek to kill a kinsman. He also attempted to rape Hera, and was punished in the underworld by being bound forever to a rotating wheel of fire.

LACEDAEMON an ancient name for Sparta and its surrounding territory.

LAERTES former king of Ithaca and father of Odysseus.

LEDA wife of the Spartan Tyndareus, mother of Helen, Clytemnestra, Castor and Pollux.

LERNA a marshy area near Argos, chiefly famous as the abode of the monstrous Hydra.

LETO a goddess or Titaness who bore Apollo and Artemis to Zeus on the island of Delos.

LEUCADIAN ROCK Leucas was an island near Ithaca, off western Greece; the Leucadian rock refers to a promontory at its southern tip.

LEUCIPPUS son of Oenomaus, king of Pisa.

LEUCOTHEA a goddess of the sea, formerly the mortal Ino.

LIBYA part of N Africa, sometimes loosely used to refer to the whole continent other than Egypt.

LOXIAS a title of Apollo, perhaps meaning 'crooked' or 'slanting', with reference to his ambiguous oracles.

LYCUS (a) a wicked Theban king, husband of Dirce, overthrown by Amphion and Zethus; (b) son of the first Lycus, a usurper of power in Thebes and persecutor of Heracles' family. The second figure is probably a Euripidean invention. The name Lycus, implying 'wolf-like', is suitable for any bad king.

MAENADS another name for the Bacchantes, followers of Dionysus. The name means 'mad ones'.

MAEOTIS, LAKE an inner lake at the far N of the Black Sea, on the border of Scythia. It was here, according to the chorus of *Heracles*, that Heracles was involved in combat with the Amazons.

MAIA one of the Pleiades, daughters of Atlas; mother of Hermes by Zeus.

MAID, THE (or 'Maiden') Persephone, consort of Hades. Although she had a kinder face, as daughter of Demeter and bringer of fertility, she is often regarded with awe, and 'the Maid' is a way of avoiding use of her name.

MALEA, CAPE a promontory at the south-easternmost point of the Peloponnese. It was a region notorious for unsettled weather, and many sailors in legend, as no doubt in life, were driven off course off Malea.

MALIA the Gulf of Malia is an inlet S of Achaea, in central Greece.

MARON a priest who, according to the *Odyssey* and Euripides' *Cyclops*, befriended Odysseus and gave him a gift of strong wine.

MEGARA in Euripides' *Heracles*, wife of Heracles and slain by him in his madness.

MEMORY mother of the Muses.

MENELAUS son of Atreus and younger brother of Agamemnon; king of Sparta; husband of Helen. The Trojan war was fought by the Greeks on his behalf, to recover her.

MENOECEUS a Theban, father of Creon and Jocasta.

MEROPS in an obscure story, mother of a companion of Artemis.

MIMAS a giant, one of those (like Enceladus) who opposed the Olympian gods and was defeated at Phlegra.

MINOTAUR, THE the monstrous offspring of Minos' queen Pasiphae, who made love to a bull; the child was half bull, half man, and was imprisoned by Minos in the Labyrinth. It was eventually slain by Theseus.

MINYANS legendary heroes of N Greece. Heracles' reference to past combat with the Minyans in *Heracles* seems to allude to his conflicts with the town of Orchomenos, in Boeotia.

MOTHER OF THE GODS, THE Cybele, a great goddess of nature and fertility, worshipped was in Phrygia and was absorbed into Greek myth, where she was sometimes identified with Demeter. Her genealogical relation to the Olympians is left vague. A major cult-centre was at Mount Dindyma.

MOUNTAIN MOTHER see previous entry. This title arises from Cybele's association with Mount Dindyma.

MUSES nine in number, goddesses of the arts and especially poetry; daughters of Memory.

MYCENAE in very ancient times, a great centre of power and wealth in the Peloponnese. By Euripides' time it was eclipsed and indeed destroyed by Argos, with which in some passages it is virtually identified.

NAUPLIA a town in the Peloponnese near Argos, serving as its port.

NAUPLIUS father of Palamedes. Because the Greeks (especially Odysseus) had brought about his son's death at Troy, Nauplius lit misleading beacons along the rockiest shores of Euboea and lured many of the returning Greek ships to destruction.

NEMEA a town in the Argolis, most famous for its sanctuary of Zeus, the centre of the Nemean Games. One legend held that the games had been founded by Heracles to commemorate his slaying of the Nemean lion.

NEREIDS sea-nymphs, daughters of Nereus; often associated with Thetis, mother of Achilles.

NEREUS a sea-divinity, often conceived as part man and part fish. He had the gift of prophecy. In *Helen* a Nereus, probably the same, is said to be one of Theonoe's grandparents.

NESTOR king of Pylos; one of the oldest Greeks to go to Troy, and because of his age and wisdom highly respected by Agamemnon and the other leaders.

NILE the chief river of Egypt and one of the great rivers of the world. In ancient times, as in modern, the question of its source was one which fascinated travellers and poets.

NISUS former king of Megara, who gave his name to the port of that city, Nisaea.

NYSA a mountain of uncertain location, usually referred to as a place where Dionysus is celebrated.

OCEAN in early Greek thought, conceived as a vast river circling the known world, and often personified as the greatest of river gods.

ODYSSEUS one of the chief leaders of the Greeks at Troy; son of Laertes, king of Ithaca, husband of Penelope. He was the favourite of Athena, and a cunning deviser of plans; often he was represented as too clever for his own good, and even as an immoral schemer.

OECHALIA a town rather vaguely located (in some versions in Euboea), sacked by Heracles on campaign.

OENOE'S HUNTRESS GODDESS Artemis. Oenoe is a place on the borders of the Argolid and Arcadia. Heracles slew the hind of Artemis but offered it to her here to placate her anger.

OENOMAUS a tyrannical king of Pisa, father of Leucippus and Hippodameia; slain by Pelops, Hippodameia's suitor.

OLYMPUS a mountain in N Greece, on the borders of Macedonia and Thessaly. Because of its majestic height, it was considered the home of the gods, though the name is sometimes used more loosely to describe a remote heavenly realm.

ORESTES son of Agamemnon and Clytemnestra, brother of Electra and Iphigenia. After growing up in Phocis near Delphi, he returned to Argos to avenge his father's death.

ORION a gigantic hunter, who pursued the Pleiades, a group of nymphs; both pursuer and pursued were transformed into constellations.

ORPHEUS a gifted poet and musician whose singing could spellbind even wild beasts and who endeavoured to charm the powers of the underworld into releasing his dead wife – in some versions successfully.

PALAEMON a sea-god, formerly a mortal called Melicertes whom Poseidon saved from drowning.

PALLAS = Athena.

PAN son of Hermes; half goat, half man, this lesser deity is a figure of the wild and is often thought to induce frenzy and fits of madness (hence 'panic').

PARIS Alexandros, son of Priam and prince of Troy. Paris was the name given to him by the shepherds who rescued him when he was exposed in infancy on Mount Ida. He judged Aphrodite the most beautiful of all goddesses, and was rewarded with Helen; but the consequence was the Trojan war.

PARNASSUS a mountain north of Delphi, sacred to Apollo and the Muses.

PELASGIA a term loosely used to refer to the area occupied by the original pre-Greek inhabitants of the Greek mainland; hence Greece generally.

PELEUS son of Aeacus, king of Phthia, in Thessaly; a hero of the generation before the Trojan war; married to the sea-nymph Thetis, he became the father of Achilles.

PELION a mountain in Thessaly, in NE Greece.

PELOPID of or associated with Pelops, and hence with his family, which included Atreus, Agamemnon and Orestes.

PELOPS son of Tantalus and an early king of Pisa; father of Atreus and Thyestes. He gave his name to the Peloponnese, the massive southern part of mainland Greece.

PENEUS the chief river of Thessaly in NE Greece.

PERSEPHONE daughter of Demeter, and often associated with her in cult. Abducted by Hades, she was eventually obliged to spend part of the year on earth and part in the underworld with her husband. See also 'Maid'.

PERSEUS one of the great heroes of Greek myth, slayer of the Gorgon, Medusa. He was a forebear of the even greater hero Heracles.

PHINEUS a Thracian king who was persecuted by the Harpies, monstrous winged women who stole his food. The Argonauts visited him on their journey to Colchis and brought an end to the Harpies' attacks.

PHLEGRA the 'Phlegrean plain' was the battleground for the conflict between the Gods and the Giants, located in the southern part of the region known as Chalcidice, a large peninsula in the NW Aegean sea.

PHOCIS the large territory surrounding Delphi, to the west of Boeotia.

PHOEBUS another name for Apollo.

PHOENICIA the territory at the easternmost end of the Mediterranean; its chief ancient cities were Sidon and Tyre.

PHOLOE a mountain in Elis, in the NW Peloponnese.

PHRYGIA area in W Asia Minor; often used more loosely to refer to Asia and the 'barbarian' territories generally. Hence 'Phrygians' often = 'Trojans'.

PHTHIA region in Thessaly, the kingdom of Achilles' father Peleus and subsequently of his son Neoptolemus.

PISA the area around Olympia in the W Peloponnese, and sometimes used to refer to Olympia itself. The name is especially associated with the festivals involving the Olympic Games. Oenomaus and Pelops were successive kings there.

PLEIAD (plural PLEIADES) the seven daughters of the Titan Atlas and of Pleione; they were pursued by Orion and turned into a constellation. They are associated with the marking of the seasons for farming activity.

PLUTO another name for Hades, ruler of the underworld and husband of Persephone.

PLUTUS the name means 'wealth', and Plutus is the name of a god who is a personification of prosperity.

POLYDEUCES Latinized as 'Pollux'; one of the Dioscuri or Heavenly Twins; see 'Castor'.

POLYPHEMUS son of Poseidon; one of the gigantic and one-eyed Cyclopes; blinded by Odysseus.

POSEIDON god of the sea and also of other threatening natural forces such as earthquakes.

PRIAM king of Troy, husband of Hecabe. He was the father of many children, especially Hector, Alexandros (also called Paris), Polyxena, Cassandra. At the sack of Troy he was killed by Neoptolemus.

PROCNE wife of Tereus; she killed her son and served him up to her husband to eat, in revenge for his rape and mutilation of her sister Philomela.

PROMETHEUS a Titan, who assisted Zeus in seizing power on Olympus and helped him in other ways (including enabling him to give birth to Athena); in some myths the creator of mankind, whom he befriended and to whom he gave the gift of fire. He was famous for his wisdom and ingenuity.

PROTEUS the old man of the sea; like Nereus, an immortal sea-god and prophet. He had the power to change into any shape, hence the term 'protean'. In Euripides' *Helen* he is rationalized as a human king, father of Theoclymenus and Theonoe.

PSAMATHE a sea-nymph, married first to Aeacus, then to Proteus, king of Egypt; mother of Theoclymenus and Theonoe.

PYLADES son of Strophius, king of Phocis, and close friend of Orestes, who was brought up in Strophius' court. He accompanied Orestes in disguise to Argos, joined him in the killing of Aegisthus and Clytemnestra, and subsequently married Electra.

PYTHIA the title of the priestess of Apollo at Delphi.

PYTHIAN a title of Apollo, commemorating his slaying of the snake Python that previously guarded the oracle at Delphi; hence also an adjective meaning 'to do with Apollo, or Delphi'.

PYTHO another name for Delphi. The story was that Apollo had killed a huge snake (python), who had possessed the shrine before him. Hence Apollo bore the title 'Pythian'. The Pythian Games were held at Delphi.

RHADAMANTHUS one of the sons of Zeus who judged the dead in the underworld; hence proverbial for stern but fair judgement.

RHION a place on the promontory at the southern entrance to the Corinthian Gulf.

ROARER, THE, or THE ROARING ONE a title of Dionysus, who was thought sometimes to transform himself into a wild beast.

SALAMIS an island off the coast of Attica, home of Telamon and his sons Ajax and Teucer. When Teucer was sent into exile, he found a new home in Cyprus and called his settlement by the same name.

SCAMANDER one of the rivers of the plain of Troy.

SIDONIAN of or from Sidon, in Phoenicia in the eastern Mediterranean.

SILENUS an old man who accompanies Dionysus on his revels and is often regarded as his teacher. Though not a satyr himself, he is sometimes called 'father' of the satyrs.

SIMOIS a river of the plain of Troy.

SINGING MAIDENS, THE daughters of Hesperus, guardians of the Golden Apples that Heracles sought as one of his labours.

SIRENS a group of female creatures, part human and part bird, dwelling on a remote island, who entranced passing sailors with their song, luring them to their deaths.

SISYPHUS a king of Corinth with a reputation for cleverness and unscrupulousness. He was sometimes said to be the real father of Odysseus. He was said even to have tried to cheat death itself. In the end he was imprisoned in the underworld and set the perpetual task of pushing a gigantic boulder up a hill; the reason for his punishment is variously reported.

SOWN MEN, THE the original citizen warriors of Thebes, who sprang up from the earth when Cadmus sowed the dragon's teeth (see under 'Cadmus'). The myth symbolizes the ferocity of the Thebans.

SPARTA chief city of Laconia, kingdom of Menelaus and Helen; in historical times one of the dominant cities of the Peloponnese and regularly opposed to Athens. This antagonism is often projected back into the mythical period.

STROPHIUS king of Phocis and ally of Agamemnon; father of Pylades.

SUNIUM a cape at the southernmost end of Attica.

TAENARUM or TAENARUS a cape in southern Laconia, which was believed to have caves which gave access to the underworld.

TANTALUS son of Zeus and father of Pelops; ancestor of Atreus, Agamemnon and Menelaus. He was a great sinner who was punished in the underworld after death; the misfortunes of the house of Agamemnon are sometimes traced back to his actions.

TAPHIANS a people in NW Greece.

TAURI, TAURIANS, TAURIC LAND these terms refer to the remote nation to which Iphigenia was transported after her father sacrificed her at Aulis. It is located on the north coast of the Black Sea, in the modern Crimea.

TELAMON son of Aeacus, brother of Peleus and father of the greater Ajax and of Teucer; king of the island of Salamis, and one of the heroes of the generation before the Trojan war.

TEUCER bastard son of Telamon, and brother of Ajax. Ajax killed himself at Troy, whereas Teucer survived. His enraged father exiled him, and he eventually founded a new settlement in Cyprus, which he called Salamis after his former home.

THEBES chief city of Boeotia, north of Athens.

THEMIS an ancient goddess, daughter of Earth and Sky, and protectress of justice. Her name means 'order, law, propriety'. In early times she presided over the Delphic oracle.

THEOCLYMENUS in Euripides' *Helen*, son of Proteus and king of Egypt; brother of Theonoe.

THEONOE The name means something like 'divine in knowledge'; according to *Helen* this was the name given to Eido, daughter of Proteus, when her prophetic gifts were discovered.

THESEUS son of Aegeus and Aethra; most famous of the mythical kings of Athens.

THESSALY region of NE Greece.

THESTIOS king of Aetolia and father of Leda, Helen's mother.

THETIS a sea-nymph, who married Peleus and bore him the hero Achilles. She abandoned Peleus and returned to the sea, but never entirely forgot her mortal connections.

THOAS in Euripides' *Iphigenia among the Taurians*, king of the Tauric people.

THRACE a region to the extreme NE of the Greek mainland, beyond Macedonia; southern Greeks regarded it as primitive and savage.

THYESTES son of Pelops and brother of Atreus; father of Aegisthus, whose usurpation of Agamemnon's throne was partly a form of revenge for the crime of Atreus, who had killed Thyestes' sons and served them up to their unsuspecting father for dinner.

TITANS an earlier race of immortals overthrown and replaced by Zeus and his fellow Olympians.

TRITON a sea-god, attendant on Poseidon.

TRITONIAN LAKE, LAKE TRITON a lake in N Africa, said to have been the birthplace of Athena; hence she is often called 'lady of Triton' or the like.

TROJANS the people of Troy, defeated by the Greeks in the Trojan war. Most famous are their king Priam and his sons Hector, the outstanding warrior killed by Achilles, and Paris, who started the war by abducting Helen.

TROPHONIUS originally a Boeotian prophet; he had an oracle not far from Delphi.

TROY city in Asia Minor, ruled by Priam and his family. In earlier times its kings included Dardanus and Laomedon. Its citadel was known as Pergama or Pergamon. The Greeks destroyed it at the end of the ten-year Trojan war.

TUSCAN another word for Etruscan, one of the peoples of early Italy. Tuscan pirates tried to abduct Dionysus in his youth.

TYNDAREUS father of Helen and Clytemnestra, Castor and Pollux (some of these had Zeus as their real father, particularly Helen, but terms such as 'daughter of Tyndareus' are still used in a loose way).

TYPHON a fire-breathing monster who defied Zeus and was struck down but not slain by the god's thunderbolt. In some accounts he was imprisoned under Mount Etna, and the volcanic eruptions were said to be his fiery breath.

UNFRIENDLY SEA, INHOSPITABLE SEA, etc. pejorative names applied to the Black Sea, also called euphemistically the Euxine ('Kind to Strangers').

URANUS the name means 'sky' in Greek. The sky was personified as one of the oldest of the pre-Olympian gods, with Earth as its consort. Cronus overthrew Uranus, and was subsequently overthrown in his turn by Zeus.

XUTHUS in Euripides' *Ion*, a Euboean general who is rewarded for helping Athens in war with the hand of the princess Creusa.

ZEPHYRUS the west wind, usually gentle and favourable.

ZETHUS see Amphion.

ZEUS the most powerful of the Olympian gods and head of the family of immortals; father of Apollo, Athena, Artemis and many other lesser gods, as well as of mortals such as Heracles.